HEARTSOUNDS

Martha Weinman Lear

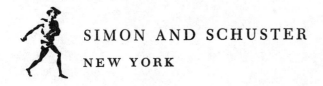

SIMON AND SCHUSTER

NEW YORK

Designed by Eve Kirch
Manufactured in the United States of America
Printed and bound by Fairfield Graphics, Inc.

Library of Congress Cataloging in Publication Data

Lear, Martha Weinman.
Heartsounds.
1. Heart—Infarction—Biography.   2. Lear, Harold
Alexander, 1920–1978.   I. Title.
RC685.I6L397   362.1′9′61209 [B]   79-23100
ISBN 0-671-24329-2

For those who loved Hal

This is a true story.
Only some names have been changed.

Part One

*H*E awoke at 7 A.M. with pain in his chest. The sort of pain that might cause panic if one were not a doctor, as he was, and did not know, as he knew, that it was heartburn.

He went into the kitchen to get some Coke, whose secret syrups often relieve heartburn. The refrigerator door seemed heavy, and he noted that he was having trouble unscrewing the bottle cap. Finally he wrenched it off, cursing the defective cap. He poured some liquid, took a sip. The pain did not go away. Another sip; still no relief.

Now he grew more attentive. He stood motionless, observing symptoms. His breath was coming hard. He felt faint. He was sweating, though the August morning was still cool. He put fingers to his pulse. It was rapid and weak. A powerful burning sensation was beginning to spread through his chest, radiating upward into his throat. Into his arm? No. But the pain was growing worse. Now it was crushing—"*crushing*," just as it is always described. And worse even than the pain was the sensation of losing all power, a terrifying seepage of strength. He could feel the entire degenerative process accelerating. He was growing fainter, faster. The pulse was growing weaker, faster. He was sweating much more profusely now—a heavy, clammy sweat.

He felt that the life juices were draining from his body. He felt that he was about to die.

On some level he stood aside and observed all this with a certain clinical detachment. Here, the preposterous spectacle of this naked man holding a tumbler of Coke and waiting to die in an orange Formica kitchen on a sunny summer morning in the fifty-third year of his life.

I'll be damned, he thought. I can't believe it.

It had crept up on him so sneakily. He had awakened earlier, at 6:30, with an ache, not a pain really, high up there in the pit of the stomach, and wondering what might have caused it, possibly the broiled-chicken snack at midnight, he had padded into the bathroom and had caught his reflection in the mirror: pallid under the tan, blue eyes dulled, the hollows beneath them deep and dark.

You look like hell, he had told himself. Go back to sleep. It's Saturday.

So he had gone back to bed, but not to sleep. It was a habit he could not break. Whether he had slept eight hours or two, alone or not, in his own bed or in some vacation spot five thousand miles from home; whether he had worked or boozed or counted his debts or fought with his wife or mourned a friend the night before; on weekends or on New Year's Day, with or without headaches, backaches, upper respiratories, whatever: even when he willed himself to linger in the bed and there was no reason at all not to do so, he was always up at 6:30, his own most reliable alarm clock, instantly alert, ready to wash, dress, gulp the coffee, scan the front page, drive to the hospital and appear at 8 A.M. in the operating room, scrubbed and ready to cut. A habit.

He had lain there thinking about this habit, and perhaps finally he had dozed for a few minutes, but then he had wakened again with the pain worse, and had gone for the Coke. And now he was at the edge of an abyss.

He made his way back to the bedroom, clutching walls for support. He eased himself onto the bed, picked up the telephone receiver and, with fingers that felt like foreign objects, dialed the Manhattan emergency number.

A woman's voice, twangy: "This is 911. Can I help you?"

He spoke slowly, struggling to enunciate each word clearly:

"My name is Dr. Harold Lear. I live at ———. I am having a heart attack. My doctor's name is ———. I am too weak to look up his number. Please call him and tell him to come right away."

"Sir, I'm sorry. This is 911. I can't call your doctor."

"But I need him."

"Well, I'm sorry. This is *strictly* an *emergency service.*"

"This is an emergency. A heart attack."

"Sir, I'm *very* sorry." Reproach in the voice. "I *can't* call your doctor. We don't *do* that."

He thought he might laugh or cry. He felt trapped in an old Nichols and May routine: I think my arm is broken. Yes, sir, what is your Blue Cross number? I don't know. You don't *know?* Well, I don't have my card, but I have this arm, you see . . . *You don't have your card?* You should *always* carry your card. . . .

Now he felt not panic, but a certain professional urgency. A familiar statistic plucked at his brain like an advertising slogan: 50 percent of all coronary victims die in the first ten minutes. "Thank you," he said to 911, and hung up.

Slowly he tugged on a robe, staggered back into the foyer and pressed for the elevator. At this hour it was on self-service. When it arrived, he entered, pushed 1 and CLOSE DOOR, and braced himself against the wall. Suddenly he knew that if he did not lie down he would fall. He lowered himself to the floor. When the elevator door opened, he rolled out into the lobby and said to the startled doorman, "Get a wheelchair. Get me to the emergency room. I am having a heart attack."

"An ambulance, Doctor? Shouldn't we get an ambulance?"

"No. No time. A wheelchair." Then he lost clarity.

He was next aware of being in a wheelchair that was careening down the street. His head was way back, resting against a softness that seemed to be a belly. He did not know whose it was, but he was so pleased to have that belly for support.

The hospital—his hospital, where he was on staff—was nearby, a few blocks from his home. He felt the wheelchair take a corner with a wild side-to-side lurch and go rattling on toward the emergency room. Though his mind was floating and he could not keep his eyes open, that curiously disengaged observer within him reached automatically for the pulse. He could no longer detect any beat. He was very cold, very clammy, and he knew that he was in shock.

I am dying now, he thought. I am dying in a creaky wheelchair that is rattling down the avenue, half a block from the emergency room. Isn't this *silly*. And then: Well, if I am dying, why isn't my life flashing in front of me? Nothing is flashing. Where is my life?

The apartment-house doorman, who was steering the wheelchair, and a janitor, who was running alongside, recalled later that he was smiling. They wondered why.

Finally the chair screeched to a halt. He opened his eyes. Crutches, pulleys, traction, all the paraphernalia of an orthopedic treatment room. Damn it, he thought, we've come to the wrong place, A uniformed security guard stood nearby, eyeing him idly. "Excuse me," he said to the guard, "but I am having a heart attack. Can you direct us to the right room?" And slipped out of consciousness again.

Then, dimly, he felt himself being lifted onto a stretcher, sensed noise and light and a sudden commotion about him. They were giving him nasal oxygen, taking his pulse, taking his blood pressure, starting an intravenous, getting a cardiogram—the total force of modern emergency care suddenly mobilized; a team clicking away with the impersonality of an overwhelmingly efficient machine.

He understood that at this moment he was no more than a body with pathology. They were not treating a person; they were treating an acute coronary case in severe shock. They were racing, very quickly, against time. He himself had run this race so often, working in just this detached silent way on nameless, faceless bodies with pathologies. He did not resent the impersonality. He simply noted it. But one of the medical team, a young woman who was taking his blood pressure, seemed concerned about *him*. She patted him on the shoulder. She said, "How do you feel?" It was the only departure from this cool efficiency, and he felt achingly grateful for it. Ah, he thought in some fogged corner of the brain, she must be a medical student. She hasn't yet learned to depersonalize. She will. We all do. What a pity.

(Later—he thought it was that same day, but it may have been the next—she came up to the coronary-care unit, and took his hand and said, "How are you doing, Dr. Lear?" and smiled at him. He never knew her name, and he never forgot her.)

The painkillers had taken effect now. He could breathe. A white-coated figure said, "Well, there's no question about your having a heart attack."

What a dumb way to put it, he thought. I don't know what he's saying. "What do you mean, 'no question'? Did I or didn't I?"

"You *did*. *Look*." The doctor, clearly irritated, thrust the cardiogram reading in front of his face. He peered at it. The fine ink lines traced a crazy path across the paper tape. Groggy as he was, he could see that he was having one hell of a heart attack.

Now administrative forces descended upon him. They asked about next-of-kin.

His wife was out of the country, he said.

Where?

He wasn't sure.

Children?

His son was traveling too. He could not remember his daughter's married name.

Siblings? None. Parents? None. Finally he gave them the name of a friend.

His own doctor was abroad. The covering doctor was a stranger to him. "Whom do you want?" they asked. He couldn't think of anyone else. This seemed to rattle them. He could not simply be admitted; he had to have an admitting doctor. They conferred for what seemed like a very long time while he lay there, feeling agreeably hazy, bittersweet strains of Nichols and May playing again in his ear. Finally they sent him upstairs, doctorless.

He remembered thinking, just before he passed into a long, deep sleep, How can I get hold of Martha? I've got to get hold of Martha, because if I die without telling her, she will never forgive me.

He knew this was the logic of a deranged mind. A nurse wondered, as his street escorts had wondered earlier, why he was smiling.

Chapter 2

———————————————————

"*M*ILD?" I screamed, for the overseas connection was dreadful. "Did you say 'mild'?"

"No, I did not say 'mild.' I said '*myo*.' " The voice muffled but smooth, cool; these strange phrases as easy as butter on his tongue. "Your husband has suffered a myocardial infarction." Pause. "A massive myocardial infarction."

Massive. I hadn't been prepared for that.

The first call had come, just an hour before, from the Paris bureau of *The New York Times*. No one else would have known where to reach me. Two days earlier I had fled a tourist-choked Cannes, driven up into the hills behind the Riviera and found a *pension* in a mountain village named Magagnosc. The place was small and quiet, not crawling with couples, and I found comfort in the fact that the proprietors called me by name. I had informed the *Times* people of my move, for we were trying to set up an interview with Simone de Beauvoir and were in daily contact.

"Lewis Bergman would like you to call him right away," a secretary from the Paris bureau had said. Bergman was then the editor of the *Times* Sunday Magazine, and a close friend.

"Oh? What's it about?"

"I don't know. This is the telephone number."

I knew the number: his home telephone in New York. Instantly I began floating, on waves of adrenaline, toward the Wailing Wall. This happens so easily. It is in the blood, this readiness for hysteria that gets passed down from mother to daughter like the family silver. Our cultural heritage: sons inherit obsessiveness; daughters inherit hysteria. Bergman, calling Paris to reach me from his home? On a Saturday? This was no business call. Hal was dead. Or had had a heart attack. There were no other possibilities.

Still, I had tried to pretend that there were others. Wait, now, I lectured myself. Don't hurry to call him. Prove to yourself that this is not *necessarily* a crisis. Think reasonable thoughts. Think that Bergman wants me to do a rush assignment. Think that he wants to say hello. Think that he wants to discuss some questions to put to de Beauvoir, questions that simply happened to occur to him on a Saturday, at home. . . .

Tell me, Mlle. de Beauvoir, do you feel as strong and independent as you sound? Do you really have it all that together? Do you ever feel lonely? Did you ever want to marry Sartre? No, no, not as a bourgeois gesture, but to . . . you understand . . . to *formalize* your commitment? Do you think about how life would be without him? Do you sit around worrying about whether he's going to have a heart attack? Do you . . .

So I sat quietly on the bed for fifteen interminable minutes, considering other possibilities, and then I went to the telephone to confirm what I absolutely knew.

Bergman, with such a harsh message to deliver, sounded nervous. "Now, look, Martha, don't get nervous, it's just that Hal is feeling a little sick. . . ."

"He's dead?" Oh, galloping now toward the Wailing Wall.

"Dead! Good heavens, no, of course he's not dead. He's just had this little . . ."

"He's had a heart attack?"

"Well, sort of. Yes. But it's nothing much, it's just this little . . ."

"Oh, God. You're sure he's not dead?"

"Of *course* he's not dead. I tell you he's fine. I saw him this afternoon. He was bitching because he can't make our tennis date tomorrow." He laughed leadenly. Much later, I learned what this call and that hospital visit had cost him. My husband, lying in an intensive-care unit at the mercy of his own heart, had nonetheless been trying to figure how to get the news to me with least trauma. In some narcotic-fogged corner of his mind, it had seemed logical that if I got the call from Bergman, I would assume it was a business matter and not be frightened. So Bergman, who had lost his dearest friends to coronaries in the past several years, had been summoned to the bedside of yet another friend who lay hovering on the brink. The two men were not that close. But still, what a wrench in such moments, what a tearsome thing! To be American, male, in one's fifties, a compulsive worker—as who of them is not?—worried about cholesterol and unpaid bills, working under stress and watching old friends succumb, one by one, to that crisis of the heart . . . I do not suppose women can fully understand that fear. Not that particular one. We agonize instead over cancer; we take as a personal threat the lump in every friend's breast.

"I'll get the next plane home," I said.

"There's no hurry. I mean, I think it would be a good idea, but Hal said to be sure to tell you that there's no hurry."

"*No hurry!* My God, he may be dying and there's no hurry."

"Now, look, I *told* you he's bitching about the tennis. Don't go to pieces, for Christ's sake. . . ."

But of course I went quite to pieces. Monsieur and Madame, the proprietors of my little *pension*, were in the kitchen. I went to them, stuttering, unable to make sense.

"*Mon mari. Un coup de coeur,*" I cried, striking my chest with a fist.

They stared uncomprehendingly. I didn't know how to get through. I kept striking my chest. "*Mon mari, malade,* ici," I cried, and finally they seemed to understand. They petted me. They made sounds of comfort. Some phrases I understood: It happens to many doctors. They work too hard, *n'est-ce pas?* Now that he has a warning, he will work less hard. He will recover and live long. And so forth, trying their best.

We then called the hospital—Monsieur yelling, "*Urgent! Urgent!*" but still it took forever. Finally a voice, blurred but unmistakably Brooklynese: "Good evening, —— Hospital."

I screamed that I wanted information about Dr. Lear. Immediately I was off on my own Nichols and May trip. Dr. Lear, the voice said; was he on staff or a patient? A patient, I yelled. His room number? I don't know. Just a moment, then, we'll transfer you to Information. . . .

"Don't cut me off!" I shouted, for I knew these hospital switchboards. "I'm calling from France. . . ."

The Brooklyn voice again, injured: "I'm *not* cutting you awf, lady."

Another voice: "Good evening, Maternity. . . ."

"Oh, please, no. My husband, his name is Dr. Lear, he's had a heart attack."

"A heart attack? Oh, well, then, he wouldn't be in Maternity. Just a moment, we'll try to switch you. . . ."

Then I heard a third voice say: "Dr. Lear? Oh, yes, he's in Coronary Care. Hold on. . . ." And finally, now, here was the resident on duty, telling me something about a massive myocardial infarction.

I couldn't understand. I had been married to a doctor for all those years, and "massive" was a common household word signifying other people's problems, no more. I knew jargon. My husband was a urologist, and I could sling around "transurethral resection" and "prostatic CA" with style, as though I knew what I was talking about. But what did I know of "massive myocardial infarction"? It wasn't his specialty.

I'd moved in a society of predominantly male doctors and their wives, and doctors' wives—especially surgeons' wives; especially in small communities, where they are known—are accustomed to homage and tithings.

In Hartford, Connecticut, where my husband had been in private practice for twenty years before moving back to New York, I had been embraced often by strangers. They would say, "Your husband saved my mother's life," or "If I could ever do anything for you, I would be so happy," or "To me, your husband is God." People say such things when lives have been in the balance. Most doctors' families are accustomed to it; the first time it happened to me, when I'd been married for two weeks and a salesclerk had gazed at my charge card, and at me, and back at the card, and that look, something of awe, had come into her eyes and she had said, "You're his *wife*? Your husband is the most wonderful man in the world," I'd gone near faint with pleasure.

But we are not accustomed to being on the other side of the equation. We are not accustomed to feeling helpless, or to asking frightened questions of awesome figures in white coats. We answer telephones in the middle of the night and speak soothingly to terrified voices. We wait in hospital lobbies for our husbands to finish work and take us to the movies, and smile soothingly into terrified faces.

We do social work among the terrified, walk with detached empathy among the terrified, but we are not accustomed to terror. We never really hear words such as "massive" and "critical"; we never grasp them. We know only that some poor bastard has trouble and our husbands are going to be late getting home again; they are going to muck up another fine dinner party.

Massive. "Is he dying? Is he in pain?"

"He is resting comfortably. But of course, it's too early to know. There could be another. . . ."

Well, of *course* there could be another, one didn't have to be married to a doctor to know that there could be another, it wasn't an illogical thing to say. And yet at 3,000 miles it seemed gratuitous.

"Can I speak to him?" Of course not. *Massive.*

And then, inexplicably: "Yes, I think we can arrange that. Hold on. . . ."

There were buzzes and gurgles on the wire, I thought we'd lost the connection, and suddenly I heard Hal's voice, weak but even: "Hi, darling," and I felt the ecstasy of reprieve. I had taken mescaline once. It was like that: ecstasy, and astonishment at one's own capacity for ecstasy.

"How are you?" he said.

From that place where I was floating, I heard myself say, "I'm fine. I'll be home tonight or tomorrow."

"There's no rush."

"I know, but I'd like to come home."

"Vacation's over?"

"Oh, I'd rather spend the rest of it with you."

"Okay," he said, and I knew from that "Okay" how close to the precipice he felt. We exchanged, ever so casually, assurances of love and good cheer, and hung up.

It was 7 P.M. There were no more night flights. I got a reservation on the 7 A.M. flight from Nice to Paris, and a 10 A.M. flight to New York.

Madame put me at a table and brought me wine and an omelet. I drank a great deal quickly. There were dinner guests now, but Monsieur came over and sat and smoked with me, as though he hadn't another thing to do. I gave him a long monologue, in English, about how my father had collapsed of a heart attack in the middle of my brother's wedding, and how Hal had tried to save him, and couldn't; and how I had twinned them in my head in so many ways, father and husband, and had often confused the two in my dreams, losing now one and then the other—crude Freudian stuff; and how so many men on both sides of Hal's family had died young, in their forties and fifties, of heart attacks; and how I had lived with some rational core of dread, for he was a genetic patsy; and how heavily he smoked and how hard he worked and so on, on and on . . . and Monsieur kept nodding his head and saying, "Oui. Oui," with the sweetest and clearest compassion, although he could not understand a word of English.

At midnight I went up to my room. I set the alarm for five, then lay listening to the half-hour and quarter-hour chimes of the church bell. I felt hazy, alienated, standing aside and watching myself in this bed. I thought, Maybe she is a widow now, and began to cry again, but in the strangest, calmest way. The tears simply flowed, soaking my hair and the sheets, and I didn't move. When the alarm went off I got up, washed, packed, carried my bags out to the car, fastened my seat belt and set out down the mountainside, just at daybreak, still with the heavy tears flowing and still with this sense of standing apart from myself, watching.

At the airport, the car-rental agency was closed. I asked the information-counter attendant to return the keys for me.

"I can't accept the responsibility," she said.

"My husband has had a heart attack," I said.

I did not understand the sequitur, and neither did she, but she took the keys.

At the Air France counter, a clerk said, "In dollars, $444."

"One way?"

"One way."

"But that's terrible. The three-week tours are $365 *round trip*."

He gave me a lifted eyebrow.

"My husband has had a heart attack," I told him accusingly, paying off in whatever little I had left—French currency, American currency, traveler's checks.

On the plane I fell asleep immediately; I changed planes in Paris and again slept. A stewardess woke me for lunch. They showed a film, a comedy. Momentarily I would become absorbed in the screen images, go with them, and everything would be all right. Then suddenly I would drop back into my own reality and think, Wait, now, something terrible is going on, I'm feeling terrible about something. What is it, what is it? Oh, yes. Hal has had a heart attack. Oh, God . . .

Finally the lights went on. Across from me sat a handsome young couple, he dark, she blond, models of cool and lust and jet travel, the kind whose pictures appear in tabloids above captions reading: ". . . in Acapulco and looking very much in love, but say they have no plans to marry. . . ."

They both wore expensive jeans. They both wore tight-fitting shirts, hers unbuttoned to show a lovely cleavage, his to show the requisite gold chain gleaming on a tanned chest. They stretched, they nuzzled. Once he reached a hand into her shirt and I watched his fingers squeezing her nipple. They smiled lazily. She pushed up his sleeve and ran her tongue slowly down the length of his forearm, licking the dark hairs. I shivered.

Once, in a plane, going off on our wedding trip—he in a dark suit and I in something new and pink; one didn't wear jeans, then, to go away—we had nuzzled and played in this way. Two women across the aisle had stared at us, and finally one had leaned over and said, ever so shyly, "Pardon me, but we were just wondering . . . Are you two on your honeymoon?"

It had made me feel marvelous. Powerful. We hadn't been so young, not nearly so young—I 30, Hal 41—that it was logical to take us for honeymooners. But the manner was unmistakable, I suppose. There is such an arrogance to new love.

Now I stared at these two across the aisle. I felt mesmerized by them. I wanted to *be* them. They both turned suddenly and caught me staring. To my horror I began to cry—not quietly, as before, but with a loud, pungent grief now, rocking and moaning.

"My husband has had a heart attack," I wailed.

They reddened and looked away.

Some hours later, at Kennedy, I broke my last $20 taking a cab into the city. Of course I told the driver too about my husband's heart attack, and he told me about his own.

Chapter 3

A *NURSE,* smiling wordlessly and bobbing her starched and stoic little cap, ushers me into the coronary-care unit.

This place is so hushed, like a church or a funeral home. It smells of danger. Everything here is hearts. Men, all men, I can see them, lying on the brink, hearts freshly broken, arteries long rotted, vital passages plugged, God knows what.

I follow her past the open cubicles and look into each and away, fast, as though from shameful sights. In each, a small tableau. The deathbed scene from countless old movies. That high holy hush, the stricken one motionless in his bed, the haggard-faced relatives grouped about him, just so, the whole scene framed by some kitschy and cliché-ridden director. And here, in this last cubicle, a tableau as unreal to me as all the rest.

Hal? Oh, come off it. What baroque bullshit is this? Hal is my healthy husband who, when last seen, picked me up at a London airport and twirled me around, I being no insignificant weight, and we gave each other a fine big kiss and a grab or two of the butt and said, So long, see you in two months, and he went off to America waving. So what does this charade have to do with him? With us?

He lies in that bed and plastic tubes are feeding oxygen into his nose. Needles are feeding some colorless potion into his arm, I can see it dripping slowly from a bottle that hangs upside down by the bed. White discs are stuck like suction cups to his chest, and wires run from these discs to a big black machine, medical surrealism, that flashes lights and makes buzzing sounds and sends yellow blips racing across a small gray screen. His heart, the rhythms of his heart, blipping like unidentified objects on a radar screen. Danger out there in inner space.

Preposterous. Come on, Hal, disentangle yourself from those gadgets. Get up and give me a hug. You know I hate discontinuities. Why, we were just at that airport and you . . . You know I can't cope with shifting planes of reality. You've given me little lectures in the past, haven't you, eh? When my father dropped dead, when Billy dropped dead, when Phil jumped off the roof, when your mother lay in the morgue, when Fanny, who always had more marbles than anybody, smiled up at me out of her arteriosclerotic mists and said, Who are you?— you gave me those neat little reasonable Hal lectures about ebbs and flows, births and deaths, natural cycles, here today gone tomorrow, and you know I rejected every word of it, you know all those natural cycles are unnatural and barbaric to me. Listen, Hal: If God had meant us to fly He would have given us wings. If God had meant us to die He would have given us different song lyrics. No Forever and a Day, no Our Love Is Here to Stay, no Yours Till The Stars Have No Glory . . . I have been inculcated with faith in immortality. It is so sweet and American. *I* am so sweet and American. I have learned all my lessons. You are supposed to be here when Gibraltar tumbles, when the mountain crumbles; you are supposed to last at least as long as the moon over Alabama. So get up, damn it, and give me a hug.

Really, he doesn't look so bad. I don't know what I expected—a coma, perhaps; a cadaverous gray; some implacable terminal look. But this is not so bad. Not the face of a dying man. He is even smiling at me and mouthing Hello. What was this "massive" business; what was that idiot doctor telling me on the overseas call last night? Can't he see? Can't he comprehend? This man is smiling. Where is the "massive"?

He looks a little pale, yes; but then, he has never been ruddy. He looks, despite those preposterous tubes in his nose, very handsome. I have always loved to look at his face. It has seemed to me simply the best sort of face a man could have. I don't know why. Something in its geometry, perhaps, sharp planes and crags, and yet with a great sweetness of expression about the eyes and the mouth.

And now his mouth is smiling and it is that same marvelous smile, ineffably sweet. His eyes, which are an extraordinary blue, the precise blue almost of a low gas flame, glow as always. His chest looks as solid as ever, tanned and smooth, which has always pleased me because I never enjoyed the look or the feel of very hairy men. He looks . . . healthy! I would swear that he is healthy! How could anything so bad, so massively bad, be inside that good sturdy chest? It must be a mistake, one of those grotesque medical mix-ups . . . No, no, doctor, you were supposed to take out the *left* kidney. . . .

But then, why those yellow blips going crazy on the small gray screen? Why all these Rube Goldberg nightmares, these wires and tubes and needles and discs? And why—oh, Jesus—why this sad little tableau?

Judy—his daughter, my stepdaughter—stands by the bed, her eyes puffed and swollen almost shut with crying. We embrace. She was a child when I married Hal, a sullen whiner, painfully split by the split of her parents and jealous of this woman who made new claims on her daddy. And I, perceptive as a cabbage, jealous of this kid who made prior claims on my husband, an 11-year-old and a 30-year-old locked in silent, raging competition for first dibs on the same man. Stepmothers and stepdaughters: what a crucible. Well, we'd both grown up and grown close. But at this moment she is a child again, terrified that her daddy may die. My heart goes out to her. I remember when my daddy died.

And her husband Mark is here, awkward in this role. What is he supposed to do? He has been in the family for only two months, after all. It was only two months ago, just before Hal and I left for England, that we gave the wedding reception in our apartment, around the corner from this hushed dangerous place, and drank champagne toasts to everything that was going to last forever, and look at us now.

And David, Hal's cousin David, to whom I had cabled the night before: HAL HEART ATTACK ———— HOSPITAL. PLEASE TAKE CHARGE. ARRIVING TOMORROW, knowing absolutely that he would do whatever had to be done. Like Hal, like all the men in that flamboyant, feverish family: monumental Type A's; responsible, reliable, guilt-ridden men, bred to bear the brunt. And my brother, Joe, bred, like me, in quite another mold, giving me nervous little kisses, jerking a thumb toward my husband and saying, with a weird, wistful, inept stab at humor, "He's fine, he's fine, he pulled this stunt just to get you home. Right, Hal?" with a wink.

And my husband, still smiling gently. He lifts an arm to wave, to motion me over, but he is too weak. It falls back on the bed.

And this seems to me the worst of anything, this small failed gesture. This breaks finally through my defenses and makes my heart pound so hard that I feel it may pound its way out of the chest wall, and I hug myself to contain it. Hal? *Hal.* My dearest with the smile and the bold blue eyes, who six weeks ago lifted me in that airport and kissed me goodbye, is too weak to lift his own arm off the bed.

The others leave the cubicle. I move toward him and kneel down beside him and cover his left hand with my own and put my cheek, ever so lightly, next to his, because now, close up, I see that he is profoundly fragile, like dried petals, and if I grab or clutch he may crumble in my hands.

"Pretty dumb," he whispers.

"Damned dumb."

"I missed you."

"Me too." Don't cry, wretched jellyfish.

"It will be all right."

"Yes."

"It will be just like it was."

"Yes. Yes."

And we are smiling sad, deceitful smiles at each other, both knowing that, whatever happens, it is not likely ever again to be just like it was.

"Five minutes are up, Mrs. Lear," says the starched little nurse.

And I go out into the corridor and fall into Judy's arms and we both cry like hell, not only for fear of losing him but for loss itself, any loss, the lifelong loss of all the lovers and all the daddies, all the fierce and insupportable systems of support.

I met the doctor on duty.

"How bad is it?" I said.

He shrugged. He reddened. He began to speak softly and cordially of "left ventricle," "severe damage," "extensive death of tissue," "danger period," "uncertain prognosis," all the while staring fixedly at my left shoulder, as though I hadn't a face.

Look at me. Tell me what matters. Tell me whether you think he is going to live or die.

Nothing.

"You'll have to get a doctor," he said.

"Whom should I get?"

"I can't tell you that. There are any number of good people on the staff."

Any number. Pick a number. For Christ's sake, tell me who is Number One; tell me whom you would pick if it were your own dearest lying in that bed.

Yet I knew he wouldn't. It wasn't done. Often enough I had heard Hal say to patients on the telephone, "I can't recommend anyone in particular, but I'll give you the names of several excellent doctors. . . ."

And I'd objected. I had said, "Why *can't* you recommend anyone in particular? If I were sick, or you, you would want the best and you would know where to find it. But most people don't know. They feel lost. Why can't you give them the one best name?"

And he would explain, patiently, as he always did when I raged against some detail of medical protocol:

"Because usually there isn't 'the one best name.' Usually there are several highly competent people, equally competent, and the rest is a matter of personality. An excellent doctor may be perfect for one patient and terrible for another. . . .

"Because doctors depend on referrals. If I always referred patients to the same internist, the other internists would never refer to me. . . .

"Because it's dangerous to recommend just one name. Suppose something goes wrong? 'Dr. Lear, it's your fault that my mother died. You told me to take her to Dr. Zilch. . . .' "

It had made sense. To me, the doctor's wife, it had made sense. To me, the patient's wife, it made no sense at all.

We all went back to the apartment and sat around in a family circle, looking at the floor.

How do you pick a doctor? In Hartford, where he had been a member of a close professional family for twenty years, I would not have had to pick. They would have embraced us, taken us in and given us their best. Here, who cared? He was a stranger, just two years on staff. The place was so immense that most of the doctors were strangers to each other anyway. He had trained in this hospital a quarter-century ago. It didn't matter now. The professors he had cherished were dead or retired; the residents he had trained with, back in those improbable days when residents earned $20 a month and sold their blood for pocket money, were cozy in their private practices in Boston and Kansas City.

I knew several cardiologists slightly. I did not doubt that he could get the best. Doctors can always get the best. But in a vast, impersonal medical community, "the best" is the best reputation, and the best reputation may be the smoothest bedside manner, the fanciest office, the biggest chauffeured limousine double-parked outside the hospital; the best reputation may belong to a bum. It happens. And how could you know unless you yourself were a doctor and had watched him work? They would never tell on one another.

I called three doctors we knew for advice. Each one came up with a different name. David called his own doctor, Moses Silverman, a hotshot cardiologist at another hospital, with a Who's Who practice that extended across the seas.

Silverman was, in fact, in Europe at the moment. I spoke to his associate, Peter Mason.

"Who does the best cardiology?" I asked.

"We do," he said.

"I mean at my husband's hospital. I've heard Werner recommended, and Roberts . . ."

"Both excellent. You couldn't go wrong with either."

So I chose Roberts. I had known him slightly, years before, when I had first come to New York to work and had been living next door to three young nurses. The interns used to come and go, dating the nurses, marrying the doctors' daughters . . . cool, smart young Jewish gods diagnosing rare tropical diseases with assurance, coming at our breasts with brash fingers, saying, "I've got to practice palpation." Vague memories of Roberts, a good-looking young man, smart and cocky as the rest; and the nurse Faye adoring him, telling me once, "He has such gentle hands, you just *know* he's going to be a great doctor. . . ."

What the hell, as good a recommendation as any other. And at least some human connection, however long ago. I telephoned him, and he agreed to take the case.

Everyone left. Did I want them to stay? they had asked. No. In fact, I wanted desperately to be alone. I had to concentrate. In my luggage was a journal. Just hours before he had been stricken in New York, I had been sitting in a hotel room in southern France, writing in that journal of my fear that he might die. In the six weeks that we had been apart, I had scribbled in that journal obsessively about dependency and death and dread of losing him.

Had it been premonition? Possibly. I am no believer in such things, but possibly.

There had been signs. We had been traveling together in England. He had been depressed by a bad work situation, and one day, in a crowded pub, he had begun to cry. It was utterly unlike him.

"What is it?" I had asked.

"I hate working for them, I hate them all, I hate the whole damn setup," he had cried, with such an urgent and impotent rage that I should have guessed it might eat like acid into his heart. But I had guessed nothing; not consciously, at any rate.

At the end of June he had gone home, to the job that so depressed him, and I had stayed on to finish magazine assignments in London and Paris. He would be returning in two months for a medical convention in Spain. I would stay abroad, do my work, meander down to the Riviera and meet him in Spain in September. A nice plan.

The work part had gone well enough. The work always went well. Press credentials, business luncheons, interviews—such things are a form of belonging, a portable set of roots. But as soon as I had finished my work and gone south to be a tourist, I was in trouble. Then I was a wife without a husband: another story.

It was my first vacation alone in twelve years of marriage. I saw it as a test. Before the marriage I had traveled alone often, carrying self-confidence like baggage around the world. Now it was a strain to go alone to a cocktail party across town.

"Do you think I can manage on my own?" I had asked him just before we'd parted in London.

"Of course you can. You always did."

"But I'm out of the habit. You've become my social security blanket."

"That's nonsense." Knowing it wasn't. "You travel alone all the time on assignments. You are a self-confident woman, a . . ."

"That's professionally. Socially is different."

And so it had been.

"Five days in this place," I had written in Cannes, "and I've yet to talk to a soul but waiters, chambermaids, hotel clerks. In some sense I seem not to exist. Only couples exist. This terrible sense of dislocation, invisibility . . . I keep wondering what the hell has happened to me. I used to be so adequate on my own. Passing a mirror, sudden shocking confrontation: Oh, yes, that's what's happened. You're 42. To be a woman alone at 25 is okay. The world moves in on you. To be alone at 42, in a Gallic Miami Beach 3,000 miles from your husband and from your women's group that talks about the expendability of husbands, is not so okay. Despite all our cool, bold talk, things really haven't changed that much.

"Ah, stop it. Hiding behind chronology. The truth is, it has very little to do with age. It's this locked-in marital state of mind: two's company, one's an aberration. . . ."

"It is his problem too, I think. Did I suppose that only women grow dependent? Bullshit. It is a symbiosis, after all. It is the price we pay for intimacy. Open Marriage, open schmarriage—elegant theories that don't work. Possibly there is no way to have intimacy without dependency. You love, you need. . . ."

"We have become so much to each other. It is so huge, this investment we have made. It scares me. Too many eggs in one mortal basket. What if something happened? How could one survive the loss of so much at once?

"What a bloody Catch-22. The better it is while you have it, the worse it will be when it's gone. . . ."

Scribbling on like that, just yesterday. And then, last night, the telephone call. Ah, Hal. How's this for irony? Our own ironies are always so much more cosmic than anyone else's.

I put aside the journal and went into our bedroom. It was a mess. Neither of us ever had given much of a damn about housekeeping; a happy meshing of domestic incompetences. Socks and shorts on the floor, tennis racket, many pounds of the Sunday *Times*. Bureau tops cluttered. On his nightstand, a glass of Coke; an ashtray packed with ancient butts; an enormous pile of medical journals; an old *Village Voice*. Bed greatly disheveled, as though by bad dreams or good sex.

I wonder, had that been what ripped his heart? The shock of unfamiliar flesh, sheets drenched with different-smelling sweat, strange strokes and groans, heart pumping harder, harder, racing faster, coming, coming, gone . . .

Not that I would ever ask him. We never asked each other those questions. We had seen marriages so open, the winds of candor came howling through and blew them away. Anyway, people talked too much about such things. There was something so ingenuously American about that, making such an earnest public fuss, as though it were a problem to be solved at the next Town Meeting: Next on the agenda, we have this question of whether it's okay for married people to screw around. How many ayes? How many nays? Any discussion? . . .

Much too much discussion. It's too complicated. It's too trivial. Work it out for yourself and keep your mouth shut. We both always knew where home was, and that was enough. Right, Hal? But now, my pale darling, if you live, you probably won't be able to play. There's an old medical joke for the occasion: Cardiac victim: "Will I be able to have sex, Doctor?" Doctor: "Yes, but only with your wife. I don't want you to get too excited. . . ." Ah, folk humor.

I went into his closet and closed the door and stood in the dark embracing his clothes, smelling him. Who will take his clothes if he dies? His son, Jon? They won't fit. But as mementos, maybe. Yes, Jon will want his clothes. His books, his desk, his easy chair. Judy will want his bathrobe—as a child, she loved to cuddle in his bathrobe— his granny glasses, his collection of petrified wood. His pictures? How will they divide the pictures? Oh, God, the pictures, hanging on walls, crammed into albums, stashed in boxes on closet floors . . . Hal sailing his Sunfish in our beautiful Provincetown Harbor. Hal fighting the bull in some Mexican town (during a medical convention, that one. They had staged a bullfight for the doctors and then asked for volunteers. And suddenly there was Hal, bounding out onto the field, I yelling, "Are you crazy? Come back here!" It was a baby bull, a mere trainee, but those modest horns could hurt. They handed him the red cape and he did damned well, swirling the cape around and holding his ground as the little thing snorted past him, the crowd cheering and whistling, I laughing and screaming in fright. The Mexican doctors loved him for that one. For the rest of the trip they would applaud whenever he appeared, chanting "To-re-ro!"). Hal in mortarboard, holding his brand-new diploma, a beaming parent on either side. Hal in ensign's uniform, World War Two. Hal cradling baby Judy. Hal and Martha cutting their wedding cake. Hal and Martha feeding pigeons in front of the Doges' Palace, leaning out of balconies in the Leaning Tower, poised in front of French châteaux, Aztec temples, Stonehenge—all the classic Kodak stuff; grinning into the camera on dance floors, at football games, picnics, birthday parties, New Year's Eves, anniversary celebrations: twelve years' worth of HalandMartha . . .

And if he dies, what will I do with all our conspicuous consumption? The stuff that crams these rooms, the lamps and Portuguese rugs and second-rate French chairs and first-rate Irish crystal and visions of him everywhere, in every single object, all the artifacts of an affluent-consumer marriage?

I will have none of it. None of it. I will run away from this place; I tell you, Hal, if you die I will close the door and run away and never look back; I won't even come to your funeral. It won't be much of a funeral anyway. We always told each other that whoever survives is to go up in a little plane and scatter the ashes over Provincetown Harbor. Well, I won't do it, Hal. Let Jon scatter the ashes. Let Judy do it. Let your goddamned bad-artery cousins do it, whose heart attacks are yet to come. I won't be there, you bloody abandoning bastard. Oh, Hal. How dare you do this to me, who loves you so?

I came out of the closet and arranged myself carefully on his side of the bed and buried my face in his pillow: faintly salty, smoky.

Such a damned big bed! At first I hadn't liked it. When I lay reading by my bedside lamp, and he by his, we couldn't touch flesh, and always I liked to have the feel of the flesh. Sleep habits define a marriage. We would fall asleep in the middle of that great bed, cupped belly-to-ass, like two spoons. But in my sleep I would push, burrowing in ever deeper, as though to imprint myself upon his body; and in the morning we were always both on his side, crowding the edge.

What would I do with the bed? In the beginning it had been only for sex and for sleep. But then it had become, as the bed does, I suppose, in any marriage that lasts long enough and is decent enough, a multifaceted thing. Our playing field, our pizza joint, our corner

pub, our library, our battleground, our voting booth, our clubhouse—
a style of life contained within its limits. A hell of a lot to give to the
Salvation Army.

I picked up the phone, dialed the hospital and asked for Patient
Information.

"Can you tell me Dr. Harold Lear's condition?" I said.

A pause, a rustle of paper. "Critical but satisfactory," a voice said.

Chapter *4*

---

*F*OR the next thirty-six hours his situation was precarious. They would answer none of my questions. They said only, "Let's wait a couple of days," with little pats on the shoulder that filled me with dread.

At the time, I thought it was deliberate evasion. It was, partly. Most doctors—at least, those I have known, and they are surely no better or worse than most—cope badly with families in times of emotional crisis. Emotions make them nervous.

But mostly, they told me nothing because they knew nothing. When there has been a massive coronary, there is no telling which way it will go. It may simply leave town like a tornado, having done its damage. It may start up again abruptly and spread, killing more heart muscle. There may be a sudden cardiac arrest, possible instant death. They watch. They say, "Let's wait a couple of days," with clumsy little pats on the shoulder. It is the best they can do, which I tried to remember. A rule of thumb: Practically everyone means well.

I sat with him for five-minute intervals, twice a day, in the cubicle bathed with that monstrous fluorescent light which gives everything white the dead waxen sheen of lilies. The nurses swayed about him like lilies. He asked short, labored questions about my trip—questions designed, I knew, to make me feel better. I had said of him once that this man would be thoughtful on his deathbed, a comment that now kept exploding softly behind my eyes.

I spoke of the food and the weather, and he listened attentively. Vallauris is like Coney Island now, I said. And you remember our secret seafood joint on that little back street in Cannes? It's everyone's secret now. We'll have to find a new place when we go back. . . . He nodded, he smiled, his lips spreading sweetly beneath the nasal tubes. His eyes shone. His eyes were like lifelines. My own notions of death have always demanded large visible traumas. A man who smiles and listens so nicely is not a dying man.

"He looks so *well*, wouldn't you say?" I prattled to a couple of the interns, and they shook their heads at me, not so much to say No as to say This woman is crazy.

I met Roberts on the third day, just after he had examined Hal. The handsome young medical student was white-haired now, slightly pudgy, his face gone to pockets and pouches of flesh. "You look wonderful," he said. "So do you," I said. Is he lying too? Of course.

"Your husband has had a bad attack, there's no doubt of that. But we can't tell yet how extensive the damage is. Right now his enzyme levels are so crazy high that we're getting a very distorted picture." When the heart muscle has been damaged, certain enzymes are released and appear in abnormally large quantities in the blood. The larger the quantity, the greater the presumed damage. A normal enzyme count is 40. A count of 80 suggests significant damage. Hal's count was then 400. "I think the house staff is being too pessimistic. When the count settles down, we might find things aren't as bad as they look right now."

"When will you know?"

"Let's give it a couple of days. Did you have any other questions?"

"Yes . . ." In fact, I had written them down. The list was in my hand. Good doctor's wife. I knew the intrusive nuisance of the telephone call during busy office hours: "Oh, Doctor, there was one question I forgot to ask you this morning. . . ."

"Okay. Let's go in here."

We went into a small visitors' lounge and sat down. A woman sat opposite us staring at nothing, like a catatonic or a mourner. Her fingers were systematically ripping Kleenex tissues into shreds, and the pieces fluttered to the floor, making a soft pile around her ankles. We ignored her. I read my first question:

"What's the prognosis?"

"I told you. We don't know yet."

"The resident said 'massive.' . . ."

"Idiot. He shouldn't have said that."

"What is the percentage of recovery from a massive attack?"

"I don't know. There's no point going by percentages."

"Can a damaged heart heal as good as new?" This seemed to me a vital question. In my mind there was a vision of this heart lying broken, rather like a bone. Hal had broken a knee playing football years ago and the past winter, in a skiing accident, his ankle. Both had mended well. Bones could break and mend strong as they ever had been. Could the same be true of a heart?

"Sure. Good as new. Next question."

"What are the chances of recurrence?"

"No telling."

I looked up from my paper. "But you must have some idea. There must be studies. How many heart-attack victims have second attacks within a year, or two, or five?"

"Oh, come on," he said. "What do you have to know all that stuff for? You reporters. Here, let's see those questions."

He took the piece of paper from my hands. "Prognosis . . . yup. Percentage of recovery . . . yup. Chances of recurrence . . . yup. Okay, I've answered all these. Anything else?"

"No."

"Are you sure? No questions about sex?"

I stared at him. "I beg your pardon?"

"Aren't you going to ask how long it will be before you can have sex?"

Sex. The prognosis for *life* is uncertain, and he wants to talk about *sex*? Is this a sick joke? Is it a Peeping Tom–ism, a quaint form of reassurance, a diversionary tactic, what?

Actually I did understand. I thought I did. Medicine has its vogues, like any other business. Sex was sexy now, as heart transplants had been sexy five years earlier. Fifteen years after Masters and Johnson, thirty years after Kinsey, the medical profession finally had acknowledged sex, and in a fine rush of overcompensation it was stomping the subject to death. Doctor, I have this wart on my backside. Ah, so; how is it affecting your sex life? And here was Roberts now, showing us both that he was of and with the moment. A misplaced impulse, but surely benign.

"No. No more questions," I said.

He looked faintly disappointed.

In the hours between our five-minute visits, I went home and did witless things. I spoke to myself in the mirror. How can this thing have happened? I said. It is inappropriate. You are a mere girl, not ready for the seriousness of life. One afternoon, out of what seemed a perfectly reasonable impulse, I opened a dust-covered box and put on my wedding dress, a limp chiffon reeking of mothballs, and my wedding cap, a little lump of a pillbox styled after those Jacqueline Kennedy used to wear, and my white silk wedding shoes with toes like needle points; and I hauled out our wedding album, which had lain at the back of a closet shelf for a dozen years, and sat for a long time weeping over our dear departed myths: the bride, chastely encased in these same veils; the groom, irreducibly strong and sure; and my father, now dead; and his mother, now dead; and aunts and uncles and cousins, now dead. How extraordinary that they were gone and silk shoes survived. Pillbox hats survived. Mere paper, here, these faint pencil marks, survived. Something is mad in molecular structure, I said.

I telephoned Hal's superior, a powerful man in the medical school, and asked him to come for a drink. He arrived bearing consolation like roses, his eyes gentle but evasive. He knew what was coming.

I sat him down and slugged back a couple of Scotches and said, "It's partly your fault. I blame you. You encouraged him to come here. You encouraged him to build up his own program. You told him he would be funded for five years. And when he had worked so hard and made a program that was big and successful, you let them take it away from him. You sabotaged him. You don't take a man like that . . . his own successful practice for twenty years . . . such pride and skill . . . demeaning him so . . . terrible stress . . ."

He listened quietly, looking pained. Finally he said, "Martha, you're not being fair."

Goddamn passive resister. Not being fair, eh? But not altogether unfair, either, eh? We both know that, don't we?

There was enough truth in what I was saying to send him home feeling guilty, and that sent me to bed feeling better.

On the fourth day, Hal's enzyme levels dropped somewhat. His life signs improved. Word went down to the Patient Information desk to change "critical" to "fair," and for the first time I had some sure sense that he might survive.

So there was no mourning to be done after all. And still I grieved, without knowing quite why or for what or for whom. Grieved, it seemed to me, for the loss of frivolous things. Probably he will never be able to play tennis again. What a terrible loss. Or ski again. How unbearably sad. Or run, or snorkle, or pick me up . . . Why is any of this important? What hurts so damned much? Why this persistent sense of mourning?

It was a mourning he had yet to do. He would, of course. Every survivor of a coronary goes through it.

On the fifth day, when I entered the cubicle, he was sitting up in bed. He was still hooked into various wires, but the nasal tubes were gone. He was fresh-shaven, and the cleft tip of his chin shone like satin, as it always did after a shave.

"This is ridiculous," he said. Big grin. "I feel great. What the hell am I doing with a heart attack? There must be a mistake."

Then, abruptly and deliberately, he began to shake his arms and upper body. Lights flashed on the big black machine, a buzzer sounded and paper began spewing out like ticker tape. He ripped off a section of the paper, studied it. Then he shook his head and gave me a small, wry smile. "It's no mistake," he said. "Wow, have I had a heart attack!"

A nurse came running, warned by the red light flashing at her own desk that the machine in this cubicle had been activated. That could mean trouble. And there sat the patient, studying his electrocardiogram.

"Dr. Lear, what are you *doing?*" she said.

"Just checking."

She rolled her eyes heavenward and went back to the nurses' station.

"Neat trick," I said. "How did you start the machine?"

"Trial and error. It gets activated by any change in pulse rate. So you just jiggle around like this . . ."

He was getting much better. Well enough, almost, to begin showing his rage.

---

Chapter 5

*H*E felt comfortable. Relieved, almost. Finally the thing had happened. Not that he had been sitting around waiting for his coronary; but he had known the genetics, he had known the odds. On some level he had always expected it to happen, he had moved through the years juggling intimations of infarctions and immortality; no cool act. And now it had come and gone and he was still alive, grateful, astonished: *Okay, I've had my heart attack. It's done.*

He knew that he had come close to the edge and that he was not yet on the high ground. The monitor beside him was like a large pinball machine, given to sudden animations, and he lay there thinking—the thought amused him, made him smile—that it might perhaps light up and say TILT: *you lose.* Those sudden beeps and hums were not random. They meant: now, at this moment, some change is happening in this man's heart. But what sort of change? Yes, there goes the beep again. *Am I developing a different rhythm? Am I going into shock? Another attack? Cardiac arrest? What is going on inside me at this moment?*

So of course he felt wary. But not greatly agitated. It was out of his hands, after all. He was no longer in charge. Other people were in charge. He could lie back now, aware that whatever they could do was being done and hoping that it was enough. It felt quite pleasant, really. No responsibility, no decisions to make. Nothing seemed crucial. Nothing could get close enough to seem crucial. If they had come to him and said, "Sir, there is war. There are bombs. There is plague. We must evacuate," he would have told them, "I don't work here. Don't bother me. Do not disturb." He felt helpless and at peace.

Later he would have to resume responsibility. He would have to take this body, in which he himself happened to be housed and which he had abused most dreadfully, treating it with a negligence he would not have shown to any other body in the world, and restore it as best he could. That would take rethinking and retooling, big changes in his life. But he didn't want to think about it yet. There was no need to do anything—anything at all; simply to float here cocooned in this soft postcardiac calm, observing how curious this familiar world looked from his new vantage point.

Curious, even amusing, to lie here observing. The doctor observing the patient. The patient observing the doctor; observing the other doctors, the nurses, the orderlies, the water pourers and bedpan fetchers, everything inverted, sights and meanings reversed, seen as through a mirror . . .

So this was how it looked to sick people. So strange! So many surprises.

Who would have believed, for example, that the nurses were so much more important to sick people than the doctors were? Doctors didn't know that at all. As a doctor, he had always thought of the nurse—it astonished him now that he could have been so dense—as a sort of executive secretary. If she (always she) kept an orderly desk, knew what was going on with the patients, took orders efficiently and gave the right pill to the right patient at the right time, she was a good nurse.

But now that he was a patient, he could see that the nurses were . . . angels! Angels of mercy!

They were with him constantly, these woman figures. They were gentle and good. They fixed his pillow. They came when he called for help. They said, "This will make you feel better" and "There, isn't that better?" They touched him with their hands, flesh to flesh. His succor. His lifesavers. His lifelines.

The male figures were with him for ten minutes a day. They were marginal figures, shadowy and cold. They touched him with instruments—stethoscopes, blood-pressure gadgets. They had condescending airs. They asked him many curt questions and grunted at him. He did not like them.

"Do you have any trouble breathing?"

"No."

"Do you have any chest pain?"

"Yes."

"How bad?"

"Slight."

"Oh. Do you have . . ."

How quickly arrogance had been bred into these kids, these baby-faced interns and residents. (So young! Had he looked this young when he himself had been an intern, feeling so old in his dewy skin and in his nifty white coat?) How early they grew pompous!

The way they managed his chest pain, for instance. At first the pain had been severe, and they had given him shots that sent him out into space. But then, as the bad pain passed and he grew stronger and more aware, he did not want to be knocked out anymore. He saw no medical indication for it. When a cardiac patient is feeling agitated, there is good reason to keep him doped up. But he himself was feeling quite calm now. Remarkably calm, really.

So he said to one of the residents, "I am having only low-grade discomfort. But whenever I report any pain at all, I get a shot. It makes me dizzy and disoriented. Could I have something milder?"

The resident got angry. He said, "There is a medication ordered for pain for you. If you want it, you can have it. If not, you'll get nothing." And walked out, leaving him lying there, helpless.

So he went through the evening with this pressure in his chest. As soon as the shift changed, he asked the next resident on duty, "Could I have aspirin instead of a shot? My pain isn't bad."

"Sure," the resident said; a jewel, a rare bird. And soon enough the pain had disappeared, and he hadn't been knocked out.

He realized then—something else he never had realized before—what huge emotional investment doctors made in the orders they wrote. It was utterly gurulike: Give the patient the green pill and say, "This is going to help you." And in fact the red pill might work every bit as well, maybe better, but the guru's omnipotence is now tied to the green pill. If the patient asks for something different, that is a challenge to medical authority and must, like all such challenges, be faced down.

This is annoying, he thought. Worse than annoying: this is bad medicine. These people do not listen to the patient, they do not think in terms of what is best for the patient. They are too enveloped in their own authority.

Had it been like this in that neat, clean, good little hospital, back there in Mount Sinai Hospital in Hartford, Connecticut, where he had been in private practice all those years?

Probably.

Had he, then, as an attending physician, been a party to bad medical care?

Surely not. Never deliberately.

Undeliberately, then? By default? By his own obliviousness?

That was what appalled him now, his obliviousness. He had never had any notion how his patients were treated by house staff. If they had been neglected or infantilized or patronized or otherwise abused (as patients were; he saw it here so clearly), he would never have known unless they complained. And patients seldom complained. They expected to take orders, as doctors expected to give orders. It was part of the unwritten contract.

He remembered an elderly man upon whom he had performed a bladder operation. The man had a catheter in his penis. In the night he rang for the nurse and told her that he was in pain and he thought the catheter was not draining properly. She had telephoned the intern on duty, who was napping in his room.

"It's just postoperative pain; there's nothing wrong with the catheter," the intern had said. "Give him fifty milligrams of Demerol."

She had given the patient the shot. But later yet, toward dawn, the old man had rung for her again and told her that he was in agony now, he couldn't stand this pain, and please, please call the doctor.

She had called Lear at home at 5 A.M.

"The intern didn't see the patient?" he had asked.

"No. He ordered the Demerol by phone."

"And is the catheter draining properly? Can you tell?"

"I can't tell."

So he had thrown on some clothes and driven over to see the agonized old man, and of course the catheter wasn't draining; it was clotted with blood, the bladder bloated with urine that had no place to go. He had cleaned out the tube, and then he had confronted the intern.

"I could understand if you had seen the patient and misdiagnosed the problem," he had said. "But not even to bother seeing him, to let him suffer unnecessarily for hours, to give orders by phone because you didn't want to get out of bed . . . If you can't do better than that, I don't want you taking care of my patients."

He had been in a deep purple rage. Such negligence!

But he would never have known there was anything wrong—not that time, not any other—unless someone complained. Damn it, doctors *should* know. They should care. Say, how're they treating you? How's the food? Accommodations comfortable? Staff courteous? Prompt service? Anything you need? Just let me know. . . .

Doctors never asked such things. He himself would never even have thought to ask. Didn't that make him negligent too?

Ah. Bingo.

Where the hell else, he thought, would you tolerate such rotten service for $185.80 a day?

And now, like a grievance committee, he began collecting grievances.

The way they distributed sleeping pills. Untenable.

He himself always had ordered sleeping pills P.R.N.: as necessary. That meant that the pill was available if his patients felt a need for it at bedtime. Whether they took it or not was irrelevant in health care. But he himself, something of a therapeutic nihilist, who resisted putting even aspirin down his own gullet, did not like those pills. Always, he had cautioned his own patients to take them only when necessary.

Now that he himself was a patient, he could see what "when necessary" really meant. It meant when necessary *for the house staff*. And for the house staff, sleeping pills were *always* necessary. Sleeping pills meant that the nights would be more peaceful, fewer pains perceived, fewer anxieties, fewer calls to the nurses' station, less disturbance for the house staff—less night work for everyone. So zap all the patients. Knock them out. P.R.N.

And now he no longer wanted sleeping pills. He knew he didn't need them. And too, one became addicted so easily, and doctors could stay addicted so gracefully: take out the prescription pad, write the order, a little of the sweet, spacy stuff for Doc's nasty old bursitis. . . . In fact the addiction rate among doctors was much higher than in the general population. It was just so damned easy.

He told a resident, "I don't want those sleeping pills routinely. Why don't you leave the order P.R.N.?"

The resident nodded as though he understood. But that night, when a nurse came in with the nighttime medications, they included the same old knockout tablets.

He said, "I'll take that one and that one and that one, but not those two."

A look of shock. "But you *have* to. The doctor *ordered* them."

"Well, the patient refuses them."

He slept beautifully.

The resident sulked.

The social atrocities committed by the staff! It was as though, by the simple act of signing in, patients forfeited the right to be treated with respect.

One day he lay in bed reading, his door closed.

Two white-coated figures came bursting in. One began yelling at him, "What gave you the right to do that? What are you trying to do, make trouble?" Loud and abrasive.

He didn't know what the fellow was talking about. He said, "Who are you?"

"I'm the medical resident."

"I know that. I can tell by your stethoscope. But what's your name?"

Flustered, the resident quieted down, mumbled a name.

"Well, I'm Dr. Lear. Now, what's the problem?"

The problem was, it turned out, that they were in the wrong room. They walked out, leaving him seething. Suppose they had been in the right room; what kind of way was that to talk to a cardiac, or to any patient at all? And where else (prisons, of course) would total strangers come bursting into your bedroom, eh? And in what medical classes, from what pig-skinned professors, did these house-staff brats learn that it was permissible to so demean and infantilize their patients? And why did no patient ever say, "Get the hell out of here! This is a private room! Knock first!"? There was a reciprocal acceptance of the ground rules, and the ground rules stank.

They should make another rule, he thought. They should make a rule that every doctor must spend one week a year in a hospital bed. That would change some things in a hurry.

"Get the hell out of here! This is a private room! Knock first!" he yelled at the still-swinging door.

The rage that he would later realize was directed at his own loss of power, he directed at these people and these routines. He did not know that he was enraged. He thought that he was annoyed. He thought that he was having great medicosociological insights about doctors and patients and medical institutions and the relationships among them all.

Actually, his observations were valid enough. The people behaved quite as badly as he thought they did; the system was quite as dehumanizing as he thought it was. It was simply that he had found a convenient mesh of truth and consequence: So long as he focused on what was wrong with the system, he did not have to deal with his own cardiac rage.

Well, now, he thought, I myself will not submit to these indignities. I will not be infantilized.

He cast about for some declaration of independence and found it in his hospital gown. This gown symbolized sickness. He was not sickness. He was on his way to health.

"Bring me my cutoff blue jeans," he told me.

"Your what?"

"You know. The ones I cut the legs off."

The ones that he wore when he sailed his Sunfish in Provincetown waters, the ones that he associated with summer and good times.

He had been yearning for the sun. For days he had been nagging for permission to lie out on the sun roof that was at the end of the corridor, perhaps twenty yards from his room. Finally permission had been granted.

"Yes, the jeans," he said. "I don't want to wear this damn thing"—slapping angrily at a fold of the white cotton gown. "I want to get some tan on my chest."

So I brought the sawed-off jeans that had seen him through ten summers, raveled and faded and patched beyond any possible redemption, which was to say, in their prime; and he put them on with soft fumbling motions and stood tall and extended an elbow to me, both of us trembling with the fineness of this moment.

"Shall we go?" he said.

He was some sight. The jeans hung loosely on him now. On the left side of the rump was a patch shaped like a fish. It said PISCES. Beneath the fringed cuffs hung his legs, wrapped from ankle to knee in the white elastic stockings that are used to keep bedridden patients from developing thrombophlebitis—blood clots; and on his feet, his favorite Provincetown sandals.

Slowly we proceeded down the corridor. Other patients, in their pink nylon dusters and their seersucker robes, eyed him curiously. Nurses smiled and winked. An orderly said, "Man, those sure are great sandals, Dr. Lear."

"Why not?" he said.

The twenty yards to the sun roof was a far longer distance than he had yet been allowed to walk. He was unsteady on his feet and, toward the end, staggering. We made it very slowly up the three steps to the roof level, and then he sank into a deck chair, breathing heavily; smiled up at the sky; nodded some warm personal greeting to the trees and gave himself up, ecstatically, to the sun.

When we came back to his room an hour later, he was exhausted but sun-warmed and mellow. Roberts was waiting.

"Hi!" Hal said.

Roberts looked silently at the jeans, the brass-studded belt, the sandals, the PISCES patch. His face wrinkled with acute distaste.

"Why can't you dress like everyone else?" he said. "You look like a bum."

There had been this bad thing between them from the beginning. Hal did not talk to me about it, not then; but he kept trying to analyze it.

The man was strange. He was too distant, too impersonal. He seemed unable to connect. It was fortunate that I can objectify myself, that I do not need much emotional support, Hal told himself, buried deep in his own defenses; I would never get it from this man.

Roberts never looked at him or talked to him directly. Roberts never called him by any name—not Hal, not Harold, not Dr. Lear, not Lear, nothing. Simply "you." He would come by twice a day, bury his head in the chart and say, "Well, you seem to be okay." As in the relationship between a building and a janitor.

Why should this be? Was it something he himself was doing? And if so, what? He wasn't being a pest, he wasn't asking any of the bad questions. The bad questions were the nuisance questions, the up-against-the-wall questions that doctors hated to hear: "Can I go home next Sunday?" "How long do I have to live?" "Will this ever happen again?"—that sort of thing.

Doctors learned soon enough to deflect such questions. Throw them back at the patient. Make the patient responsible. This had never occurred to him before, because doctors did such things unconsciously, more or less; but now that he was watching and listening so hard, he could see that it really was a game, one of the tricky little substructures of doctor–patient relationships. A professional ploy that might be called "It's Your Fault." As in:

"Why did the operation take so long?"
"Because you lost so much blood."
Not: *"Because the surgeon blew it."*
"Why do you keep making these tests?"
"Because you have a very stubborn infection."
Not: *"Because I cannot diagnose your case."*
"Why did I get sick again?"
"Because you were very weak."
Not: *"Because I did not treat you competently the first time."*
"When can I go home?"
"That's up to you. There's a lot of moisture in your lungs. . . ."

Well, he asked no such questions. He had asked one, once. "How long will I be in the C.C.U.?" he had asked. "That depends on you," Roberts had replied coolly, and he had asked no more.

So that was not the reason for Roberts' hostility. He could smell this hostility; it hung on the man's skin like sweat.

Could it be because he himself was a doctor? That would be the most obvious thing. Many doctors got jittery when they were treating other doctors. It was nervous-making to know that the patient beneath your stethoscope also was looking over your shoulder.

Yes, perhaps that. Or perhaps—this was a reach, but not impossible —because he worked in sex research and sex therapy. And not only because he worked on that dark and pungent side of the tracks, but because he had given up urology, a fine old rep-tie specialty, to do it.

Roberts might be hostile to that. Many doctors were. Every reputable sex researcher and therapist he knew, from Masters and Johnson on down, was accustomed to the professional hostility.

"*Sex* therapy!" the gynecologists and proctologists would say, reddening, their laughter coming in too tight and too fast on the words. "You call that medicine? Why don't you go back to practicing *real* medicine?"

For sex was something they hadn't been trained to consider at all. They had been pointed toward some reverse goal, in fact, trained to look at the human body with dispassionate eyes and touch it with dispassionate hands, sterile, antiseptic.

Most clinicians were less defensive these days. But there were still the inveterate tight-asses, and Roberts might be one such.

Whatever it was, it was bad. Roberts clearly was tense and uncomfortable. Not that a doctor must play psychic toesies with his patients, but there should be a certain emotional rapport in a cardiological relationship. A heart attack, after all, is an emotional trip.

He also seemed, in some odd, quirky way, uninterested. Plumped up with ennui. Only once did he show real animation. It was one day when he stood at the foot of the bed reading the chart, fiddling around meanwhile in his jacket pocket, and his hand came out with a scrap of paper. His face lit up.

"Oh, my gosh, I almost forgot," he said. "I'm supposed to make arrangements for a stable for my daughter's pony."

Stable? Pony? I happened to be in the room at the time. Hal had been in the middle of some question about his medications. We were both startled.

"Pony? Oh, how nice. Now, about those pills . . ."

"Does that kid love her pony! You should see her ride that pony. Boy, that kid . . ."

Like someone who assembles ironing boards for a living. As though he had been too long on this particular assembly line, it was too dull and predictable now, a heart attack was a heart attack and what else was new?; and the anxieties of the cardiac had become a bore as well, a broken record clicking forever in his ears; and the questions and the depressions and the fearful tearful relatives and the anginal sweats and the emergency admissions and the sudden collapses upon suburban tennis courts and the terrified calls in the night and every known variation upon the malfunction of a pump—boring now, all of it, and the only satisfaction left in being a doctor was that it provided the wherewithal to maintain his daughter's pony.

Of course Hal couldn't let it go. He brooded about it that night, muttering "Pony!" to himself, and the next day he said, "Well, I did have a question about my medications, but if there is something *more important* you want to talk about, like your daughter's pony, we're *certainly* interested. . . ."

"Is he always this impossible?" Roberts said to me. Furious, trying to sound amused.

"Not always. Hal, cut it out."

"Oh. You mean we're *not* interested in his daughter's pony?"

Thus they kept outraging each other. The chemistry between them positively reeked. Hal tried to analyze it, and probably all the reasons he found were substantially correct. But the most obvious one never occurred to him: he was being a pain in the ass.

Most cardiac patients are difficult, and perhaps he was even worse than most. Doctors make notoriously bad patients. In some mystic way they consider themselves immune. Disease is something they treat, not something that happens to them; and when it does happen to them, it is a terrible affront, a traitorous inside job. So indeed he was hostile. But cardiologists are used to that, and most of them learn to transcend it. Roberts wasn't even generous enough to try.

Roberts: "We're discharging you Sunday. Let's go over the instructions. Food: stay on the low-sodium diet. Exercise: You can start walking a block a day. Do not walk uphill or into the wind. Resumption of normal activities: you should be able to start working part-time in three weeks; full-time in six weeks. And I want to see you in my office a week from Monday. Do you have questions about anything else?"

Lear: "Yes. When can I start having wet dreams?"

Roberts' lips go prunelike and he walks out.

"I knew it!" Hal said. "I knew that tight-ass wouldn't mention sex. Can you imagine giving a cardiac instructions about everything you think he may be wondering about, and never even mentioning sex?"

"He mentioned it to me," I said.

"He did? When?"

"The first time I met him. When you were still in the C.C.U. He asked if I wanted to know how long it would be before we could have sex."

He smiled. "Not long," he said. "That hostile bastard."

Chapter 6

---

*A*T home, I fussed about him as though he were a newborn. The simile is too precise. In just that way I fussed and fluttered, kitchy-kooing, endlessly rearranging his atmosphere, bearing chicken soup and other placebos for my own nourishment; tiptoeing into the bedroom, in the way of nervous new mothers, to put my hands and ears down close to various body parts and satisfy myself that the baby still breathed in his crib.

Once, when I could see no rise and fall of the bedsheets, I even held a pocket mirror under his nose, as I had seen them do in the movies. He stirred and understood in half-sleep this idiot thing I was doing. "What are you so afraid of?" he murmured sadly.

I didn't know what I was afraid of. A crib death. That he might die silently in his sleep. That he might wake, clutching his heart. That he might . . .

He was so tired all the time. He looked sick—far sicker here at home than in the hospital, where his had been simply one of many pallors. He was having chest pains. "Healing pains," Roberts called them, explaining something about the fusing of scar tissue. Still: pains. I felt uneasy. And the support system of the hospital was gone;

no oxygen tanks, no instant intravenous. I sent secret instructions down to our building staff: If I ever give *three short buzzes* and *two long buzzes* on the intercom, call the police; call 911; call an ambulance; run like hell to the hospital, get a wheelchair, just like last time, and get it up here fast.

At first we went together for his short daily walks. Then he wanted to go alone. ("Why must you go with me? What do you think will happen?" "Nothing, nothing." "Then why do you infantilize me like this?" "*Infantilize?* I don't do any such . . .") I watched the clock. It seemed that the block a day—and then, as he worked his way up, the two, three, four blocks a day—took too long. Five minutes; where the hell can he be? Ten minutes; oh, Jesus—skipping ahead now into fantasy visions: he is lying down there on the curb, a crowd is gathering round him, you know those cool native spirits, they'll simply stand there ho-humming, better get down there now, run, run . . . *No!* Stop this craziness, control yourself. That's all he needs, eh?, is a crazy wife chasing him down the street: *Yoo-hoo, Harold, are you still alive?*

When I myself was out of the house, marketing or whatever, the ambulance sirens, constant in this hospital zone, made me crazy. That murderous shriek which I hated, anyway, beyond all other mechanical sounds, that sound which had been a horror for me since the night ten years before when I had sat in one of those vans beside my father's body, an attendant screaming to me above the siren shriek, "It's no use, I'm sorry, he's dead," I screaming back, "No, please, keep the oxygen mask on him, Daddy, Daddy, *listen* to me," screaming like that to a dead body above the siren shriek of a dark van that went hurtling through the deserted country roads of Canton, Massachusetts, where we had been in attendance at my brother's wedding reception . . . Oh, some night. Some exit Daddy made. Give me any sound rather than the shriek of an ambulance siren.

And now, walking along Madison Avenue, I would hear that sound and the gooseflesh would spread over me: Could that ambulance be for my husband? Does he lie dying, purpling as my father did, the elevator men standing as the wedding guests had stood in helpless horror, and I down here unaware, down here with the chopped sirloin and the cottage cheese? I would begin to rush along the street. Jesus! That siren is close. Here it comes; is it going to turn into our block? Running now. Oh, please, don't turn into our block. . . . Good! It passed on. Saved again. And homeward now with the cottage cheese; nothing better for the appetite than somebody else's disaster. . . .

When he had been home a week, we went for the first time to Roberts' office. A wet, nasty day, but Hal refused to take a cab. "I am supposed to walk *every day*," he said. "It is *good* for me."

We took a bus and walked two blocks to Roberts' office in what was now a downpour. I tried to hold the umbrella over him. "Stop *protecting* me," he said. "I won't *melt*." And in truth I was driving even myself crazy with the constant hovering, and I couldn't seem to stop.

Roberts greeted us austerely and disappeared with Hal, and twenty minutes later the nurse beckoned me into his consulting room. Everything anal-compulsive neat, pictures of a boy and girl—ah, the *pony* girl—upon his desk, paper clips in a brown leather cup, not a shred of paper in sight.

"He's doing well," he told me, quite as though Hal weren't sitting there too. "His cardiogram looks stable, his chest sounds clear. I've told him he can start walking three blocks a day. We should keep him in shape, get his body toned up. . . . I want to see him in two weeks."

A swift shake of the hands, and we were back out on the street. It still poured. There were no cabs. We had to walk slightly uphill to get to a bus stop. When we got there, we were both soaked and he was too tired to stand. We stumbled into a coffee shop next door.

"Hal!"

It was a casual friend. We hadn't seen her in months, but I knew she had heard of his illness. Now she stared at him. I turned to see what she saw; a sick man huddled in a black raincoat. A man in whom some insidious process clearly lingered on, despite what his doctor said; a man whom she has seen robust and now saw frail, stoop-shouldered, with an aged gaunt gray face, the eyes—even the eyes!—lusterless. She was an actress and good at her craft. But for a moment, before she could hide it, the horror stood clear in her face.

"Why, Hal!" she said. "Why, don't you look *marvelous!*"

He lay out on our terrace in his cutoff blue jeans, his thoughts sober and inward. He had seen his most recent cardiogram. It was, as they said in medicine, "stabilized." He could not read the subtleties of a cardiogram, but he could read gross abnormalities, and this last one had shown exactly the same gross abnormalities as he had had in the coronary-care unit. Stabilized at the level of grossly abnormal.

Very well, then. There had been a garden-variety massive infarction. Now the patient seemed to be doing well. He was following the usual course: three weeks in hospital, three weeks at home with gradually increasing ambulation; next six weeks, gradual return to work—"resumption of normal activity." Three months after the attack, a cardiac is theoretically healed.

Of course, he would never be quite the same again. One is not, after a part of the heart is gone. They had told him that he had been stricken in the anterior wall of the left ventricle. For all he knew, the whole damned wall might be gone. For certain, his cardiac reserve would be limited now. But if he took care, if he minimized the risks, he could make a decent recovery and hope for a decent life-span.

Minimize the risks. That was a tough one. There were seven acknowledged risk factors. Of these seven, the only true immutable was the genetic factor, and the genetic vulnerability of his family was catastrophic.

Himself an only child, with both parents dead of heart attacks.

Five brothers on his father's side, all dead of coronaries in their fifties.

Seven siblings on his mother's side, all but two dead by sixty; all but one dead of coronaries—including two women, in a generation in which it had been rare for women to die of coronaries. All those genetically poisoned siblings living at the top of their lungs, denying all the signs until they dropped—his Uncle Mac, *a cardiologist*, for Christ's sake, denying his way right through two heart attacks and into the final third—"It's my gall bladder, it's my gall bladder . . ."

So there was a genetic factor, carved in stone. Now he looked at the other risk factors:

Weight: Good; it had never been a problem, and would not be.

Physical activity: Good; probably no more tennis or skiing but he would be able to walk and perhaps, in time, to jog. He had always exercised sensibly and would continue to do so.

Diabetes: No history in family.

Cholesterol: Sky-high, even with the low-cholesterol diet he had been on for years. All he could do was keep dieting. There had been a drug that lowered cholesterol levels. It happened also to cause cataracts, a side effect which the drug company had managed to suppress

for some time, so that a number of poor bastards with high cholesterols got themselves blinded before the stuff finally was taken off the
market. Later, another drug house had come up with a pill which
lowered cholesterols *without* causing cataracts: a pharmaceutical triumph. Reports in the literature had been consistently good, and finally he had ordered some, just weeks before his attack. Then he had
read the Framingham Group Study, a huge follow-up study of cardiacs. And according to that report, it didn't seem to matter one bit
whether you took cholesterol-reducing drugs or not, you would die
just as fast either way. The bottle of pills still sat on his bureau,
unopened. You had to get up mighty early in the morning to keep up
with medical progress.

Smoking: a ghastly history: three packs a day for thirty-five years,
come rain, sleet, sore throats, sinusitis, laryngitis, day in, day out,
faithful as a postman.

Stress: bad. He handled stress in very bad ways, internalizing. And
there had been so much stress in his life of late. That miserable work
situation which had filled him with impotent rage, and impotent rage
was a poison, a gun to the head, nails in the coffin; impotent rage
killed more people than all the holiday traffic combined.

These he would have to work on. He would have to stop smoking.
And he would have to change his responses to stress: cool his compul-
sions, change this intolerable work situation, clear the guilt-producing
garbage out of his life, simplify, simplify . . .

The Framingham Group Study was on his desk. He had clipped
and read it just before his attack, operating off some anticipatory
vibration. Now he reread it. There it was again, that taut mean statistic: 50 percent of all coronary victims die before reaching the hospital. And then this one: of those who survive, 35 percent die within
two years.

He thought a lot about that. In Urology, he thought, lying out there
on the terrace, squinting into the soft September sun, we can say that
forty out of a hundred people with carcinomas of the kidney will die
within ten years. A 40-percent mortality rate. Of course, for those
who die and for those who love them, the mortality rate is 100 percent. To make a prognosis, I would need to know the variables: How
big was the tumor? Did it involve any veins? How long had the
patient had symptoms? And so forth.

Now, if we say that roughly one out of three heart-attack survivors
will be dead within two years, we must consider another set of vari-

ables: How severe was the attack? Where was it located? He knew that damage to the rear wall of the heart was worse than damage to the sides, and that damage to the front wall—the anterior, where he had gotten his—was the worst. How much heart muscle had died? What was the recovery course? And so forth.

I need to know these things, he said to himself. And finally, on the next office visit, he did ask Roberts a bad question:

"I have a wife, two kids. I want to be able to make realistic plans. Can you give me some idea of my prognosis?"

"No. You're doing fine. Don't worry about it."

Well, then. He would have to push.

"I've read the Framingham Group Study. It said that thirty-five percent of survivors die within two to three years after the first attack, depending on variables. I'd like to know . . ."

Roberts rose abruptly. His face was red. "It is nonsense to talk about this kind of thing. You're all right," he said. He closed the patient's folder, suppressed rage in the neat small gesture, and the interview was terminated.

Hal understood Roberts' anger. If a patient asks, "What are my chances, Doc?" Doc can select from the standard repertory: "Everything is fine, fine!" But if the patient says, "I read in the Framingham Group Report that thirty-five percent . . ." it is hard to be evasive. Doc must talk plain. Roberts hadn't liked that at all.

Well, tough. The patient had come to him asking, "What is my prognosis?" (playing the scene over again in his mind, as though he had been a detached observer in that consulting room, able to peer past his own defenses). What was that patient really asking him? What was *I* really asking him? To give me encouragement that my life wasn't over.

If I were treating another doctor for cancer of the kidney and he said to me, "I know the mortality rate. What is my prognosis?" I would hear him between the lines. I would know that he was looking for hope. I wouldn't lie. I would stress the positive. Even when things are quite bad, there is a positive. I might say:

"Yes, those are the statistics. But they don't take into account the variables. We caught this early. Your tumor was small and encapsulated. We saw no evidence whatever of spread. . . .

And even if the damn thing *had* spread, even if the prognosis seemed rotten, you could in perfect truth speak supportively. You could say:

"We never know the rate of progression of these things. That tumor that I took out of you last week may have been in you for ten years. It may be another ten years before you get another symptom. You're—let's see, sixty-two? Let's see what happens when you're seventy-two. And by that time, who knows what cures they may have for cancer!"

It was a doctor's responsibility to respond to a patient's anxiety, Roberts could have done it. But Roberts hadn't.

Well. He would just have to work it out for himself.

Dr. Lear: "Yes, one in three die. But those are the old, fat, feeble ones. You are healthy but for this accident of the heart; you are in otherwise good condition. . . ."

Patient Lear: "I want to help myself. Life is sweet. What can I do?"

Dr. Lear: "Oh, *lots.* Let's take a look at how you can minimize the risk factors. . . ."

In the third week at home, as he lay in the sun thinking these thoughts, something terrible began to come upon him.

Something prodromal. A strange awareness of a *thing* that was happening or about to happen in his heart. Not just in his chest but in his *heart*, he knew it: a low-grade aching in there, an ominousness, a time bomb ticking quietly, about to explode.

Relax. Relax! But this *thing* persisted, dreadful, impending. . . .

He called Roberts.

"Healing pains, maybe," Roberts said.

"No, not this time. I don't think so."

"Okay. Come over to the cardiology clinic."

"Is it all right to walk?"

"Oh, sure."

He got off the phone and said to me, "Let's get over there. Something bad is happening."

My guts trembled. This wasn't at all his style. His style was to deny. If he called this thing bad, it must be catastrophic.

"I think we should get a wheelchair," I said.

"If my doctor says I can walk, I'll walk. Don't be my doctor."

We walked the two blocks very slowly. Something hovering, like storm clouds, but from within. Not looking at each other, angry about the wheelchair, and very scared.

"Tell me again, what kind of sensation?" Roberts said.

"Dull, persistent, prodromal. Sort of . . . I don't know how else to describe it . . . as though something terrible is happening or about to happen."

"Well, I've found nothing on examination, and your cardiogram is unchanged. It must be healing pains."

"But it is like no other kind of pain I've ever had."

"It happens like that. Very common. Why don't you just go home and relax."

"Okay."

He went home and to bed.

"Do *you* believe it's healing pains?" I said.

"No."

"What *do* you think it is?"

"I don't know."

He knew as a surgeon that this period, from four to six weeks after a trauma, is a dangerous time for the flesh. What is going on in this period is a tension, in some sense a contest, between opposite processes: dead tissue is rotting, like a carcass in the sun, while the live tissue around it is struggling to mend. In these weeks, if the balance tips the wrong way—if the dying outpaces the healing—the surgeon sees wounds begin to bulge and grow weak; vital parts rupture; seams burst.

Could any of that be happening to his heart? If so, he was a damned fool to have insisted upon walking. And Roberts was a damned fool to have let him walk.

In about a day, the sensation disappeared completely. He wondered if he would ever know what had caused it.

Chapter 7

*H*E knelt in the center of the big bed, seemingly lost in some fine fit of passion. Surreptitiously he checked his pulse. Not with his fingers to the wrist. Nothing so vulgar. Just a hand resting casually at his throat, up there against the carotid artery, so that it would look as though he were simply, in the gallant old way, supporting his weight on his elbows.

His pulse was a little fast, but nothing worrisome. Good, so far. He was sweating. But it was the hot sweat of exercise, not the clammy sweat of shock. He was panting. But it was normal enough to pant. His heart was pounding. Oh, damn, pounding very hard now. But that was normal too. Wasn't it?

That was the trouble. How could he be sure? How could you tell a heart that pounded toward orgasm from a heart that pounded toward its own destruction? No *petit mal*, that.

Better rest a moment. Catch my breath. But smoothly, gracefully, so that she will not suspect. It would be terrible if she knew how scared I am. The thing would be ruined for her.

This was rich. Not to laugh aloud, but funny. Maybe some day, if he survived this sweet fearsome screw, he would get up the courage to tell about it in his lecture. The lecture called "Sexual Aspects of Medical Practice," which he had given so many times, with such success, to audiences of doctors.

". . . Now, as to the sexual aspects of heart disease, we know that twenty-four percent of coronary patients are impotent sexually, although there is no physiological basis for it. Why should such a large group be impotent?

"The most obvious reason is the fear that they may overexert themselves and die in the act of sex. But beyond that, there is the psychological association of a heart attack with loss of symbolic potency. The cardiac is no longer the hard-driving money earner, no longer the weight lifter, no longer the macho man; his self-image is devastated and he loses his potency. . . .

"We know from nurses in the intensive-care units that there is a very high incidence of masturbation among the male cardiac patients. Here, too, evidence of anxiety. . . .

"In studying the impotent group, we find that over ninety percent of their doctors never mentioned sex during convalescence . . . important to understand the role we ourselves may play in perpetuating the patient's fears. . . . When discussing resumption of physical activity, important to discuss sex. . . . Emphasize that there is no need to be afraid. . . .

"Now, a small personal note, a leaf from my own book, as it were: There I knelt in my bed one day, about six weeks after my heart attack, making love to my wife. . . . And I want you to know, ladies and gentlemen, that despite all the talk and theory, despite all the research and the statistics and the cool nifty bits of advice, I want you to know that yours truly, El Professor here, was scared absolutely shitless."

Yes, that would be useful and informative. It was always a good idea to include a personal anecdote in a lecture.

It had been a pretty good lecture, actually. An important subject. Because doctors could be (and usually were) grossly negligent in these ways, doctors could make sexual cripples out of their patients—not just cardiacs: people with mastectomies, colostomies, other body mutilations, living silently with God knows what agonizing urgencies and anxieties—cripple them for good, simply by saying nothing. Or by saying the wrong thing, which could be even worse. Just before his own heart attack a man had come into his office, impotent, not knowing why. They soon found out. He'd had a coronary. In time he had found himself waking up with erections and with the nice old fevers, but he had been too scared to do anything. Finally, at the end of an office visit, he had asked his internist, "Is it safe to have sex?"

"Perfectly safe," the doctor had said.

"Are you sure?"

"Oh, absolutely. And if I'm wrong"—here the doctor had leaned way back in his swivel chair, folded his hands behind his head and laughed—"and if I'm wrong, what a way to go!"

From that moment, impotent.

So an informed doctor could make a powerful difference. He had been glad for the opportunity to give this lecture, and physicians always had listened to him with respect, since he was an expert, after all; and he had always spoken with confidence and authority, since he knew what he was talking about, after all.

Except that he hadn't known bugger-all. Not about the fear. None of his expertise had prepared him for the fact that the fear went this deep, choking desire out like a weed.

And then, kneeling there, wondering what might happen to him before this act was done, he had a sudden astonishing thought. Astonishing in that he had never discussed it as a doctor, he had never heard any other doctor discuss it, he had never even thought of it before. It was: Jesus! What about *her* fear?

Why had it never occurred to him to talk to the doctors about this? Of course, quite possibly, it would have occurred to women doctors.

I had so wanted this. It was a symbol, reassuring beyond all medical reports, reassuring beyond description. I hadn't anticipated that I would be so scared.

It seemed crucial that he not know how scared I was. Lying there silently, as though my mind were on my pleasure. Watching him in the half-light that came from the bathroom, seeing the fingers pressed so slyly against his carotid artery, wondering what the pressure told him. Feeling his rhythm, the contact so sweet, and hearing him breathe heavily like that, and wondering if it was okay or too much. Then feeling his body go still. Was he all right? Did I dare ask?

I felt poised at the edge of an irredeemable mistake. It would be dreadful to make him feel like an invalid here, of all places, in the bed. One wrong word and I might ruin it, erection gone, impulse gone, confidence gone, goodbye, and maybe for good.

And yet it might be even more dangerous to say nothing. For his body was in motion again now, and what if he was feeling pain, denying it, pushing himself to perform?

"Do you want to rest a moment?" I whispered.

Wrong. He made a sound like a sob and fell away from me, and we lay silent, not touching in any way.

I was having a bad time with the cigarettes. Smoking more and enjoying it less, and desperately wanting to quit because, after all, he had quit just weeks before under the large duress of a heart attack, and things were hard enough for him without my inhaling and exhaling about the house.

Yet I felt unable to stop. It agitated me even to think of sitting at the typewriter without cigarettes. This was where all my writing friends lost the battle, right here at the typewriter. A habit absorbed into the bloodstream: the typewriter and the smoke, the smoke and the typewriter; how could one think even of spelling or simple grammar without that vital sense of *presence*, pulmonary eroticism, deep in the lungs?

So I concealed. In his presence I clenched plastic placebos between my teeth and sneaked real smokes in the bathroom. When he slept, I smoked at my desk. I hid packs at the backs of bookshelves, in pillow covers, in a soup tureen.

It amused him that I thought I had him fooled. He would sniff the smoke in the bathrooms and laugh. It became a challenge to find my hiding places, while I was out smoking in the A&P; grinning expectantly as he searched the bookshelves, marveling at my slyness when he got to the pillow covers; when he found a pack in the soup tureen, there was, he said later, a sense of triumph as pure as if he had made a hard, clean strike deep into enemy territory. Of course, it was only a game.

Finally he said, "Look, I know you're smoking. It's okay. Just don't do it directly in front of me, and please don't leave cigarettes lying around."

That was a great relief. It reduced the guilt to a tenable level. I was very careful with the cigarettes, but once, having worked very late and boozed a bit much, I forgot and left them on the dining table. In the morning he was icy with rage.

"You did this deliberately," he said. "You left them here to tempt me."

"Deliberately! Are you crazy?"

"*Don't* call me crazy."

"Okay, not crazy. *Paranoid.* If you believe that, you're paranoid! You should see a shrink!"

"Don't tell *me* I should see a shrink. Maybe *you* should see a shrink!"

And such and so. Tensions, as I say.

He thought it quite possible that I was counting the number in each pack before I hid them, and so he never smoked mine. Several times, when he was out on those solitary walks, he bought a pack, smoked a couple and threw the rest away.

But this was too gross an admission of failure. It became a point of honor not to buy cigarettes.

Instead, he grubbed for them in gutters.

The grubbing had begun in the hospital. A thing done in surreptitious ways. Picking up matches at the nurses' station. ("Anyone have a pack of matches?" he would ask, and someone would say, "Sure," and hand them to him without even looking up.) Padding down to the visitors' lounge at night, after visiting hours, to pick butts out of the ashtrays. The first time, he had felt revulsion. But this qualm was soon conquered. It became a sport to find the best butts—of good length, uncrumpled, preferably filtered, nonmentholated, with no visible stains. He cached these in his shaving kit and smoked them behind the locked bathroom door.

When he came home, he had to switch to the street supply. This was more noxious yet. Surgeons typically are clean, sensitive to sanitary precautions, and he was no exception. Yet here he was, not only doing this revolting thing but doing it in just this way, sneakily: strolling along Fifth Avenue looking in the gutter; spotting a good butt, pausing to look left and right and across the street, to make sure no one observed him; leaning over, as though tying a shoelace, and meanwhile palming the butt. Like a Bowery wino.

In just this way he happened one day, while seeming to tie his shoelace near a parked car, to glance up and catch his image in the car's rearview mirror; and to look down then and see the butt he had just picked up, the yellow stain of dried saliva on its edge.

You are disgusting, he said to the mirror image. You disgust me.

And began to cry.

He knew that it had more, infinitely more, to do with self-image than with the simple desire for a smoke. He knew that this behavior which was so repugnant to him, and which he could not seem to stop, was dictated by a sense of worthlessness; and that this sense of worthlessness, of being a cipher amid the significant high-stepping sports of Fifth Avenue and environs, was tied in intimate ways to the wound in his heart; but that this very sense of worthlessness (self-loathing, to be more precise; for nothing less could have inspired him to court humiliation in the street gutters) had not been *caused* by the heart attack but had been *released* by the heart attack, a dam broken and the torrents of self-loathing rushing through; and he knew finally that he had better do something about it, or all this rage turned inside out and all this self-abuse would get him nothing more or less than another heart attack.

"You should see a shrink!" I had screamed. And he had been furious because he agreed.

Oh, God. To have slid so far down so fast. He'd been doing pretty well, hadn't he? His father, who had always laid on the expectations with a heavy hand, with a big heavy fist, would not have been displeased: Harold the Urologist, making, if not the big money that his cousins were making, why, at least, a *very* nice living, and (what was more important) with the stature of a man who does *good works*, with plenty of respect, including his own. Chief of Staff at the hospital, president of the state urological society, all those estimable *of*'s. And then the founder and the director of this sexuality program at a great medical school—his father would not have liked the sexuality part, but he would have recognized the *achievement*—a good sex-therapy clinic, one of the best and busiest, and some damned good sex-research programs, and his papers in the medical journals and his picture in the newsmagazines, the press coming around to interview him all the time now in this crazy year in which sex therapy suddenly had become a national preoccupation and the number one media event, riding high, no money but this dizzying mini-celebrity, new absorbing work, the gratitude of patients, plenty of self-esteem . . .

And now this. Now this in the gutter. How had he plummeted so?

Chapter *8*

---

*T*HREE years earlier we had been living in West Hartford, Connecticut, a suburban dream incarnate. His practice was as successful as he could want or need—a corporation, three partners, all working too hard already. He was a much-respected man. Safety shone like sun upon our house, our dogwood in bloom, our two-car garage, our health and our affections. His two children, who lived nearby with their mother, came and went freely between both households. We had many friends. We gave frequent dinner parties. We drove often into New York to go to the theater and walk in peace marches.

Blessings. For me they were mixed. I had come to that town to live with that man nine years earlier, given up my town, my friends, an editorship at *The New York Times*, the pleasures of a close professional circle, given them up not because of who was the man and who the woman but because it is easier to move a typewriter than a medical practice. And lived there with the constant sense that it was the right marriage in the wrong place. For I never could make my peace with the landscapes and cadences of suburban life, they did bad things to my metabolism, and I always said that if I could have this man in this marriage in New York City, I would have everything that I could want in life. I even believed it.

If it hadn't been for my discontents, he might never have moved. Not that he was some model of contentment. He went through what so many doctors go through, that crisis of confrontation with their own limitations. Almost all the doctors I knew in West Hartford were men, and most of them at one time or another mucked around in the depression we call male menopause. So did many of the lawyers and the builders and the shopkeepers, but most of all it was the doctors, I think. I don't know why. Perhaps it is because they are trained to do such noble things in life, and then there aren't any.

Probably, without my prodding, he would have done as most of them do. Settled in, passed from a mild discontent into a subdued resignation. But he had always been a surprise package. Partly the conservatism of the breed, partly always something of a maverick about him, a drive to do good, to *earn* the comforts of his life, a nose-thumbing at medical proprieties. (When the A.M.A. opposed Medicare, early in our marriage, he sent a letter to both Hartford newspapers supporting national health insurance. There was talk of expelling him from the County Medical Society, and some doctors never spoke to him cordially again. Oh, my, how I loved it.)

Vacations, several years, we spent not in the swell places to which many of his colleagues went, but in a jungle hospital in Haiti, where he would do six months' worth of urological surgery in a month, working on the wretched of the earth, and emerge from that ordeal rested, strengthened, nourished by the sense that he had come for that small time at least within shouting distance of the Hippocratic Oath.

So the busy partnership did not altogether fulfill him. And my restlessness fed his own.

Often I have wondered if any of it would have happened, the heart attack or any of the rest of it, if we had stayed put. If I had not encouraged him to leave the warm embrace of his professional community back there in that polite, pretty suburb, to leave his private practice and go into public health, which in theory is a noble calling but in fact turned out to be the pits. Probably his coronary crisis would have come anyway. Not so soon, not so devastatingly. But it would have come. It was written in the blood. I knew that, and still I gave myself the business. I never could resist a *Mea culpa*; a cheap romance.

What happened was a classic in its way. I couldn't have known it at the time, but I understood later that the research fitted him like a rubber glove. A classic coronary profile. A classic American stress story.

We lay one mellow West Hartford summer Sunday out on the patio, the dog and the Sunday *Times* spread between us, the rubber lining of the pool sending up a fine azure glow, when he leaned back in his chaise and announced apropos of nothing that I can recall:

"Do you realize that I have examined twenty thousand cunts?"

A curse on the chauvinist pigs! But no, that was not until the next year.

"Why, no," I said, "I hadn't realized that."

"Twenty years. A thousand a year, *conservatively*. It's enough. I want to quit."

The pool was not yet paid for. "Quit medicine?" I said.

"Quit one-to-one medicine. Do something more . . . socially useful. Community medicine, maybe. Planning health-care programs for communities. Research. Teaching. A teaching hospital, maybe Boston, maybe New York . . ."

His voice faded. I understood that he was testing. "A pogrom is a pogrom," I said. I was ecstatic.

Once he had made the decision to move, he wanted to do it quickly. He spent the fall months talking to directors of medical schools and public-health programs. They lived in another world: a world not of fee-for-service but of grant proposals, funding agencies, foundation money, government-agency money, hard money, soft money. Most people in public health did not deal with patients. They dealt with statistics, bell curves, projections, pins on district maps.

The people he talked to were charmed by the idea that an experienced clinician would willingly give up a thriving private practice to come into this world. But he would have to find his own funding. They were all strapped.

He didn't know how he might do it, but a neighbor, an academician, supplied the answer:

"Sex!" he said. "The foundations are interested in sex research now.

Put together a good grant proposal and with your experience as a urologist, you'll have no trouble getting funded. Sex, Hal!"

Plastics, Benjamin!

Actually, it was a good idea. Masters and Johnson were about to publish their second book, in which they would describe their techniques of sexual therapy, and soon a small revolution would be in progress, a citizenry inflamed, demanding satisfaction in the bed as though it were a fifth freedom, lines forming beneath the shingles of any fools or quacks who cared to call themselves sex therapists, and practically no one adequately trained. Oh, it was going to be a mess. Medicine caught with its pants down.

He did have experience. Not much, but more than most clinicians at that time. Sex had not existed in medical school, but he had seen the connections in his own practice. He had recognized that there might be sexual dimensions to all medical specialties—urology, gynecology, dermatology, neurology, all of them. And clinicians generally could probe those depths no better than their patients could, and generally did not want to.

"How's your sex life?" they would ask, rustling through papers.

And if the patient replied, "Okay, I guess," despite a clear and desperate hidden agenda of sexual complaints, they would say, "Fine, fine," and ask no more.

He himself had been doing a primitive sort of sex therapy for years, long before Masters and Johnson—no research to guide him, but aware that patients were coming to him with those complaints high on their hidden agendas. He would do the best he could with simple reassurances:

"You know, sometimes a man . . ." (never a woman; the women did not report their sexual miseries to a urologist, if indeed they confided in any doctor at all) ". . . sometimes a man has trouble performing sexually because he is too tired, or he has had too much to drink. And that makes him tense. And the next time, he has trouble because he's tense about the last time, and he can get into this vicious circle . . ."

That sort of thing. Raw, unsophisticated. But often it seemed to help.

Then he had had his first true sex-therapy case. A man had come to him complaining of impotence. His wife had died of cancer, he had married again ten months later and as yet, now a month remarried, he had been unable to consummate the deal.

Hal had examined him carefully, found no organic problem and recommended a psychiatric consultation.

A year and a half later, the patient again had appeared in his office. He had been in psychiatric treatment all that time. He still could not have erections. He was desperate. The marriage, despite deep mutual affection, was headed for the rocks.

"The psychiatrist did not help at all?" Hal had asked.

"No. He said I could not be helped. He said I should buy a dildo."

A *dildo*! Eighteen months and countless thousands of dollars and this is the payoff: the poor limp cull is told to go buy a *dildo*. . . .

He was enraged. There is no way, he thought, that I can do any worse than that psychiatrist.

He told the patient to come back in a week. He read a couple of books on behavior modification, a relatively new technique about which he had vague but hopeful notions. If people could be cured of various phobic fears—fear of heights, say, or of water—by desensitization techniques, why could they not be cured in the same way of sexual fears? It seemed at least worth a try.

When the patient returned, he laid out the treatment in stages, seeking gradually to reduce the levels of anxiety:

"This first week, you and your wife may be naked together, and you may kiss and stroke each other any way you like, *except*: She must *not* touch your genitals. And you are *not under any circumstances to attempt intercourse*"—coming on as dictatorially as he could, easing anxiety by forbidding the patient to do the undo-able— "and come back in a week. . . ."

And the next week: "Now she can touch your genitals. And if you want to, you may put your penis between her legs. But no penetration. *Absolutely not*. . . ." Waving his finger, patient nodding soberly.

And so on, for several weeks more. And damned if the week did not come when the patient walked into his office pridefully shamefaced and said, "Doc, I didn't follow your orders last night."

"What happened?"

"Well, I was moving around between her legs and it felt so good that I just said The hell with it, and we went ahead."

"How did it go?"

Beatific smile. "Great! Gee, Doc, I don't know how to tell you . . ."

It worked! That had stunned him, delighted him. He had never thought that clinicians could or should play psychiatrist, and he did not think so now. Still: Eighty-five percent of the people who walked into a doctor's office had nothing physically wrong with them. That was a generally accepted fact in medicine. And astoundingly often, their problems were sexual. (That was less generally accepted. "Sex?" a nationally renowned urologist had said to him once. "What does sex have to do with urology?") And routinely, medical students emerged as doctors with absolutely no awareness of the sexual implications of their work. That was, he thought, a grossly deficient medical education.

So it seemed, when he made the decision to move, that this would be a good way to go. The timing was right. The issue was important. He would learn everything he could about sex education in medicine. And then he would educate.

He got a modest grant from the National Institute of Mental Health to fund his own training for two years. The first year he would study at the University of Pennsylvania, in the Center for Sex Education in Medicine. The next year he would spend in New York, at the medical center where he had trained a quarter-century ago, and study public health. And then he would stay on, developing sex-education programs for medical students and health-care workers, and perhaps setting up a sex-therapy clinic for residents of the community. A cluster of programs and services to be called The Medical Center Sexuality Program.

It was a nice package. Service to the community. Prestige for the medical center. Programs that might attract money to the department.

"*Exactly* what we are looking for," the Director of Special Projects, Dr. Koerner, told him. "And don't worry about money. No worry. The first year we won't expect you to do a thing but learn public health. And after your grant money runs out, we'll fund you for the next five years. By then you'll have your own programs going, you'll be attracting your own funding. . . ." Koerner beamed assurances.

So we left West Hartford. We had no savings, no income other than the N.I.M.H. grant. But hell, we would manage. One managed. What an adventure! And in fact, we hedged the bet. We rented our house instead of selling. Hal kept the option of returning to practice within a year. He wouldn't go back, I knew he wouldn't, but the option was there; a safety net.

The hospital staff gave him a farewell dinner. Heartfelt speeches, a handsome attaché case. Someone gave him a book. It was John Gardner's *Self-Renewal,* on the virtues of starting a new life in mid-life, and it was inscribed, "Good Luck! I wish I had your nerve."

I think many of them thought he was crazy. I also think some of them were jealous, contemplating those visions of change, second chances, self-renewals which seemed that night to shimmer like sugar-plums in the air.

Philadelphia was a good year for him. It was a small training program within the Department of Psychiatry for perhaps a dozen people, mostly M.D.'s, who wanted to change or broaden their specialties. He was at lectures and workshops all day, and at night he read voraciously: social psychiatry, psychology, techniques of psychotherapy—all the fine, imprecise, human stuff for which there had never been time when he had been memorizing the nine little bones of the wrist back in medical school. Medical doctors have an awful education, really. Bones and microbes, never much time for anything else. Few Renaissance men.

Now he loved being a student again. He blossomed. Nosing around in these corners of the psyche, he himself became far more introspective. He had sudden startling insights about his father, which came back to haunt both of us later.

"I am so sorry you never knew my father," he had told me often. "He was so warm, he had such *joie.* You would have loved him."

A poor but happy man, he had told me, who brought turkeys to his poorer neighbors each Thanksgiving and never went into the street without pocketfuls of candy for the children. If I had heard once I had heard fifty times about the candy in the pockets.

Now, in Philadelphia, there came an evening when we were sitting at dinner with guests and someone asked about his family, and he said:

"My father was a fine, moral man." Taking off his wristwatch and regarding it thoughtfully. "A *very* moral man." Tapping the watch lightly against his palm. "Stern, but good. I mean, he was *righteous . . .*" And Hal was slapping the watch now into his palm, wholly unaware that he was punctuating each word with a vicious slam of the watch into his palm, ". . . *so damned righteous, Jesus, always right, always right, always right . . .*" slamming, slamming, slamming; and stopped suddenly, listening with wonder to the rage in his voice and looking at his hands with astonishment. That kind of sudden insight. Disturbing, but not unwelcome. Exhilarating, somehow.

I thought about the father often, later, when the bad things began happening to the son. Good Eddie, I called him. He had been the oldest of five brothers, all of them sweet-talking and larcenous except for Good Eddie himself, who had been righteous.

It interested me that while Hal had always recalled his father with such affection and respect, Hal's cousins hadn't liked him at all. Every cousin had a story, a trauma, an Uncle Eddie Special. The best and the worst I heard many times from Hal's cousin Norman, who told it *con brio*.

The cousins had been kids, 10 or 12, and the Lear clan had gathered one summer weekend in the Lear family cottage in Woodmont, Connecticut, Uncle Eddie presiding as always. And the elders were downstairs doing whatever, and the kids were upstairs in the bathroom doing whatever, and suddenly the bathroom door burst open and Uncle Eddie crashed in upon them like a madman, screaming:

"Not like that! Not like that! We can all hear you downstairs. *Pee in the side of the bowl. Like this!*" And unzippered and proceeded to show them how one could do it soundlessly, genteelly, simply by aiming at the side of the bowl.

He meant it, too, that dreary self-righteous man. Just as he meant it when he said, "Children should be seen and not heard," and when he gave whippings with his belt and said, "This is for your own good." Good Eddie.

At 15 the son came home late one night and undressed in the bathroom so as not to wake his parents. He left his pants hanging there, and it was his rotten luck that his wallet fell out of the pants and in the morning the father picked it up and found a rubber in it. *Ai.*

This rubber was chaste. It had lain in the wallet so long, this small white hope, that its ring shape was permanently embossed in the leather.

"What's this?" Good Eddie held it at arm's length, as though it were contagious. "What's this? *Answer me.*"

Hal, shrinking back: "A condom."

"Who do you use this with, eh?"

"I don't. I just carry it. All the fellows carry them."

"You *carry* it and you don't *use* it? Don't tell me that. The truth! Who do you use it with?"

"I don't."

"Ruth Jules? You use this thing with Ruth Jules?"

"No, Dad."

"Cydele Bender?"

"No."

"Amy Lerman?"

"No, Dad."

And on down through the roster of neighborhood princesses, who in those days would as soon have sacrificed an arm as a hymen.

"Not Ruby Morton? Well, then, you bum: *Are you doing it with a shiksa?*"

Eddie stories. Fond memories. "Christ, I was terrified of him," Hal would say, smiling, as though that were somehow *sweet*, to remember being terrified. It was odd because he was always so sensitive to the ways in which others had been traumatized. He could see all that clearly. But he could never see it in himself, never until that night in Philadelphia when he had started slamming his wristwatch into the palm of his hand and growling, "*always right, always right, always right . . .*"

It was not insignificant about the father. It rarely is. Fathers play big parts in coronary dramas. From the grave, perhaps, but *big*. I see them standing tall in those coronary arteries, standing in the middle of the road blowing their whistles and shouting their commands, blocking traffic, plugging the flow. Good Eddie had fixed it so that his boy would never for the rest of his life be able to tell the boss to go to hell. As long as he had been his own boss, in his own practice amid respectful peers, it hadn't mattered. But when we got to New York, where there were small men in high places and cockfights and cool, mean maneuverings, he reacted as he had done with Good Eddie. Suppressed his anger, turned it inward. And that wasn't so good.

They liked him tremendously in Philadelphia. They wanted him to stay and teach. In fact, he was tempted, because they were nice people and they were doing good work. But he had made his commitments. By now he was teaching a human-sexuality course to medical students and practicing sex and marital therapy, enjoying it all and looking forward to the programs he would create in New York. There was no reason to keep our bets hedged. He resigned from the West Hartford practice. We sold the house and bought an apartment near the medical center in New York. When Koerner heard about that, he whistled.

"What an act of faith!" he said. And kept saying it:

"This is Dr. Lear, who is coming into our division in September. He just bought a co-op a few blocks away. How's *that* for an act of faith!"

Again and again, with such awe in his voice that Hal wondered, What's the man making such a fuss about? If I have made a commitment to work here, why is it such an act of faith to buy a home here?

Oh, he was some babe in those woods.

They gave him office space: a galley kitchen in a minimally converted apartment. A desk, a chair and two books on epidemiology. On one side of his desk was a table holding a coffee percolator. On the other side was the kitchen sink. On the linoleum floor were many rubber toys belonging to a small poodle that was brought in to work each day by its owner, a medical sociologist. The kitchen aisle was three feet wide. The dog would lie in this aisle, chewing its toys, and whenever Hal would push away from his desk to get up, his chair would bounce off the wall behind him and the animal would begin to bark and he would have to step with care to avoid tripping over the toys, or over the dog itself, which all the while would keep barking in that high, shrill yawp small poodles have. It drove him crazy.

What might one do? Say to its owner, "Keep your dog the hell out of my kitchen"? But these quarters were too close for intensity. She was, in any case, a nervous, troubled woman, squabbling constantly with another medical sociologist who sat in the dining room, the two of them sounding rather like the poodle itself.

Or might one say to Koerner, "What kind of craziness is this, to put me in a kitchen? Give me a proper office. Immediately"? Had he given up a seven-room medical suite in a fancy office building, corporation, corner office, straw-cloth walls to sit with a dog in a kitchen?

But it seemed not quite right to complain so fast, as though one were showing a petty set of priorities. Others in the department, after all, were hardly more elegantly housed. Public Health was where the money was not. Staff members were scattered about in several shabby old apartment buildings owned by the medical center. Presumably one went into Public Health to do good works, not to sit in fancy offices with straw cloth on the walls. This kitchen was preposterous, it was dire, but it was nothing more, really, than a small problem to be solved. In a short time he would solve it. "Look, Fritz," he would say to Koerner, "I know space is tight. But really, this kitchen . . ."

What bothered him more, far more, was the way people worked

in this place. What they worked at. His two neighbors seemed, even with their bickering, to be very busy, and so did a pediatrician down the hall. But he soon learned that the medical sociologists did no medical sociology. The pediatrician did no pediatrics.

"How long has it been since you treated a child?" he asked her.

"Three years," she said.

Instead, she wrote grant proposals. They all wrote grant proposals. As he got to know others in the department, he found that he was surrounded by highly trained specialists who did very little work in their specialties because most of the time they were writing grant proposals to get money to enable them to work in their specialties.

That was the first nasty discovery. The second was that there was no training program for him.

There was a Dr. Wood, Koerner's assistant, who had been assigned to train him. Dr. Wood came by once a week. He would sit and talk to the staff for a while in the foreign language of epidemiology, and then he would say how glad he was that Dr. Lear was on the team, and then he would leave. Nothing more.

Hal sat for three weeks with the two books on epidemiology. Finally he went to Wood and said, "I am doing nothing but sitting and reading those books, and I am not learning much about public health that way. How about my spending time with you?"

"Great idea!" Wood said. "You can come to all the meetings with me."

So then, each day, he would go with Wood from one meeting to another. They would meet with a neighborhood council of this and a community group of that, and they would have daily staff meetings to discuss vastly complicated community-health projects for which there were no funds. He did not understand what they were talking about.

Sometimes, after a meeting, he would say to Wood, "What exactly are you trying to do here?" and get back the most enthusiastic gobbledygook. He kept struggling to get a fix on this thing, to understand what Wood was doing, and gradually he came to realize that he *did* understand: Wood was doing nothing. He was making committees to hold meetings to make more committees to hold more meetings. Endless hours of meetings about wonderful projects that did not exist, colossi built on hot air, a system geared simply to perpetuate itself.

That was discovery number three.

"I'd like to get to work on some project of my own," he told Wood.

"Great! We're putting together a project to study the emergency-care system in an old-age home. I'll get you involved in that."

"But I know nothing about geriatrics. My field is sexuality."

"Great! You'll study the sexual activity in an old-age home."

I began urging him to leave. I hated the desk in the kitchen. It demeaned him. It demeaned me. Ah, the rub. I understood only dimly how much I resented him for that. Went there and looked at that kitchen and felt such contempt I couldn't even look him in the face. For God's sake, you were never much good at cocktail-party chatter and you never could tip a headwaiter with aplomb and you were never able to flag down a cab in the rain and now this: you, my husband, big urologist from the North and sex expert from the South, twenty years of honor (power) down the drain, sitting here in this kitchen and putting up with this crap? Listen, Hal, tell them this is crap and shove it, goodbye. Be strong, damn it, the way I want you to be strong.

In fact there was tremendous strength involved, but of another sort. Staying power. It was always like that between us: I made the showy starts, he went the distance.

"Damn it, tell them this is crap and shove it."

"And go where? Do what?"

"Go into private practice here. Do sex therapy. Or do urology. Or go back to urology in Hartford. As long as you're your own boss again."

"No. I'm not going backward."

Still, he could not do nothing. Sit there in the kitchen amid these people who would teach him nothing, demand nothing of him, until he moldered or his grant money ran out, whichever came first. That repelled him, to be paid for doing nothing.

There were the projects he had hoped to do. Good, inventive projects. "*Exactly* the sort of thing we're looking for!" Koerner had said months earlier. But for those projects he needed space and staff, and he understood now that when Koerner had said, "We'll fund you for the next five years," Koerner had meant that the department would carry him at this desk in this kitchen; no more. If he wanted more, he would have to find money.

He wrote up a modest proposal to train nurses and social workers to run sex-education courses in the community. Then he went with Koerner to sell this proposal to a foundation. And he sat with three blue-vested men in a wood-paneled office in a splendid town house that housed one of the richest, most powerful foundations in the world, and he explained his little project, feeling nervous and awkward and somehow demeaned, asking these banker types to give him money so that he might get to work, and at the end, one of them said:

"Sex education is too general for us, Dr. Lear. If you could give us something specific . . . for example, a proposal for controlling venereal disease in East Harlem . . ."

"What do you think?" Koerner asked later.

"I'm sure it would be a nice thing to control venereal disease in East Harlem, but that project doesn't really interest me," Hal said.

"*Interest* you?" said Koerner, genuinely perplexed. "But *they want to fund it.*"

At a meeting, he met a professional fund raiser for the medical center.

"The thing you should do," said the fund raiser, "is come up with a project for putting one big condom on all of Harlem. Do *that*, and we'll get you all the money you want."

So besides the gross political underbelly of the thing, which he suspected that these people did not understand, it was necessary to grasp that in this world, the proper way to move was ass-backward. You did not apply for grant money to do what you wanted to do, or what your training had best prepared you to do. No. You found out what the money givers wanted to give money for, and then you wrote a proposal for *that*. An *a priori* pretzling.

Discovery number four.

All those years, taking out the kidneys and repairing the bladders, he had thought how fine it must be to work in some larger social cause. The very phrases—"public health," "community medicine"—had conjured up a generosity of spirit, a kind of caring that one did not find in private practice.

Now he looked about him and saw that the caring was mostly talk. The caring had long since dried up, like an old riverbed, and what remained was a parched political pit. The pits. And in this pit were frightened, incompetent people who would stay forever, as some students clung forever to the cloisters; and also highly skilled people who had come in with energy and hope and stayed to find their energies depleted in this constant grubby game of grantsmanship.

Well, he thought, here I am. Plenty of bridges burned. If I'm sitting around on my ass, I may as well offer my services to students.

He went to the director of student health services, told of his training in treating couples and volunteered to see any medical student or nurse who wanted help. Immediately he was swamped.

He helped plan a small sex-education program for students, just two hours a semester. Soon the students were asking him to expand it.

Professional groups in the community—psychologists, nurses, social workers—began asking him to speak on the sexual aspects of health care.

He said to an audience of three hundred nurses:

"How many of you have seen a patient who has had a mastectomy?"

Almost every hand in the room went up.

"Have you ever heard a doctor talk to a mastectomy patient about her self-image? Her anxieties about sex?"

Silence.

"And what of yourselves—how many of you have encouraged mastectomy patients to talk about such things?"

A couple of hands were raised. One woman said:

"Often I know the patients would like to talk about it, but I am never sure what to say. Nobody ever taught me. I think it is just terrible how medicine ignores . . ."

The meeting grew lively. He was asked to return and organize a workshop. Other nurses' groups invited him to speak. Invitations began to come from other medical schools, and then from medical societies across the country. Each appearance brought more requests for lectures, seminars, workshops.

Now he was getting calls from local people who wanted therapy. This meant income. Koerner gave him a suite. He hired a secretary and a psychologist, a woman with a strong analytic background and training in sex therapy. They began seeing couples jointly, on the Masters and Johnson model.

They were doing good work and getting dramatic results. The gratitude of a patient who is cured of impotence, or inability to have orgasms, is not the gratitude of a patient cured of gastric distress. It is a form of ecstasy. Most patients referred others, and by spring he was getting more calls than he could handle.

Early on, he had been exquisitely careful to explain himself and his intentions to various department chiefs. He mightn't have known much about public health, but he knew all about the sensitivities of department chiefs. Fiefdoms. Turf wars. He had gone to the chiefs of Urology and Obstetrics-Gynecology and Psychiatry. He had described his training and said that if they could use him in their teaching programs, he would be happy to help in whatever way they wished. No takers.

He had been especially careful with Psychiatry. Psychiatrists were deeply edgy about sex therapy. It threatened to crack their Freudian bedrock. It was short-term. It claimed to solve problems that, in the traditional view, could not be solved without scraping the bottom of the psyche. It was practiced by people who had no psychiatric training—Bill Masters himself was a mere *gynecologist*, for God's sake! (It interested me that two years later, when it was clear beyond doubt that the damned thing *worked*, and also clear that Psychiatry had better concede the fact or be left looking ossified, the very psychiatrists who had bad-mouthed Masters and Johnson were giving them standing ovations wherever they spoke.)

So there was plenty of defensive hostility among the psychiatrists back then, and Hal had known that he had to be careful. He had stressed to the co-chief, Dr. Gross, that he himself was not a psychiatrist and that he had no desire to tread on psychiatric turf. But if any members of the department were interested in short-term sex therapy, he had said, he hoped they would participate in his program.

Nice of you, Gross had said. We'll keep it in mind.

Now he went back to Gross and told him, "We've got more patients than we can possibly handle, and if any of your psychiatrists are interested in what we're doing, we'd very much like to have them involved."

Swell, said Gross. You people are doing a nice job over there in that little program of yours. We'll get in touch with you.

And didn't.

The thing kept snowballing. He had a waiting list backed up for six months. He was seeing patients nine to nine and running workshops for professionals on the weekends. He was working harder even than in the private-practice days.

Still, since he had set his fees according to ability to pay, the program was not making much money. Enough to cover his staff and his space, but not his own salary.

Koerner sent a lieutenant. "We're having money problems," the lieutenant said. "You're going to have to find other funding for your own upkeep."

"But Dr. Koerner told me that I wouldn't have to worry about personal funding for five years."

"Well, that's changed now. You'll have to earn enough to pay your own salary, or you're in serious trouble."

Oh, yes, he thought, I am in serious trouble. But not because I am not making enough money. Because I trusted you people.

There was this anachronism which had always been one of the charms of him, though it kept him vulnerable: this capacity for trust. He took people at their word. A charming, dangerous quality, so strongly fixed that even now it was painful to give up, like gambling or cigarettes. Suspicion lodged uncomfortably in his craw.

He began working even longer hours to make more money. His program at this point was a fine thing he had created from scratch, scratched out of the arid soil of that pit. He did not want it endangered.

Now the mini-celebrity began moving in on him. That was the season the media were keen on sex-therapy programs, and very few medical schools had them. He was profiled in professional journals. He was asked to speak on educational TV. The talk shows wanted him. There were dozens of requests for interviews from newspapers and magazines. There were even overseas calls, especially from the German press, which was smitten with sex therapy; *ach*, a new technology. All of this he cleared through appropriate channels, for medicine had always been dainty about publicity. *Low profile, low profile.* But now appropriate channels said, Go, full steam ahead; it's great publicity for the hospital. So it built.

In the dark we giggled at it.

Oh, you kid, you sex expert, I said. I taught you everything you know.

Sh! he said.

It was an instructive look from the inside at the mechanics of Media Event, and we both watched, dazed, as it happened. A kind of madness, this tension between the public success and the private reality: the media chasing him and Koerner's hatchet man coming around to tell him that unless he made more money, he was in serious trouble.

It was then that the screws began to turn down.

The Chiefs of Psychiatry sponsored a symposium on short-range sex therapies. Lear was not invited to speak; he was not even invited to attend.

Gross contacted the director of the Center for Sex Education in Medicine, in Philadelphia, and asked if one of his psychiatrists could come down there to learn sex therapy. He needn't come here, the director said. He can learn from Dr. Lear, right there at your own hospital. I'd rather send him to Philadelphia, Gross said.

Students—students!—began coming to him, saying, "Dr. Lear, I hear they're going to take your program away from you. Is it true?"

They were so concerned, those kids. A floating dozen of them came to our house each week to sit around and talk about Caring in Medicine. I think they found in him something of the spirit they still entertained, that sense of service which fades so soon after medical school. They tried in the sweetest ways to protect him; they even talked of going on strike when the barracudas came gliding in. But they were just kids, and powerless. There was nothing they could do.

He confronted Koerner with the rumors.

"Why, no," Koerner said. "No one is going to take your program away from you. But it *is* true, Hal, that Psychiatry is, uh, unhappy about the program. They feel it belongs in their department. I'm not sure what we should do. I don't want to jeopardize our good relations with them."

Hal understood. Public Health is an expendable department. It needs the goodwill of other departments to survive. If anything had to be sacrificed, it would not be goodwill. It would be his program.

Now, something stirring in his belly, he said:

"I've always thought Psychiatry should participate in the sex-therapy part of my program. I've tried to get them involved. Suppose we divide the program into two parts: the sex-education work will continue under your aegis, and now the sex-therapy clinic will be under their aegis, and I'll be working for both of you with a joint appointment."

Good, Koerner said. We'll have a meeting. We'll resolve it just that way.

Okay, Hal said; and waited for the meeting. And then learned, one day, that the meeting was to be the next day, and he had not been invited. Just Koerner and Gross and the director of the hospital and Lord knew who else, but not himself.

"You're going to meet to decide the fate of my program without *me*?" he said to Koerner. "Why are you doing this?"

"Don't worry about it," Koerner said. "It will all be settled just as you and I discussed."

Then he was summoned to Koerner's office. There sat Gross with a stranger: a Dr. Peron. Dr. Peron, the psychiatrist who was traveling to Philadelphia twice a week to learn how to do sex therapy.

"Well, we have no problems at all," said Koerner. "Everything has been arranged."

"What are the arrangements?" Hal asked.

"The sex-therapy program will be under the Department of Psychiatry, just as you suggested . . ."

"That's fine."

". . . and Dr. Peron is going to be head of the program," Gross said.

Hal stared at him, stunned. He should not have been. The sign of the double cross had been hanging for weeks in the air, like a terrible smell. But still, stunned.

"I don't understand. It's my program."

Peron, pink-faced, weak-featured, small-voiced, smiled gently.

Gross said, "I'm sorry, Hal. I can't have someone who is not a psychiatrist be the head of the program. So Dr. Peron will be in charge."

"But it's *my program*."

"Well, you'll work with him."

He looked at Koerner. Koerner the bearer of good news: Don't worry about funding, No one will take away your program, Just bought a co-op a few blocks away, how's *that* for an act of faith . . .

Koerner looked away.

Hal heard his own voice, desperate, hating himself for the desperate edge of it: "Will we be codirectors, then?"

Gross: "I'm afraid we can't do that, Hal. It would be all right with *me*. But if we made you, a nonpsychiatrist, codirector of a program in Psychiatry, the other psychiatrists would . . . I'd have a revolution on my hands. We'll make you . . . let's see, now"—thoughtfully, just as though it hadn't all been set up—"we'll make you an associate director of the program."

Their voices droned on. He sat deaf with inchoate rage, his pulses pounding. *But it's my program. It's my program. It's my program.*

The classical double bind. The more he had succeeded, the more he had failed. When it had been a little bud of a program, nobody had cared. But when it had become a big, shiny plum, well known and prestigious, a source for research, getting press and generating publicity for the hospital, they had clawed for it. They had stolen it.

He blamed himself, and rightly. If he had come into a jungle and chosen to see a rose garden, that was his problem. But he blamed them too, and rightly. They had lied to him and deceived him.

And what could he do? Nothing. If he walked out, they would have his program and he would have nothing. When he had been Chief of Staff back there in Hartford, he had had a power base. He had represented a constituency of doctors. Here, he had no voice. He could be wiped out, and there was no recourse, no way to avoid it, nowhere to turn for help. His own chief had betrayed him.

He remembered reading about learned helplessness: those experiments in which they put animals into cages and administered electric shock. The animals could not avoid it. No matter how they maneuvered to avoid painful stimulus, they got only more stimulus. Eventually they stopped trying. They broke down. They simply lay on the floor and whimpered. Learned helplessness. It's like that, he said to me.

It was vacation time. We went to England. Psychiatry would take over his program when he returned. We sat in pubs, he crouching silently over his pints of stout, so deeply depressed; I urging him again: Leave! But more softly than before, for his pain was clear.

And he, as softly, would reply: "I'll see. Maybe I can still work it out."

Work *what* out, for heaven's sake? How long will you keep taking it, biting the bullets of your rage, impotent rage . . . Keep this up, Hal, you'll get a heart attack.

And on and on in that way, inner furies that I thought were *for* him but were in fact *at* him, the classic bilious furies of a woman whose sense of self is hopelessly tangled in somebody else's skein.

And why didn't he leave? He simply couldn't. The lessons of a lifetime, not all of them wise, dictated that one must not quit. One must work it out.

It was not unlike that time twenty-five years earlier, when he had felt trapped in a marriage that was just a year old and already a disaster, patently beyond hope, and had told his father that he was thinking of getting a divorce.

Good Eddie had thumped the tabletop. "There has never been a divorce in our family," he had said. "Try harder. *Make it work.*" And damned if the son had not kept trying for ten more hopeless, wasted years before he had finally said No and walked away. Ah, Good Eddie.

And now again there was this urgency to *make it work*, all virtue and self-respect being on the line. And there was no way to make it work, no way at all.

So there came that day when he stood in a crowded pub and cried out, "I hate them all; I hate the whole damned setup!"

And then he came home and had his heart attack.

You can't fire me, you fuckers. I quit!

Chapter 9

*S*O there he was, almost two months postcoronary, with his self-esteem sunk as low as those gutters in which he grubbed for butts.

"You should see a shrink!" I had screamed. I did not know that it was common, even classic, for cardiacs to experience a lowering of self-esteem. It is part of the process of loss; and, in him, exacerbated by the battering he had taken at work.

Now he felt miserable enough to try anything. Anything that might get him off those cursed butts and make him feel better about himself.

He went first to see a locally celebrated psychoanalyst who used hypnosis to help people stop smoking. It was a one-shot deal, $75, and if it worked it was because the doctor was good and if it failed it was because the patient was bad, unhypnotizable, a poor subject.

Hal was a poor subject. He wanted to be good. He tried hard to respond to the suggestions that his eyelids were growing heavy, that he was getting sleepy as he rolled his eyes way back in his head, that his arm was now rising involuntarily from the chair rest; but he was in no way hypnotized.

The doctor asked him to repeat several phrases. They were phrases of a simian simplicity, such as "Smoking is harmful to my body. I need my body to live. Therefore . . ."

Then the doctor told him that whenever he wanted a smoke, he was to raise his arm and roll back his eyes in just this way, thus inducing self-hypnosis, and to repeat these phrases to himself. And Hal kept trying to concentrate but he couldn't push off this mischievous image that hopped like an animated cartoon around the edges of his mind: himself in a posh restaurant, say, suddenly raising his arm high in the air and rolling his eyes back in his head while other diners gaped, their soup growing cold, or politely averted their gaze, and the headwaiter hovered nervously nearby. . . . No, no, *concentrate*; listen to the doctor's voice.

But now it was not the doctor's voice live. It was the doctor on tape, a stereophonic blast repeating the idiot phrases again and again, while the doctor himself might be out having lunch. For the doctor, he saw upon peeking, was no longer in the room. And this made him stir, the resentments rising, the resentments he had always felt both as doctor and as patient in the face of impersonal care, but risen now to some nth degree because this was impersonality of the nth degree— *literally* faceless care, technology gone crazy, the patient sitting here listening to a taped voice that hummed on and on, inanely, and the doctor not even in the room.

Why, I could have made this therapeutic process even more efficient, he thought. What I could have done, certainly *would* have done if I'd known, was send my tape recorder down to listen to his tape recorder, an apotheosis of medical technology.

He paid the receptionist (couldn't this transaction too have been handled on tape? "That will be $75," says the shrink's machine. "Bill me," says his own machine) and walked out so incensed that he went immediately, his martyrdom shining like sequins, into a drugstore and bought a pack and lit up and pulled in heavily and exhaled hard, heaving the smoke out toward the doctor's office in a paroxysm of pleasure and rage.

Then we had a fight. We went to a dinner party, our first social event since the heart attack. He seemed in good shape, but he kept going to the bathroom so often that I thought he might not be feeling well, until it happened that I stood waiting to get in and the door opened and he came out, and there was the smoke cloud behind him.

I was livid. In just this way my father had betrayed me, promising after his first heart attack that he would smoke no more, and smoking then on to his second attack, and onward, as the coronary-artery disease and the Buerger's Disease crept onward, smoking and choking out all the small capillaries of his limbs, smoking even as he lay in a hospital bed waiting to have his smoke-choked leg cut off . . . Traitors, fathers who abandoned us then and husbands waiting to widow us now. Listen, *if you loved me,* you wouldn't . . .

Oh, one hell of a fight that night. Lessons learned at Mother's knee. The grievously injured look, the *What about me?* the cold shoulder in bed, the whole damned business.

So then he went to a psychiatrist. A well-recommended man who specialized in helping people cope with classic depressions, such as coronary depressions, cancer depressions and bereavement depressions; in short, people who had every right to be depressed.

The trouble was that this doctor himself seemed depressed; rather more so than the patient. The doctor's office—a room in his apartment, actually, filled with cooking smells—looked like a depressed area, and so, when he finally appeared, did the doctor himself. A small, unkempt man reflecting not the shabbiness of a well-worn analytic couch but the shabbiness of egg on the vest; a man who seemed to consider himself an object not worth sprucing up.

Of course, one could not judge in this way.

"I have come to you," Hal said, looking determinedly away from the vest, as though he might in fact find a trace of dried egg yolk there, "because I have had a heart attack and I am still smoking and I want to stop. And also . . ."—letting this out grudgingly, as though he really hadn't intended to say it at all—". . . also, because I want to . . . to be able to cope better with certain kinds of stress."

The doctor nodded. The doctor looked stressed too.

He saw Dr. Ackerman perhaps ten times, and each time he was increasingly disenchanted.

"I think the fellow is mediocre," he said to me once.

I trotted out the predictable cliché.

"Maybe you are resisting treatment," I said. "Has that possibility occurred to you?"

"Sure."

"And what would you say to it?"

"I would say bullshit."

But he could not be sure. He could not know beyond doubt

whether he was a difficult patient or Ackerman was an incompetent doctor.

This shocked him. If he, a medical doctor with psychiatric training, could not tell the difference, how could the layman—vulnerable, as everyone who goes to a psychiatrist is vulnerable—possibly know?

In any nonpsychiatric speciality one would know soon enough whether the doctor was any good or not, simply by watching him work. And there would be checkpoints—hospital review boards, pathology committees, systems of quality control. There were firm, clear standards. They mightn't be applied stringently enough, there were yo-yos on the staff of every hospital who really shouldn't be practicing at all, but at least the standards *existed*; a medical staff could apply them if it wanted to.

But here, what standards could one apply? My God, he thought, it's the old psychiatry joke come to life. Some poor bastard really *could* lie on that couch three times a week, $50 a session ($75, in this crazy New York), for two or five or eleven years, parsing the Oedipal parts unto exhaustion and still getting no better, still no relief; and maybe at some point he rises up on that couch—nothing mean, you understand, just up on one elbow—and asks in a mildly querulous voice why he doesn't seem to be getting any better, and what might he be told? Why, that he is *still resisting treatment*!

The thing of it with Dr. Ackerman was how he listened. Hal talked of his recent past and of stress situations that he had handled well, trying to isolate them from the stress situations that he had handled badly—the stresses that he seemed to thrive on, such as those of the operating room, or of changing a career, or of building a new program from zip; and as he talked of how successful that program had been, he could sense hostile vibrations coming from Dr. Ackerman; and the vibrations seemed to grow strongest when he spoke of those waiting lists, patients backed up for six months, and how he hadn't been able to handle them all and hadn't wanted to keep them waiting for months, and how he would look around the city for experienced doctors to give them to, and there were so few; as he told this part, he could see the sullenness come over Dr. Ackerman's face—Dr. Ackerman who sat in this dark, malodorous dump surveying his future and all the empty spaces in his appointment book.

Well, what is to be done? he wondered. I too would be sullen if I were he, sitting here listening to this hotshot talk of giving patients away while I myself scrounge around, twiddle my thumbs. . . . An impasse. The patient is resisting the doctor. The doctor is resisting the patient. Pick one.

He brought Dr. Ackerman a dream: He was driving on a highway. He fell out of the car. He was lying in the middle of the road and did not know which way to turn and understood that this was crucial, for if he turned the wrong way he would be killed, run over by traffic.

Subtle as a blow to the head. He was in a professional crux. Which way should he turn? Could he or should he try further to fight those vultures at the hospital, maybe killing himself in the process? Should he surrender and work for them? Should he retreat, go back into private practice? It seemed clear enough, that dream.

But Dr. Ackerman did not ask what he thought it meant. Dr. Ackerman said:

"What kind of car were you driving in the dream?"

"A Volkswagen."

"What kind of car do you really own?"

"A Cadillac."

"Aha! I'll tell you what that dream meant. You think you are superior to me. You think that *I* am a Volkswagen and *you* are a Cadillac . . ."

Oh, God. It is embarrassing to listen. Now I know. The problem is not my resistance. The problem is that Dr. Ackerman has egg on his vest.

Weeks later, he met the physician who had recommended Ackerman so highly.

"Why did you recommend that guy?" he asked.

The physician blushed. "Oh, my goodness. I didn't realize you were asking for *yourself*," he said. "He was looking for referrals and I wanted to help him out. He's my wife's cousin."

Oh, my goodness.

He had never put great stock in psychoanalysis. It simply didn't seem to be successful enough, often enough. But now he wanted very much to do a specific thing: he wanted to explore the ways in which he dealt with stress. Finally he found a psychiatrist who had written good stuff on postcoronary depressions, a smart, reflective man whom he liked immediately. With this man's help, he began moving in on himself. Probing carefully, like a surgeon. If genetics could produce a heart attack, so could the toxic seepages of the mind. Stress. *Stress.*

Two million overly stressed Americans were stricken by heart attacks each year. It wasn't that the octogenarians lived without stress—who lived without stress anymore, or ever had?—but perhaps that they handled it differently. Would his odds change if he learned to detoxify stress? The idea fascinated him, and he pursued it, probing.

Chapter 10

"**Y**OU'RE doing well," Roberts said, stethoscope in place.

"You know, I still get those funny pains in my chest."

"Healing pains."

"And another thing: after I've walked four or five blocks, I start getting quite short of breath."

"What do you expect? You've had a heart attack. It takes time. Keep doing what you're doing. I want you to keep walking a mile a day. And you can go back to work now, too."

"Fine. How much work can I do?"

"As much as you want. Full time, if you want. And remember, keep walking."

So he was back at work now, detesting to be back there and I detesting for him to be there, but what could he do? He was in no condition to look for another job. And in some secret place he still nursed the perverse notion, a notion he no longer shared with me because he knew it was perverse, that he might yet reason with unreasonable men; direct his own programs again or, at the least, codirect them with the neophyte Peron.

He wanted to work full time. Not for the pleasure of it, but for the *principle* of the thing, the good old Right is right. If Roberts had said that he *could*, then of course he *should*.

In the early days of our marriage he had driven me cuckoo with the Right is right. Later it eased, it lightened, but in the beginning it had been a stern, judgmental thing—hardworking, standard-setting, duty-minding, with a small touch of the sanctimonious up there around the edges. It was the way in which he came most precariously close, and there were happily few such ways, to the spirit of Good Eddie; Good Eddie and all those other good Judeo-Christian spirits that floated within, pieces of moral plaque floating forever upstream in the blood-stream, clogging the works.

I had joked about it, or tried to. Once, just a year married, he had frozen into that righteous stance about something-or-other, and I had made my face go sour and dour, quite like the faces of *American Gothic*, and held up a table fork as though it were the farmer's pitchfork and said, "Quick! What painting am I?" He had broken into laughter, which was the part that wasn't at all like Good Eddie. And after that, anytime he started getting righteous, I would hold up a fork, or three fingers, and yell, "Pitchfork! Pitchfork!" and he would laugh. My sense of responsibility had never been overdeveloped, and neither had his sense of play, and we helped each other make a balance.

So now, Roberts having told him that he could work full time, he said, "I have to get strong enough to work full time," and I said, "Pitchfork! Pitchfork!" but nobody laughed. Not he, not I.

At work, they were all enormously solicitous now. Peron would call each morning and ask solicitous questions in his soft, timid, virtuous voice: How are you feeling today, Harold? Better? Ah, I am so glad. You must not overwork. Perhaps we can have lunch? Coffee? Talk about this project, develop that project, discuss some of our sex-therapy cases? But only if you feel strong enough, of course. . . .

Peron had trouble. Patients were still calling every day, and many of them were not asking for a doctor in the Medical Center Sexuality Program. They were asking for Dr. Harold Lear. And they could be told that Dr. Lear was recovering from illness and was not yet treating patients, but what then? Somebody had to treat them, and Peron was just now learning the techniques. Peron needed help.

In fact, Hal would have wanted to help. (Not I. Husband, where is your honor? Do as I would do: avenge, maim, bomb the place down, make large, clever sabotages in the night!) Why punish the patients?

He would do the best job he could, and that would be the way to keep his honor and cope with his stress.

But he could not do much. Each morning the tiredness would come closing in on him like fog; it was impossible not to see it, and the others would become alarmed and insist that he quit early.

So he would come home each day and have lunch, and those were not pretty picnics. I hostile, nagging, with the most adamant sense that I was *right: Damn* it, I can *see* it, why can't *you* see it?

"I'm warning you, leave that damned place before you get another heart attack."

"Let me alone."

"Listen to me. I beg you. You'll be sorry."

"Please. Don't be my doctor."

And so on, table talk.

Then he would rest. And then he would go out to do his daily mile, and that was very hard.

Should it be this hard to walk a mile?

That ominous pain which had come and gone so mysteriously when he had been lying out on the terrace, weeks before, had never returned. But the old healing pains were with him constantly when he walked, and this new shortness of breath, and this other matter, this unsettling sensation which he could describe to Roberts only as a sort of *gurgling* in his chest, like water flushing sluggishly down a drain.

Even at rest, he did not feel well. Nothing acute. Simply a weakness, a chronic dragging of the ass. But since Roberts had said to keep walking, he assumed that he was running a normal recovery course. A mile a day was the standard routine now, two months postcoronary. If he was finding it so hard to walk, perhaps it was *supposed* to be hard. Perhaps next week will be easier, he thought.

So he kept walking, and it got no easier.

Some inner voice, the doctor voice, kept warning darkly that anything that felt this bad could not be good. But how could he be sure? He could be sure what was normal, and when, for a bladder or a kidney or a prostate gland, but how accurately could he gauge the recovery of a heart?

He had never felt a lack of confidence in Roberts. A lack of rapport —yes, indeed—but not of confidence. Now he pondered it. Perhaps I should get a consultation, he thought. Because I am not feeling well, and yet Roberts tells me that I am doing well, and I am confused.

One day as he was walking along Madison Avenue, breathing hard, trying to navigate a slight incline that had magically, within these past weeks, been transformed into a hill, he ran into Roberts.

"How are you doing?" Roberts said.

"I'm not sure." Panting. "I still seem to get awfully short of breath."

Roberts said, "Short of breath, eh? Getting a bit of a double chin there, aren't you?" Chucked him under the chin. "You putting on weight? You should watch the weight." And gave that tight little laugh of his, that distancing laugh, and walked off.

It was then that Hal decided beyond doubt to get a consultation.

He wanted someone who had no association with Roberts or with Roberts' hospital; no silent loyalty oaths. Maybe this fellow Silverman, his cousin David's doctor. David thought he was excellent. The man had a Park Avenue reputation, but that didn't necessarily mean he was *not* excellent.

He made an appointment for three weeks later, which would be three months postcoronary. It was a polite interval; three months was the traditional period of active medical care. Then he telephoned Roberts. This might be sticky. No doctor should ever resent a consultation, but many did.

"I thought it might be a good idea to get another opinion," he said.

"Of course," Roberts said. "That's perfectly all right."

"Then you'll send Dr. Silverman the summary of my case history?"

"Sure."

Moses Silverman kept the right people coming to him not because they knew that he practiced good medicine—as it happened, he did, but lay people do not always know the difference—but because he practiced with authority. He had the quintessentially right paternal air: attentive, supportive, loving but firm. One could imagine him on the overseas call, soothing a merchant prince: "Constantine, I want you to get into bed and stay there for the next twenty-four hours. . . . What? Lunch with the Prime Minister? Cancel it. Don't worry, you'll be fine, but you must do *exactly* as I say. . . . No, I can't fly over. . . . Do I *care* about you? Of *course* I care. But for heaven's sake, I am not your private physician, you know. I have other patients. They have a right to expect . . ."

He looked like an amiable giraffe. Homely in a most pleasant way, not tall but with a startling length of neck and a sharp forward pitch of the torso, as though it were forever trying to catch up with the head.

Photographs of famous people sat on every surface in his consulting room, endearingly autographed: "For Moe, With Gratitude and Affection, Always"—that sort of thing.

There were several quite good oils on the walls. He waved toward one of them.

"Pretty nice, eh? A gift from one of my patients." He mentioned the name: a social eminence. "You know how much that painting is worth? Twenty-seven thousand . . ." His intercom buzzed, and he said into the telephone, "No, no, I'm with a patient. Where's he calling from—Beverly Hills? . . . I'll call him back. Oh, and on that overseas call—did you get the Ambassador yet?"

A show, a spectacle. As long as I knew him he never stopped playing it, and always at the level of a *sotto voce* meant to be overheard.

But when he began to take the patient's history, the professional authority was solid. He heard with cleverness. He heard what the patient was not saying—one could almost hear him hearing it—and he asked the acute questions. A doctor tells universes about himself in the way he takes a history.

"I am coming to you for just one purpose," Hal had said in the first moments. "I want a totally independent opinion as to my condition." Said it coolly; and Silverman's ear had gathered in like a suction cup all the hot debris of uncertainty and anxiety buried beneath the words.

After the examination, he said, "How do you think you're doing?"

"Pretty well," Hal said. "What do *you* think?"

"I don't think you're doing so well. You have râles in your chest. Your liver is enlarged and tender. You are in heart failure. Your cardiogram is abnormal, but I can't comment on it because I have no basis for comparison."

"You got no records from Dr. Roberts?"

"No."

Roberts had sent nothing.

They arranged that Silverman would consult with Roberts. Then Hal left, feeling shaken. Heart failure! How could Roberts have missed such a thing? How could he have missed the râles, those crackling sounds which would indicate the presence of fluid in the lungs; sounds that any senior medical student should be able to detect?

And even if there had been no râles at the other end of Roberts' stethoscope, even if the lungs had been bone dry whenever Roberts listened, he should have been alerted by the symptoms. The weakness, the shortness of breath. It fit.

He wasn't sure what to think. One had to be cautious. There were doctors who played a tacky game when they were seen in consultation. They built themselves up by knocking down the referring physician: "You say he gave you the *green* pill? *Not* the pink one? Tch, tch."

He could not be sure yet whether Silverman had diagnosed correctly, or whether he was playing that kind of game.

"Can you check him out?" he asked a friend who was on staff at Silverman's hospital; and the word came back good. Several of Silverman's colleagues thought that he was a bit odd; silly in the way of social affectations; but beyond all that, an excellent cardiologist, with good gut sense.

Two days later, Silverman called.

"I'm a little concerned about you," he told Hal. "I'd like you to try these medications for a couple of days"—he mentioned digitalis and a mild diuretic—"and call me back and let me know how you're doing."

This is very strange, Hal thought. This man is only my consultant. How come he is calling me and ordering medicines for me?

On the other hand: if Silverman is right and I *am* in failure, I want nothing more to do with Roberts.

Let us see. It cannot hurt to take these medicines for a couple of days. It may not help, but it cannot hurt.

So he took the medicines. Within two days he had lost several pounds of fluid; he was walking better, feeling less weak, and his shortness of breath was greatly eased.

He never returned to Roberts' office.

The next week, he ran into Roberts on the street again.

"I must say, I was very much surprised that Dr. Silverman found me in failure," he said. It was a question.

"What did you expect?" Snarling out the words. "You refused to take the medicine I ordered for you."

Hal had not refused any medicine ordered by Roberts. Not once, not ever.

Much later, many months later, Silverman told me:

"What I found on that first visit was a very, very sick, very courageous man. Here was a man who had been pushing himself, who would not resign himself, who kept walking, walking, walking, doing everything *he could* to get better, in the face of a condition that was not overcomable. It was not denial. Denial is when I say to a patient, 'You've had a bad heart attack and now you must do so-and-so' . . . and the patient does not do so-and-so. That is denial. Hal did what his doctor told him to do. In this case, the *doctor* was denying."

"Why?" I said. "Why should the doctor have denied that his patient was in heart failure?"

Silverman shrugged. Frowned. Furrowed his brow.

"The doctor in question is a good doctor," he said. "I can only think that he didn't know. Quite possibly he did not examine the patient in relation to his symptoms. I mean, patients not only get biases about doctors. Doctors get biases about patients. Maybe he thought Hal's complaints were exaggerated."

"Not good enough," I said.

He shrugged again. I knew that shrug. I had seen Hal shrug, shoulders humping upward within his white coat. At the bottom line, there was a fraternity.

Chapter 11

*I*T started modestly enough. No dramatic production this time.
Not like that other one, with the sweat and the shock and the
creeping crushing pain and the fear that he might be crushed to death,
back there in his orange Formica kitchen on a sunny August morning.

This was midday, mid-December, a month after he had first seen
Silverman. He was sitting in his office, feet up on the desk, no tension,
no nothing, thinking about a speech he was scheduled to give to a
group of doctors. The season's first snow, large furry flakes, floated
softly by his window. He was sitting there thinking about the speech,
looking with pleasure at the snow, when he became aware of some
new sensation in his chest. Not the old healing pains, not the old
gurgling; really nothing much at all except that it was *there*. He
might have called it casual. But for anyone who has ever had a heart
attack, there is no such thing as a casual sensation in the chest.

It was a Friday afternoon. If this pain (no, no, not pain; simply
this unfamiliar *presence*) persisted or grew worse, he might have
trouble reaching Silverman later. He picked up the telephone.

"It's nothing much, but I thought I should let you know," he said.
"It's just a sort of vague, dull pressure. More an awareness than a
pain."

"Come down here right away," Silverman said.

He called me at the house, sounding ever so cool. Just going to check it out, mere routine, not to worry, absolutely no need for you to come.

Sure, sure. But wait for me.

We took a cab down together, holding hands.

"No pain?" I said.

"None. It was just a funny little feeling, and now it's almost gone. Probably Silverman was being overcautious."

"Better over than under."

"Yes, of course."

I sat in the waiting room thumbing ancient *Newsweek*s while they examined him. In half an hour Silverman came out and said to me:

"It may be nothing, but there's a change in his electrocardiogram. I want to play it safe and admit him."

"Okay." Feeling the trembling start. "When should he go to the hospital?"

"Now. We've already booked a room."

Within an hour he was lying in a hospital bed hooked up to a monitor, nasal oxygen, intravenous tubing. His enzyme tests came back abnormal. Probable diagnosis: a mild myocardial infarction.

Mild? Did you say mild? Screaming the words, months back, in that high-panic telephone call from France. *No, I did not say "mild." I said "myo."* . . .

But this time, yes. Mild.

Probable diagnosis? How can a heart attack be *probable?* How can they not be sure? Even when it is mild, surely there must be signs from the standard Hollywood repertory, moans, groans, gaspings for breath, clutching the heart, a wild fear in the eyes, doubling over, slumping to the floor, all or several in any combination; at least a purple sign or two worthy of such an occasion?

But I was wrong, of course. A heart attack can come and go so quietly that one may never know it has happened. And in fact, many heart attacks happen in just that way.

Silverman was reassuring. "We are quite certain there's been some degree of infarction, but not transmural; not clean through the wall of the heart," he said, causing me to see, in my mind's eye, a heart only pleasingly pierced by an arrow.

They kept him in hospital just a week. That was reassuring too. If he had had to have another coronary, this one seemed choice.

We had no way to know, until he came home and started trying to move around, that this one, this diffident mild one, had left him crippled.

Angina. The pain was unbelievable. He would be walking along the street, moving in the most cautious and conservative way, and suddenly it would hit him like a lead weight in the chest, doubling him up, blotting out his vision, making him gasp, Help, *help*, and he would have to stop and lean helplessly against a telephone pole, a parking meter, whatever was handy. Wait till it eased, start out again, then get slammed again by that solid-lead fist, and stop, and start, and stop, Help, *help*, and so on down the street.

Soon he was living like the classic cardiac cripple: afraid to walk; afraid that he might drop dead within steps; afraid even to leave the house.

Silverman said, "Let's take some pictures."

Coronary angiography. X-ray of the heart. Pictures to show whether the heart is a candidate for surgery.

Part Two

*H*E didn't want the test. In the worst way, he didn't want it. He was afraid of it.

That was the nastiest part of being a doctor-patient: one knew when to be afraid.

The test had been developed only a few years earlier. It was not just another X-ray. Not like chest X-rays, not like belly X-rays. It was, in fact, a form of surgery, and a supremely delicate form.

Among the stacks of medical literature that came across his desk each day, he had seen, just the week before, a disturbing report. There had been a meeting of cardiologists and cardiovascular surgeons in Texas. They had heard the latest findings on the complications and mortality rates of coronary angiography. In that blisteringly cool way of medical language, surreal as military language, it had been noted that the major complication of coronary angiography was death.

The mortality rate was 5 percent. Not bad. Anything involving general anesthesia, even the removal of an ingrown toenail, has a mortality rate of at least 1 percent.

But among patients whose hearts were X-rayed within six weeks after a heart attack, the mortality rate was 35 percent.

And he was within that period. His second coronary had occurred just a month before.

He had carefully read and clipped the article, as he read and clipped everything, these days, that had to do with hearts. Not out of any macabre self-interest, but because he simply had to know. That was the doctor in him, the part he couldn't shake off, even when the angina seemed to be crushing him to death: he had to feel in control.

So he had clipped out this article. And then, when Silverman had begun muttering, "I think we should take some pictures," he had hidden it away in some back corner of his desk. He didn't want me to see it. And he didn't tell me that he was afraid.

The heart attacks had not frightened him. Not in this way. He understood why: Because there had been no element of choice. A coronary was a coronary; you couldn't choose *not* to have it. You went with the pathological process, and if you were lucky enough to survive, you coped as best you could.

But here, he had a choice: he could submit or not submit to a test that might kill him—and he was not at all sure that the test was essential.

It bothered him, too, that his doctor was so casual: "We should take some pictures. . . ." Such benign words. A 35-percent mortality rate was not benign.

He knew what would be done to him: they would stick a tube—a catheter—into his femoral artery, at the groin, and push that tube up into his heart. It was a technique he himself had used many times to X-ray kidneys. Renal angiography, that was called: sticking a catheter into the kidney, injecting a dye and taking pictures of the vascular system.

He remembered that when he had prepared patients for this test, he had sounded as casual as Silverman. "Oh, it's nothing much," he would say. "We're just going to take some pictures of your kidney."

If they expressed anxiety, he would talk about it further, trying to reassure them. But generally he minimized the detail. It was simpler that way. And the truth was, the test *was* relatively innocuous. You could fill the entire vascular system of a kidney with dye and get excellent pictures without harming the organ, because the substance was washed out in a minute or two.

But when you stick a tube up into the *heart*, and fill an artery of the heart with dye, you are depriving that artery of oxygen. Functionally, it is the same as if you jammed a plug into that artery. Functionally, it is the same as having a heart attack; and if the heart is thus deprived for moments too long, there may be disaster.

If you didn't inject enough dye, you couldn't get good pictures. If you injected too much, it was all over. The trick was this: to inject precisely enough, and at precisely such a speed as would let sufficient blood flow through the artery at the same time as the dye.

And he lay there, in our bed at home, staring up at the ceiling and thinking that this would be a mighty delicate balance.

He asked Silverman, "What about the radiologist who will do it—what are his mortality rates?"

"Don't worry. He's the best."

"But what are his mortality rates?"

"I told you, he's the best. What more do you have to know?"

The mortality rates, that's what.

No answers; never any answers. Damn it, he thought, why don't doctors give you straight answers?

And then: Did my patients feel that way about me?

At the same time, Silverman was coming on heavily to me. He would duck that long neck down and put his head conspiratorially close to mine—not in the least unpleasant, even somehow flattering, we two professors working this thing out together—and murmur:

"Look, whaddya need this for? You want this guy to spend the rest of his life under wraps? You call that living? Let's take the pictures and see what's there and get it fixed up and *fachtig* (finished, taken care of). Right?"

Of course right. I wasn't asking any questions. What did I know of mortality rates?

But Hal felt doubt. The doubt distorted his judgment just enough to make him do what his own patients had so often done: lie to himself, deny his own symptoms. This pain isn't so awfully bad, is it? Why, at this very moment, it's really quite mild. Maybe it isn't even angina. Maybe it's heartburn. Maybe it's those "healing pains" again. . . .

In this mood he went to a consultant, a sharp and highly respected young cardiologist, and managed to tell just enough of the truth so that he would get back what he wanted to hear. Not quite lying, but selecting his facts, minimizing his symptoms to some degree, and not even doing it consciously.

He said, "I want your opinion because I am really not positive that these attacks are angina, and I really do not want the angiography now if I can avoid it."

And the heart specialist obliged. There was no collusion. He was simply responding to what he heard, which is a perfectly reasonable thing to do and which, in medicine, can be disastrous.

He ran Hal through the tests. He said that he didn't think there was any hurry. If the pain persisted, the X-ray could be taken later, when it was safer, when the heart had had more time to recover from its second attack.

Good enough. Hal told Silverman, and Silverman said, "I think you're making a mistake," but what the hell. The patient was a big boy. A *doctor*. He had a right to make his own mistakes.

The trouble was, the pain persisted. It got worse. In the next couple of days he tested himself, going out for little walks, and before he'd walked a half block from home the pain would hit him and he would be stopping and leaning again against cars, mailboxes, telephone poles, gasping and clutching his chest.

On the second day a woman approached him and said, "Are you all right? Can I help you?"

He managed to smile. "Thanks, I'm all right."

"You look awfully sick. I could help you get to the hospital. It's right down the block, you know."

Yes, he knew. He also knew, fully aware of it now, that he had been cheating on himself. This pain was of course angina, there was no way it could be anything *but* angina, and who the hell was he kidding?

But how frightened he was of the test!

He wondered, Whose opinion could I accept with peace of mind? And thought immediately of his Uncle Victor. Victor Kay, a Miami cardiologist with a national reputation, the only one of the uncles who hadn't dropped dead at some preposterously early age.

He was about 70 now, a superb clinician, and cautious, conservative, not one of the hotshot new breed who had been weaned on open-heart surgery and would reach, when in doubt, for the knife. And of course, Vic would care. It was family.

So Hal called Miami. They had conferred several times after the first heart attack, but Hal hadn't told him of the second.

He told it straight now, underplaying nothing. And he hadn't even finished reporting his recent medical history, the second attack, the angina, the frequency and degree of pain, when this conservative uncle interrupted him and said:

"No question. Do it. Go in and get the angiography. There is danger, but there is a greater danger if you don't."

So he went.

Chapter 13

*H*IS room was on the fifteenth floor of the hospital, with a splendid southern view. The last time, he'd faced west. This was better. If you had to be in a hospital in New York City, you couldn't have a better view. The skyline peered in at us. The river shimmered like clean water. We watched the Tinker Toys cruising on the river and talked of friends who had called, mail that had arrived, the reviews of a new Broadway play, whatever. He was medicated for pain, and he looked and sounded so relaxed that I would not for a moment have guessed that he was playacting.

He was scheduled for angiography the next morning.

A nurse came in while he was eating dinner.

"Dr. Lear," she said, "after angiography the patients always seem to have the same complaints, and I thought you might want to know about them. It might help."

This was a good nurse. I didn't know it then, because I didn't know how scared he was. But later I understood that this was a damned good nurse.

"Thanks; it would help," he said.

"It's mostly two things. The first is, they say that during the test, they feel a tremendous flush. It's very sudden, and it can be scary."

Oh, yes, the flush. Whenever he had done kidney X-rays, patients had complained of the flush. It was caused by the injection of a large volume of dye. He had always warned them beforehand, but not putting too sharp a point on it, because then the anticipation would make it far worse.

"You may feel a flushing sensation when I inject the dye," he would say. "It's normal. It's nothing to be frightened of. . . ."

Now, he told the nurse, "Okay, the flush. And what's the other thing?"

"It's . . . well, they say that at a certain point, they feel as though they're about to die. But that feeling passes quickly."

He thanked her again. He was very grateful.

He wouldn't have known that. It didn't happen in renal angiography. But he could understand it. Of course: When the dye is injected, less oxygen is going into the heart. The sense that you are dying is caused by the lack of oxygen. And if that lack is prolonged, you *do* die.

Too much dye, I die, he thought. He laughed at his lousy little pun, and I asked what he was laughing about.

"Ah, nothing," he said.

I stayed until eight. I sat in a chair with my shoes off and my feet up on the bed, playing toesies with him. Skin hunger. And he sounding so easy-cool that it seemed there was nothing on his mind except the lazy play of our toes.

When the bell sounded and the stern little voice on the loudspeaker announced, "Ladies and gentlemen, visiting hours are over," I put my shoes and coat on and bent down to kiss him.

"See you tomorrow," I said.

"Right. Listen, come late. I'll probably be pretty much out of it until midafternoon."

"Okay. Is there anything I can bring you?"

"No. Just . . ."

Suddenly he pulled my head down to his again and gripped my shoulders, hard.

"You know I love you very, very much," he said.

And for the first time, quick study that I was, I caught a glimmering of what lay behind his cool.

"Are you worried about tomorrow?" I said. "Silverman said it was nothing to worry about. . . ."

"No, no, I'm not worried. I just thought you'd like to know you're loved. Don't you always like to know it?"

"Always!" I said. And kissed him again, and turned at the doorway to do a silly little soft-shoe number which had become my signing-in and signing-out of his various hospital rooms. He laughed and applauded, and I left.

I didn't know that he had called Jon to his room before I arrived and given him careful instructions as to where everything might be found—his insurance policies and his will and all that business, neatly labeled and tucked away in folders in his study at home. Because he had seen the horror that it could be for widows when the legal trappings of a lifetime must get pulled together and nobody knows where or how.

He might have told it all to me. But it was no chauvinist impulse that made him tell it to his son instead. It was simply that he knew I wouldn't listen. "I don't want to *talk* about it," I would say (and had said, often, over the years). I never wanted to know about insurance policies, last wills and testaments, all those bleak papers contingent on death; I didn't want to know they existed. Bad omens.

So he had told Jon. Just in case anything happened, he had said. Not that he *expected* anything to happen, but just in case, he wanted to know that it would all be managed tidily. And Jon, sober and pale-faced, had promised him that it would all be managed tidily.

When I had gone he lay there, surrendering himself to the tension. Those persistent little denial mechanisms began to creep in on him again.

Well, now, he thought, If I'm having that test done tomorrow, I really should take one last little test of my own tonight. Just to see if I get pain.

He decided to walk the corridor—it was a city block long—twenty times. A mile.

He got up and began to walk vigorously. Nobody seemed to notice. Visiting hours over, the corridors quiet, nurses bustling into and out of rooms with medications, doctors sitting at the nurses' station writing orders, a patient with a bad heart who was scheduled for angiography at 8 A.M. marching back and forth like a demented robot, and nobody seemed to notice.

While he walked, he kept checking himself. Do you feel pain now?

Just a bit. That's okay. Is your pulse rate up? No, not much. Heart pounding? Only a little. Shortness of breath? Not too bad . . . And such and so, until he had completed his mile.

Then he went to a resident at the nurses' station. He said:

"I have just walked the length of this corridor twenty times. I have no pain. I am not short of breath, and I have a minimal tachycardia. Therefore, I am not sure I really need the angiogram tomorrow."

"I think that was very foolish of you," the resident said.

Skewered.

He went back to bed. Still, this stupid bravado: Well, I've shown them. I do not need this test. What the hell, I'll go through with it. I am already scheduled, the pre-op orders are already written, I am on this particular conveyor belt and there is really not any getting off. But I've shown *them*.

On the other hand: How weak he felt now! How his heart was racing! How he was gasping for breath! *Shmuck*, he thought, what are you out to prove?

Finally, ironically, it was the terrible pounding of his own heart that gave him peace of mind. It told him that the thing had to be done. He could no longer bluff anyone out of it, including himself.

And the moment it was clear, *in his own medical opinion*, that there was really no element of choice, he relaxed and fell asleep.

The next day, when they saw what was in his heart, they marveled that he hadn't dropped dead during his little demonstration stroll.

Chapter 14

*T*HEY strapped him into a stretcher with high safety rails and wheeled him through labyrinths down to the X-ray room.

He gazed upward and around. A large, dim, windowless space painted a pale, dull green. And the attendants in this space wore pale green caps and gowns and masks. And around the walls were the usual stainless-steel equipment tables, draped in pale green cloths. He had the sensation of being awash in green light, something vaguely underwater.

The X-ray table stood in the center of the room. Opposite the head of the table, on the pale green wall, was a television screen. An image intensifier, it was called. Very sophisticated stuff. He knew that whatever the X-ray camera saw would be projected onto that screen. They had just been developing the equipment when he had quit practice.

Orderlies rolled his stretcher up against the X-ray table and helped him slide over. They flung straps across his body, all but his right arm. He noted with surprise that the straps stuck to each other: they were Velcro, not like the buckled canvas straps he had used to use. He had last worked in an operating room three years ago—eons ago, in medicine. Ah, progress, he thought. Velcro. If they have to tilt me much, I hope the stuff holds and I don't fall off this fucking table.

Beneath him, he knew, were foot pedals that could tilt the table sideways, forward, backward, and buttons that could direct the camera to take moving pictures and stills. Above loomed the X-ray machine, a huge cone-shaped weight which honed down to a small opening focused on him.

There was something schizoid here. It was all so familiar, yet so utterly strange. He had never been in such a setting lying down. He had always been one of those masked faces that floated way up there, in the semilight, peering down at bodies stretched on tables like this.

So this is how it looks from the other side, he thought. A room with a different view. Worm's-eye views. Infants in their cradles gazing up at giants. Alice in Wonderland, that was it: Alice walking through the looking-glass and seeing everything from the other side.

Someone slipped an arm board under him, strapped his right arm to the board and said, "You'll be getting intravenous anesthesia. You won't be asleep, but you'll feel pretty groggy."

Good. He felt no great agitation, but there was a tightness in his stomach. He would like to feel more relaxed.

A green-masked figure stood over him. The mask came up almost to the eyes and the cap came down almost to the eyes and the space between the two was covered with eyeglasses, so that he could get no sense whatever of a type, a look.

"Dr. Lear, I'm Dr. X," the face said. "I'll be doing this procedure."

"How do you do, Dr. X."

"How do you do."

Oh, yes, Alice in Wonderland.

"The anesthetist isn't here, but we're going to get started."

The Team clustered about him: the chief radiologist, a resident assisting him, a couple of interns there to watch and learn and keep their mouths shut, two nurses, an X-ray technician. He could feel them painting his lower body with an antiseptic solution, then draping his groin area. The familiar metal bar, shaped like a two-foot-high croquet wicket, straddled his body, just under his chin, and now a pale green drape was thrown over the bar. This sort of screen was used in every surgical procedure. It separated the sterile area from the nonsterile. Also, if the patient was awake, it obscured his line of vision.

So now he couldn't see what they were doing to him. But he could feel them working and, of course, he knew precisely what they were doing because he had done it so many times himself.

He felt the pressure down there, fingers pressing into the right side of his groin, and knew that they were searching for the femoral artery. Then a pushing sensation, and he knew that the large hollow needle called a trocar was going in, probing. It didn't hurt, but he could feel it. He was starting to sweat.

Very timidly, he asked, "The anesthetist hasn't come yet, right?"

A voice said soothingly, "No, but it's okay. She'll be right here."

This was always a tricky moment. The artery lay right next to the femoral nerve and the femoral vein, all three running parallel and within millimeters of each other. You could hit the nerve—which would hurt like hell and could cause neurological damage. It didn't happen often, but it could happen. Or you could hit the vein, ripping right through it. Veins are like tissue paper. Or the tip of the trocar might just slide off the artery, just by a fraction, and nick the vein. The whole area would swell with blood and you might have to stop and go into the other leg.

That was the most common. It had happened to him once, early in his practice. He had been working on a child. In children the vessels are smaller, even closer together, and it is harder to find the artery. He had inserted the trocar. Those big needles are fitted with plugs called stylettes. When you have pushed in the needle you pull out the stylette, and that is how you know whether you're in the right place: If the blood whooshes out at you in a bright, strong spurt, you've hit the artery. If it comes out in a dark ooze, you've hit the vein.

And that time, working on the child, he had removed the stylette and seen the blood oozing out toward him, dark and slow, and he had had to pull out the needle quickly and press down hard on the vein to stop the bleeding. It had been all right, no damage, but it had shaken him, and he still remembered it twenty years later. It was so terrifyingly easy for a surgeon, any surgeon, no matter how careful and skilled, to make that kind of mistake.

Suddenly he felt something pop within him, and knew that they had made a good hit. Because the wall of the artery is thick with muscle, not at all like the fragile vein, it is more like going through a rubber tube: first resistance, and then that sudden *pop*, and you know you've gotten through. When he had been the doctor, when it had been his hand guiding the needle, there would come a moment when he would feel that same pop, and know that he had landed cleanly in the artery.

Now, he thought, They've pulled out the stylette and my blood is spurting out at them. Now they will start pushing a catheter up through the needle. Now I will see the catheter entering me.

He looked up at the screen. There he was. Live on TV. He saw his pelvis, his bones, his spinal column. And then, in a corner of the screen, he saw this *thing*, this intrusion, this snakelike tube beginning to creep into his pelvis.

He was sweating harder. His body was rigid. His heart was pounding.

Someone yelled out, urgently, "Tell that anesthetist to get in here, we've started."

He closed his eyes. He said to himself:

You are too tense. You are getting very frightened. It is not good to get this frightened. Your heart is racing and it's a weak heart, it can't afford to race. You must relax. Keep your eyes closed. Shut out what frightens you. Don't watch.

Instead, pretend: What if they had already given you the anesthesia? You would be lying here awake, but you wouldn't be tense. Your heart wouldn't be pounding like this. Your fists wouldn't be clenched. Unclench them. Your muscles wouldn't be knotted. Relax them. You would be breathing slower and deeper, like this. Your body would go loose, like this. Yes, like this, now, breathing easy, staying loose, you would be feeling relaxed, relaxed, completely relaxed. . . .

And soon he *was* feeling relaxed. He thought, Maybe they've already given me the anesthesia. I wonder what I look like on the screen now.

So he opened his eyes again. There was the catheter creeping upward slowly; he could see it climbing up behind his bladder and moving into his lower aorta, just above the small of his spine. He watched, then, filled with wonder, as the thing snaked up along the back of his belly, behind his intestines, up between his kidneys, and crawled through an opening in his diaphram and entered his chest. He watched his ribs move with his breathing. He watched the tube climb high up in his chest and make a curve to the left, and he thought, Oh, yes, that's the arch of my aorta. And he watched the tube curve a little bit more and creep finally into a cavity, and he thought, My God, this cavity is my heart. I am looking at the inside of my heart. That is my own heart, beating, contracting and expanding, up there on the television screen.

He felt awestricken. He felt overwhelmed with emotion. It was like . . . what? Like seeing God? Like God suddenly making an appearance? Almost, yes, like a profound religious experience.

A voice said, "We're going to inject dye now. You may feel this."

He kept staring at the screen. Now he could see one of his coronary arteries. This is unbelievable, he thought. He felt astonishment at this thing which was happening to him. And yet, even now, a kind of detachment. That old clinical detachment. Detached astonishment.

And then, all at once, he felt it: that flush, that tremendous flush, as though his whole body had been thrust into an oven. It wasn't scary. There was an almost amused recognition: right on, the flush.

But then—*wham*. Suddenly a massive pain in his chest, a life-sucking pain, as though the life were being squeezed out of him. He felt on the verge of a fatal heart attack. And that sudden total loss of strength, that dread, that foreboding. Terror.

"I am having pain," he said aloud.

No answer.

And to himself, with his eyes squeezed shut: Easy. Easy. You're supposed to feel this way. This is precisely what the nurse described. The moment when you feel you are dying.

But also the moment when you *can* die. Moments of truth. At this moment I am having the equivalent of a heart attack. The dye is filling my arteries, choking my arteries, choking off oxygen.

My God, this pain is awfully bad. Maybe I *am* dying. Is this it? I may be dead within seconds.

People drop dead of heart attacks. They get hit by cars. They die in comas with terminal cancer. But to lie here in a fully conscious moment, waiting to see whether I am going to live or die . . .

And he lay there, in this unbearably attenuated moment, the longest moment of his life, with every atom of himself like fingertips, focused on his heart, waiting.

Suddenly, the pain seemed a fraction less. And then less. The heat began to subside, retreating in diminishing waves down through his body. He felt a near swoon of the soul. I am safe now. I am going to live.

Soon all that remained was a deep burning sensation in his rectum.

He thought, So this is the ending to that endless moment; to be left finally with a pain in the ass.

He opened his eyes again and saw a masked figure approach and give him a shot through the intravenous tubing.

"What are you giving me?" he said.

"That was your anesthesia," she said.

And just moments later, he heard another voice say, "Okay, we're finished."

So that he had time to marvel, until the shot sent him into space, at the crazy thing that seemed to have happened:

They had forgotten the anesthesia.

They had been concentrating so intensely that they hadn't realized nobody had given him the anesthesia.

And he had somehow managed, in those first moments of terror, to hypnotize himself.

Chapter 15

*T*HEY got a good set of pictures. It showed that he was an arterial disaster area.

One of his three coronary arteries—the major one, the left anterior descending—no longer existed. It had simply rotted away. They could find no trace of it on the angiogram.

The other two arteries were almost completely blocked, so badly plugged and narrowed in certain places that the blood could barely dribble through. Like very old pipe. Like the ancient rust-ridden galvanized pipes they had had to take out of our house in Provincetown and replace with copper tubing.

"Like the insides of an eighty-year-old man," Silverman told me.

"They should have something like Drano for people," I said, dreading what now would come; yearning after the image of some pill that could be taken by mouth, some Good Housekeeping Seal of Approval pill that would foam up nicely and loosen the buildup of dirt and grease from the plumbing and flush it all away, leaving every inner surface clean and fresh-smelling.

But of course, there would have to be surgery. He needed new pipe. How fortunate that they now had pipes for people.

A decade ago they could have done nothing for him. He would have had to take his angina to bed and more or less live in bed until he died; maybe months, maybe years; in either case, a cardiac cripple living in bed.

But in this decade they had made the most astonishing advances in cardiac surgery. Now there were surgical procedures tailor-made for hearts like his.

Coronary-bypass surgery: They would cut a half-yard of vein from the leg. Good clean vein, wide open, for cholesterol does not clog the veins as it does the arteries; and big, with the diameter almost of a drinking straw, whereas a coronary artery has more the circumference of a spaghetti strand. Then they would cut open the chest, break the chest bone (in the old days they had done it with cutting shears; now they used an electrical saw, neat, cool) and expose the heart; and they would use that nice piece of vein from the leg literally to bypass the plugged portion of the coronary artery. They would graft onto the artery above and below the occlusion, making a detour around the roadblock.

They could do this to one artery; or to two, which would be called a double bypass; or to three, which would be called a triple bypass. The angiogram showed that Hal was a candidate for a double bypass.

Nobody claimed that bypass surgery prolonged life or prevented future heart attacks. The likelihood was that it did neither. But what it could do, almost like magic, was provide total relief for patients with severe angina and permit them to lead normal lives. The surgeons were not sure why. Perhaps because of the improved flow of blood; perhaps because they severed some pain fibers when they opened the chest cavity. They simply did not know. They knew only that the angina disappeared.

The operation was very popular at the moment. Too popular, perhaps; almost a form of medical *chic*, as the heart transplant had been in its time. It was being performed sometimes, in some places, on people who might have been better off without it. People whose angina wasn't all that bad. People who were too old, or too sick in many vital organs, to withstand the trauma of heart surgery. People in whom the bypass would be useless because their coronary arteries were too pervasively clogged.

And not very many hospitals were set up for the surgery, really. And not very many surgical teams had much experience. It was too new. Too many mediocre surgeons from obscure hospitals were reaching too impulsively for the knife, eager to get into the action—Angina? Oh, now, we're going to fix that up just *fine*—and chalking up atrocious mortality rates. At one suburban Boston hospital, a scandal later revealed, half the bypass cases were ending up dead.

So there was all that, as there always is with a fashionable surgical procedure. But in good surgical hands, and performed upon a good candidate, the coronary bypass worked wonders.

Hal was a good candidate. He was in superb shape except for his heart, they said. (I smiled nervously, thinking of the old analytic joke: I've got everything solved but sex and my mother.) And he had enough decent coronary artery left so that the bypasses might work well.

He would be in competent hands. The best. There were just two surgeons in New York who were said to rank with the best in the country for bypass surgery; one of them was Dr. Evan Bell, the chief of cardiovascular surgery right here at Silverman's hospital. "Golden hands," Silverman said.

Anyway, there were no reasonable options. The thing had to be done, and fast. For many patients it would have been an elective procedure. Probably severe angina would not kill them. It would simply cripple them. You decided whether you wanted to live your life under wraps, or take your chances in the operating room and maybe emerge pain-free and maybe emerge dead. There was a choice.

With Hal, there was no choice, for the angiography had revealed a terrible surprise.

They had anticipated the rotten state of his arteries. What they could not have anticipated was the time bomb he carried within: a large aneurysm in the left ventricle, a section of heart wall stretched so thin that it could no longer function. Stretched almost to the breaking point, like the inner tube of a tire just before the blowout; like the bubble of gum just before it bursts.

This big cardiac bubble had ballooned outward into his chest cavity and lay there, lifeless, a sort of dead heart lying beside the live heart. When his good heart muscle, or what was left of it, contracted, blood should have been pushed out to the major vessels of his body. Instead, it was pouring into this inert sac, pooling up in there, depriving his body of blood and stretching that perilously thin section of heart wall ever thinner and thinner. Left to itself, it would probably burst open and kill him.

When they told him of the aneurysm, he thought back with horror to his mile-long walk along the hospital corridors, just the night before; to all the mile-long walks of the past several months and all the labored steps, with any one of which the deadly bubble within him might have burst.

He felt instantly sure of when the aneurysm had happened. That fearful day three months before, lying out on the terrace with an ominous stirring in his heart, a deep, certain sense that something terrible was happening or about to happen . . . just then. Exactly then.

Probably healing pains, Roberts had said on the telephone. And he himself had said, No, I don't think so, and Roberts had told him to come to the cardiology clinic, two blocks away. Is it all right to walk? he had asked. Sure, Roberts had said.

And what was it Martha had said? Oh, yes: I think we should get a wheelchair.

He remembered how impatient he had felt. Listen, don't wheelchair me. If my doctor says I can walk, I'll damn well walk. And he had walked.

But how stupid! Stupid of Roberts, stupid of himself. A coronary patient calls you and says he has pains in the chest, you don't tell him to walk. You don't have to be a cardiologist to know that. If Roberts had been careless enough or indifferent enough to make such a gross mistake, what was his own excuse? He was a doctor too. And it was his heart. Why had he walked? Some vestigial *machismo*; some dumb denial mechanism . . .

Okay. It didn't matter now. What mattered was that his crazy luck had held. This time bomb within him had not exploded. But it still ticked. Now (he thought, moving gingerly about in the bed; cautious as a bomb squad, gloved and soft-footed), let's get it dismantled and removed. And let's get the bypasses in there, and *fachtig*.

That was a Friday. They scheduled him for surgery on Monday. Dr. Bell came and told Hal how he would proceed, the two surgeons discussing this matter together.

Hal said, "I would appreciate your talking to my wife about this. She might be less apprehensive if she knew just what you're going to do."

Bell spent an hour with me, explaining. I do not think he did it simply because his patient was a doctor. He was a most decent man who had managed somehow never to cut the human connection. That happens so easily to surgeons, with all the cutting they do. We sat beside each other in the visitors' lounge and he made doodles on paper, doodles for the left ventricle and the bad places in the arteries and where he would make the bypasses and where the aneurysm was located and how he would get rid of it. ("Technically," he said, pointing to the aneurysm doodle, "this is a very simple thing to correct"), and such and so. And I could not make much sense of his doodles and no sense at all of his technical talk, but it soothed me. It sounded so calm, so safe. And Silverman ("Moe" I was calling him now, in the cordiality of shared traumas) was calming me too. This thing would be done, Bell's golden hands would do it with dispatch, and then I would have—presto!—a healthy Hal again. A normal Hal.

And Hal himself, working on me like a tranquilizer. He was genuinely not scared now. Before the angiography, yes. He had been scared and I had been blithe, not knowing enough to be scared. Now I was plenty scared, and he was surely not complacent, but he felt as a surgeon that the surgery had to be done, and faced with this inexorability, he was utterly cool. And in some way he conned me, they all conned me into a kind of cool. Not so much a confidence as a spaced-out daze, as though I had awakened in somebody else's dream and it would be bad form to make a fuss. In this dream, everything was neutralized. The savaging of a chest, the unbearable vision against which I had been squeezing my eyes shut, a chestbone cracked open (how? Bell hadn't told me that; by shears, by saw, by ax, by a massive fist?), vital organs shoved aside, lungs collapsed, a heart exposed, Hal's heart, a mere lump of bloody liver which hands would push and tear, upon which hands would perform obscene acts with scissors and needles and disembodied pieces of vein—all this was transformed, in this cool, polite WASP dream in which I now wandered, into something as safe and unevocative as a top-sirloin roast at the A&P. A hernia repair, maybe; something on that order, without imagery.

For himself, of course, there could be no escape to the A&P. He lay there with the surgeon's projective imagery, a total evocation in living color. He had been often enough in people's chests. He had handled hearts that were beating and hearts that were not, and he knew what that looked like and how it felt.

Of course, his own heart would not be beating. His body would rest on the operating table like a dead body. A computerized machine, the heart-lung machine, would perform his vital functions for him while he was dead.

His blood, every last drop of it, would go out of him into this machine, which would do all the good things a heart and lungs should do for blood—purifying it, oxygenating it—and feed it back into him through some system, staggering even to the medical imagination, of tubes and rollers and membranes and pumps, some Rube Goldbergian system—no, no, not Goldbergian; that image was too lighthearted; *lighthearted!*—but more in the nature of some brooding, mysterious, omnipotent Supersystem, a Supermachine. He thought of HAL, the cosmic computer from *2001*. HAL feeding Hal.

Knowing it was silly, he nonetheless began, in the twenty-four hours before surgery, to anthropomorphize this machine, to assign it traits of personality (stern, meticulous, arrogant, clever, contained, cosmic cool cat), to reflect upon the awesome relationship that would exist between it and himself, HAL and Hal, and to hope that they might develop a good, healthy, death-defying rapport. There was nothing morbid in this. It amused him.

Saturday, visitors came bearing smiles. There was something almost celebratory: Gonna get you *fixed up*, boy! Edgy smiles, like New Year's Eve, but still with some real sense that there would be things to celebrate. *Fixed up!*

His cousin David brought vodka and we all hoisted a few. "You'll be a fifty-three-year-old machine with a brand-new motor," somebody said, and I, as ignorant of medical realities as that sweet believer, said, "Hear, hear," and we drank again.

Jon brought a bag of red dollars. I think that is what they are called, those loathsome red licorice discs that grab the teeth like glue. Hal had a passion for them. He said they were the closest you could get to the Saturday-movie-matinee Jujubes of his childhood. I think also that he liked to encourage his children to poke a certain kind of fun: Oh, yeah, Dad and his crazy red dollars! Dad thinks he's Mr. Fix-It, but he always fucks up the toaster! Dad has the worst singing voice you ever heard; sing it again, Dad! Family anecdotes, an oral history of love.

And so here was Jon, age 24; a philosopher, working toward his doctorate at Rockefeller University, just blocks away; a reflective, sophisticated, immensely intelligent man, nodding with a child's delight to see his father chomping away on the red dollars. "These things are *terrible*," Hal mumbled happily, and Jon nodded harder, smiled bigger, basking in the comforts of continuity.

He and I left together in the evening.

"How are you doing?" he asked.

"Fine. And you?"

"Pretty *good*. Pretty *good*."

"Dad seems good too, doesn't he?"

"Oh, fine. He seems in *great* spirits!"

"He was so happy you brought the red dollars."

"Jesus, yes. Dad and his red dollars."

"What are you doing tonight?"

"I have a date. But listen, if you'd like company . . ."

"No, no. I was just wondering if *you* had company."

"I do. But how about *you*?"

"The Honans invited me to dinner."

"Great. So you're doing all right?"

"Fine. And you?"

"Pretty *good*."

Smiling. Trading little hugs, little soft-sell pats on the shoulder.

He went off on his date and I went to visit friends who had just moved into a new apartment. They hadn't yet decided upon a furniture arrangement. "I love to move furniture," I said, and set to like a maniac, shoving the sofas and tables and chests around as though they were on wheels, pushing them to this wall and that, to the middle of the room, to the fireplace, freestanding, catercorner, pseudo conversation-pit, scratching the hell out of newly polished floors, refusing to stop—"Now, look, wouldn't it be nice by this window? Let me just try it by this window." My hosts stood silent, tactful. At midnight, leaving them to straighten out the mess, I went home and attacked my own living room, dragging furniture across the flokati, arranging and rearranging until near dawn, when I fell into bed exhausted.

Sunday, we telephoned Judy from Hal's hospital room. She was pregnant now, and coping with morning sickness. We had told her not to come to New York.

"I hope you've told them to do a good job on you, Daddy," she said.

"They damned well better. I'll be very angry if they don't."

"Oh, Daddy." A breathy delight in her voice. *Daddy will make them make it all right.* "I love you so much, Daddy."

"Me too, darling."

In the evening, Jon laid his head upon his father's broad, deceptive chest and cried.

"It's going to be all right, darling," Hal said.

"I know," Jon said.

They embraced, and he left, and Hal and I sat together in the dim room, holding hands, talking into the shadows.

"Are you afraid of dying?"

"No. Yes, of course. I know that I could die on the table. But it has to be done. So I feel at peace, really."

"I'm frightened. But it's unreal. I feel as though it is appropriate to be frightened, but I don't for a moment believe that you are going to die."

"Of course I'm not. How could I do such a thing to my Mushie?"

"Oh, darling." Oh, Daddy.

When it was quite late, an orderly appeared.

"I have to prep you now, Dr. Lear," he said. "Will you excuse us, ma'am?" Apologetic.

"Excuse you? You mean I have to leave? What do you have to do to him?"

"I have to shave him."

"Shave him?" An unreasonable nervousness rising inside me. Shave him, eh? Starting already to do things with small knives. This man is no doctor. Are his hands steady? I do not want to leave.

"What is your name?"

"Brown, ma'am."

"Mr. Brown, do you mind if I stay?"

"Well, ma'am, it might be better if . . ." He looked helplessly at Hal.

"Suppose we draw the curtain around the bed and I sit on the other side of it. Would that be all right?"

"All right, ma'am." Reluctantly.

So we did that. I sat outside their enclosure making chatter, giggles, nervous noise.

"I hope you have a steady hand, Mr. Brown?"

"Yes, ma'am. Quite steady."

A long silence. Then: "Where are you shaving now, Mr. Brown?"

A small strained laugh. "Well, ma'am, right now . . ."

"*Oh.* Well, then, *do* be careful, Mr. Brown. . . ." Oh, *do* shut up, Martha. Pest. Vulgar. Quit it.

Within the circle of the green curtain, they shared a hushed intimate space. Hal lay naked amid shadows, his body spotlighted like a painting. The orderly, Brown, loomed over him. He was a huge dark man with a puffy Afro. He murmured as he worked; crooned, almost, cozy, comforting sounds, as he first soaped the body and then began to shave it, crooning, working gently and deftly.

He began at the neck and moved steadily downward with his razor over the lathered skin, over the chest and the arms and the underarms, crooning signals to lift this arm higher and turn a bit more on that side, razoring downward then over the belly to the pubis, so strange to feel the shaving there, and down then between the legs and upon the legs—everywhere hair grew.

And when Brown had shaved the body completely, he started from the top again and painted it to the toes with a sticky brown liquid, strong-smelling: tincture of benzoin, an antiseptic. And Hal, newly shorn, now being painted from head to toe with the tannic stuff, gazed up at Brown's large, neutral milk-chocolate–colored face and wondered what this reminded him of: some familiar ritual, some powerful *déjà-vu* that lingered here, and he didn't quite know what it was.

Brown finished. Drew a fresh sheet up over the anointed body. Gathered his tools; swung open the green curtain, instantly destroying a space, a universe; smiled at us both; whispered, "Good luck," and was gone.

And what to do now? What would be appropriate? What sort of good-night does one say to a husband whose heart they will cut open tomorrow? Good night, then, love, and here is a special kiss, a big ripe wet saliva-running, tongue-sucking wonder of a kiss, because perhaps I will never get to kiss you again. Good night. Break a leg. Take no wooden nickels.

We kissed casually.

"Go home," he said. "Get a good night's sleep."

When I had left, he went to the window and stood looking out at the skyline and the river and a near-full moon, thinking, in a quite peaceful way, I wonder if I shall ever see these again.

He stood there a long while. Then he got into bed and waited for the terror to come. Twenty years in operating rooms: he knew exactly how they would make the incision, how they would saw through his sternum and hold his chest walls apart with retractors.

But the terror never came. There was still this strange deep peace. At eight the next morning, when they wheeled him into the operating room, he said, "Where is the heart-lung machine?" They pointed it out. Though he was sedated already into a semistupor, he lifted his head several inches off the stretcher and stared with what seemed to be great clarity at the machine.

HAL, he thought. And saluted it silently, wishing them both well, and then lay back and prepared to sleep.

We waited in the visitors' lounge, Jon and I and David's wife, Joyce. She was good company for such occasions; blond, soft, made of metal. She would not whimper. And if one must sit for hours through this sort of scene, the obligatory waiting-for-the-doctor scene, at least she greatly improved the scenery. *At least.* Hal's old partner in urology always had told patients who called in the middle of the night to get into a warm bath. It might ease their pains. And if it didn't, he had said, and he ended up having to see them, *at least* they would be clean.

We sat around a bridge-type table and talked nonsense for two hours. At noon she looked toward the doorway, which was behind me, and I saw her eyes and mouth move in an odd, unguarded way and I knew she had seen something that distressed her, but before I could ask, she had pulled it all together again into the stunning poker face, and a moment later Silverman was standing beside us.

She said afterward—it was a fragment she seemed always to remember, as we remember the fragments of our hours on the day John Kennedy was killed—that she had glanced up and seen these things: Silverman emerged from an elevator, came to the door of the visitors' lounge, looked at us sitting there, turned away fast, crossed the corridor toward a water fountain, bent down, drank, and then headed back toward us slowly; and Joyce had thought, Oh-oh, we have had it. Hal is dead.

"Well, it's finished. They're just sewing him up," Silverman said. He sat down at our little table as though making a fourth for bridge. He would have been my partner.

"And?"

"Well, he's all right. He's all right. Of course, it was one hell of an operation."

He said this without looking at me. He did not meet my eyes for a moment—Silverman, who knew the full therapeutic value of eye contact. Abruptly he turned toward Joyce.

"So, did you see me on your husband's show last night? How did you like it?"

Easy, Martha. Cool it. He's anxious about something. Give him time.

"Moe . . . what about Hal?"

"Well, I told you. He's all right. I mean, considering . . . If you could have seen that aneurysm"—shaking his head morosely—"that thing was the size of an orange. An orange!" And one understood that he did not mean the wizened little eight-for-a-dollar juice oranges but some monster citrus, a 4-H prizewinner. "I can't remember when I've seen a bigger one. Dr. Bell did a beautiful job, a beautiful job. So"— back now to Joyce—"it was a pretty interesting show, wasn't it? Did you see the part where I talked about . . ."

Jon sat tight-lipped. I thought Jon might hit him. I too felt close to violence. Yes, I understand why he is doing this, but fuck his anxiety. What about *our* anxiety?

"*Moses. Fuck the TV show. What about Hal?*"

"I'm *telling* you. He's *all right*. He came through; the grafts were made satisfactorily—Jesus, he had a lot of disease in there! Terrible! —the aneurysm was sutured off, his heart started beating immediately when they took him off the pump, his vital signs were pretty good. . . . Of course, he's going to be pretty sick for a while now. What do you expect?" Finally, saying this, he looked at me directly. "After all, he's had one hell of a shock. It was a massive operation. *Massive*. I mean, they did everything you can do to a human heart without ripping it out of the body."

Without ripping it out of the body. Fancy that.

"Is he out of danger?"

"We can't say anything like that yet."

"When can I see him?"

"He'll be in the recovery room all afternoon. Come down to the intensive-care unit tonight. Say about six. I'll meet you there."

128

We picked ourselves up as though we were large awkward parcels and carried ourselves out.

Arms across the chest are a bad bit of body language. I am creating space, they say, between you and me. I am uncomfortable. I am defending myself. I am braced for your attack. You have reason to attack, which I know and which I am prepared to deny.

So they stood, Drs. Bell and Silverman, with their arms folded tightly across their chests, and they addressed themselves to David and to me but they looked only at their arms or at each other, glances meeting briefly to exchange cues and warnings of various sorts and then dropping again to their tightly folded arms.

"We're having a little trouble with his blood pressure," Moe said. "His pressure is a little low. That's worrying us a little. But, uh . . ." Eyes flash to Bell.

". . . but, uh," says Bell, "if we can keep his pressure up through the night, why, then, we hope . . ." Take it, Silverman.

". . . yes, uh, we hope, we are very hopeful that, uh . . ."

Watch it, Silverman. Easy on the hopeful. Hedge.

"What are you saying?" David asked.

"Well, we're telling you that we have this problem with the blood pressure. But otherwise . . ." Come on, Bell, help.

". . . otherwise, yes, yes, he seems well. He went through the operation well. We're very encouraged. . . ."

Careful, Bell. Remember. We agreed. Just name, rank and serial number.

"I want to see him," I said.

"Oh, Martha, you don't want to see him now. It will just upset you."

"It will upset me *not* to see him." I was trying not to cry. I was trembling; visibly, I suppose.

"Oh, all right. Take it easy. Let me go see . . ."

Moses went through the swinging doors into the intensive-care unit. Moments later, he reappeared.

"Listen, he doesn't want you to go in there now. He's embarrassed to have you see him with all those tubes stuck in him."

"*Embarrassed!* What's going on? What are you hiding? *I want to see him.*"

The two exchanged another significant look. We'd better let her in there. She's getting hysterical.

"Martha, nobody's *hiding* anything. Oh, all right, come on. . . ."

Moses took my arm and led me through the doors and into a large, brilliantly lit space, and over to a bed partly curtained off from the rest of the space, and there he lay. And I knew that color, oh, yes. Can it be mixed on any palette? I had seen that color when I had been writing a profile for the *Times* Sunday Magazine on the Medical Examiner of New York City, and I had gone down to the autopsy room ("That's no place for a woman. Do you *have* to go down there?" the late, legendary coroner Milton Helpern had said, and "Yes, I have to," I had said, dutiful reporter, pissed feminist. "Well," he had said, "we'll bring a wheelchair, just in case." "Just in case what?" "Just in case you faint"). And stood in that huge brilliant space, stainless steel, clean as a milk-bottling plant, with many autopsy tables lined up in a row and three or four of them now occupied, pathologists hunched over them, the rigid blue bodies in various stages of disarray: one with the scalp neatly peeled back to bare the skull, one with its torso slit and gut things exposed, one seemingly intact but for a large blue hand that was being carved into at the moment, ever so carefully, a large round of skin being carved and excised from the palm, and merry Dr. Helpern saying to the white-coated carver, "Mike, this is Martha Weinman Lear of *The New York Times*"; "Hi!" says Mike, smiling, giving an affable wave with his carving knife over the stiff blue palm; oh, shit, the sights, the sights, and *No*, you merry bastards, *I will not faint,* and coolly averted my gaze from those butchered blue corpses, blue toes pointed serenely heavenward, and ran upstairs to vomit in the bathroom; and for weeks after, I dreamed of those bodies and woke screaming from those dreams.

So I knew that particular color, and I saw it here now: this death mask, my dearest, this blue inert object with a fat tube stuck in its mouth.

"He is dead," I said.

"He is *not* dead. Hal! Listen!" Loudly, as though to an old man with a faulty hearing aid: "Listen! Your wife is here. She is worried about you. Give her a sign to show her you're all right."

And I stand, the tears running like sheets of rain down my face, peering through the rain for a sign. And moments pass, and I strain to see, although I know of course that there can be no sign because he is dead. And then, like a mummy bestirring itself in old horror flicks, like the coffin lid squeaking open from within, his right hand, embedded with needles and wires, lifts a fraction off the bed and the fingers twitch a bit, as though to wave; and his right eyelid, faintly, almost imperceptibly, flutters open and shut.

"Oh, my God," I moan, burying my head in Moe's chest, drenching Moe's nifty coat, "my God, my God, he *winked* at me."

"There!" says Moe. Holds me out at arm's length. Triumphant, grinning, flushed, a little dewy-eyed himself. "There, you see? I *told* you he wasn't dead!"

Chapter 16

*H*E rose to consciousness and went down again. He was in a thick fog, a true pea soup of a fog, and sometimes it would clear and there would be lights and shadows, but mostly pain, and then he would sink blessedly down again into the fog.

There was an awareness of a tube that filled his mouth and went down his throat. It felt thick as a garden hose. It gave him a choking feeling. He could not breathe. A machine breathed for him. There was the horrible sensation of not being able to take a breath; but soon, in those moments of consciousness, he learned that he could trust the machine. He had simply to go with the machine, go with it, not fight it, not try to breathe, because in a moment it would push more air into his lungs.

Sometimes he would open his eyes to see faces peering in at him. The faces he recognized, Jon's and Martha's, looked greatly worried, and he wanted to tell them, "Don't worry," but of course he could not talk.

He thought he remembered a loud voice telling him that Martha was worried, and that he must make some signal to show her that he was all right, and that he had winked at her; but this might have been a dream.

Gradually he became aware of his connection to things. There was his old friend the monitor. There was this miserable hose in his mouth. There was the familiar intravenous. But now there were many other connections, large numbers of tubes—lines, they were called—going into and coming out of his body.

There was a line connected to his left radial artery to furnish arterial blood that could be run through machines for chemical tests. The artery was tied off. This made a great pain in his hand from lack of blood. His hand felt like ice.

There was a line in his neck. He knew vaguely that this one must be something very special, but he wasn't sure what. Later he learned that it went to the subclavian vein. From it they drew for analysis blood that was returning to his heart.

There was a tube in his urethra.

There were two tubes in his chest, one sticking out of each side of his chest cavity. They were attached to a device which automatically suctioned out any air or fluid that might accumulate between his lungs and his chest wall.

Sometimes they would come with another suctioning device. They would insert it into the tube in his throat to pull moisture out of his lungs. This would surely choke him to death. And he could not cry out, he could make no protest, he could do nothing but lie there utterly passively silently choking to death.

He seemed to be in an ice bath. He shook violently. He felt that he was not a body but a solid block of pain, packed in ice. He wanted to ask the shadows that bustled about him why they had packed him in ice, he wanted to beg them to take him out of the ice, but there was no way.

He had forgotten to tell them before the surgery that he was left-handed. So that, bound as he was by those lines going into his left hand and arm, and gagged by the garden hose, he could communicate only with his eyes. He seemed not to be very good at that. Try as he did to convey that it was intolerable to be immersed in ice, and to plead with his eyes for relief, they seemed not to understand. They kept him immersed. As the lucid moments grew more frequent, he longed only to get his shot, get his fix, and sink into unconsciousness again, back down under the ice.

What an awesome place this was! Less a place than a sensation, a cluster of sensations: order, calm, essence of pain, controlled tension; constant muted background sounds—the soft padding of feet, the low murmur of voices, the steady tick and whir of machines; human shadows approaching and receding, ministering to him in ways he only dimly perceived; all around him, auras and mysteries; above him, a cyclops kind of light; no world beyond, no day, no night, no time, just constant hypnotic rhythms.

That was his sense of it as a patient. But sometimes the rhythms broke and changed abruptly. He would hear a whole new set of sounds, urgent sounds that might startle him as a patient but which he knew so grimly well as a doctor that even when he could see nothing, he knew with his doctor's ears exactly what was going on. It was strange how he seemed to be in both heads at once, sensing this place in two such different ways.

The first time it happened, he suddenly heard many footsteps and a high-pitched rush of voices. All sounds and shadows converged just to the left of him. The curtain was drawn between his bed and the bed to his left, and he heard then the rolling of a cart, and he knew exactly what kind of trouble, big trouble, was in that bed.

He knew what sound he would hear before he actually heard it, the distinctive *click* of the defibrillator, and in his own darkness he could see clearly how the body in that bed went stiff, as from an electric shock. A quiet, and then the *click* again, and he could see in his mind how they were working desperately upon his desperately ill neighbor, upon a heart that had stopped beating or had gone from a beat to a quiver. They worked a long time. Then everything went silent. Deathly silent. One by one the white shadows moved soundlessly away from that area to his left. He heard them rolling off the defibrillation cart. A bit later they drew the curtains around all the beds, so that no one could see to the left or to the right or to the center, and then he heard heavier wheels rolling, and he knew that the body was being rolled away. Sorry, neighbor. There but for the grace.

A spaceship of the senses: that was what this place was. Doctors understood nothing of that. Nothing.

Once he woke and saw Dr. Bell. Could it have been hours after surgery? Days? He had no idea. Dr. Bell examined him and said, "Well, it looks like you're going the right way," and though he could not answer because of the tube in his throat, silently he giggled at the soft, laconic Gary Cooper air . . . Which way did the patient go? *Thataway*.

Another time he looked up and saw us, Jon and Martha, coming toward him. We seemed to be clothed in brilliant colors; especially Jon, who wore something neon and marvelous.

He felt alert. For the first time—it was on the third postoperative day—he made a strong gesture, using his right hand to make a writing motion in the air. It seemed to take a terribly long time for anyone to catch his meaning, though surely he was gesturing clearly enough.

Finally Jon said, "I think he wants to write something," and he blinked his eyes, Yes, *yes*, and they put a pencil into his right hand and held a pad for him, and he wrote, *I like your coat. Is it new?*

He wrote it clearly for a left-handed person, and he could not understand why we stared at it and smiled and shrugged politely and seemed not to be able to read his message.

It was the sort of scrawl a two-year-old might make, random squiggles and lines. He became agitated. With his right hand he pointed to the coat and blinked his eyes repeatedly, ferociously frustrated not to be understood. The coat was, in fact, an old orange parka that he had seen dozens of times. We could not begin to understand what he was trying to say.

When they removed the tube from his throat (he had no sense how long it had lodged there; it had been three days), he felt euphoric. What a wonder to be able to draw his own breath! His throat was raw and it was painful to talk, but he could summon up enough of a voice to ask about this frozen block in which he was still encased.

"Why am I in ice?" he said.

A nurse said, "It is not ice, Dr. Lear. You have had a very high temperature. We have been running cold water through the mattress and keeping you wrapped in thermal blankets."

"It hurts," he said.

"I know," she said.

She took his temperature, and he asked, "Do you have to do it again?"

"I'm afraid so, Doctor. Your temp is over 104."

He pleaded: "Please don't do it again." Plea-bargained: "Please try aspirin first. That will bring the fever down."

But of course they couldn't. They had their orders. So back he went into the icy torture chamber, and began to shake again, and the nurse repeated, "I am so sorry."

I saw—he, of course, did not; his vision was still blurred—that her own eyes were filled with tears.

They were fighting for his life.

Dr. Bell had told him that he would be kept in the intensive-care unit for forty-eight hours, possibly seventy-two; certainly no more. He was there for nine days.

Throughout that period, his fevers were perilously high and his blood pressure was almost nonexistent. They had him on massive doses of drugs to keep the pressure up. *Up* meant 80 over 60. Without these drugs, it slid immediately to 60 over 40, and would have slid lower, and he would simply have slid out of life. Without the drugs, he had no blood pressure.

Much later, I saw the operative note. It gave no indication why he should have gone so bad. Portions read:

> The left leg was incised. . . . A long piece of . . . vein was isolated and removed. . . . The chest was opened. . . . The pericardium was opened longitudinally. . . . The heart was electrically fibrillated. . . . We elevated the heart and then identified the posterior descending branch of the circumflex artery and with body temperature reduced to 32 degrees Centigrade, opened this artery and anastomosed [grafted] the . . . vein. . . . A good anastomosis was accomplished and a probe could easily be passed in both directions. . . . The heart was then replaced in its normal position. . . .
>
> The diagonal branch of the anterior descending artery . . . was identified and an anastomosis accomplished. . . .
>
> The left ventricular aneurysm which was fairly modest in size in comparison to what we had expected . . . was opened. . . . We . . . excluded this aneurysm from the remaining portion of the ventricle. The everted edges were then oversewn . . . and a good closure seemed to have been accomplished.
>
> The patient came off bypass [the heart-lung machine] without difficulty and although he had some mild amount of rhythm disturbance, he maintained an arterial pressure of approximately 130/90 without difficulty. . . .
>
> The chest was closed in the usual fashion.
>
> The patient was taken to the Intensive Care Unit in satisfactory condition.

In short, an uneventful event. But clearly something had happened. Something had happened to this patient who was to be in the I.C.U. for two days, maybe three, and remained in fact for nine, teetering on the very edge.

On the sixth day—or perhaps the seventh; he himself was not sure —Moses Silverman's young associate Peter Mason came into the I.C.U. and saw the patient for the first time; saw with astonishment this patient who was still hanging on, his life sustained by such medications in such amounts as to suggest that he should have died days earlier. Mason could not believe it. He could not believe that this patient was still alive.

Why didn't they tell us? He, or Silverman, or Bell, or anyone who knew, or might have known, or might simply have suspected what had happened in this routine bypass case? Was it possible, as I was later desperately willing to believe, that they themselves did not yet know what had happened? Which was this: that the patient had suffered another heart atack.

I learned it a year later when I interviewed Mason, by that time a valued friend. I was preparing to write a book. In fact, it was originally to have been Hal's project. He had been describing to a friend, an editor, how it is when a doctor becomes a patient, how it turns his perceptions inside out. "You should write about that," the friend had said. And Hal the patient had thought, Oh, yes, I would like to write on that subject; and Hal the doctor had thought, It would be a good thing for this patient to do: a form of therapy, an ordering of experience. And he had tried but, lacking the stamina, had asked me to help, and it had in this way become a collaboration, I the interviewer, Hal the interviewee, the technical consultant: a therapy and an ordering, as it developed, for us both.

Were it not for that project, I suppose I would never have sought answers beyond those which were given at the time ("Why is he still in the I.C.U.? Why has he gone so bad?" "Because his blood pressure dropped way down"). We would never have known. From the doctors' point of view, there would have been no purpose in telling us. Events occur. Often nobody is to blame. Why torture us with might-have-beens?

The interview with Mason proceeded, in part, like this:

MASON: "When people die because the heart can't pump anymore, normally more than fifty percent of the heart muscle has been injured; whereas those people who die from arrhythmias [irregular heartbeats] may look as though they're doing perfectly well. Autopsy data show that maybe only fifteen percent of the heart muscle was involved. So the reason for pump failure or heart failure is really the massive amount of muscle that has been destroyed.

"With Hal, you have to put together how much muscle was destroyed in the first infarct with how much was destroyed in subsequent problems."

LEAR: "When you say 'problems,' you mean heart attacks?"

MASON: "Yeah. A small heart attack. Now go back to that magic number I mentioned before, of fifty percent. You take a patient who has a forty-percent infarct, he may do all right. Then he has a small, ten-percent infarct. . . . Well, now it's fifty percent and that's enough, just having that small additional injury, to turn the situation over to persistent heart failure. And then . . . Well, now, postoperatively, Martha, in reviewing the chart, it's pretty clear that there was some mild injury during surgery to the back wall of the heart. . . ."

LEAR: "Are you telling me that he had another heart attack during surgery?"

MASON: "Yeah. I just want to make sure . . . I just want to tell you exactly what happened . . . and actually I must admit I didn't realize it until reviewing the chart, or, if I did realize, I didn't . . . I just . . . I mean . . . But clearly, reviewing the cardiogram, we saw some mild injury to the back wall of the heart. So now there was that first big front-wall injury, then that possible small problem six weeks before the surgery, and perhaps a small additional injury during surgery. However, small injuries occur in twenty percent of surgical cases. This is well known."

LEAR: "Would the surgical procedure itself be likely to cause the heart attack?"

MASON: "Yeah, the surgery can cause that. But despite this injury, if the patient has had angina, the patient is usually better. They don't have angina anymore or it is markedly decreased. *Despite* an injury. But in a man who had a big infarct like Hal's, and then another little problem, and then a third little problem during surgery, the end result was that they had problems postoperatively in maintaining his blood pressure."

LEAR: "His blood pressure went down because he had a heart attack, and he had a heart attack because of the surgery?"

138

MASON: "We don't know that. The attack could have occurred after surgery, because of the vasopressor drips [medications to maintain blood pressure]. They make the heart work harder. They could have caused it. But . . . because of the low blood pressure, you might suspect that it occurred during the operation. But whether that was the main factor in causing the low blood pressure is still unclear. Just the insult of major surgery to an already damaged heart might have done it."

LEAR: "Was there any choice as to whether or not he should have that major surgery?"

MASON: "No. The indications were clear: persistent angina and a large aneurysm dictate intervention. . . .

"Now, my first recollection of Hal was an amazing sight of a man . . . I couldn't believe this . . . *walking* in the I.C.U. hooked up to an I.V. in which was medication meant to raise his blood pressure. In contrast to other bypass patients, who would leave that unit within seventy-two hours, I think this was his sixth or seventh day. I had never before seen a patient walking around with that medication. . . .

"He went into the operation, Martha, with a blood pressure of 100 over 50. His low blood pressure after surgery led to poor profusion to his kidneys and head, and because of this they were using many different agents for a prolonged period of time to raise the blood pressure and improve the performance of the heart. . . . This is very unusual for a cardiac patient."

LEAR: "Usually someone might get these medications for no more than seventy-two hours?"

MASON: "At maximum."

LEAR: "Why? Is it dangerous to give this medicine for so long?"

MASON: "No. It's not that. It's that you only give this medication in the worst situations. . . . It was a borderline situation . . . and only with prolonged administration could he actually survive. I was just amazed that a man could look so good and yet be on his sixth or seventh day of that medication."

LEAR: "You mean that usually, if a patient is bad enough to require this medication, he is on it for a couple of days and then either he is improved enough to be taken off it or he is dead?"

MASON: "That's right."

LEAR: "So what amazed you was that Hal was walking around, whereas normally anyone who is being maintained on this stuff is in very bad shape?"

MASON: "Yes. They're in shock, sweaty, no urine output, no blood flow to the head, so they're disoriented. . . . I was just amazed. He looked so vital. He looked young and healthy . . . and sort of . . . *alive*, despite what you read in the chart. Handsome guy. Young guy. Even *elegant* in some ways. Surely different from most of our patients . . . and yet when you looked at the numbers, you would have predicted that this was an eighty-year-old man who had no chance of surviving!"

LEAR: "Would the surgical team have known during surgery that there had been this injury . . . this heart attack?"

MASON: "You would only know from the electrocardiogram afterward. However, the surgeon's operative note suggests that he questioned the graft on the back part of the heart. He wasn't totally happy with it. And even the vessel that he bypassed on the front wall, he noted that there was a considerable amount of plaque in there. . . . Martha, what are you going to think tonight, at midnight, about all this?"

LEAR: "If you mean, is it going to make me uneasier than I have been, the answer is No. [This is a lie.] I would have presumed that the picture was quite like this."

MASON: "Uh-huh."

LEAR: "Would he be alive today if he hadn't had the surgery?"

MASON: "There is no way of answering that question, to be honest. . . . The operation is not meant to make people live longer. It's meant to help people do their normal day-to-day living without being disabled by angina, so the fifty-year-old man can keep his job so he can support his family and send his kids to school.

"At that time, you have to remember, Hal's problem was not heart failure but disabling angina . . . And indeed, Hal's problem since the surgery has not been that of angina."

Indeed not. After the surgery the problem was no longer angina. After the surgery the problem was, inescapably, the surgery itself: what it had caused, what it had exacerbated.

There was no one to blame. Not really. That made it worse, I suppose. However much we assured each other that good people had done their best; however we repeated like a catechism that the operation, after all, had been a necessity; however we tried rationalizing it, taking it apart and putting it all together again in prettier combinations, we never did get the damned thing to spell Mother and we never escaped completely from the might-have-been's.

One of the medications they were using to maintain Hal's blood pressure was a powerful drug called Levophed. It contracts the small vessels so that they need less blood. Some of the stuff spilled out of his vein and into the tissue of his left arm, and one day he noticed that an oval patch on his forearm, perhaps two by four inches, had turned starkly white, as if with frostbite. They packed it with wet compresses. Later, when it turned black, it did not hurt at all. Dead tissue does not hurt. But at the time, it was painful.

The next day, he told me that his left hand was paining him, too, at the site of a needle that fed into a small vein. I myself could see that the area was becoming inflamed. Such inflammations not only hurt like hell but can be serious, for they can spread along the entire course of the vein.

We rang for a nurse. He showed her the inflamed hand and asked her to get a doctor.

It was a Sunday. Just beyond the glass partition of Hal's cubicle, the intern on duty, a tall, hulking fellow, sat with his feet propped up on a desk and his face buried in the Sunday *Times*. The nurse approached him. He looked up, clearly annoyed to be interrupted. They conferred. Then his face disappeared again behind the newspaper and she returned and began loosening the dressing on Hal's forearm.

"That's not the problem," Hal said. "It's this needle in my hand. Please ask him to come and fix the needle."

Again she went out to the intern. Again he looked up, annoyed; again they conferred; again he went back to his paper and she came back to the cubicle. She was blushing.

"I'm sorry, Dr. Lear," she said. "He said there is nothing wrong with the needle. He said I should change the dressing."

"You told him about the inflammation?"

"Yes."

"What did he say?"

"He said there is nothing wrong with the needle."

She removed the compress. The forearm was green and pustulant, pregangrenous. I turned away. Hal lay helpless in his glass cage, looking at the intern who sat just five feet away, motionless, totally absorbed in the sports section, legs still up on the desk.

"What is that doctor's name?" Hal asked.

"B———," she said.

"My God. What an irony. One of the great hospitals of the world, one of the great names in medicine, and the guy is a lousy doctor."

"Maybe he hasn't learned yet," I said.

"No. He will never be any good, because he doesn't care about people. It doesn't matter how much technique he learns. That son-of-a-bitch will never be a good doctor."

Within ten minutes the intern rose, folded his newspaper neatly under his arm and walked off. He never glanced in Hal's direction.

Later, when he went off duty, the nurse—I don't suppose she dared intervene until then—approached another intern, and the intravenous needle was fixed immediately. By that time the hand was swollen and throbbing, and the inflammation required treatment with antibiotics.

It became, as such things do, a part of our personal vocabulary. From that time on, "to pull a B———" meant to perform some obscenely selfish act.

For the most part, they were deeply caring. The nurses, especially, were wonderful. So gentle with him; so regretful for the pain they had to cause him. Through it all, even when he was wrapped in the thermal blankets, he felt an overwhelming gratitude. It was not that he thought they kept him from death. It never occurred to him that he might die, neither in his most clouded nor in his most lucid moments, not even when we were sure that he lay dying. It was rather that he felt that he already *had been* dead, and that they brought him, through this unavoidably painful path, back to life.

At the same time, he felt a horrible sadness. He had the sense that his body had been grotesquely violated; mutilated; and for this there was a sadness that flowed in him like blood. Images flickered on and off: scenes from a short story he had read long ago—a Roald Dahl story, he thought it was—about a slaughterhouse where animals were stunned with a blow to the head and then moved upon a conveyor belt to a place where their throats were slit and they were bled on meat hooks and carried thus on the conveyor belt to the end of the story, where it turned out that the animals were humans.

He felt like that: like a slab of meat on a rack. He thought with awe of the tension between this hushed hospital atmosphere and the things that were happening here: in this polite, muted, ordered way, people were being torn open, ripped apart, bones cracked, holes made and tubes stuck into holes, and they moved passive as cattle along the conveyor belt—oh, yes, passive, not even breathing for themselves; the tube that had been in his throat was like the slaughterhouse hook, embedded in the animal's throat, by which it, he, was hung.

These were not hostile thoughts. He understood completely that violent acts had had to be performed to keep him alive. He himself had performed them any number of times in any number of operating rooms, and often he had felt it, this sense of inflicting horrible mutilations. As in a total cystectomy, for example: removing a malignant bladder; removing the rectum, to which almost inevitably the cancer would have spread by the time it was discovered; cutting out as much surrounding tissue as possible; creating a new outlet for urine, an artificial bladder made from a section of bowel; reconnecting the kidney to this artificial bladder and making a hole in the belly through which the urine would drain into an exterior baglike contraption, and another hole for the intestinal tract to empty out . . .

And hadn't he done these things? And he had felt, My God, this is a terrible, mutilating thing I am doing. But if I do it well, this person may live. If I do not do it, this person will die.

So he lay here now, grateful to be breathing; and still he could not shake off the horror and the sadness, nor escape the sense of awe. What have they done to me? he thought, touching the lines and tubes that, everywhere, went into and out of him. I have been anatomically raped.

"I felt like crying all the time," he told me later. Later, when we both understood more about these things.

There is a small, special body of literature in the medical libraries. It describes what happens emotionally to survivors of open-heart surgery. It describes how they experience precisely that sense of horror and of awe; how many of them simply refuse to face what has happened, barricading themselves behind amnesias, delusions, hallucinations, psychotic episodes, deliberate miscomprehensions and other baroque forms of denial.

No other surgery affects people in quite this way. For it is unthinkable, finally, that one's heart should be cut open. It is the one unthinkable cut. There are other vital organs, but they are vital only to life. This is more. This is other. No high priest ever offered up a lung to the gods. Nobody ever wrote a poem about a bladder.

"But you never did cry. Not then," I said much later, at home, when we understood all this.

"No," he said. "I was afraid to cry."

"Afraid? Why?"

"I was afraid that if I ever began to cry, I might cry my heart out," he said; and then stared at me, stunned, over his tuna-fish sandwich.

Certain moments bond me back into themselves. Instantly they make me feel and will always make me feel, by however long I may survive them, that I too could cry my heart out.

The moment when I knelt by his hospital bed, after his first heart attack, and he whispered, "Don't cry. It will be just like it was."

The moment just after surgery when he tried to wink at me, to show that he still lived.

The moment when I entered the I.C.U. on the seventh day and saw him, ravaged, supported by a nurse on either side and hooked up to the vital intravenous solutions that trailed him on their portable stands, stumbling slowly toward me, grinning.

I do not remember much of what I had felt or done in that week when we had watched his agony and thought he would die. Days, I was mostly numb with fear. Nights, I was mostly spaced on liquor. But in that moment, watching him wobble toward me, I felt as he himself had felt: as though I had died and been reborn.

He was off the intravenous now, his blood pressure maintained at 80 over 60 without drugs. They could push it no higher, which augured badly, though I didn't know it then.

His forearm was still packed in compresses. He felt nothing there. It was necrotic tissue now. The leg incision, which ran from his groin to several inches below his knee, never bothered him much either. But the pain from the chest incision was constant and very bad.

He had to cough to bring up mucus. That was imperative. If mucus were to block a bronchial tube, lung infections might develop.

But in order to cough, he had to do what was diametrically opposed to instinct, which was to immobilize the chest. He forced himself, emitting faint sounds that seemed to be no more than the discreet clearing of a throat, and even this was terrible. It was like tearing apart the sutures. It was like rubbing together the raw edges of a broken bone.

One day a nurse suggested that he clutch a pillow tightly against his chest when he coughed, to help hold the chest wall together. That helped tremendously. He also discovered that if someone slapped his back, midway between the lungs, he could get up the mucus more easily.

And so we developed a routine: He would sit up, legs hanging over the edge of the bed, pillow clutched in his arms. "Okay, hit me," he would say. "Again—a little higher, a little to the left; there, *there*, *hit*," and at the moment I hit he would squeeze the pillow hard and cough and up would come, sometimes, a bit of mucoid matter—such a pathetic return for what it cost him, but a triumph nonetheless, a costly affirmation of life, health, restoration.

"I'll beat this damned thing!" he said once, grinning fiercely, and I was reminded immediately of my father standing in the middle of the kitchen in Malden, Massachusetts, several months after his leg had been amputated; standing there with the empty pajama leg neatly pinned up and his one leg lifted off the floor, swinging back and forth between his crutches like a kid on some playground contraption and yelling, with the gusto that had never deserted him for a moment, "You can't keep a good man down!" before one crutch slipped and he fell heavily to the floor and lay there, on a hip that would be black-and-blue for months, laughing up at us. I am never surprised by the crocks of the world, but such gallantry always astonishes me.

It was from that coughing routine—from that, and also from the instinctive desire to protect his chest against all comers, all violations, all accidents of contact—that Hal became as attached to the pillow as a child to a security blanket. Long after there was any need to cough, long after the raw red scar had healed hard and shiny, and required no protection, he would lie holding pillows and sleep holding pillows; and sometimes, sitting in the living room and talking to guests, unconsciously he would pick up a sofa pillow and cradle it in his arms, against his chest.

Finally he was back in a private room. He felt stronger, but still emotionally labile. The sadness persisted. Anything might trigger it. Someone might say, "Well, I'm glad you're better," and he would feel ready to cry.

He would lie watching television, and if anything verged in the faintest way upon violence he would push the button fast to switch channels. Even pratfalls bothered him. He realized that he, twenty years a surgeon, inured by long habit to gore, had lost all tolerance for sights of violence, brutality, inflictions of pain, however slight. He felt—knew, for a certainty—that he would never again be able to go into an operating room and wield a knife.

I sat with him one day, watching some old movie that seemed to be benign, and suddenly, altogether without warning, somebody on that screen swung a knife toward somebody else's back.

"*Oh, no, oh, no, oh, no,*" he cried, clicked off the TV and buried his head in the ever present pillow, and I thought finally that he might be weeping. But no. In a moment he swung around to a sitting position and said, "I think I can cough now. Hit me; *hit* me," and I hit and he brought up a slug of mucoid matter and lay back spent, white with pain, grinning.

"Good shot, Mushie," he said.

It would soon be his birthday. I asked, "What shall I give you?"

"A bedspread," he said.

Indeed, a bedspread. In that sloppy king-sized universe in which we had spent most of the nights of our marriage, there had never been a bedspread. I did not understand bedspreads. Periodically he would make some protest, pure form. "For Christ's sake," he had said once, "we've been married for ten years. Why can't we have a bedspread?"

And now he lay in his hospital bed making this request that, beyond form, embodied a future. Marvelous! I went to Bloomingdale's and bought a quilt, a soft, light thing patterned in lovely earth colors. And matching dust ruffle and sheets and pillowcases. "I did it!" I told him. "Good for you!" he said. And I explained, with some pride, the efficaciousness of the arrangement: the quilt, you see, will be both our blanket and our bedspread, lying neatly on our bed at all times, no fat formality we have to fold up at night and open out again by day; and pillows, plenty of pillows, covered in the same pretty stuff, so that we can sink back and take our ease, and we are *always prepared for company.* He smiled, hugging his white hospital pillow, nodding Yes.

And I bought new chests—unfinished ones, well crafted in a good hardwood—and rubbed oil into their surfaces, and in the noonday sun they glowed, and sunlight filtered in through the new bamboo blinds, making everything glow. As though it were a nursery I made the room ready, filling it with new things, fresh starts, fresh hopes.

I thought of another good gift. He had always enjoyed sculpting. Back in the Hartford days he had taken a couple of art courses and puttered quite handsomely with stone and clay. There hadn't been much time then. Now, of course, there would be plenty of time, a long convalescence, probably boredom. The clay seemed a fine idea. I bought an armature and twenty pounds of modeling clay and many modeling tools and two books of instructions, and on his birthday I dragged it all to the hospital.

A birthday cake, courtesy of the staff, was on his bed table. A friend had sent six splits of a perfectly splendid white wine from his own château. Several guests had come to celebrate. The only trouble was the guest of honor, who appeared to be in shock.

Two hours earlier, they had injected him for the first time with a powerful diuretic. Soon he felt keenly sick. He rang the nurses' station.

"Something bad is happening to me," he said. "Please ask the doctor to come in."

He waited twenty minutes, half an hour, then rang for the nurse again.

"Listen, I am getting very sick," he said. "Where is a doctor?"

"I'm sorry, Dr. Lear. They're all busy. They said they'll get here as soon as they can." Apologetic. She took his blood pressure. It struck him how often nurses seemed to be apologizing for doctors. He wondered if nurses ever had apologized for him.

He felt himself getting progressively weaker. At one point several nurses brought in the cake and wished him happy birthday. "Thank you," he said. "Please, a doctor."

When I got there, he was cold and clammy. By the time a friend who was a staff psychiatrist arrived, he was in incipient shock. She went out to the nurses' station and raised hell. Soon two doctors appeared. They put him on oxygen and intravenous fluids. The diuretic had dehydrated him severely.

Very soon he felt better; and fighting mad.

"Why did it take hours before anyone came to take care of me?" he demanded.

The doctors opted for jovial reassurance. One said, "Oh, we were watching you closely all the time."

"Bullshit," he said. "How were you watching me closely? A nurse came in and took my blood pressure once. I was in near-shock for almost an hour! You had a patient in near-shock and nobody came!"

"It's too bad you were sensitive to that medication, Dr. Lear. . . ."

Aha. The old It's Your Fault. "Damn it, don't you blame my sensitivity. *It is not the patient's fault!* You have a patient here who is *very* weak, *very* hypotensive. You do *not* give a patient in that condition such a strong diuretic. *Don't you know that? Don't you?"*

They left with heads hanging. He fell back, very pale and breathing hard; wiped out, but feisty. "That's *one* mistake they won't make again," he muttered.

It settled then into a subdued but sweet birthday party. Gratitude was in that room as palpable as any solid object. I unwrapped the present and showed him each component part and he glowed weakly but steadily, like a low-watt bulb. "Oh, thank you, darling," he said. "How lovely. How perfect. When I come home I'll enjoy using these things so much."

Jon and I went then to a restaurant to celebrate the occasion. I carried the sculpture supplies. He carried the six splits of wine in a sack. At dinner we toasted the birthday boy, his father, my husband, our incomparable friend. Afterward, on the sidewalk, Jon dropped the sack of splits and they shattered.

We stared at each other, horrified. Bad omen? Ah, surely not, but such a wine! I never dared tell the giver.

I got the clay home and put it in a corner of Hal's study. It was never unwrapped again. For it appeared that postsurgically, among his souvenirs, was some inexplicable injury to that part of his brain which once had liked to sculpt.

Chapter 17

---

*T*HE first intimation that something might be wrong with his mind came one morning, shortly after his birthday, when he tried for the first time since his surgery to read a newspaper.

He could not understand the headline.

It was not that he couldn't *read* it. He saw a printed word that was a familiar word, composed of letters that he could recognize and pronounce, but he could not understand what it meant.

There was the word DOES. How funny-looking, he thought. "D-O-E-S." Whatever is it? I cannot grasp it. Well, isn't this silly. Isn't this crazy.

It occurred to him that since his eyes could not take the thing in, perhaps his mind would comprehend it if he pronounced it aloud. So he switched to his auditory system:

" 'D-O.' Okay, 'do.' 'D-O-E' is . . . uh . . . 'doe.' 'D-O-E-S' is . . . what? A bunch of deer?"

He laughed aloud. No, not deer. That made no sense in the context, for the word that preceded it—PRESIDENT—he had grasped immediately. He glanced at several other headlines. The long words seemed easier. It was the short ones that looked foreign. Then he went back to the mystery and played around some more with phonetics, and finally he got it: Ah . . . " 'duz'!"

Christ, how curious! Certainly there had been confusion in the last several weeks—a confusion about dates, about night and day, about people who came and went, and so forth. Certainly he had been aware that he was having trouble with his memory. Someone would call, a guest would come, and moments later he couldn't remember who. He would wait to ask his doctors a question, and when they appeared, the question would have vanished from his mind.

He had accepted all this as natural. Undoubtedly it was due to sedations and other drugs; undoubtedly it was transient. He had asked me to bring him a clipboard and paper and pencil, and he kept these always by the bed to make notes, to help himself remember. This was not easy to do, because he seemed to have trouble spelling. He had to proceed phonetically, which was slow work. And his handwriting looked odd. It had never been model penmanship, but now it sprawled like a child's; often he could not decipher it at all.

But this inability to read was qualitatively different. It astonished him. It was as though some wires were crossed, some plugs pulled out of the switchboard in his head.

Then he discovered that he had problems with numbers, too. There was an airline advertisement in the paper: Jamaica, $121 round trip.

Well, now, was that 121 or 1121 or 1211? He could not get a fix on the numbers. They kept expanding and contracting. How strange. Maybe his eye muscles were weak, could not converge, owing perhaps to some postoperative physiological quirk. Or was it possible, he asked himself, that he had suffered some impairment of binocular vision? All right, then, try monocular vision: close one eye and look again.

So he did that, and damned if it didn't work! Clear and steady: $121.

Wow, he thought, this is simply incredible! Look what has happened to this patient's eyes! Look what has happened to this patient's mind!

He was not in the least apprehensive. He was simply fascinated, as by an interesting case. A particularly interesting condition.

There were dull conditions and interesting conditions. The dull ones were those in which the pathology was known, the condition was static and there wasn't a bloody thing you could do about it. A stroke was dull. Cerebral palsy was dull. The most horrifying metastatic cancer, agonizing for the victim and the family and the friends, was in this particular sense monumentally dull. There was even an appropriate medical stance for these dull occasions, taught and approved by the medical schools: detached concern.

But if you found anemia, an enlarged spleen and enlargement of the bowel on X-ray—ah, that was an interesting condition! You could do some detective work. Even if it turned out to be something untreatable, at least it enlivened lunch in the staff dining room: Say, I've got this interesting case . . .

As for his own case, now: *very* interesting. This trouble reading, this difficulty with numbers—all this was probably some exotic by-product of being on the heart-lung machine. Of course, it was temporary, like his memory problem; like his general weakness and bone-deep fatigue; like having to stay in bed for a time. As he got stronger, it would all disappear. But in the meantime, he thought, squinting with bemusement at the $121, how extraordinary!

Finally I brought him home, a ghost in clothes that hung on him like sheets.

He lay clutching pretty pillows, staring into space. He knew secrets I did not know. When I or anyone else came toward him he would throw up his arms reflexively, protecting his chest from assault. I learned to approach him slowly and deliberately and always within his line of vision. No surprises. And even so, as I would move smoothly toward him with a pill or a tray, his arms would jerk upward as though pulled on strings. Once I bent to kiss him. The hands flew up, fingers spread wide across his scar.

"Easy," I said. "It's all right. It's only a kiss."

He smiled, knowing better.

Often he would be seized by coughing spells that could not be controlled. They were dreadful, wearing him out, grinding him down, and he was so weak, so exhausted, because the heart, of course, had taken that additional blow which we then knew nothing about, and pain is always so much worse when the body is exhausted.

"Hit me, hit me!" he cried one night, and suddenly he went battle-weary. "*Where is my adversary?*" he yelled out.

It seemed to come unbidden, in a voice that was hardly his own.

"Come on, you fucking demon!" he screamed. "Come out here so I can fight you!"

I thought perhaps he was momentarily delusional. But it was the medical voice coming through. It was the neat surgical mind demanding an adversary, an enemy, a pathology, recognizable forces of death and disease against which he might pit his own skills.

They were trained like that, to anthropomorphize disease. Some diseases were enemies you could not vanquish: terminal cancers, inexorable progressions downward. Others were mischievous little bastards—sleepers, simple prostates and kidney stones that should have been an easy win but might put up a hell of a fight, even to the death.

But what was he fighting now? *"Where is my adversary?"* It was not a *thing*, not a germ, not a kidney stone, not a cancer or an infection. It was simply this process which was wearing him out, filling him with pain and frustration, and he wanted to fight it aggressively, as he had been trained to do; not ineptly, like this, with a pillow in his arms and his wife tapping his back.

And I could do nothing for him. It was his fight.

It was damned weird, what had happened to his mind. He still could not read. He still could not grasp numbers. Now he noticed other symptoms:

If two things happened at once, two quite simple things—if he was pouring orange juice, for example, and the telephone began to ring—he was utterly thrown. What should he do with the glass and the pitcher? How could he answer the phone without a pencil? Where was paper? He would become agitated and confused.

If the record player was going just a bit loud, and several people around him were talking, he would begin to feel dazed and his hands would start shaking. Noise made him dizzy.

His voice, which had always been deep, often turned squeaky.

He was expressing himself strangely, using fancier words than usual, speaking in stilted polysyllabic ways.

One day he was trying to explain to me how noise and activity affected him. Instead of saying, "Too much going on at once makes me nervous," which would have been just his style, he said, "I cannot cope with the simultaneous convergence of multiple visual and auditory stimuli."

We both sat contemplating this as though it were a foreign object lying on the floor.

"Hal, that simply doesn't sound like you," I said finally.

"I know," he said, looking totally puzzled.

He could not count money. After several weeks he began going out a bit, doing small errands in neighborhood stores, and made this discovery about the money.

A store clerk would say, "That will be $3.85," and he would try to put the sum together, sweating with the effort, and he would not be able to do it.

He bought a small pocket calculator to compensate. He could not read the instructions. Rather, he could read them *literally*, with strain, but he could not keep the details in sequence. He put the gadget away and never used it.

He could not dial telephone numbers. Midway, he would forget how many digits he had dialed.

Or the telephone would ring; he would pick it up from the bedroom, or perhaps from his study, and talk for a time. When I no longer heard the murmur of his voice, I would come to him and ask:

"Who called just now?"

"I don't remember."

"I thought I heard you say Jon's name."

"Oh, yeah. Jon."

"What did he have to say?"

"I don't remember."

He went to the surgeon, Bell, for a routine postoperative examination.

"You seem to be doing well," Bell said. "How do you feel?"

"Dr. Bell, some very strange things seem to have happened to my mind. I am very emotionally labile, I have trouble with words and numbers, and I have a terrible loss of memory."

"These things often happen after surgery," Bell said. "Give it time. You'll be all right."

"Oh, yes, I'm sure of that," Hal said.

In fact, it was common to experience memory loss or various forms of mental confusion after open-heart surgery. It had to do, in ways that were not clearly understood, with being on the heart-lung machine for a time. It may have been because the machine permitted air to get to the brain; or because the machine pumped blood in an artificial rhythm, steadily, instead of intermittently, as the heart pumps—possibly that affected the brain; or because the machine somehow broke down fragments of red blood cells, and these fragments perhaps lodged in very small capillaries and obstructed a certain amount of blood flow to the brain. Whatever. The resultant confusion might be acute, but it was always transient. If there are millions of capillaries in the brain and a few thousand get plugged, there is no significant damage. The blood finds other pathways. It may take hours, sometimes days, maybe even weeks, a month; no more.

Well, it is taking me a bit longer, he thought. He was still physically pained and exhausted. As his body healed, so would his mind.

When he had been home four weeks—two months after surgery—he went out walking one day and met a psychiatrist whom he knew slightly. This man had done research on the psychological effects of open-heart surgery.

"You might be interested," Hal said. "Some funny things have happened to my head since the operation."

"Like what?"

"Like I have trouble reading. And I can't remember things."

"And your surgery was how long ago?"

"Eight weeks."

"My goodness. I *am* interested. Should we take some time to talk?"

"Oh, it's not necessary. I'm okay."

"I don't mean for your sake," the psychiatrist said. "I'm very interested professionally."

So they had lunch together. Hal described the symptoms in detail. "Of course," he said, "I know that it will all go away."

"How do you know that?" the psychiatrist asked.

"Well, everything else is getting better. My body is getting better. I assume my mind will too."

"Yes, but how can you be *sure*?" Smiling; staring at him intently, something Cheshirish there; interested, clinically, in how the subject might handle the possibility of permanent damage.

And that was the first time that Hal felt doubt. As they shook hands and said goodbye, he thought, Oh, my God. What if it *doesn't* go away?

At first, Silverman and Mason said simply that it was all due to his weakness. Don't worry, they said. You have been through a great deal. It takes time.

As time passed and the condition persisted, they switched gears.

"Peter," he would say, "something is wrong with my mind. My mind is not getting any better."

"Hal, nobody's mind is getting any better. We're all getting older."
Mason, age 35.

"Peter, I don't think you understand. Here, you see this?" Pulling a
piece of paper out of his breast pocket. "This is your address. I always
write it down on a piece of paper because I can't remenber it. Peter, I
have been coming here for six months and *I still can't remember your
address.*"

"Oh, well," says Peter, smiling, "that's just *psychological*, Hal!
That's just because you don't want to come see us!" How else to
reassure than with humor? For they simply did not know what was
going on here, they had never seen anything quite like it before, and
they were groping around in his dark.

"Moe," he would say, "what has happened to my head? I still have
no memory."

"Listen, we all forget things. I can't remember names either. I
forget phone numbers too. Nothing is wrong with you. It happens to
all of us. You're fine." Meaning so well, and driving him crazy with
these phony assurances.

Always bits of paper were clutched in his hands: addresses, notes,
lists. He would go to their office with lists of questions. Know what
you want to ask; don't waste their time. Always he took his clipboard
to write down the answers.

"Please go slowly," he would say. "I have to write down what you
tell me, otherwise I won't remember."

"That's all right. Take your time."

Several visits in a row, just as he was leaving, he would remember a
question that had not been on his list, and he would pause at the
consulting-room door and say, "I'm sorry, but I have just one more
question."

Each time this happened, Moses, with a small grimace of impatience,
would tell the same joke about the old guy who always had just one
more question.

Moses loved jokes. He had jokes for everything. They were always
terrible jokes, but he enjoyed them so much that one had to enjoy his
enjoyment. Once, in the office, I held out my hand to shake his and
he gave me in return his little finger, bent, like a teacup finger.

"Is something wrong with your hand, or is this some kind of affectation?" I said.

"Affectation! Affectation! Hey, I just heard a great joke about affectation: Goldberg meets Schwartz in the street and he says, 'Schvartz, vot's dis I hear dot lately you're hecting so heffected?' '*Heffected?*' Schwartz says. 'Who, *moi?*'"

Referring to someone we knew in common, I said once, "I think Charlie's a bit of an ass."

"Ass!" says Moses. "Say, did you hear about that research that won the Lasker Award in genetics?"

"No. What research?"

"They crossed a donkey with an onion. No, no, this is *serious*. Do you know what they got?"

"What did they get?"

"A piece of ass, ha, ha," says Moses, beaming wide now, moving in for the hilarious kill. "Such a piece of ass, it could bring tears to your eyes!"

Hal did not mind the jokes. He didn't even mind the occasional show of impatience. He knew how annoying it could be to have three patients waiting on tables in three separate examining rooms and a dozen more in the waiting room, the whole day backed up for hours because he'd been unavoidably delayed at the hospital, and in the midst of all this to have someone hovering at the door, saying, "I have just one more question . . ."—he remembered very well how annoying that could be.

But he did not think that Moses should tell the joke about the old guy who always had just one more question. That was, although of course it was not meant to be, like pouring salt into the holes in his mind.

"Please try again. Please try to explain it to me."

"You know that character in *Peanuts*, or maybe it's *Li'l Abner*—the one who always has a black cloud hanging over his head? It's like that for me. Except that it is not a black cloud, it is a *fog* cloud. And it is not hanging over my head. I am *in* it. I am enveloped. It envelops me down to my neck."

"Is it like vertigo?"

"No. Vertigo is when you stand still and the external world spins. With me, the world stands still and *I* spin. I am like a top spinning in my own head. Do you understand?"

I nod uncomprehendingly. He tries again, the voice growing desperate-edged:

"I see the world like this." Holding a paper napkin in front of his face. "All my senses perceive it like this. This applies to everything. Objects, conversations, numbers, lights, sounds, people moving toward me and away from me—all sensory stimuli are muffled. The world is clear, but there is a thick fog between *me* and *it*. I am spinning within this fog. I have a sense of impending disorientation. The world is receding. Pretty soon"—he buries his face in the napkin, and his voice comes out at me as everything is coming in at him, muffled—"pretty soon I won't know who I am."

"Oh, Hal. Oh, darling." The enormity of what he is saying overwhelms me. I want to gather him up, to embrace him, not just some embraceable body part but the whole of him, as one embraces precious bundles. "Hal. You said that you might start seeing the psychiatrist again when you felt stronger. Why not start now?"

"Jesus. You think it's psychological too? You think I forget my doctors' address because I don't want to go there?"

"Hal, no!" Though in fact I wasn't at all sure. "I just mean . . . maybe Dr. Russ would understand. It's so hard when nobody understands."

"Tell me about it," he said.

But he did go, and it was helpful. The psychiatrist, Russ, whom he had seen for a brief time before surgery, could do nothing about the symptoms. But at least he acknowledged them. He listened with care and respect. He made no affable jokes. He did not try to jolly the patient out of his blues, or deny that there was trouble, or gather him up like a helpless child and protect him from the menace of his own feelings.

We saw few people. Friends called and were caring, but he was in no mood. With those few we did see, especially with his children, he pretended a vitality he did not feel.

Judy, very pregnant now, called often from her home in western Massachusetts.

"How're you doing, Daddy?"

"Great, darling, great! I'm getting better every day. How're *you* doing?"

"Great too. I'm getting *bigger* every day."

"Ah, Judy." Hearty laughter. "Judy, you're really making me a grandfather? That's ridiculous. I'm much too young."

Jon came over often from Rockefeller University. The three of us would sit at dinner, Hal straining visibly for animation, and then he would go to bed to rest and Jon and I would stare at each other.

"How do you think he's doing?"

"Not so great. How do *you* think he's doing?"

"Not so great."

Sometimes Jon brought his friends to dinner. It was easier for Hal to entertain Jon's friends than to confront his own. They hadn't known him in the before. They could make no before-and-after comparisons. They could not know how easily he had spoken and listened once, what a competent host he had been at this table.

Probably he seemed well enough to them. But he, suspended there in his fog, knew better.

Through the fine, clear spring, the fog did not lift. Certain things grew worse. Simple words eluded him more and more. His sense of direction, which had always been superb, deserted him entirely. The first time he tried to drive was a disaster. He sat forward rigidly, fingers white-knuckled upon the wheel. Someplace in the Forties, waiting at a light, with the traffic noises around us and the buses snorting smoke and the pedestrians squeezing past, he began to sweat. "Which way, quick?" he said.

"Uptown," I said.

"Which way is uptown?"

"That way."

"Martha, don't point. I can't watch your hand. Just tell me *which way*. Oh, God," he moaned, as the light changed and the horns began honking behind us, "I can't. I can't do it. Let's switch. You drive." He would not drive after that.

At every office visit, he asked now, with rising anxiety and insistence, "What can be done about my mind?"

My mind, my mind. They began to turn off. I could see it, I could smell it, that faint wisp of hostility rising and hanging in the air. They had no answers for him, and they wished, on some dim level which they themselves may not have perceived at all, that he would stop asking those questions. Or go away.

He did perceive it. He told me later that he knew I was trying to understand, and could not, and this saddened him; but it seemed to him that they themselves did not want to understand and would continue to deny, because it was somehow too threatening to acknowledge that there was *brain damage* here—and this stumped him. He would have to find help elsewhere. But where?

He began to talk of getting a neurological consultation. The psychiatrist Russ approved.

Moses said to me, "Listen, try to dissuade him. He is very demoralized. If he starts getting his mind checked out, he'll find out that his I.Q. is twenty points lower than it used to be, which happens to all of us as we age, and that will demoralize him even more."

"You mean you think it's all just emotional?"

"Well, who can say how much is emotional and how much is organic? Sometimes there are behavioral changes after cardiac surgery, you know."

Certainly he was the portrait of depression. Wearing the same clothes day after day, and surely no accident that they were the dullest-colored things in his closet. Lying on the bed near-motionless for hours on end, fully dressed, staring at nothing, fiddling mindlessly with the middle button of his shirt, the one over the center of his scar; buttoning and unbuttoning, buttoning and unbuttoning.

I began to grow impatient with him myself. Shave, for heaven's sake. Comb your hair. There are worse things in life than a bad memory.

Once I said it aloud. We sat at the table, he poking at his food, and he was trying to say something but the simple word he wanted was not there; he struggled for it and grimaced and banged his head with his fist, crying out, *"What has happened to my mind?"* and I said, "Oh, come on, stop doing that number. It's no tragedy if you can't think of a word."

He looked at me not with anger, which would have been tolerable, but with the deepest sadness. It hurt my eyes. I felt ashamed. But was it, after all, a tragedy if one couldn't think of a word? Was it a metastatic cancer, a spinal paralysis, a death in the family? Did it merit such ostentations of misery?

A friend telephoned and asked, "How is he doing?"

"He is going down the tube," I said, listening to the soundlessness of his body on the bed, buttoning and unbuttoning the shirt button. "He is simply going down the tube, and I don't want to go with him."

But I love him. What in God's name do I mean?

I didn't understand myself at all.

Chapter 18

O NE June day he came in from the terrace looking strangely flushed. I felt his cheek. "You feel very hot," I said.

"I've been lying out in the sun."

"No, this is more than sun."

His temperature was 101. He seemed short of breath as well. We called the doctors' office. Fevers, flushes—meat and potatoes; proper adversaries. "Come down here," Mason said.

They found him in mild heart failure, fluid in his lungs. So much for the shortness of breath.

There were several guesses about the fever. One was the old arm infection. It was now a heavily encrusted gangrenous patch, black, flaking. Moses thought perhaps there was a transient bacterial infection from that arm.

Peter thought it might be something called postpericardiotomy syndrome.

"What is that?" I asked. We sat in his consultation room. Hal was in an examining room, having bloods drawn.

"It's a clinical syndrome we find sometimes from three to six months after open-heart surgery. Hal doesn't fit the typical profile, but he's close. The symptoms are chest discomfort, which he doesn't have; fever, and the presence of fluid either around the heart or in the lungs."

"What causes it?"

"Well, it's rather mysterious. It's thought that when you operate on the heart, the body actually makes antibodies that attack the injured heart cells—a reaction against the surgery. In other words, the body fights the surgery by making this antibody that attacks the heart itself. That causes irritation around the lining of the heart. The heart becomes inflamed and rubs against the cavity in which it sits, causing pain, and when it rubs it makes a noise that you can actually hear through the stethoscope. It's called a pericardial rub."

"Can you hear it in Hal?"

"Not clearly. But I'd be willing to bet that's the problem."

"What's the treatment?"

"Aspirin to start. Then steroids, if aspirin doesn't do the trick."

"Oh, Peter," I said. "He's been through so much. He's been through the surgery that was supposed to make him well again, and then, because of the surgery . . ."

"*Hold* it, Martha. That surgery was not done to make him *well*. That surgery was done to save his *life*." Dim echoes of Moses, months earlier, saying, "Whaddya need this for? You want this guy to spend the rest of his life under wraps? Let's see what's there and get it fixed up and *fachtig* . . ."

They increased his diuretics and sent him home on aspirin.

The fever persisted, low-grade, on and off. He was visibly weaker. He felt dazed all the time. His speech began to grow slurred, as though he were talking off the bottom of the third martini.

Ten days later he was admitted to the hospital with chest pain, shortness of breath, moisture in the lungs and 102-degree fever. The diagnosis was "Probable postpericardiotomy syndrome."

The blood cultures came back negative, which put the diagnosis in doubt. The fever disappeared spontaneously within forty-eight hours. The chest pain went away with more diuretics.

"As long as I'm here, I would like a neurological consultation," he said to a resident.

"Sure," the resident said. But somehow it never happened.

He was discharged after two more days, with the notation on his chart: "Etiology of fever is not clear, although congestive heart failure may play a role."

The treatment was still aspirin.

I awoke thinking there was an earthquake. The bed had moved. Was it a dream? No. The bed moved again.

I snapped on the light, filled already with dread. He lay huddled beneath the sheet, shaking violently. His eyes were closed. His lips were blue. He seemed barely conscious.

"C-cold," he said. He stuttered this out on a faint exhalation, more like a hiccup than a word.

He was burning hot to the touch. I put a thermometer into his mouth and his teeth clattered so upon it that I thought it might break, and I tried to hold it steady between his lips.

One hundred and five. Oh, God. He must be dying; no mistake this time; surely he is dying. One hundred and five is surely death's door.

"C-cold," he said again. It was hot in the room; July; hot even with the air conditioner on High. We had been sleeping only under a sheet. I wrapped the quilt around him, and then a blanket, and still he shook like nothing I had ever seen.

I called the doctors' office. It was 3 A.M.

"They're both off tonight," the answering service said. "Dr. Warren is covering."

"Tell him to call right away."

"Is this an emergency?"

"Yes."

I hung up and turned toward him. Cold, he said again. And opened his eyes and looked at me pleadingly, or so it seemed to me, as though his eyes were begging me to keep him from slipping away, and I piled another blanket on him, and another, and then, as he shook still, I piled myself upon him and lay there, spread-eagled, my face pressed to his, shaking with him, waiting for the telephone to ring before he died.

It rang in ten minutes. Warren did not know the case. He started to ask questions that required long answers, almost as though he were taking a history, and I panicked and said:

"Look, never mind that! Never mind that! I tell you, he has 105 and he is shaking like crazy. What should I do?"

"Well, I suppose you'd better get him down to the hospital."

162

"To the hospital? How?" Mad visions of picking him up wrapped in all those blankets, carrying him downstairs, hailing a cab.

"You can call an ambulance service. I'll give you the number. . . ."

"No!" Hal was shaking his head fiercely from side to side. "No hospital!"

"Why, Hal? Why, darling?"

"I w—won't make it."

"He doesn't want to go to the hospital," I said into the telephone, *sotto voce,* like someone relaying secrets. "He says he won't make it."

"Oh. Well, if he feels like that, why don't you give him some aspirin to bring down the fever and call me at 10 and let me know how he's doing."

"Yes. Yes, Doctor." Quite as though this were a reasonable course of action. Aspirin, yes, of course. And with that heavy calm that comes sometimes in our most demented moments, I went and got the aspirin and opened his mouth and put the pills way at the back, as one does with dogs and babies, and poured water and somehow got them down his gullet, and then I arranged myself upon him again, like a blanket, and pressed my body down hard and gripped him around as tightly as I could. "Hal, listen, we must concentrate." Whispering urgently into his ear. "Concentrate. Hal, listen, do not die; you must not die; you promised me; do not die; concentrate."

"Uh. Uh," he said, nodding and shaking.

Madness. He had his excuse. He was in a near-delirium, and in this state it never occurred to him that he could be taken by ambulance to the hospital. He imagined that he would somehow have to get there himself, and knew that he could not possibly do it, that he would surely die if he tried, that it was safer here, in his own bed, where he had at least some chance to survive.

That was how it appeared to him. But what excuse was there for me? For that doctor? "Never mind what he says, get him to the hospital immediately." That is what the doctor should have said. And given an irresponsible doctor, or a cretin, or a tousled sleepyhead, or whatever he was, any sane person should have known to hang up on him and call an ambulance immediately. So I can only believe that I was not altogether sane. I had perhaps entered Hal's delirium.

He survived our irresponsibility, that doctor's and mine. I lay for hours on top of him, whispering into his ear, waiting for the crisis to go one way or the other, and the dawn and his fever broke at about the same time and he stopped shaking and fell into a sleep that, but for the faint sound of his breathing, could have been the sleep of the dead.

The medical file later noted: "Prior to admission, severe shaking and chills, temp 105, patient refused to come to emergency room as requested by Dr. Warren. . . ."

He awoke at noon. His eyes were dazed. "I am limp," he said.

I called Silverman and arranged for an admission.

I dressed him. He did not want an ambulance. "There is no need," he said. "I'll make it." The elevator man and I helped him out and got him into a taxi. He leaned his head back against the seat, eyes closed, lids blue and thin. "Poor Mushie," he said.

At the emergency-room entrance, he said to the cab driver, "Don't leave yet," and to me, "Ask them to bring a wheelchair," and he drooped against the car door, waiting.

A guard came out with a chair and wheeled him into the emergency room. It was mobbed. People stared, as they do in emergency rooms and at the scenes of accidents, with that avid, unblinking curiosity.

I approached the admitting desk. "This patient is Dr. Lear," I said. "Dr. Silverman has booked a room for him."

The nurse looked up expectantly, ready to pay all due deference to this patient who was a doctor; blinked, and looked back at me.

"*That*," she said, "is Dr. Lear?"

He huddled in the chair, this six-foot-tall man, stoop-shouldered, chin retracted, hands nestled together in his lap, like a little old man in a high wind. Only his jacket bespoke the doctor. It was an obviously costly thing of softest suede, a gift from me on some healthy, well-heeled occasion. It was paler than straw in color, with the faintest tinge of green; and I remember thinking, as I looked at him huddled there, shrunken into its supple folds, that it matched his skin exactly.

Chapter 19

CONSULTANTS came. They clustered around him and pulled at their noses and stroked their chins. He was an interesting case again.

Moses had thought that it was an S.B.E.—subacute bacterial endocarditis—which might have been caused by pus seeping into the heart from the gangrenous arm. The standard treatment was penicillin administered constantly, intravenously, in massive doses, over a six-week period.

"The weeks will go by quickly," he had said to Hal.

Oh, no, Hal had said to himself. I do not agree with that diagnosis.

It simply didn't fit. He had seen plenty of endocarditis in the days when it had been rampant, before antibiotics. Always there had been specific confirming physical findings. A typical pattern of temperature spikes that was not his pattern. Fragments of bacterial colonies breaking off and traveling through the body. You would always find them, these little bacterial clots called *petechiae*, at terminal points—in the fingernail beds and the toenail beds, under the lids of the eyes, on the eyeballs. And the clincher was in the blood tests: you should always be able to culture the bacteria from blood samples.

As for himself, there was no such confirming evidence. There were only speculations. And he did not want this penicillin treatment, not only for lack of evidence, but because once they had you labeled as a case of S.B.E., it was like a police record. For the rest of your life, anytime you developed a high fever, they would slap you right back in the hospital and start up the penicillin.

Moses had left for a medical conference in France. "Peter will be in charge," he had said.

So Hal had asked Mason, "Do I have any *petechiae*?"

"No."

"How many blood cultures have you taken?"

"About thirty."

"And have you gotten any positive ones?"

"No."

"I presume the lab is good and that you've done both aerobic and anaerobic [in and out of oxygen] cultures?"

"Oh, yes. Of course."

"And they were all negative?"

"All negative."

"Well, then, I do not want to be labeled an S.B.E. Not yet. I want a consultation."

So now consultants came. Came and went, stumped.

An expert on tropical diseases came and started hunting around for malaria. Possibly Hal had been transfused with some bad blood during surgery. That was an interesting guess, a good medical-detective guess, but it wasn't malaria. I was terribly disappointed. Malaria is easy to treat.

An internist thought that it might be hepatitis. The tests were negative.

They checked for a pulmonary embolus. The lung scan was normal.

An intravenous pyelogram was normal.

The upper and lower G.I. series were normal.

The blood cultures were all negative.

Stumped.

He had been seen now by three consultants. He would have asked for a fourth, a sixth, a tenth, until he had heard what he wanted to hear: without evidence, he should not be treated for endocarditis. Doctor-shopping again.

He did not have to shop for long. They agreed with him. But what, he wondered, would have happened to a layman? A layman would be lying in that bed right now with the penicillin coursing through his veins, no questions asked, no questions that he would ever know to ask or dare to ask, not the next time, not ever again, not for the rest of his life, whenever he might start running a high fever and they would say, "Oh, yes, the old S.B.E.," and put him back into the hospital and stick the needle back into his vein. He felt frightened by the vulnerability of laymen; not simply when they were in bad medical hands, but even when they were, like himself, in the best of hands.

The only diagnosis that came close was the postpericardiotomy syndrome. He still didn't quite fit that picture. He hadn't the characteristic chest pain. It simply seemed closer than anything else. But the aspirin had not worked, and the next option was steroids, and that was no easy thing. They couldn't just give him the stuff. Cortisone might be unsafe in some cases—if the patient had TB, for example. First they would have to do a liver biopsy and a bone-marrow biopsy and various other tests, none of them innocuous, to make sure he was free of certain infections.

"Let's do nothing," one of the consultants said. "Let's just send him home. If he starts running a fever again, we can bring him back in and do the tests and decide whether to start him on steroids."

That was the consensus. So they sent him home again, doing nothing, which was the most reasonable thing to do. Faced with the alternatives, he would have done it himself.

This time, just as he had done the last time, he asked for a neurological consultation. "By the way, before I am discharged . . ." he said.

Sure, they said. No problem. And again, somehow, it did not happen.

At home, a low-grade fever persisted. His memory seemed worse. The slur in his speech grew heavier. Sometimes I could hardly understand him. Now something seemed to be wrong with his sense of balance. Ataxia, it is called. He stumbled about the apartment, looking dazed, hanging onto walls. "Are you all right? Are you all right?" I would say, hands fluttering about him as though he were a toddler taking his first tenuous steps, wanting in fact to keep my mouth shut and my hands to myself. "*Of coursh* I'm all right," he would say, drawing himself up with the dignity of a Gatsby drunk.

Sounds unnerved me. The sudden slamming of a door and I would jump, my mind flooded with images of his body hitting the floor, a dead weight. One night I walked into the bedroom and found the television going and his body in the bed; but his head was not in the bed, it was slumped down against his nightstand, and his glasses were crooked on his face and his mouth was wide open and he was totally motionless and soundless.

I bent down and whispered, "Hal? Hal?" Then, trembling, demanded loudly, "Hal!" And still he did not stir or sigh, and I grabbed his shoulders and shook him violently, shouting, "Hal! Hal! Hal!"

He awoke, frightened, the specs falling off his face. "What? What?" Then saw my agitation and understood instantly; pulled me down; held me in his arms, crooning, "It's all right, baby, it's all right. . . ." Wordplay, protective words standing in for protection. Why should a grown woman find such comfort in being called *baby*?

On the street he lurched from one support to the next. A Bowery wino, unshaven, sloppily dressed. People walked wide swaths around him. This made him laugh aloud. "They think I'm shtinking drunk," he said.

He staggered along Fifth Avenue playing Whodunit: *Why* this weakness? *Why* the fever, which still came and went, low-grade? *Why* the blurred speech, and now the ataxia? Had the balance part of his brain been damaged? Was he possibly missing electrolytes, vital chemistries drained out of him by the diuretics? What should be done? And even as he strained for answers, the physical weakness grew worse and the mental fog grew thicker, making it even harder for him to observe himself as the doctor; giving him more and more the sense that reality was receding.

"Should we push for more diagnostic tests? Should we talk to them again about steroids?" I said.

"Who knowsh?" he said.

Now his face had developed the gaunt, wild-eyed look of crazy people and concentration-camp survivors.

Now I watched this wild-eyed, thick-tongued stumbling man, slipping and stumbling away from me, and I pushed down fears which reared up again in the night.

Now in my dreams the walls of a house are crumbling, and I say to my husband, "Look here, you must mend these walls. You promised," and he smiles sadly. My dreams have never been obscure. Houses, crumbling walls, labyrinths, flights, falls, screams that freeze in the throat; all the simple, sturdy stuff of Psychology 1.

Now in my dreams the image of my husband shifts and merges sometimes with the image of my dead father. My husband is my father and my father is my husband and I am my mother and myself. We move into and out of each other. The crumbling house is the house I live in now and the house of my childhood. I wake whimpering for my father. I reach out gently to my husband and touch my cheek to his arm or his chest; and when I sense the soft heave of the flesh, I fall back on my own pillow exhausted, and sleep again. I feel in double jeopardy.

When he was healthy he used to wake up hours earlier than I, but now he sleeps much later. I hate to wake first. I lie watching. He does not stir, which makes me nervous. Since his heart got sick the ferocious old snore has disappeared, and the thrusting of limbs too, and his breathing has turned to something too delicate, almost tenuous, as though the whole body were conserving energy for the sake of the heart. When he wakes finally, I say, "Are you all right?" and he says, "I am *fine*," and smiles sadly, just as in the dream. Then I nuzzle him. I bury my face in his throat, which is lean, not plump like my father's throat, but there is something reminiscent in the smell. I burrow in deeply and stay for a long time. He lies still. He understands everything. Finally he says, "Let's have some breakfast," and I get up and make coffee, like an adult.

My father had dropped dead during my brother's wedding reception, eleven years earlier. A hundred-odd guests had just sat down to fruit cocktail at tables-for-ten covered with pink cloths. My father sat at the head table, to the left of the pretty bride. He looked tired, but immensely happy. Already, I think, he was dreaming of grandchildren.

He stood up, rapped a glass for attention, then raised the glass of pale pink wine to make a toast, a poem that he had composed and memorized for the occasion:

"On this day, one of the best of our life,

I want to say to my son and his dear little wife . . ."

And then he slumped down, and was dead.

I remember that someone quickly brought a coat rack and threw over it several pink tablecloths to make a sort of screen in front of the head table. I remember going behind the screen and seeing that my husband, to whom I had then been married two years, was breathing into my father's mouth and pounding on my father's chest. I remember thinking that if he really loved me he would breathe life back into that body; and for months afterward, I secretly blamed him for failing.

An ambulance came. An attendant said, "This man is dead," and my husband, gray with fatigue—he had been working on the body, steadily, for what seemed to be hours; it was twenty minutes—snapped, "How do *you* know he is dead? Where is your stethoscope? Are you a doctor? Get the oxygen on him! Get him to the hospital!"

They put the body upon a stretcher and hoisted it into the ambulance. I climbed in. They put a mask on the face. The ambulance took off with sirens screaming through the serene summer streets of Canton, Massachusetts, and all the way to the hospital, I kept talking to the masked face. I kept saying, "Daddy, don't do this to me. You promised."

It was a long time in the hospital lobby. I kept talking. A man who was sitting near me, in the otherwise empty lobby, got up and moved several seats away.

Finally my husband came out of the emergency room. A white-coated doctor was with him. The doctor said, "I'm sorry." My husband said, "Darling, I'm sorry." I remember feeling rage at them both, but a far greater rage at my father. They had merely failed me. He had abandoned me. For a long time after, lying beside my husband, in bed, at night, I would curse my father: How dared you do this to me? I, who loved you so?

Hal and I drove back to the wedding reception. The guests had not stirred. I went to my mother and put my arms around her and shook my head No, and she wailed. The bride sat with her own parents, pale. She was to have left for Bermuda in the morning.

The guests began to leave, weeping, murmuring, gripping our shoulders. When they had all gone, when the new bride and groom had left with her parents, the new widow went with my husband and me to our car. The hotel manager ran after us. "Please," he cried, "take the chicken! Take the chicken!" He was desperate. For two hours a hundred chicken dinners had sat in the kitchen cooling, unpaid-for. His staff had boxed them nicely, like picnic lunches, and now he pleaded with my husband to open the trunk of the car, and a hundred white boxes were being stacked neatly in the trunk.

We used up many of them during the first days of mourning. We fed guests. For a year afterward, I could not eat chicken, or look at chicken, or tolerate its odor.

Hal returned to work the day after the funeral. My brother and his bride and I stayed on for the mourning rites.

I got drunk one night and wrote a ten-page letter to my old analyst. "For God's sake, help me," I wrote. "My father has died." Drinking steadily, I wrote on, reminding my analyst of how I had adored my father, recalling how I used to say to him that I was frightened of my father's death, that I feared I would not be able to bear my father's death, and how he used to say to me that when it came, I would be able to bear it. "You were wrong," I wrote. In the morning I could not decipher most of the letter, and threw it away.

Now, eleven years later, I wished that I understood better what it was that I had felt for my father. The glib Freudian phrases do not explain, they only describe. And now that my husband was sick, I thought that if only I had figured it out all those years ago, perhaps it would have helped me to understand why I, an independent woman in most of the practical ways of life, should feel at the core such fearful dependencies. I wished that I had parsed the subject down to the last Oedipal syllable, because now that I was merging my father and my husband in my dreams, now that the walls of my house were crumbling in my dreams and, in my waking hours, I was watching my husband slip away, I felt that if only I had understood more about those mysteries, those old habits of need and love and men and what it meant in my life to love and be loved by men, protected by men, sustained by men—if only I had understood all that, I would be stronger and better able to face what must, I thought, now be faced, as I watched him slipping and lurching seemingly toward his death.

He staggered into Mason's office.

"You must do something," he said.

"What do you mean?"

"I am dying. You cannot sit and observe me any longer, or you will simply observe me die."

So Mason, who was in good and bad ways a foil to Silverman—gentler, less directive, more patient, more passive—made a command decision. And made it on the basis of no certain diagnosis and without doing tests, the liver biopsy and the bone-marrow biopsy and whatever else, because these would require hospitalization and he sensed, quite rightly, that the patient's morale would not stand up to another hospitalization.

"I am starting you on steroids," he said.

"Fine."

Many months later, I asked Mason, "What were your thoughts then? This patient came to you weak, befogged, staggering, lethargic, depressed. He expected to die. What did you think? What did you feel?"

Peter said:

"I wish I could tell you what I felt that day. I can only tell you what I *think* I felt. This was an extremely disabled and frustrated individual, who had had possibly the single roughest year one person could have. It was—let's see—August, wasn't it? Almost a year to the day since his first heart attack. He was physically and emotionally exhausted from everything that was going on. He had gotten no relief from any of the therapeutic trials; no diagnosis had been firmly established. It really was like he was begging for something to be done . . . that some change be made to alter this inexorable course . . . this course which had been made up of three heart attacks, four hospitalizations, massive surgery and persistent illness and disability."

I wondered, and did not dare to ask, what would have been done—anything?—had this patient not come and said, as probably only a doctor would say, "You cannot sit and observe me any longer, or you will simply observe me die."

"And in the face of all that, what were your thoughts?"

"I felt that we had to take a drastic step. It was drastic in the sense that there was no specific diagnosis. But going on the possibility of postpericardiotomy syndrome, I started him on steroids.

"I saw him three days later. He was still weak and woozy. Then Moe saw him and noted that he was weak and occasionally ataxic, but without fever for the first time in several weeks. Moe decided to go along with the prednisone [steroid] schedule that I had laid out. My notes said: 'Rx: Prednisone 20 milligrams Q.I.D. for two weeks.' Moe's notes said: 'Rx: Same; reassure.'"

" 'Reassure'? What does that mean?"

"That's a word Moe uses very frequently in his notes. He is able to take patients who are anxious about real problems, and . . . *reassure* them that things are going to be better, so the patients go out really confident that things will work out. . . . And actually, a great deal will

172

have been gained from that visit, just from the words 'Rx: Reassure.' It certainly is a very important thing with patients who have cardiac phobias—*no* heart disease, but come in every three weeks for a cardiogram because they've had some chest pain. And you contrast that with a patient like Hal, who—"

"Cardiac phobias!" I said, carried elsewhere for the moment on a wave of pure reportorial pleasure. "What a takeout! Heart patients who have no heart problems!"

"Oh, that's not uncommon. We have maybe a dozen of those."

Cardiac phobias! Ah, sweet dreams.

Immediately, on the steroids, he felt a surge of energy. The first dose was like a triple shot of speed, a fantastic high. He held himself back, afraid to trust that possibly they had hit the right answer. He simply said to me, "Well, I feel better. Let's hope it works."

But soon he could allow himself to believe it. For he was taking the steroids on alternate days, and when he took them he felt strong, and when he didn't, he was immediately back to staggering and feeling half-alive. Within a week, he dared say to himself, This is it! I'm alive again!

Gradually there was less of a roller-coaster effect. He came down off the highs and up off the lows and evened out at some level that was limited, but at least it was level. He was no longer sliding downhill. He could walk a straight line.

He was euphoric. "I think we've made it," he said, flashing something livelier than a ghost of the old grin. "Now, if my mind will just get better . . ."

In a sense, it did. It stopped spinning like a top—that old reverse vertigo. But he was still enveloped in what he called *the fog*, his own personal cloud, thick as ever; and in the wake of those very high fevers, his memory impairment seemed even worse.

For him, that was what mattered most. That was far harder to bear than the physical limitations. For me, of course, what mattered most was that he was physically better. He had stopped dying. My nightmares stopped too.

Chapter 20

*O*UR bags had been packed for Provincetown since Memorial Day. In August they still sat, waiting, in a corner of the bedroom.

Two summers gone by, now, without Provincetown. Strange, for we had begun in Provincetown, or almost begun there, and we had spent all the summers of our shared life there, and it was our favorite place in the world, and far more than a place: a state of mind, a style, an extension of ourselves.

We had begun, actually, farcically, in Nantucket. No one had heard of Woody Allen back then, but I have often thought since that it was a precise Woody Allen metaphor: We met, spent a day together and decided most urgently to go to bed together, but he could not find the bed. He was a stranger to Nantucket and couldn't make his way back to his lodgings. And it was very late, not a soul in the streets, not a store open, nobody to ask. We kept circling in his car, turning this way and that, and always winding up at a windmill. Driving around in that car for almost an hour, snorting and sweating, sniffing at each other, pawing body parts and laughing too, near-hysterically, at this preposterous pair who panted to get lost in the pit of passion and were lost instead in the center of Nantucket, panting left and panting right and winding up always at that same goddamned windmill.

Finally we found our way, and the impulse, luckily, survived us.

He stunned me with the simplicity and directness of his drive. I was working then at the *Times*, moving freely about the city, dating hip, fragile men who always got the right tables in restaurants, or cared terribly if they did not get the right tables in restaurants, and often had problems of one sort or another in bed. He seemed, in sex as in everything else, extraordinarily whole.

We had mutual friends in Nantucket and we wanted to be alone. So we went the next day to Provincetown, which he knew well. We lay in a motel room looking out at that incomparable bay, and up at a spectacular happening in the sky that I learned later was called the Northern Lights, and congratulated each other upon its appearance. A celestial sign. We walked across the flats in the silver dawn and watched the shabby little trawlers setting out, souvenirs of a once-great fleet; and looked back at the semicircle of houses that stood, jammed together and faintly askew, like everything else in Province-town, at the water's edge.

On the tacky main drag, with the art galleries open but deserted— Kline was dead, Rothko was dead, Hans Hofmann was long since dead, the glory days were over; Motherwell and Frankenthaler, then still married, were the only true giants left in town—we wandered amid the improbable mix: hippies sitting on the curbs stoned sense-less, college kids, gays strolling arm in arm—they were doing that comfortably in Provincetown years before anywhere else—conven-tioneers in business suits trying not to stare at the drag queens, leather-jacketed sons of the Portuguese fishermen standing around on corners, defending turf. He drove me out to Highland Light, a Coast Guard station on the ocean side: blackness but for the lighthouse beam circling the sky, a sudden bluff, a near-sheer drop to the beach far below, and the waves far below, great lacy arcs booming silently on the shore. I yowled in pleasure, which delighted him, for it was the place he liked best. And then we went back to the motel and made love some more and spoke, cautiously, of the dangers of falling in love.

A month later he pinned me up against a wall in his apartment in Hartford, Connecticut—patently a bachelor apartment, the psychic spilling-over of a man recently divorced, with his books and his clay and his easels and his records and his driftwood and petrified-wood collections mounded up on every surface, defying order—pinned me against the wall and said:

"Enough of this crapping around. When are we going to get married?"

I was ecstatic. I was appalled. A Jewish doctor. Two children. Suburbia. Light-years removed from my style and self-image. Well. I would have to adjust as best I could to the realities of his life because, in fact, I adored him.

In the spring we married.

We went to Provincetown that summer, and every summer thereafter. At first we took rental quarters. Then we decided to buy a piece of the place for ourselves, and one nasty November day, friends called and said that a waterfront house had suddenly come on the market. Those were rare. We drove up from Connecticut and were shown into a dark, dank, sprawling, monumentally ugly house—a true Provincetown bastard, part old boathouse, part old toolshed, with other odd wings tacked on over the generations—four stories high, a mess of roof lines, twelve bedrooms, one bath, with the windows boarded, so we had no idea of the view, and the electricity off and the gas off and the water off, so we could not even test-flush the toilet—we walked into this architectural monstrosity, and I said, "Hal, it *speaks to us.*"

"Yes," he said, "it's saying, 'Get the fuck out of here.' "

"Oh, Hal, please. Just close your eyes"—standing there in the dark —"and imagine tearing down walls, opening out these tiny spaces. . . . It'll be *gorgeous.*"

"I assure you it will never be gorgeous," he said. "But okay, let's make an offer."

He named a figure, substantially lower than the asking price. It was accepted. He was shocked and suspicious.

"You will *never be sorry,*" the agent said as she took our deposit.

Dazed, we went off to one of the few restaurants in town that served dinner through the winter, and toasted each other and our house with vodka Gibsons.

The place was mobbed, the year-rounders packed together for inner and outer warmth. The last of the Bohemians, those year-rounders—rebels, loners, losers, boozers, flower children past their bloom; poets who fished for a living, artists who did carpentry. We knew several of them. Word spread, and soon strangers were coming over to wish us well. A woman said cheerily, "Oh, *you're* the couple who bought the house with the leaky roof," and some man said, "Congratulations! Of course, you know about the roof?" and Hal eyed me grimly.

"Gorgeous," he said.

But it never did leak. And we never were sorry.

We tore down many walls. Remade the crazy old bastard into two duplex apartments, renting the lower and keeping the upper for ourselves. The fourth floor was no more than an odd peaked space, raw, no windows, an abandoned romantic impulse. We broke it out on the water side with a big glass wall. It became our bedroom, a glittering white space suspended high over the bay like a flying bridge, higher than any other house, higher even than the circling sea gulls; a room to fly in.

And Provincetown and that house became part of the rhythm of our lives, a measure of our seasons, like the growth charts of children. Every summer, taking off with Jon and Judy in the back seat—later, as young adults, they would come and go on their own with chums and lovers, making their own arrangements in the back bedrooms while we shrugged silently at each other, helpless as to protocol— with the kids in the back seat, counting the hours and the miles, and with the Sunfish on its hitch and the hibachi in the trunk.

And now, for two summers, we hadn't been there. And I didn't care.

Safety now was in this bedroom in New York. This space, in which for the past year he had not only slept but spent most of his waking hours, had become in a sense our permanent I.C.U. The pills and the pillows were at hand, the prednisone was at hand, the telephone, the doctors, the emergency room, the cardiac team, all at hand, in this space that held us like a womb.

So the suitcases sat there crammed with his sawed-off jeans, my requisite caftans, the Provincetown leather sandals, the woven belts and white ducks and tanning lotions, and yes, of course, it would be glorious to get to our bay again, but if we didn't, it would be quite all right. We were safe here.

"Well, if you keep getting better and the doctors say you can go in mid-August, what do you think? Would you like to go?"

"I don't care."

"You must have some preference."

"No."

Ah, this won't do. Show me a preference. Give me a yes, give me a no, give me something. Don't give me nothing.

"Come on, Hal. What do you *prefer*? To go or not to go?"

"What about you?" he said.

"I don't care."

"Neither do I."

Chapter **21**

"**I**'M good news and bad news," he said.

And so he was. Something schizoid was happening here, some strange split, or so it seemed, between his body and his mind, as though the two were deeply estranged.

The body kept growing stronger. He devised little exercises to help it along: filled half-gallon vodka jugs with water and swung them in circles to build up his atrophied arm muscles; lay flat and lifted book-filled briefcases by their handles, with his toes, to build up the legs.

The memory seemed worse.

"I can *feel* it," he would say, slapping his stomach. "I can feel the strength coming back into my body. I did a terrific new exercise and it didn't strain me a bit."

"Good. What was the exercise?"

"I don't remember."

I do not know whether it was because of this, the discomfort of dealing with some unnamed, uncharted brain damage, or simply because he was now considered a routine case that Silverman turned him increasingly over to Mason. It was done gently enough.

"Peter feels hurt that you never see him in the office," Silverman said during an examination. "Why don't you book some appointments with him?"

Hal understood. It was a prerogative of senior men. Medically, he was stabilized. Socially, he was no star.

"I didn't scout the whole city to be your associate's patient. I chose you," he said. "But I respect Peter and I'm perfectly willing to see him on routine office visits. As long as we understand that if there is any change in my condition or my treatment, you're my doctor."

"Of course," Silverman said.

I took offense. It was nothing personal. I respected Mason too. But I felt the sting of second-class citizenship. The senior man would not have palmed off a plum—a patient, say, such as Cousin David, who was a television eminence and could create eminences. "And with us tonight," David could say—and had said, more than once—"is Dr. Moses Silverman, one of the most distinguished cardiologists in the country. . . ." The senior man would hang on to such a patient through head colds, hemorrhoids, warts, whatever.

And something more. In his own practice Hal often had turned over new or stabilized patients, those who were willing, to his young associate. That was common in partnership medicine: one helps the junior partner build up a following. But there was a protocol. He would not have turned over a patient who happened to be a doctor. A doctor becomes ill, he surveys the field, he makes a choice. It is a compliment. One does not slough off such a compliment onto a junior partner. One accepts it with respect.

"Don't be angry," he said to me. "They've both looked after me. They're both devoted. And after all, they've given me good care for almost a year, and I'm a courtesy patient. . . ."

Ah, my Pollyanna. I blew up. "Damn it, *you've* given. You gave plenty. You gave courtesy for twenty years, to doctors and their kids and their in-laws, and when did you ever palm off any of them?"

"There's a difference."

"What?"

"I'm not in practice anymore. I can't refer patients."

"You mean that's all professional courtesy is about? Referrals? You mean if a retired doctor had chosen you to take care of him, you would have turned him over?"

"No. I wouldn't have."

"Well, then?"

"Well, then, *what?* Let it alone. Just let it alone."

Of course he minded. His pride was hurt. But he had no sense of having been thrust into lesser hands. Both men were good.

As his body continued to mend, his libido returned. It had been fragile for months and gone, totally, since the last hospitalization. He had cursed it. He had refused to understand where it had gone, or why. Never a sudden heat wave, never a stirring in a body that had always responded with such urgency and ease—it infuriated him.

Had this been a patient in treatment, he would have explained and reassured. But it is different when one's own penis lies limp. This was foreign matter. This was some unfortunate case history that he had heard a thousand times, but not, damn it, his own.

The provocations I brought to that bedroom! Subtle and deft as a crutch, even unto the black lace nightgown, quintessence of crutch, in which I had appeared one night to our mutual astonishment. I, who never wore nightclothes of any sort.

"Martha, *really*," he had said, trying to salvage some modicum of dignity for us both. "What would your women's group say?"

And then the old stuff began to flow in him again, like early sap.

"Guess what? I woke up with an erection last night," he told me, gleeful as a boy. And to Mason, he said, "Is it all right to start having sex again?"

Peter blushed. Rose from his chair. "Let me close this door," he said, "so the people in the waiting room won't be embarrassed." And then said that Yes, it would be all right, if we . . . uh . . . took it easy.

So. The missionary way is not the treatment of choice for cardiacs. It had always been my own choice—cultural compaction, I suppose— but one rises above such handicaps. Soon there seemed no need to take it easy, and it was fine. Having lost it and regained it, we made love now at the top of our senses.

"I think you ought to start going to a gym," Mason said in late September. "Start working out; do a little swimming."

Working out! Swimming! He was jubilant.

He joined the health club of a local Y, nine blocks from home. It was a longer distance than he had ever thought to walk again.

Always he would recall that first walk with absolute clarity, the precise sensation of it, the extraordinary joy he found himself taking in ordinary things—the feel of the sun on his flesh, the reddening of a leaf. He knew it was predictable, even banal, for someone in his circumstance. The old redemption rapture. Patients who had almost died, or had been bedridden for months, had often described it to him, or tried to.

"You wouldn't believe it, Doc," a cancer victim in his last remission had said once, embarrassed by his own intensity, "just looking at the sky, that *blue* . . ."

He had believed it. But to experience it himself was remarkable. It was the start of a time in which he would live frequently at the top of his senses, not just in bed, and he would communicate his exultation to me, and we would walk down city streets peering, listening, pressing palms, marvéling at our own capacity for joy. I did not think we could stay way up there. We didn't. But we never plummeted. Our senses never went dormant again.

Now, on that first trip to the Y, he cruised slowly through the side streets, gazing at grillwork, gargoyles, minor miracles that he had never seen before. Some kids were playing ball. He stopped to watch, loving their exuberance. But he watched at a distance. There might be a wild ball. A kid might come chasing it, bump into him, crash into his chest. The ball did in fact bounce toward him. "Hey, mister!" a boy cried, and Hal picked it up and threw. A bad throw, but it felt good.

On Madison Avenue troops of men marched grim-faced with their briefcases. He stared in wonder. They looked like soldiers, or insane.

On Lexington he browsed past the little shops, delighting in the plenty, the great rounds of Brie, the Belugas and Malassols, the old porcelains that Martha might like. He bought one, a small, exquisite Ming plate with its sixteenth-century provenance—preposterously expensive, but it was that kind of day—and had trouble with the writing of a check and the presentation of identification cards. And finally, thrilled to find that he had made it—somewhat foggy, it was true; feeling not altogether right in the head; but strong in the body, secure, his feet following each other in good sequence and his pulse beating strong and slow—he arrived at the Y and was welcomed to the health club.

He was assigned a locker: a dial lock, with turnings to the left and right, which he couldn't manage at all.

A man, large, ruddy, perhaps a decade older than he, was standing at the next locker.

"These things are a nuisance, aren't they?" the man said.

"Yes. They are." He was beginning to sweat, fingers fumbling with this damned dial contraption.

"This is my first day here."

"Mine too."

"Oh? What's brought you here?"

"I've been sick," Hal said, "and my doctors thought this would be good rehabilitation."

"What's been the matter?"

"I'm a cardiac. I've had bypass surgery. . . ."

"You don't say! Me too!"

Shyly they eyed each other. The eyes moved to that telltale place, to the second shirt button from the top, where the scar began. It was like children feeling out friendships, he said later. Tentative. Breathy. Emanations of love.

His name was Chelsea. Reality sat hard on Chelsea. He had fought in the Spanish Civil War, been a labor-union organizer, a Communist, a scrapper all his life, and then had come his angina and his heart attack ("It had my name on it," he said) and his surgery, and he scrapped no more. It gnawed.

They became buddies. They went together each morning from the exercise room to the pool to the sauna to the showers to the weigh-in to the lockers, and then they would sit in the lounge talking of the surgery, the constant awareness of the chest, the sense of loss.

Hal had lost more. More physically, and in the head. He told Chelsea about that. How he had been on the heart machine and then, when he woke up, he had seemed to have no head. Chelsea was shocked. His head was whole. He knew several others who had been on the machine, and their heads were whole.

It was odd with those two, how their roles seemed reversed. For Hal, despite the fog in his head, felt exhilarated by everything physical. Sharp sensual pleasure in the mildest exercise, bending and stretching, lifting small weights, feeling the slap of water against his face as he floated there in the pool, buoyant, sensations of strength seeping back into his body. It filled him with joy.

But there was no joy in Chelsea. Chelsea was a deeply depressed man.

"What's the matter, Chelsea?" Hal would say.

"I don't know." Fingers at his pulse, listening. "I just feel low."

Chelsea would swim two laps effortlessly. "You're looking good," Hal would say, and Chelsea would shake his head. "Ah, my friend.

You should have seen me in the old days. I was some swimmer." "But Chelsea"—hanging on to the pool wall, breathless after a half-dozen strokes—"isn't it wonderful to be able to swim!"

They meshed, those polar spirits. Hal helped Chelsea with his moods. And Chelsea, in the kindest way, helped Hal with this mysterious disability of the mind, leading him about the building like a stranger or a blind man, for even after weeks in the place, even after months, Hal could never remember which way to go to the exercise room, left or right, or what route to take to the swimming pool, one flight up or down, or how to get back to his locker with the difficult dial lock. He kept the combination on a piece of paper in his wallet, and consulted it every day.

So there was this schizoid quality: a celebration in the physicality of his life; a growing despair about his mind.

Sequences were beyond him. He would go out to shop in the neighborhood. (He insisted upon doing homely errands, and house-work too—"Get out of my kitchen," he would say, cleaning up after dinner. And I, who before his illness had made all the predictable noises about division of work—"Listen, while you're at the office I'm at the typewriter. Why can't you help with the dishes? Have you ever in your life cleaned a toilet bowl?"—I now could not bear for him to do domestic things, could not bear to see what it revealed of his self-image. But he insisted.)

He could not manage the logistics of errands—a route, a plan. He wandered rudderless in the streets.

Finally he tried to lay it all out on paper:

1. Leave off shirts at laundry.
2. Go to corner pharmacy for shampoo.
3. Cross street to supermarket. Buy:
   orange juice
   English muffins
   cottage cheese
   dishwasher powder . . .

Then he would go, and do, but by the time he got to the third store he would be so confused that he no longer knew what he was doing. Clutching that piece of paper desperately, as a foreigner clutches a street address, he would wander through the supermarket aisles squinting at labels, seeking out clerks to ask repeatedly where was the canned-soup section, losing his cart, and before he'd crossed out half the items on his list he would be feeling dazed and faint and he would stumble toward the cashier and hold out a bill, pocket whatever change was given him, for he couldn't count at all, and get out and weave toward home, proceeding often in the wrong direction. Once, three blocks from home, he had to ask the way. He came through our front door pale and shaky.

I said the utterly wrong thing. "Oh, well, you never *could* find your way home. Remember in Nantucket, the night you almost didn't get laid because you couldn't find your way home?" Trying, as his doctors did, to jolly it through.

He stared as though I were someone he ought to know, but didn't. "Oh, God," he said. And went into the bedroom and gently closed the door.

Now he made lists for everything. Lists were his coping mechanism. Lists were his memory. He trusted nothing to his own memory. Except once, and it failed him.

We had resumed a bit of social life. One morning we went to meet friends for brunch in a midtown restaurant. I drove. I circled the blocks several times, but there were no parking spots, and we were late.

"You go in and meet them. I'll park the car," he said.

"Are you sure?" For months he had refused to get behind the wheel.

"Yes. I'm sure. My head feels good."

I joined our party. We went through one round of Bloody Marys, and then another, and it was a half-hour and no Hal. I began to sweat.

"I think I should go look for him," I mumbled.

"Take it easy. He's a big boy."

Ah, marvelous. Everybody's a psychologist.

Finally I spotted him out the window. He was walking very slowly, staggering a bit, in a mini-version of the old lurch. He looked desolate.

He faltered toward us and slid heavily into a chair.

"What happened, Hal?"

"I got lost."

"Lost! You're kidding," somebody laughed.

Hal put his arms on the table and laid his head upon them.

He had driven round and round, bewildered by the uptowns and the downtowns, no sense of where he was. At some point he had made the wrong turn into a one-way street and had been honked out by a cabbie who had pointed to a sign and screamed, "One way, you asshole. Can't you *read*?" He had pulled over and waited until the trembling stopped. Then started circling again, finally found a spot, parked the car, got out and reached for paper to mark down the location.

No! he had told himself ferociously. Memorize it! Damn you, *memorize* it!

He had put away the paper and begun to walk, repeating to himself, Sixty-sixth and York, Sixty-sixth and York, Sixty-sixth and York, and had gone some distance before he realized that he did not remember where the restaurant was and he did not remember its name.

He had stepped into a drugstore and sat sipping a Coke, waiting for his head to clear. *Concentrate*. But the name wouldn't come.

Finally, with some sense of concession that he hated to make, he had said to the clerk:

"There's a restaurant near here. A popular place for brunch . . ."

"We got hundreds of them."

"But this place is on a corner."

The clerk snorted.

"It has a lot of windows. Like a closed-in porch. And, uh, a stained-glass ceiling . . ."

"Oh, yeah. Maxwell's Plum. Eight blocks south and over on First."

South. He had been walking north. He copied the address from a telephone book. His hand was shaking badly and he used the other to steady it.

"You all right?" the clerk said.

"Yes, thank you. I'm fine."

And so he had arrived. Now he lifted his head from the table as though it were an object too heavy to bear, and shook it in despair.

"Martha," he said, "I can't remember where I parked the car."

We picked at the eggs Benedict for a time. After, in a friend's car, we circled the blocks again, and it was almost an hour before we found what we needed to find at Sixty-sixth and York and took it home. I drove.

Fog. Foggy. Foggier. They were the words he used constantly, the best he could summon to describe an indescribable state.

It was like a daily weather report. We gauged his internal weather

186

by these words. "Foggier today." "Clear this morning, and then, walking home from the gym, I got foggy. . . ."

Listening, Mason or Silverman would ask, "You mean dizzy?"

"No, not dizzy. *Foggy*. Not with it."

"You mean withdrawn?"

"*No*." Voice rising in frustration. "Not withdrawn. Sort of . . . *foggy*. Like, I look at a street sign and I can't . . . figure it out. I can read it, but I can't figure out which way to go. I buy something, they tell me how much it costs, and I can't understand how much that is. The money is in my hand, but I can't . . . Do you know what I mean?"

They (we) nod gravely. They make scribbles on their charts: *October 20: complained of feeling foggy . . .*

At least now they listen with respect. No more jollies. Now they make gestures of respect for some disability that *may or may not,* their solemn faces seem to say, be beyond understanding. There were fevers of 105 just months ago, and such things command respect. But in fact they understand no more now than they did before of whatever the hell he is talking about, and he knows it now as he knew it then.

"Listen," he says in desperation, "my mind is *shit*."

Silverman reddens and wags a forefinger sternly in his face. "Don't you *ever* say a thing like that again," he says. He means well. Everybody means well. But what then?

How are they to help him? Open-heart surgery. Oxygenation by proxy. The mind bone connected to the body bone—how? There is so much they do not know. "We pool our ignorance," a friend, a heart specialist, once said to me. *Fog.* The thing fits no clinical profile. It yields no diagnosis. It submits to none of their tests, invites no technique, and so what are they to do?

Technique! Land of technology. Doctors of technology. Give them the abnormal heartbeat, the stricture, the germ, the tumor, things they can hear, see, palpate, capture on camera and tape. But what the hell kind of adversary is *fog*? Whatever cannot be diagnosed or treated by technique is suspect, vaguely inauthentic, and quite possibly does not exist.

So there was something here, in the way they listened to him, doing their very best, that was in the deepest native vein. Some implicit rebuke: Shape up. Get with it. Your potassium is *normal*. Your adrenal function is *normal*. All your chemistries are *normal*. *Stop being complicated.*

He did not know where to turn. I could only say, "I understand," when in fact I did not. His pal Chelsea, back there at the gym where he reveled in that other, physical part of his life, could only listen and, out of the depths of his own depression, commiserate. The psychiatrist Russ, whom he was still seeing once a week, listened better than anyone else. But Russ could not treat the problem; he could only help—*try* to help—the patient adjust to it.

"Nobody wants to deal with a brain-damaged person," he said to Russ. "Nobody really wants to talk about it." He gave up on his doctors and went back to his lists.

He made a list of what he saw as his mental disabilities. It said:

1. Fogginess
2. Trouble with sequences
3. Trouble with spatial relationships
4. Can't handle multiple stimuli
5. Can't handle noise
6. Can't manage numbers
7. Can't read well
8. *No memory.*

It was not, of course, *no* memory. It was damaged memory. Of all his disabilities, this was the most devastating. He had always taken memory so for granted. Who does not, when it works? He'd had no awareness how paralyzed one might be without it. Now he understood the obvious as philosophers do, profoundly. He understood that without memory, life was not human life but vegetation. Without memory, one could not tie a shoe.

It was strange, or seemed to be, that he could remember events long past with no trouble whatever. A journalist called one day for an interview on the psychological effects of vasectomy. He talked for an hour, and was astounded to find that he could do it with ease, thoughtful and fluent, and everything he said was based on material he had researched and written two years earlier.

But new memory was something else.

Guests came to dinner, and hosts invited us to dinner, and he could not function. He could not follow conversations. He could not remember names. I do not think others were acutely aware of it; only he.

Once he walked into a roomful of people he didn't know and

settled upon a project for the evening: he would commit at least two names to memory. He concentrated hard upon his dinner partners, speaking first to one, and then to the other, and each time repeating her name. But then the woman to his right got up from the table briefly, the rhythm was broken, and when she returned he looked at her and he didn't know who she was. Not simply her name, but *who she was*, as though he had never seen her before. He could not, he said later, describe the awfulness of that to anyone—not even to me, not even to Russ.

In conversation he tried to fake it. He could remember only the sentence of the moment. He would cling to it fiercely, physically; but then the sentences would move on, rushing past him like accelerating vehicles, he would be stalled way back there hearing only faraway sounds, and soon he would stop trying to catch up and simply sink down into his fog and watch the mouths move and whenever the mouths came to rest he would smile and say, "Uh-huh," and "Um-hm," hoping these would do. He did not want others to know how damaged he was. He did not want to hear that their memories were failing too. He had heard enough of that.

Sometime later he stopped trying to fake through. He began to talk about it compulsively, telling anyone who would listen exactly how it was with his head. Of course, it was a catharsis. But it was also a form of special pleading: It's not really *me*, you see, it's this thing that was done to my head. Later yet, he would learn to laugh it off. "Sorry, but I have a memory problem," he would say. "What were we just talking about?" But back then, it was a thing he had to hide.

The most awkward social moments came when people said, "Oh, a doctor? What kind of doctor?" Or: "What do you do?"

He could not say, "I do nothing."

He could not say, "I cannot work." For then they might wonder how it was that he was well enough to go to parties, but not to work.

When he said, "I am convalescing," they asked how long he had been convalescing ("A *year*?"), and why, and how long he would continue to convalesce before returning to normal life, which meant work, and he didn't know the answers. He did not know what to call himself, or what he could do, or when or if he might ever do it again.

"Well, pretty soon you'll be able to go back to work," Mason had said.

He had stared in horror at Peter's good, artless face. Back to work doing *what*? *Surgery*? Oh, yes, he would be swell in an operating room. *Hemostat. No, not the hemostat. Give me the uh . . . the uh . . . the whatchamacallit. Hold on, now, let's wait until my head clears.* . . . With somebody's exposed renal artery pulsating there in his hand . . . Or seeing patients in therapy? When he lost track in moments of whatever was being discussed?

The very thought of not being able to work again was intolerable. It engulfed him with guilt. Not to work! Where he had grown up, it was the sin of sins. Scum did not work. Basket cases did not work. Crazy people, senile people, worthless people, women (this legacy he had escaped) did not work.

For months this had been the pivotal issue in the psychiatrist's office: to throw off the burden of guilt and come to terms with himself as a worthwhile human being who did not work.

Russ, ordinarily a mild man, was fiery on this point. "Absolutely not!" he had said, and thumped his desk, when Hal, weak and woozy, had spoken through the months of returning to that pit where he had worked before—"I think I could cope with the stresses better now," he had said—or perhaps taking a job elsewhere. There had been offers. Money men, frothing, had spoken urgently to him of backing a national chain of sex-therapy clinics that he would direct. A fortune! they had told him. He had rejected them outright. But he had been beguiled when a large, good hospital in Long Island had asked if he would be interested in creating and chairing a well-financed department of sex research and therapy.

He had sat at his desk for days, trying to draft a reply. Yellow legal pads covered with drafts, disjointed sentences, execrable spelling . . . "I am curently recovering from cardiac surgery. But your offer interests me. I antisipate that within another two months I antisipate I will be ready to . . ."

It was impossible, anyway. "Absolutely not!" said Russ, knowing that this was not a man who could ever do any job by halves. "You have had two heart attacks"—we did not know back then of the third, during surgery—"and surgery that has left you with limited cardiac reserve and some degree of brain damage. You worked for twenty-five years. What more do you need? Do you need another heart attack? *It is okay not to work.* Don't you feel that you have earned the right to retire?"

No, of course he didn't. Retired? He could not even spit out the word. Not the son of Good Eddie, not all the sons of all the good fathers; for one could not be honorably retired, one could be retired only to the city dump. That message too was in their blood.

In his journal, which he kept with no consistency, he wrote:

A dream last night: I was working in the kitchen, washing dishes and feeling irritable. Walter [his former partner in the urology practice in Hartford] walked by and said, "Is he always like this?"

When I told it to Martha, she related it to our change in roles, my cleaning the kitchen and so forth. But when I verbalized it, I related it instantly to *the* kitchen, that damned kitchen where I tried to work, with that damned dog yapping and all my rages and frustrations of those times . . .

How it moldered in him, that kitchen! "I don't think it bothers me anymore," he told me often; while it gnawed like acid.

The psychiatrist Peron, who had taken over his Medical Center Sexuality Program, had had it handed to him like a Venus off the half-shell, called him for lunch. Peron did that occasionally. He was just being decent, Hal would say. He wasn't a bad fellow, really. It wasn't *his* fault that they had given him the program. Hal was always willing to reevaluate. Ah, but I, who pounced once and forever, knew better. Peron the chinless swindler asked my husband to lunch to pick his brain over the salad, and to dissolve his own guilts in the tea.

Hal went. This time, even he could find no silver lining. He wrote:

Lunch with Peron. He gives me a progress report on my program. New suite of offices, expanded staff. Plenty of money now. They got the grant for the research re impotence and sleep—my research idea.

He tells me he gave a paper at American Psychiatric Association meeting in Chicago. Paper was about the sleep cycle and sexual dysfunction, and he actually used my cases as examples.

I listen, smiling and nodding. Yet in me I cry out that this is all *my* work and *my* ideas. And I am so frustrated that I cannot do it, and that my role is not even acknowledged. I rage at those stealing bastards. And at the same time, another part of me says, What difference? I should be far removed from all of that by now. If I were truly "retired," I would not give a damn. Perhaps someday I won't. But today it hurt like hell. . . .

Later, when he had it worked out—not totally, never totally, but enough so that he could talk about it without wincing—we lay sprawled in the big bed one night, looking around and backward, and I said, "Was that the most painful thing for you, that retirement business?" And he said softly, as though talking to himself:

"No. The most painful thing was what happened to my mind. Nothing in my life was ever worse than that, or ever will be. But the retirement thing was bad. You take someone like myself, who was taught that you are what you achieve, you are what marks you get, you are what society says you are. I had been an 'A.' A *macher*, a leader in my profession, running around giving papers, getting kudos and green stamps. And suddenly your public persona is wiped off the board. And then, who are you?

"I used to wander through those blocks between home and the gym, asking myself: If who I am is what I can do, who am I? When I was Dr. Lear of Urology Associates, or Dr. Lear, head of the Medical Center Sexuality Program, that's who I was. But now, *who the fuck am I?* That question tortured me. It went round and round in my head day and night . . ."

Lying motionless there in the bed, I took one of my graceful flying leaps: "I could have told you. You are a man who is loved beyond measure by his wife and his children. That is a huge thing, to be loved as you are."

And, "Thank you, kid," he said. "That *is* a huge thing, and I always knew it and felt lucky for it. But it wasn't enough."

My God. He sounds like the women. I sound like the men. All those women who talked to me in one way or another over the years of the big Who Am I? Zoe, back there in Hartford, who had asked it of her husband, and he had said, "What kind of question is that? You are the wife of a man and the mother of three great kids." And "Yes, yes, I *know*," she had said, "but *that's not enough*."

So why do I speak to him, here, of love? Why should it be enough? For whom is it ever enough?

For me! For me!

". . . round and round in my head day and night, and I could never find an answer. I had gone from an 'A' to an 'F.' A disabled cardiac with a blown-out mind, useless, junk, an annoyance and an embarrassment to my culture, and I hadn't even had the grace to die. That was my perception of it—I mean, that is *real*: useless people are always an annoyance and an embarrassment to the culture, unless they are rich or decorative, and I was neither. [No, no, Hal, listen, you are *extremely decorative*.] That's *real*. What was wrong was my acceptance of it.

"Somehow I stumbled my way through that. I began to understand: I am *not* as society defines me. I am as I define myself. Hell, I'm pretty good. I don't need titles. I have intelligence. I have decent qualities. I have certain strengths and sensitivities. I am still a *mensch* I can be proud of."

"What made you think so?" I said, aching to hear it.

"I realized that I have more character than most people."

"Oh, now, Harold . . ." With my fingers I made the pitchfork sign, our old *American Gothic* joke.

"Bullshit. It's true," he said.

Aha! I loved it.

But that was later. Back then, when Mason had said, "Pretty soon you'll be able to go back to work," Hal had still been stumbling around in the debris of old values.

"Work?" he had said. Mason of course had splendid intentions. Your values are my values. Congratulations, you are about to become a man; again. But Russ had been tugging so long, so hard, in the other direction, and they had just begun to make progress, and now this. Hal was racked.

"I would love to go back to work," he said, "but I . . . Do you think . . . Peter, you *do* understand how badly I function? I'm almost a year post-op and I still can't remember. I can't learn. I can't do things you take for granted. Hell, I can't even drive a car."

"You can't *drive?*" Mason looked stunned. This, finally, was a calamity a native mind could grasp. "What do you *mean*, you can't drive?"

"I just can't."

"Why not?"

"I've been *telling* you, Peter. I get foggy."

He began to read about cerebral function and split-brain phenomena. Always he had been fascinated by the exquisite localization of brain functions. Delgado's bulls that would stop charging, instantly, when he pressed a button wired to certain parts of their brains. Those Yerkes monkeys that would start copulating wildly when researchers stimulated specific brain centers. In his own field, the crazy business with Parkinson's Disease: They had found a drug that relieved the symptoms and also, incidentally, activated the libido. Even advanced geriatrics who hadn't had a sexual impulse in years— they took this pill, stopped shaking and got horny. Why?

So little had been known about brain function until very recent years. What little had been learned was deductive, mostly, based on observation of trauma—what happened when people had strokes, or had parts of their brains blown away.

In right-handed people, the left side of the brain was dominant. Their speech centers were on the left side. If they had strokes and were paralyzed on the left, they couldn't talk. But if they were paralyzed on the right side, speech was unimpaired.

For left-handed people, these equations were murkier. In some the left side of the brain dominated; in others, the right. Hal himself was left-handed. Now he wanted to fathom precisely what parts of his brain had gone bad, and what functions they controlled.

He absorbed very little of what he read. But enough. He had spurts of insight. Suddenly he understood, or thought he understood, why he could not tell uptown from downtown; why he had felt no desire— none, which had perplexed him—to use the sculpture materials that I had bought him almost a year earlier. What did the two have in common, after all? Spatial relationships! It must be that injury had been done to that portion of his brain which controlled spatial relationships. Now, then, where was it located—left or right?

It was fun, in a way. It became not just a means of distancing himself but a sort of diagnostic game, a series of elegant puzzles to be solved. Isolate the symptom, pinpoint its source, devise a compensation mechanism. Okay, on to memory: where in those pale convolutions was it stored?

But as he plodded on, he realized that there was nothing whatever to be gained from being able to say, Ah, this must be left-side damage, this must be right-side damage. No arrow had pierced his brain. It had been more like buckshot. He envisioned it as micropellets knocking out brain cells diffusely, on both sides. Or as wires, God knew how many wires, that had somehow gotten pulled loose in the switchboard system. The damage had not been repaired—*yet*. There was always a *yet*.

And what difference, anyway? Left side, right side. What was, was.

So he put away the literature and continued making lists, which was the only way he could find to organize experience.

And he continued going to the gym, which was terrific.

The state of his mind never seemed to me anywhere near as bad as it did to him. I even thought that in purely intellectual terms, it was better than ever. He had always been a deeply reflective man. Now he had trouble finding the words, and trouble speaking them, and of course the bad memory made it hard to organize thought. But it did seem to me that his sheer thinking power had been somehow refined, as though by fire.

I told him this once. He laughed, not merrily.

And what did it matter, really, how I, with my pencil and my notes and my underwrought little comments on his improved thinking power, perceived his mental state? He lived there. It pained.

"Poor Mushie," he said once. "What a life you've got, stuck with me."

"Stuck! That's preposterous. I'd rather have my life with you than any other. I think I'm lucky."

"I think you're crazy."

"Then tell me: who has a better life? Jeanette, with her healthy husband? Margot, with her healthy lover? Elsa, with her . . ."

I named a half-dozen women we both admired, joylessly attached to men we admired not so much. He smiled. But I don't know that I ever convinced him.

His pain was altogether beyond my reach. I think he would rather have lived in an iron lung with his mind intact.

"I'm quite limited physically, but if I stay within my limits, I'm okay," he would say to friends. I heard him repeat it dozens of times, word for word, as the limits closed down inexorably from ten-block walks to five-block walks to one-block walks navigated with strain. And then, lying on the bed, speaking softly into the telephone mouthpiece: "I can't talk too long because it makes me short of breath. But if I stay within my limits, I'm okay."

That part was bearable. People adjust, however painfully, to such limits, and those who love them can comprehend the pain.

But the mind! "It doesn't *work*," he would cry out, banging his head with his fist as one bangs a broken vending machine.

He was locked into an incomprehensible state of brain damage in which he was utterly isolated from the understanding of his doctors, his family and his friends. This he bore alone.

He thought he was coping well. Even arrived at the point at which he could say, "I don't work," although he never quite managed the close-ended "I am retired."

Still, managing well enough, he thought.

Then, toward Christmas, he read an article in *New York* magazine. It had been written by Fred J. Cook, a solid journalist. It was titled "The Unnecessary Death of My Wife."

Julia Cook had undergone open-heart surgery for repair of a mitral valve. The job had been done in New York Hospital by the surgeon Paul Ebert, and apparently done well. But nobody had prepared Julia or her family for the terrors to which she might awaken: amnesia; disorientation; hallucinations (*temporary*, they assured the husband later, while the wife agonized that she was going crazy; *temporary*, and due no doubt to some momentarily imperfect mix of blood and oxygen from the heart-lung machine).

She had it all. She saw things that were not there. She forgot her husband's visits. She called him in the night to say that she had seen an accident in which their children had been killed. She feared that she was dying. She told the house staff that she felt "bubbles" in her head.

But the *clinical* reports were satisfactory, and so she was sent home, and scolded by a family physician, who knew bugger-all about such things, for her fears and her depression. She ought to be thrilled, he said, with such a fine surgical result. "This mental attitude of hers is a crock," he said.

Then had come a series of nightmarish mistakes, faulty communication, imprecise instructions for medications, inadequate monitoring of a powerful anti-coagulant that finally turned her blood to water, and days later she was dead.

Hal read it through. He grew increasingly distressed. He came to the part about the callousness of the doctors—"Oh, yeah, baby, that's how it is," he said to the dead Julia; and then to the part about the bubbles in her head, the memory loss, the fear that she was going mad, nobody, anywhere, to understand, and suddenly he broke.

"Oh, that poor woman, that poor woman, that poor woman, how she must have suffered!" he wept. And buried his head in the pages of the miserable thing and cried, finally, for the first time, and it was precisely as he had feared it would be: as though he might cry his very heart out.

"Did you read that article in *New York* magazine?" he asked Mason.

Peter shrugged. "Oh, you know how they sensationalize things. I'm sure it wasn't like that."

"How do *you* know it wasn't like that? How could you *possibly* know? A lot of it was like that for *me*."

He was himself taken aback by his outburst. He felt convulsed with rage. Not really at Mason, for Mason was at that moment mere metaphor. Rage at all of institutionalized medicine, that fat, cool, smug entrenchment in which he had lived his own professional lifetime, protected, as by a moat, from contact with anything more human than blood and bones. *You know how they sensationalize things.* Jesus!

Well, then, he said to himself, I have made no peace with it after all. I have a volcano in here, and I had better do something about it before it erupts.

He called a friend who was an expert on brain waves and biofeedback. Listed his own symptoms one two three, like a proper doctor.

"You are describing a classical case of organic brain damage," the friend said. "I think you should have a complete neurological workup."

The neurologist was thorough, a fine technician. Did the patient's knee jerk when hit with a percussion hammer? Did that quick probing across his body surface feel like a pin or a feather? When the soles of his feet were stimulated, did his toes bend forward or back? When his eyes were examined through an ophthalmoscope, what pathology was hidden there? The instrument could show minute distortions of the blood vessels inside the eyes. It could show increased pressure within the cranium, an abnormality, a disease—perhaps a tumor— within the brain itself.

"Gee, even your eye grounds are normal," the doctor said. He sounded disappointed. The history had fascinated him—an interesting case, he had said—and he had perhaps expected to peer into some high secret drama. He did not. He could make no diagnosis.

Hal sent him a letter later, asking if he had any recommendations. Guesses, suppositions, anything at all to help him cope with a disability that, despite the normal eye grounds, persisted.

The neurologist sent back a cordial platitude. Patience, he wrote;

time heals. As to *what* time might heal, there was no clue. His will hardened.

"I do not accept that I can't get an evaluation," he told Russ. "I need a thorough testing with someone who has worked with brain-damaged people."

Russ made inquiries. A neurologist at an uptown hospital specialized in interpretation of psychological tests. Her reputaton was superb.

Immediately Hal made an appointment.

"Are you sure you want to do this?" I said. Uneasy, not knowing quite why.

"Yes. I want to know what happened to my mind. I don't care what I find out, but I've got to know."

"What do you expect to find out?"

"That I have organic brain damage. I trust my own diagnosis, no matter what the others say. But I need more. I need an honest evaluation. I need to learn how to cope with it."

The consultation was in two parts. For the first he went alone. He gave the doctor all of it: the D-O-E-S and the memory fade-outs, the spatial confusions, the supermarket fiascos, the crisis of Maxwell's Plum and a dozen other such; the imporous fog.

"Okay," she said. "How does all this affect your functioning now?"

"Well. There was something . . . I'm not sure when. I think this morning."

Yes, just that morning. A typical, trifling, crazy-making thing.

The day before, we had bought a silk scarf for my mother. He himself had chosen it, rifling patiently through the piles until he found one that he thought would suit her especially well.

And in the morning, just hours ago, he had seen that scarf lying on my bureau and he had picked it up and held it to the light and said, "Oh, this is pretty. When did you get it?"

The doctor nodded. She called in a psychologist, and they got to work: memory-scale tests, attention-span tests, perception tests, word association, image association, time-and-place orientation, progressive-number tests. He grew increasingly fatigued. In some exercises he had to write for extended periods, with time limits. His hands began to shake, his writing became illegible, the sweat poured, the fog descended. Finally he said, "I'm sorry. I can't. I've got to stop and rest," and put his head down on the desk.

"Don't apologize," she said.

She told him little stories which he had to tell back. He listened hard, but had trouble in the retelling. And in the paired-word test, he saw instantly that unless the words were related in some obvious way, he was lost.

"Finger—hand," she said. "Radiator—green. Salt—pepper. East—west. Rock—shoe. Now tell me: Finger . . ."

"Hand."

"Radiator . . ."

"Hot. No. I can't remember."

"Salt . . ."

"Pepper."

"East . . ."

"West."

"Rock . . ."

"Uh . . . uh . . . uh . . . I don't know."

She repeated that test three times. He flunked each time.

The session lasted two hours. At the end, she said, "You have a marked verbal-memory problem. There are standard coping mechanisms. The most useful one you seem to have developed on your own."

"What is that?"

"Making lists."

Lists. For this he didn't need her. His pockets were full of lists.

"Another is to make word and idea associations. You do that to some degree already. And I have a third suggestion: Try using visual imagery. When you have to go somewhere, or do something, close your eyes and visualize each detail of it as fully as possible."

He came home exhausted and discouraged.

"It was very hard. I don't think I did well," he said.

"What sort of tests were they?"

He didn't remember much. Except for one test, which he recalled very well. He had been given partial sentences to complete. One sentence said, "I feel guilty about . . ."

And immediately, reflexively, he had scrawled, "being sick."

They were to meet again three weeks later. In the interim he worked hard on the memory exercises. Sometimes I worked with him.

"Street—pear," I would say, and he would shut his eyes tight and concentrate on the image of a pear-shaped street.

Setting out to meet someone for lunch at the Plaza, he visualized, in as lavish detail as he could muster, the facade and precise placement of the hotel; the glass canopy; the fountain that fronted it; the movie house that sat there to the side, just past Bergdorf's windows; the horse-drawn carriages lined up along Central Park. It seemed to help.

I went with him to the second session.

The doctor began with the old paired-word test.

"Radiator . . ."

"Green," he said promptly; yes, green grass in the sun might feel warm, like a radiator.

"Salt . . ."

"Pepper."

"Rock . . ."

"*Shoe.*"

"*Good.* I see you've been doing your homework." She gave him another paired-word test, harder. He did rather well. "Now, then . . ." she fanned out a deck of picture cards. "Now, tell me the names of these things."

"Glove. Bagpipe. Typewriter. Clock. Onions. Ah . . . ah . . . xy . . . xy"—banging the table with his fist—"xy-lo . . ."

"Yes, go on."

"Xy-lo-*phone.*"

"Good!"

And then to color cards. And then to block-letter cards, and number cards.

"Colors and objects are generally harder than numbers and letters," she said.

Harder for *what?* I wondered. For *whom?*

"I'm beat," he said when they were done.

She shook her head. "This easy fatigue may be partly because of your heart, but I think it's also cerebral," she said. "You get a diminution of blood flow to the brain. I don't know why we disassociate mental from physical things. If I put you on a bicycle now, you would huff and puff and not be at all surprised."

He knew that, of course. No need to be a doctor to know that. But it was the first time that any clinician had spoken to him reasonably of the mind–body connection, and he was comforted. There would be no patronizing here. She would be straight.

"Well, what can you tell me?"

"I'll send you a full report, but I can already tell you that you were a very accurate diagnostician of your own problem, Dr. Lear. You have organic brain damage."

The room was still. He nodded Yes into the silence.

"Do you know what caused my brain damage?"

"Sure." Just like that. A year of denials, artful dodges, shoulder pattings, kitchy-koo, and now, *Sure.* "Your severe hypotension post-surgically. The parts of the brain that have to do with memory are the most vulnerable to hypotension. The brain cells that were damaged are the same cells as are affected in the normal aging process. It's the classic pattern we find in senile people. The symptoms you reported are to the letter what a man in his seventies will say to me when he comes in complaining about his memory."

Images of senility doddering into the tiny room. Pervasive smells of senility. What a brutal thing to tell him! Is this supposed to be comforting? Validating? Some esoteric form of therapy? *What?* It took me a long while, because I myself wanted euphemisms, to accept that she was saying not merely doctor to doctor but person to person, respectfully, what had to be said.

"Is it reversible?"

"No. Compensatory, yes. But not reversible."

We walked down Broadway in the cold dusk, he so silent, and I asked if he didn't want to get a cab and he shook his head No and we walked on like that, holding hands tightly, and finally I said, "You said you'd feel better if you could get an honest evaluation. . . ."

And he said, "Yes. And I do. But I'm sad."

Brain damage. Compensatory, but not reversible. It was no triumph of self-validation.

The doctor's report came later. It read in part:

. . . There is little question in my mind that this loss of memory function followed upon the period of prolonged hypotension coupled with fever which you described to me as having taken place during your long stay in the Intensive Care Unit. This is not directly a "post-surgical" situation and therefore one can understand the reaction of many physicians in stating that your particular problem did not follow the pattern of the open-heart surgery mental syndrome. Indeed it did not, for it followed the pattern of the sequelae of severe hypotension exacerbated by fever. You have already done a very good job of giving yourself lessons in compensatory therapy and since you have so many intact mechanisms I have every confidence that you will continue to improve, although I am fatalistic enough to state that I am sure you will not regain ease and automaticity of new-learning or recent-memory functions . . .

And though he knew that her diagnosis was right, he was less certain than she of the cause. Yes, it could have been the hypotension. It could also have been—he hated the thought, shrank from it, but it persisted—a mistake: some minute, monumental, brain-cell-killing mistake made with the anesthesia.

He wrote to the anesthetist, asking for particulars. He never got an answer.

He did not show the neurologist's report to his doctors. It could only make them defensive, and to what point?

> . . . although I am fatalistic enough to state that I am sure you will not regain ease and automaticity of new-learning and recent-memory functions . . .

He took the fancy phrase between his teeth and gnashed it like a hound, down to the bone splinters: Could he still learn?

She had said it was compensatory. Then he would compensate.

Start small. At the Metropolitan Museum, at the grandest exhibit of Impressionist paintings ever assembled.

He went four times; I tagged along, marveling at a tenacity I could never have brought to this enterprise, or to any other. I think in his place I might have said, What I know, I know, and if my learning days are done, the hell with it. Peace. But he!

The first time, he rented one of those talk-along gadgets that deliver a taped lecture as the viewer proceeds through the galleries. He moved slowly, oblivious of the jostling queues, pausing to stare at each painting as Hoving's taped voice spoke soothingly into his ear: *Now, in this monumental work by Monet, note how the plane of the horizon tilts toward you. Compare this with the earlier work in Gallery Three, in which we saw* . . . And he pushed his way back into Gallery Three, working against the traffic, to make the comparison; but by the time he got there, he'd forgotten what he had seen in Gallery Four, and he was exhausted.

He bought the catalogue and studied it at home, for hours.

On the second visit, he again rented the taped lecture and repeated the entire procedure.

On the third, he hugged in close to each canvas, staking it out, resisting elbows. He lip-read each label repeatedly, trying not to memorize it but to extract its thought process and move from this into his own thought process: Ah, yes, ah, yes, here we see the influence of Cézanne, and this is why, and furthermore, I think . . . pausing often to rest on benches, sitting with his eyes shut, hoarding visions.

By the fourth visit, standing back from the paintings and asking himself, How does this compare with what I just saw, and what do I think about it, and why? he found with elation that he knew a great deal more than he had known when he began. It was not simply that he could remember. He could learn.

I think he would have gone back a fifth time, and a tenth, but the grand stepped approach to the Metropolitan seemed a bit steeper on the last visit; he was puffing slightly when he got to the top, and puffing more as he went through the galleries, and the puffing interfered with his concentration.

Still, he was high. "My mind *is* getting better. I'm *sure* of it," he said.

But then we walked out of Lincoln Center one night, with the snow coming down heavy and the wind blowing hard, we were striding along the great plaza into the wind, and I said, "Oh, Hal, isn't it wonderful that we can do these things, go to the theater and walk in this wind!" and suddenly he dead-stopped and began to cry, because he realized that he could remember nothing, absolutely nothing, about the play we had just seen. He stood there with a white knit hat tilted over one eye, jaunty, and the tears freezing on his cheeks.

"Oh, Mushie, please tell me the truth. Is my mind *really* getting better, do you think?" he said.

And I put my arms about him, wanting in that old way to gather him in, to shield him from the wind and from the pain, and said, "*Of course* it's getting better, darling!"

But what or how did I know? I didn't know.

I gave a party for him on the first anniversary of his surgery, shortly before his fifty-fifth birthday.

I had billed it as a combination birthday and rebirthday, and the rebirthday part of it went to my head and I made a toast, which was not at all my sort of thing to do. I toasted my husband, who sat there looking marvelous, boyish somehow, belying his innards. I toasted his doctors and our friends and the graces and the fates, going on at some martini-propped length about my appreciations; hell, I would have toasted my enemies that night, and maybe I did; and afterward Moses said, "You're some woman"—such a silly little thing, but it pleased me inordinately: the *doctor*, who dealt constantly with nervous wives and incipient widows, saluting this wife for her courage, her stamina, her style . . . Earthwoman. Oh, nice.

When they had all left, we made love. It was slow and quiet, and it seemed to me exquisite, open in every pore, an extension of the sense of gratitude that had pervaded the evening.

He didn't tell me how much it tired him. He didn't tell me that hours earlier, feeling unaccountably short of breath and not wanting to spoil the party, he had gone quietly into our bedroom and popped an extra diuretic.

He did that often, quietly. On his last birthday, there in the hospital, they had given him 40 milligrams of diuretics intravenously and he had gone into near-shock. Now he was taking 80 milligrams a day, two pills, and it was like nothing. The body adapts. And when it didn't seem quite enough, when he felt a bit dyspneic—short of breath—which meant that the two pills hadn't wrung quite enough fluid out of him, he simply did as he did that night, popped an extra pill, and usually he didn't tell me. Why tell me? It might have made me nervous, earthwoman that I was.

The transition was slow and subtle. In later winter he noticed, almost casually, that it seemed to be getting more difficult to walk to the gym. The hills were growing a bit steeper, the distances longer, the rest periods more frequent. He began changing his route to avoid the hills.

"I must be redeveloping my muscles. I've gained five pounds," he said one day. And then, slowly: "I don't know what it is, but I don't seem to have the strength I did. I get awfully tired walking home. . . ."

In fact he looked a bit bloated. I didn't know, then, what it meant to look bloated. And more and more often, there were comments on the tiredness, the shortness of breath. But nothing dramatic.

They talked of cutting back on his diuretics, since he seemed to be doing so well. And he, Dr. Lear, sitting in on these consultations about the patient, said, "No, I don't think we should cut back. I really don't think I'm doing all that well."

"You're swimming every day? Marvelous!"

"Yes. It is marvelous. But I can only swim a few yards. Then I get short of breath."

"Riding the exercycle a mile a day? Great!"

"Yes. But then my pulse is at 110 and my breath is coming hard."

Through the winter they had encouraged him to exercise.

"It's good, it's good, you'll strengthen the heart muscle," Silverman would say. And Mason: "Walk to the gym every day, no matter what the weather. Walk briskly."

Often Mason urged him to go to another gym as well. A place that specialized in cardiac rehabilitation.

"On the same day as I go to the Y?"

"Sure! Sure! It's good for you!"

Several times Peter asked, "Have you gone to that gym yet?"

"No. Not yet."

"Oh, Hal." Disappointment, faint reprimand. "You really should. It would help build you up."

"I'm sorry. I don't feel strong enough now. Maybe next month."

His cousin Frankie was dying of cancer, in Boston. It was a long, bad show, with many intermissions and remissions, moving now into its final act. They had been close as boys and had grown apart as adults. But cancer tugs at old family ties, cancer pulls them taut, and now Frankie was calling often to say that he was ever so much better and to ask, lightly, "Do you think you can get up here soon? I'd really love to see you," and for weeks Hal had been saying, "Maybe next week, Frankie. As soon as the snow lets up," and never feeling quite strong enough to make the trip.

But Frankie's voice was getting lighter and lighter, and Hal decided to put it off no more.

He wanted to go alone. That seemed right. I hardly knew Frankie.

It was the first time he had been out of New York since his illness. The simple logistics of taking a cab to LaGuardia, walking to the gate, boarding the plane seemed not simple at all. He felt weak when they took off and weaker yet when they landed at Logan, and he arrived at Frankie's house light-headed, with his pulse racing; and it was dreadfully hard to behave in a natural way, not only because of how he felt but because of how Frankie looked, lying in the bedroom that had been transformed into a hospital room, with the bed that went up and down electrically. He had known, of course, how Frankie would look, he had anticipated precisely this degree of ravage, but it is always worse in the flesh than in the mind's eye. He shook Frankie's emaciated hand and said, "Well," and Frankie said, "Well, well," both of them smiling hard.

Hal was looking like no prize either. Frankie's wife, Rhoda, had not expected, she told me later, that he would look so . . . *fragile*. Maybe he should rest for a while, she said, and they could visit after, and Hal said Yes, he could use a spot of rest, and went into the guest room and collapsed on the bed and cried.

As he lay in the dusk, coexistent with the sadness and the familial sense of loss, sensations that were soft and predictable, and to which he had already given himself over, there was this sudden guilt, out of nowhere, and so harsh and of such an intensity that it made him writhe and moan on the bed.

Guilt. Guilt. He could not stop Frankie's cancer. Soon Frankie would die and he himself would not, at least not *necessarily*, at least not so soon; but Frankie, yes; necessarily.

They had dinner in the bedroom, for Frankie could not move much since they'd severed a nerve to stop the pain in his leg, and they talked, of course, of the past. They no longer had much in common but the past. On this occasion it was enough. Those summers at the family cottage, when they'd competed to see who could pee the best trajectory and Uncle Eddie had given them all an exegesis on the proper pee, demonstrating there in the side of the bowl—talk like that, with much laughter.

Then Frankie, whose voice had grown more vital now, and whose sunken eyes had taken on a glow, wanted to go through the family picture album.

So they sat with the pictures. There were the elders, all gone now, and themselves as children, in the bathing suits with striped tank tops. And Hal, turning the pages, peering at faces he had not seen for decades, remembered when he had closed the summer place after his mother's death and had gone through her old picture albums and wondered, Why am I saving these? Who will want to inherit them from me? Why should anyone want them? These pale images, which were meant to immortalize, trivialized instead. For no face pasted into these pages would any longer mean anything to anyone.

He left in the morning. Frankie wanted him to take a tie. "*Please.* Look through the rack and pick one out. What do you like? Blue? Brown? I've got so many ties," Frankie said, "I just don't know what to do with them."

So Hal picked a tie and put it on, feeling guilty. He embraced what was left of Frankie, and promised to return soon for another visit, and flew home and lay on his own bed fingering the tie. Not a sweater, not a belt, but a *tie*—had Frankie understood that? Of course not.

Frankie would never, knowingly, play to any grandstand. Frankie was as discreet as his foulards.

It worried me, the look of him and the way he was breathing.

"Perhaps it was a mistake to go," I said.

But as it turned out, he had gone just in time. The next day, Frankie died.

I too felt the guilt. I felt it whenever I talked to Rhoda, who mourned with grace, as I felt I could never mourn. I wondered whether somewhere beneath the grace, so deep beneath that she herself might not have been conscious of it at all, she resented that Frankie had died and Hal lived. I felt awkward, always, when she said, "How is he doing?" and I said, "He could be better," because I wondered if she might not be thinking, as surely I would think in her place, what is this woman complaining about? Her husband still lives. It was a thing I would experience often with widowed friends. When it became too disquieting I avoided them, or chose to believe that this was why I avoided them. A certain shame, a nagging: Does she resent me for not being the widow?

Of course, it may never have entered their thoughts. Only mine.

After that, Hal started taking cabs to the gym.

"If I walk, I'm too tired to exercise when I get there," he said.

"Maybe you're trying to do too much exercise."

"I don't know. Peter and Moe seem to think I should do more."

He complained again of the shortness of breath. They examined him and heard faint râles. That is left heart failure, when the left ventricle is not pumping as well as it should, and fluid pools up in the lung tissue. Right heart failure is when the right ventricle cannot pump fluid from the rest of the body strongly or quickly enough, and a swelling may begin in the legs. Hal was a little wet, they said. This is the language of heart failure—"a little wet," "a little moisture in there"; in severe cases, "bubbling." He had been a little wet before. It was to be expected with a heart as damaged as his. We must be careful about his fluid intake. And was I watching his salt intake? These are the questions for the wives, paramedicals in the kitchen. Oh, yes, I said. I no longer used any salt at table or in food preparation, and I had learned to mask the blandness with garlic, ginger, herbal consolation prizes. Yes, I was watching the salt intake carefully. "Well, be even more careful," Mason said.

They increased his diuretics. On three pills a day, 120 milligrams, he was no longer short of breath, but very weak. Washed out, literally. They switched to three pills a day for five days and two for two days. On that regimen he was erratic. One day he would walk a half-mile with no symptoms. The next, he could hardly walk at all. They continued switching dosages in search of a winning combination, at least a tenable combination, and it continued to elude them. He went up and down like a yo-yo.

At one point he felt well for forty-eight hours. His spirits rose readily to the occasion.

"I think we've reached a homeostasis," he said.

I put a message on his desk:

> Home the place is
> Where homeostasis.

He put a message on mine:

> Homeostasis
> Is going places.
> Movie tonight?

But by evening, he was too weak for the movies.

He made a note to himself:

> So little resiliency. *Why?* Potassium deficiency? Electrolyte imbalance? Are diuretics washing trace elements out of my system? Why do I feel better after eating? Possibly food replaces trace elements. Possibly change in blood-sugar level—any bearing there? Must discuss with Moe and Peter. . . .

One morning I woke to find him standing at my bedside with a glass of orange juice. A good sign. Always, whichever of us woke first brought the orange juice to the other. It had been a long while since he had wakened first.

"You're feeling all right?" I asked cautiously.

"Not all right. Fantastic. I feel *fantastic*, Mushie. I think we've turned a corner."

Sick was okay and okay was good and good was fantastic. We were always turning corners. These were the siren songs he sang, and for a time I was beguiled. "I'm well, Mushie. I'm over the sickness." "You promise?" "I promise." Ah, Hal, sing another song of safety. You're a doctor, you surely know the tune. But as we kept turning corners and winding up in dangerous places, I stopped trusting. Tin-eared bastard, you'll wreck us both. There are *rocks* out there.

Feeling fantastic, he went off for a haircut. A half-hour later he was back, staggering, and he looked like a walking fraternity prank. On one side his hair was neatly trimmed and shaped. On the other side it stood out in great wet clumps and cowlicks.

"Hal, what ever . . .? You've been *butchered*."

Sitting in the barber's chair, with the scissors clicking about his ears, he'd been stricken suddenly by a great faintness. He had known that he was about to lose consciousness, and had ducked his head down between his knees to bring the blood back to his brain.

The spell had passed in moments. Afterward, he had said, "I don't feel well. We'd better stop now."

"You don't want me to finish the shaping?" A terrible consternation. How could they let such a head walk out into the street? "Maybe if you rest a few minutes . . ."

"No. Not today. Just let me pay you and get out."

They had conferred, and charged him $6. Half-price for a half-head. He had walked home. The air had helped, he said.

"Shouldn't we call Peter?"

"No need. It's probably just hypotension. If I eat something, I'll be fine."

The next evening we sat with guests, talking quietly. Suddenly he began to gasp. He was struggling to breathe, opening his mouth wide to suck in oxygen. I'd never seen such a thing before. It was dreadful to watch. "Air hunger" he called it.

It passed shortly. Just a bit of heart failure, he said, a little *moisture in there*. And in fact it had been of such brief duration, and he seemed so well in its wake, that we agreed, my fingers itching to press all panic buttons, to do nothing until morning.

In the morning, he got up and dressed for the gym.

"Won't you at least call the doctor?" Oh, how dreary to hear myself nagging. I am sick of the sound of my own voice nagging; I have nagged so much of late and it gets his back up.

"Okay," he said. Translation: I feel sick.

They heard no râles. *Dry as a bone*, they said. No sign of failure. Perhaps he had developed an irregular heartbeat. That could have caused the episode.

They fitted him out with a portable cardiac monitor, a recent technological triumph. Of course, Silverman's office had one of the first in the city. The beauty part, they explained, was that you could wear it strapped about the body just like this, it went under a jacket with diffidence, you could wear it to a restaurant, to the theater, anywhere. Whenever there was a change in the heartbeat, the monitor emitted a beep; then all you had to do was press this button, and automatically the machine would start printing out an electrocardiogram. So you wear it for the weekend, eating, sleeping, everything, and next Monday morning you bring it back and we simply read the tape.

We went that night to a dinner party in our apartment building. He was pale and quiet. Suddenly, over cocktails, a distinct beep emanated from the vicinity of his jacket. I jumped, sloshing my drink. Another beep. Conversation faltered. Several guests looked at him sternly, then away, as though suspecting that he had passed gas. I saw a hand resting casually at his wrist, and knew that he was taking his pulse. Then the hand pressed mine. Nothing to worry about, he whispered. Probably a sudden body movement had activated the machine; his pulse was completely regular.

At dinner the talk turned to politics—ghosts of Watergate still hovered, then, over many dinner tables—to Nixon and his crew, some already in prison, some still in the midst of plea bargainings. There were several corporation lawyers at the table. Our building was full of them, tall thin men in vested suits striding out each morning with their attaché cases, en route to The Street; and one of them had gone to law school with the long-dishonored Kleindienst, and he knew that his old school buddy was innocent. And how did he know that? I asked. Why, because the man had *told* him so; and if there was one thing he himself knew, would stake his life on, he said, as his wife sat there digging fork tines into the damask, it was that this old buddy of his would never tell a lie.

Ah, come on, I said. Our hostess sat stiffly with nostrils aquiver, sniffing smoke. I liked her and wished her party well, but still. Must we simply sit here listening to this twit? Ah, come on. Your honorable old buddy, who got off with a mere misdemeanor, perjured himself plenty. Those transcripts in the *Times* and the *Post* . . . My point *exactly*, he said: the *Times*, the *Post*, *Newsweek* too, pinko sheets, pinko editors, crucifying honorable men, and Nixon, poor Nixon, history would show that he was the best . . . You've got to be *kidding*, I said. Can you really believe that that wretched deceitful man . . . And didn't *you* once work for the *Times*, Mrs. Lear? he said, unctuous as the hollandaise; so you know about those pinkos, I don't have to tell *you* . . . Listen, I said, no offense, but that is the most monumentally dumb . . . As our hostess darted up like a fawn and said, Uh, uh, why don't we go into the living room, and not too slowly they all drifted from the table, my husband drifting with the twit's wife, as though to apologize to her for my crassness, and we sat on, nose to nose, he smirking and his voice corporation-law steady while mine rose and trembled with indignation. And I'll bet you're a feminist, too, he said; I must say you people have some strange notions. . . . My God, I said, I can't *believe* this. . . . Some *very* strange notions, Mrs. Lear. . . . Why, you dodo! Almost shouting now. Are you *real*? Can you smell *coffee*? Can you *possibly* be as dumb as you *sound*? . . . And on and on like that, going rapidly out of control, until suddenly I heard my own voice moving to the very edge of a scream, and I stopped abruptly, and listened to the timbre of it, and wondered, Why am I getting so crazy? Why am I sitting here trading cretinous insults? And in a moment's small insight, but I was always grateful for whatever size I could get, I realized that it had nothing to do with him. Absolutely nothing. I was raging at the bloody *beep*, coiled up and waiting to spring at the next sound of the *beep*, I was angry at the *beep*, angry at Hal's symptoms, angry at Hal's heart, angry at Hal's sickness, angry at *Hal*, with his ceaseless siren songs, Getting Better, Turning Corners, Feel Fantastic, No More Fog . . .

Oh, this is dangerous. Deal with it later. Merely accept, for the moment, that what is going on here is a mess of displaced rage.

And accepting this, I uncoiled myself and said to the twit, Why don't we join the others? and refused to be further engaged.

My hostess said it was quite all right, there was nothing she liked better than a lively table. But I don't know that she ever forgave me.

Later, in the bed, in the dark, I tried to face it down. Angry at *Hal*? Oh, this is a worm I never knew was in me. This is monstrous. Anger against the disease, yes. Against the card we drew, yes. But against *Hal*! What do I do with such anger?

And finally I said, "I must tell you something because I can't manage it alone. I realized tonight that I resent you for being sick."

"No shit," he said.

"But it's obscene!"

"Stop breast-beating. It's normal."

He stayed asymptomatic through the weekend. "What I had was heart failure," he said. "They won't find any rhythm irregularities."

On Monday, he returned the cardiac monitor. No rhythm irregularities.

On Tuesday, he turned another corner.

Chapter 22

O N Tuesday he turned the corner from the psychiatrist Russ's office into Third Avenue, walking fast and thinking hard. He felt vital. It had been an animated session.

The episode had been heart failure, he'd told Russ. He was sure of it. He was sure that his doctors had missed a diagnosis, mucking around with that portable monitor. Well, all right. It was easy to miss. The episode had been transient; by the time they listened to his lungs he had been clear. But he, the patient, had given them a classic description of failure; they should have listened to the patient, and he was not only a patient but a doctor; he knew failure, the sound and the look of it, he had seen it often enough. . . .

And further, he was sure that he did not have to bounce around like a yo-yo. He did not have to feel so sick and lethargic. There were precise correlations between the sickness and the pills. He was sure that the sickness was to some degree iatrogenic—caused by the treatment itself: too much treatment, too little treatment, wrong treatment, he didn't know what, but he knew it was caused by the treatment.

And he knew all about the perils of being one's own doctor, but still, he could not *stop* being a doctor, he could not simply lie back, unquestioning, and surrender himself to sickness and to their earnest gropings. . . . And Russ had been fiercely supportive. Yes, absolutely, he had said, you must keep an active role in your own care. For Russ understood, as he himself understood, that this was a patient who needed urgently, an urgent characterological need, to feel in control of his affairs; and Russ understood too that this patient was a damned good doctor.

Anyway, the episode is over, Russ had said. You are not in failure now. Perhaps it will not recur.

Perhaps, the patient had said. But I wouldn't bet on it. Failure does not come from nothing. Failure comes from something. *Something happened.*

So now he took the corner briskly, thinking about all this, and suddenly, out of nowhere, it hit him. Suddenly he was gasping, leaning against a storefront for support, pulling air as hard and as fast and as deep as he could and still not nearly enough coming in, mouth clawing at air, and then he heard the wheezings begin, he felt his lungs filling with fluid, he felt the fluid bubbling deep inside him, he knew he could not walk, he thought if he got off his feet his distress might subside, and somehow he managed to get himself into a cab and gasp out his home address.

I'd been out. The doorman got to me first: "Dr. Lear just came home. He's not feeling well."

Panic.

Then Siegfried, the elevator operator: "Dr. Lear no could . . . He no could"—casting about in his German head for the proper word and then retreating into pantomime, clutching his chest and panting elaborately—"but ve help him valk. He iss *bet*-ter now. . . ."

I broke into the apartment shouting his name. No answer. I found him sitting like an angle iron on the bed, propped high against pillows, white, gasping. He couldn't talk. Instead he winked; a fat, fruity wink. *Give her a sign,* Moses had said, in those bad hours after the surgery, *to show her you're all right.*

Of course I knelt by the bed and began to cry. He winks, I cry. He needs me like a poison. Of course he patted my head.

"Have you called the doctors?" He shook his head No. "Have you any pain?" *No,* emphatically. "Shall I call them now?" Yes.

Both doctors were with patients, the receptionist said. Was this urgent?

214

"Hal, they're busy. Is this urgent?" Of course this is urgent; how can it not be urgent? But let him decide; give him that.

He shrugged. Semiurgent.

"Not urgent but important. Ask them to call back as soon as they can."

We sat and waited for the call, smiling at each other.

"Boring," he said.

"*Damn* boring. Listen, Hal, you need a new act." Oh, my, what a WASPy crisis. This is not my style at all. I would do better with an *Oy gevalt*. I would sooner rip a few buttons and wail *Oy gevalt*, as my mother did. But he would not like that. His mother had never done that.

The intercom buzzed from the lobby. A gentleman to see Dr. Lear. He says it's Chelsea from the gym.

"You want him to come up?"

He nodded Yes.

And there was Chelsea, of whom I'd heard so much, a hulk with a large, ruddy face etched by depression, shoulders hunched by depression, giving me a small depressed smile and, with his great paw, a defeated shake. ". . . haven't seen Doc at the gym for a while, the boys were a little worried, just thought I'd drop by . . ."

He followed me into the bedroom. Hal, who sat gasping still, gave him a sprightly salute, and "Oh, my, oh, my, oh, my," said Chelsea, cracking his big knuckles, "I was afraid of this, I'm so afraid of this, I'm so afraid . . ."

Come on, Chelsea. Get hold of yourself, Chelsea. And Chelsea starting to sob now, soft, depression-smothered sobs, and Hal gasping, "Chelsea, it's okay, it's going to be okay," and suddenly Hal in paroxysm again, desperately sucking air again, wheezing: "Oxygen."

Oxygen. Where? How? Should I breathe into his mouth, as he had breathed into my father's mouth? Should I lie him down, pinch his nose, what?

I came toward him and he waved me away. "In the closet."

Oh, yes. In the closet. He'd ordered a canister the week before, a twenty-minute supply, and shown me how to administer it. "You never know," he had said, knowing.

I got out the squat green thing and fumbled with the dial. "Easy," he wheezed; even I could hear the râles. "No rush." I got the mask on his face and he began pulling deep, fast swigs of the stuff, and there was Chelsea, wringing his paws and moaning, "What can I do, what can I do, what can I do?"

You can shut up. You can shut up. You can shut up. *Oy gevalt.*

"It's amazing," he said in the cab to the emergency room, the canister cuddled like a pet in his arms. "I feel completely well now. It's over."

And you can shut up too. No more siren songs for me.

So he was back in the hospital again. I hadn't reckoned on that. Death, yes, but not another hospitalization.

Acute heart failure, they said. They told him, when they examined him upon admission, that he had loud râles at the base of both lungs.

That first day was a pip.

They gave him a huge dose of potassium. The stuff burns. It should be given with food or drink. They gave it to him with neither, and sent him downstairs for a lung scan, an hour-long procedure in which the patient lies motionless on a hard, flat table. Midway through it he began to develop pain, and by the time they wheeled him back to his room, he was writhing.

"I have terrible stomach pains," he told them; and Hal had high tolerance for pain. "I need something to drink."

"You can't have anything." He was scheduled for certain tests, X-rays, that required an empty stomach. "You're on N.P.O. [*nil per os:* nothing by mouth] until after the tests."

"But I must have fluids to relieve this pain."

"The orders are N.P.O. Do you want a shot for the pain?"

"No, damn it, I don't want a shot! I want fluid to keep this stuff from burning a hole in my stomach!"

"Sorry."

In a rage he called Mason's office. "If they don't give me fluids I'm going to disconnect the I.V. and get the hell out of here," he said.

All right, Mason told the nurses' station: give him fluids.

Soon a nurse came with fruit juice and a resident behind her, purple to be countermanded: "Dr. Lear, I don't understand what you expect us to—"

"What I expect you to do? I'll *tell* you what I expect you to do. I expect you to know what you're doing, *that's* what I expect you to do." He reared forward so violently that the cardiac monitor by his bed came to life. "If you have me on N.P.O., either you postpone the potassium or you postpone the tests. But you do not, you do not *ever*, give a corrosive substance to a patient A.C. [*ante cibum:* before eating]. You could burn the mucous membrane. You could cause an ulceration. You could cause a perforation. That is gross ignorance. That is indefensible treatment. That is *malpractice*. That is . . ."

Good, Hal! Give it to him! Show him who's the doctor! Fuming and blasting; these fumes warm my heart. Pompous punks who have been nowhere, know nothing, they're not accustomed to being called on their mistakes; no back talk from these beds, just *cases* lying in these beds, scared, passive, deferential, Yes, Doctor, No, Doctor, Thank you, Doctor, If you say so, Doctor . . . Oh, Hal, why can't it be he lying here and you standing there? Hit him again!

". . . that is total disregard for the welfare of the patient. And the name of this game, goddamn it, is *the welfare of the patient*. Do you understand *that?*"

The resident pivoted and stomped out.

Later Peter came. Edgy, shy. "I hear you've been making trouble."

"Trouble! For Christ's sake, Peter—"

"Hal, I know. I know. It shouldn't have happened. But you know how it is in a teaching hospital, advantages and disadvantages . . ."

Indeed he knew. Every attending physician knew. The advantages were around-the-clock medical coverage, continuity of care, a swarm of residents and interns who knew the case exceedingly well. The disadvantage was that they had authority and inexperience, no winning combination. And it was not easy for the attending physician, especially a tender attending physician like Peter here, who liked very much to be liked, not just by his patients but by the house staff, and the house staff did not like an attending physician who countermanded their orders. The house staff could make life better or worse for an attending physician, and for his patients too. It was bad politics to antagonize the house staff.

". . . and disadvantages, you know that. So please try to ride with it. Okay, Hal?" he said, and flashed a tense grin, and left.

"Let *his* stomach ride with it," Hal said.

Next came a medical student to draw blood.

"I understand you're a doctor," the student said, busying himself with the tourniquet.

Hal nodded.

"I'm always nervous around doctors. I hope I don't have trouble getting this needle in."

"Don't be nervous. You won't have trouble."

The boy jabbed in the needle and perforated clear through the vein. They both watched glumly as blood began spreading beneath the skin.

"There," he said. "You see? I *told* you I'd have trouble."

"That's all right. Try it again."

Again he perforated. "Darn!" he said.

"Relax. Look, just angle it in right here. . . ."

But the boy couldn't do it. His hand trembled. He apologized profusely and left the room, and minutes later a nurse came in and went *ping ping* and the needle came to rest neatly within the vein.

Soon there was a large swelling in the crook of his arm. The nurse applied compresses. He was uncomfortable, but not in the least angry.

"That kid was nervous, but he wasn't a snot," he said. "He was concerned. You can learn to give an injection, but you can't learn concern. He'll be okay."

Toward evening a chunky intern ambled in and slapped Hal's leg, locker-room style.

"We're going to take you off the monitor tomorrow and discontinue the I.V. Isn't that nice?"

Hal, still squirming with stomach pain, yet never one to resist the available pun, said, "Oh, I don't know. I've gotten rather attached to them."

"What? *Oh.* I get it. Well, your enzymes this afternoon were a little elevated, but we don't think you've had more coronary damage. We think it's probably a reflection of your heart failure."

"Then I've a question," Hal said. "Why did I go into failure?"

"We're not sure yet. Could be"—the intern shrugged and scratched his head—"could be that one of your bypasses plugged up. In which case—it's up to your doctors, of course, but I would assume they would want angiography. . . ." And shrugged again, and gave another smart slap to the patient's leg and said, "Take it easy, now," and ambled out.

We stared at each other. *Could be that one of your bypasses plugged up.* Could he really have said that? If Hal were a layman, this casual conjuring up of a plugged lifeline, shooting dye into the heart again, possibly slitting open the chest again, might be enough to produce another coronary. Oh, he looks so scared.

"Don't look so scared," he said.

"Who's scared?" *Oy gevalt.* "But I can't *believe* those bedside manners."

"Unbelievable. It's so callous it's funny."

"I don't hear you laughing."

"I can't," he said. "My stomach hurts."

Probably, that day, they did cause a small ulceration. I know at least that before that business with the potassium he'd never had stomach problems of any sort, he hadn't known what it meant to take a Tum; and afterward, he had persistent, severe stomach pains that often woke him in the night, and we kept bottles of chalky antacid around the house and he swigged it down like soda pop, sometimes in hiding, because he knew how I seethed to recall the incident, but I could always tell by the faint ring of white around his mouth.

Chapter 23

*H*E has been in hospital a week, and still they do not speak of causes. Moses says there is no reason to think that a bypass closed. The cardiogram is stable. Dumb intern, shooting off his dumb mouth . . . Moses was furious about that, and I think he gave the intern what for. But nobody says what caused the failure.

His illness is at the center of my life. Sometimes I think that his illness *is* my life. My unconscious erupts not just in dreams but in all my waking moments.

I walk into his room wearing red shoes.

"I like those," he says. "Are they new?"

"Oh, no," I tell him. "I bought them before my first heart attack."

Someone calls to ask if I can play poker Saturday night.

"I wish I could," I say, "but I'm still in the hospital."

I go into a sandwich shop with a friend. It's lunchtime, the place is jammed and noisy, I want another cup of coffee and I keep waving at the waitress but she manages not to see me. Finally, loudly, I call, "*Nurse!*"

The odd thing is, she comes right over.

I am beginning to act strangely. Friends invite me to dinner. I say I am busy, and then I go by myself to eat in the Soup-Burger. "I feel like a fifth wheel," my mother said. I have the sense that I should practice it, become accustomed to the rhythm and feel of it, before the fact. But I do not want to practice yet.

Alone, I never go to a proper restaurant. I lecture myself: "Listen, tonight you will make a reservation for one, and you will put on fine duds, and you will go like a person who does not have to be alone, and you will order oysters and a good bottle of wine." But I seem no more able to do that than I ever was—even less, for his sickness depletes my self-confidence, as though it were my sickness. It is like the time in Cannes, before he got sick, when I walked invisible along the promenades and ate in the back-street joints.

We have talked so often of this, in my women's group and elsewhere. When we try to convey this particular sense of vulnerability, we focus always on the restaurant. The sociology of restaurants. Alone, we cannot sit in fancy places without twitching. Betty tells me that she can do it with small deceptions: She reserves a table for two and sits with a drink—and with a book, of course—and keeps looking ostentatiously at her watch. Finally, she says to the captain, "I don't want to wait any longer. I'll order now." Joyce says that she used to do it like this: At some point she would rise from her table for two and go to the telephone, then come back and tell the captain, "I don't know how late he will be. I'll order now." Then she resolved to throw away the crutches. She worked at it. She said, "One, please," and willed herself to walk cool and sit tall, without twitching, and now, she says, she can dine alone anytime, anywhere, and it's all right, so long as she knows that she's looking swell. If it's not one crutch it's another.

Four A.M. As always, when alone, huddled on his side of the bed, amid his pillows, his contour in the mattress, his smell in the sheets.

There has been no sex for so long. Many weeks. Months, perhaps. I do not miss it. I feel dry down there. Dried up. The thought of another man disgusts me. It never used to disgust me. It was no insult to him. He was fine in this bed and he knew it. But now it would seem a consummate insult. It would be unbearable.

I am afraid to sleep. I scribble. The dreams have been dreadful. The crumbling walls are back again, and last night there was something new: last night a man in a white coat was bending me backward as the circus strong man bends iron, breaking my back, and I awoke just as my spine was about to snap, crying out in pain.

They say Hal is completely out of failure now. But he has that look again, that concentration-camp look, with the prevalence of bones, with the terrible hot glitter of the eyes, that he had last fall—or was it the spring before?—when I said he was going down the tube. So I don't know.

Today they told him that he still had a gallop rhythm. *Still?* That jolted me. Nobody had ever told me that he had a gallop rhythm.

I asked him, "What is a gallop rhythm?"

He said, "You know how, when you listen to a heart, the beat goes 'clip-clop, clip-clop'?"

"Yes."

"When you have a gallop rhythm, there is an extra beat. It goes, 'clippity-clop, clippity-clop.' "

"You've got rhythm, eh?"

"Right!" Smiling strained smiles at each other.

"Is it a very bad thing to have?"

"It's better not to have it. But it's not necessarily dangerous."

I could feel my smile beginning to twitch.

He said, "Try not to get tense about it. It's just words."

The *Times* dropping through the mail slot. Six A.M.

And fearing to dream of that dark, dank house in which walls eternally crumbled, I slept finally and dreamed instead of a horse named Râle galloping, clippity-clop, toward the finish line.

It didn't hit me then, the small sly trick: that *Râle*, but for the circumflex, was an anagram for *Lear*.

Somewhere in this wakeful period came a telephone call from Boston: my mother, who lived in a suburb north of the city, had been hospitalized under vague and distressing circumstances.

Her doctor was an old man. He had treated me in childhood. My mother had taken me to him once when I had fallen off a chair and bled. He had written a note, at her request and virtually dictated by her:

> To Whom It May Concern: This is to certify that I have examined Martha Weinman, age 6½, and found her to have a ruptured hymen, probably due to falling off a chair.

My mother had wrapped this note in tissue paper and had put it into her hope chest, among her treasures, and it had remained there until the day that I, age 30, had brought home the man I would marry. Then, gravely, and with the sweetest propriety, she had presented it to him. My dowry.

So that this doctor had long been in some sense a member of the family, and was himself now highly distraught.

He said, "She called me in the middle of the night. Apparently she woke up and reached for water and swallowed some denture-cleaning solution by mistake. She was very frightened, so I called the police and asked them to take her to the hospital. She was all right physically, but sort of disoriented. They had a psychiatrist see her. He said he thought it might be Alzheimer's Disease."

"What is Alzheimer's Disease?"

"It's a form of dementia. All I can tell you is, I hope he was wrong. We had that with my mother-in-law, and it's an awful business."

I flew immediately to Boston. She seemed fine to me. Soothed now by the attentions of several kind nurses, glowing to see me, but embarrassed too.

"It was a *nothing*. I got scared, that's all. I thought maybe it was poison. And the policemen! All of a sudden, they're banging on the door. You know me: when I get scared, I get *a bissel meshugge* [a little crazy]. So they bring me here and then they bring a psychiatrist. And he asked me the *stupidest things*. 'What year did the war end?' I said, 'What war?' There have been *so many wars*, how am I supposed to know what war he means? He asks how old I was in 1933. *Azamin frage* [such a question]! Who remembers such things? Especially when you're scared. He says, 'Where were you born?' I said, 'I don't know.' Mashala, you *know* I don't know. Who knows, these days, if it was Poland or Russia?"

The psychiatrist was very young. He had an accent I could not place. He spoke almost in a whisper, as supply carts rattled past us in the hospital corridor, and I kept edging toward him to hear, and he kept edging backward.

". . . and sometimes they appear to get better, and there are no further episodes for a time," he whispered. "Or there may be steady deterioration . . . and certainly . . . she lives alone . . . I think you may have to start making plans . . ."

"What makes you think it's Alzheimer's Disease?"

"I did not say it was." Edging back. "That was a tentative diagnosis."

"On what basis did you arrive at this tentative diagnosis?"

"There were signs of a personality breakdown. She could not tell me the most basic facts: where she was born, her own telephone number . . ."

"Listen," I said, "imagine that you are elderly, you are all alone, you are very timid, you have had many bad illnesses, you don't see too well, you are frightened of authority, and you have a language problem, and in the middle of the night you think you have taken poison. Then police come and put you in a car, and they take you to a place with bright lights, and strangers start throwing questions at you, and *you think you are going to die.* Can you imagine what that would be like? Tell me, Doctor, *how old* were you in 1961?" And I knew this was displacement again, just as with that Nixon twit at dinner, but I couldn't seem to stop. "*Where* did you live when you were nine? *Who* was the President during the Korean War?"

He clicked his tongue reproachfully. "Madam, I am not from this country," he said.

I took her home the next day and stayed with her overnight, then telephoned her from New York.

"How are you feeling, Mom?" I said.

"Fine!" she said. "In the pinks!"

And I knew in my bones there was no Alzheimer's Disease. But still, there were loneliness and fear. There was fragility. Things happen. I had friends who had come recently to that crisis with their parents, a broken hip, a fading memory, creeping depression; and the impossible guilt-laden alternatives—disruption of households, obscenity of nursing homes, that whole damned agonizing business; and no one had found a good way. What could be done? With her, frightened in her bed, and I, frightened in mine, and Hal, surely frightened in his, however much his hot sunken eyes tried to reassure me.

Spinning off her, and off him, and sleepless again and half-zonked, I began writing one night:

My mother's mother lived with us, with my parents and my brother and me, from the time she was widowed until her death a quarter-century later. It was the last generation that pretended to any natural feel for extended-family life. She sensed that the divine right of parents was slipping, that she lived in this household by the largess of hosts, and she strove to keep their goodwill by being invisible.

When my father came home from work she murmured good evening and disappeared immediately, so that he and his wife might have their privacy. She never trespassed in any way upon our nuclear circle: When a quarrel arose between husband and wife, or parent and child, she fled to her room. She cooked, insisted upon cooking, but rarely joined us at the dinner table (on Mother's Day, yes). Instead, well before we sat down to eat, she would take a small plate of food, finish it quickly, clean up after herself, and disappear. "Why don't you eat with us?" I once asked. "I don't have all my teeth," she said. "It doesn't look nice." I never realized until my own adulthood that she seemed, in some dim way that she herself may not have perceived at all, to want my mother to realize the burden of her own invisibility. See how much I love you.

When she was very old, about 90, she suffered a stroke and lost her speech but began to scream—strange, high, sudden caws, as though she were in the most unbearable pain. The doctor assured my mother that she was in no pain at all; it was an involuntary sound caused, he said, by vocal chords in spasm. I was by this time no longer living at home, but I came to visit on a weekend. She knew no one, which shook my mother's soul and even mine—that ghastly threat, that childhood nightmare materialized, when our parents do not know us!—and the sound she made was terrifying. It racked our nerves. It broke our sleep. And she could tend to none of her bodily functions, and her daughter had become her anxious, bitter keeper.

My father, dangling finally at the end of a quarter-century's tether of patience, insisted that she be placed in a nursing home. My mother at first said no, then relented. A week later I went with her to see the old woman. It was an awful place, dour and dirty, with those wretched elders sitting and lying about, catatonic, and my grandmother struggling down a corridor with the aid of a walker and emitting those terrible caws. I cried. My mother said, "No, I can't stand it. I'm taking her out," and transferred her to a hospital, where she died within days. To this time, a dozen years later, my mother weeps on Mother's Day with the most bitter remorse, and intones: "I shouldn't have let her go to that place."

What I remember vividly is that in my late adolescence, my mother bought a fine big white stove. It was her pride, replacing a despised cast-iron model, and she cleaned it carefully after each meal. My grandmother, whose sight by then had gone quite bad, would drop food on the stove and leave greasy finger marks, and I can remember my mother cleaning up after her, scrubbing and rubbing and muttering angrily to herself.

Now my mother is widowed and lives alone in another city. Sometimes she comes to visit. She comes for two weeks and stays for a week, and in that time she lives like a shadow, silent and fleeting. Her self-effacement infuriates me. It fills me with guilt, and I can't cope with the guilt, and what comes out is rage. She is blameless, almost. So am I, almost. We are locked into one another, dancing that ineffably sad old mother-daughter waltz. Who leads?

She tries to help in the kitchen, paying her dues, as her mother used to. And her sight is not good, and sometimes she takes dirty dishes out of the dishwasher and stacks them up on the shelves, and she leaves charred bits of food and grease on my fine copper-colored stove, and I find myself standing there scrubbing and rubbing, muttering angrily.

She is arthritic. Sometimes we talk, cautiously, about what will happen if the time comes when she can no longer maintain her own home. "Mothers cannot live with daughters," she says. And: "I will never go to a nursing home. It is better to die." "You will never have to worry. We will take care of you," I say. "May I never need you," she says.

It astonishes me how often, in my women's group, we talk about our mothers. "What shall we talk about tonight?" we say. And the topic, most often, is ourselves in relation to men, or our sexuality; or our children; or our work, our ambitions, our struggles with sex roles. But so often, wherever we set out, we end up talking about our mothers. Bitter-sweet. Love-hate. We are in our thirties and forties and fifties, some of us with grown daughters of our own. But we cannot escape that vise, and possibly we never will.

One of our group, a woman who manages so intelligently a complex and creative life, tells us that the worst hours of her week have been spent shopping for a birthday present for her mother. Imagine it: She has work deadlines to meet, a household, a husband, three children, and she has spent two days wandering anxiously from store to store, in search of the perfect gift. The perfect gift from the perfect daughter. A gift (a daughter) so *good* as to insure love, recognition, approval. Where do you buy such a thing? The despair of having to settle for something as imperfect as herself, and then the day-long wait, tense as a hospital vigil, to learn how it had been received. And then, finally, that pre-posterous sense of relief and reprieve: Her mother *liked* it.

As she told the story she laughed a little, near-cried a little. We all did. Who could understand such a *madness?* she said. We all could.

Liberation. Extrication. Our mothers grow old and we watch them becoming us, and ourselves becoming them, and whom do we extricate from what? And how? And do we pass this dear, murderous entangle-ment on to our daughters with the family silver? Often I wonder if this is not some ultimate form of liberation: the most painful, and the most elusive. . . .

It stopped there. I'd had no goal. Later I thought that it might be reworked into the start of a piece about aging parents and how people cope—nursing homes were then much in the news—a reportorial piece, but opening perhaps on a personal note.

"What do you think?" I asked my friend Bergman at the *Times* Sunday Magazine.

He wanted to use the fragment as it stood. They ran it as the lead story on Mother's Day. The reaction astounded me. This was not sedate *Times* mail, it was the passion of the tabloids. Ah, thank you, God bless you, what comfort to know I am not alone, I have never dared to say, I have always felt such guilt . . . And the others, filled with the wrath of Mom's mythic children, I hope God punishes you, She'll die and you'll be sorry, We happily nursed our angel Mother through twenty years of cancer . . . and with foul name-callings— monster, scum, whore, mother-fucker . . . the twitchings of some unspeakably tender nerve. One writes hoping sometimes to do this, to touch a nerve; and yet in those weeks when the letters kept coming, and the threatening calls, too, from psychotics who looked me up in the telephone book, I was filled with remorse.

And my mother: I had called to tell her of the thing, and had sent an advance copy. Silence. Finally I called again.

"How did you like your picture?" I said. The magazine had published her wedding portrait on the cover.

"It's a picture. So what? I've seen it before."

"What did you think of the article?"

"I guess nobody will want to visit me," she said, "now that they think my dishes are dirty."

Christ, how I cried. So did she.

Chapter 24

*T*HEY sent him home dried out. *Dry as a bone down there.*

But now it required far more to keep him dry. Now he took six diuretic pills a day, 240 milligrams, double his former dose—enough, the corner pharmacist assured me cordially, to knock a horse on its ass. He took more potassium to replace what the diuretics washed out of him, and this gave him stomach pains. He took antacids to relieve the stomach pains. He took digoxin to strengthen the heartbeat. He took Sorbitrate to ease the heart's work. He took Allopurinal to inhibit certain actions of the diuretics, which could produce uric acid, which could produce gout. He took aspirin as an anticoagulant. He had been taking a supplementary diuretic that helped the body to retain potassium. Then his right breast had grown slightly enlarged, a condition which in men is called gynecomastia, and can lead to cancer; and he had become totally impotent. He had consulted his *P.D.R.* —*Physician's Desk Reference*—which describes every drug on the market, to check out the side effects of this medication. There it was: *Possible side effects: Gynecomastia; loss of libido; impotence.* No one had told him of the possible side effects. Imagine, he thought, if I weren't a doctor. To Moses he had said, "I've developed a unilateral gynecomastia and I'm impotent. Don't you think we should stop that supplementary diuretic?" "Absolutely," Moses had said. And they had switched to a drug that was thought to be somewhat less effective but hadn't these side effects; compromises must be made. His potency and his breast returned to normal.

The diagnostician in him nagged. "No matter how we go around in circles, they're still not explaining it. How in winter I could walk a half-mile to the gym, swim, exercise, come home, eat, take another walk and say, 'I feel fantastic.' And now I need twice as much of that crap"—jerking a thumb toward his bureau top, where the vials stood in rows—"just to keep me out of failure, and I can barely walk around the block."

"It's rotten," I said.

He arched an eyebrow. "It could be better."

"Yes."

"On the *other* hand"—with that sweet shrewd smile, pointing a Talmudic forefinger in the air—"it could be worse. *L'chaim.*" Raising his glass.

On the other hand. It became another fragment of our shorthand.

"I'm so sick of being sick," he would say. A pause. And then: "On the *other* hand . . ."

We would go out walking, and he would begin to gasp, and my eye would begin to twitch; and he would reach out a finger to still my twitching lid and say, "On the *other* hand . . ."

It worked wonders for us both. Usually.

"What happened? Why did I go into failure?" he asked Silverman. He had been home from hospital a week.

"You were trying to do too much."

The old It's Your Fault again. Why could no doctor ever say, "It's my fault?" (Had he himself ever said it? He couldn't remember.) Or at least a Maybe. Listen, Hal, *maybe* it's our fault, *perhaps*, in some limited insignificant way, we have stirred a drop of culpability into this mess, *possibly*, Hal, we're not sure, but *possibly*, we told you to exercise too much, we did not appreciate how little cardiac reserve you had, instead of looking for irregular heartbeats we should have diagnosed heart failure, we should have caught it faster, dried you out sooner, maybe even saved you that trip to the hospital. We hate to admit it, Hal, but perhaps that trip was unnecessary. . . .

Oh, no. Never. It's Your Fault. Patient gets recurrent hernia, surgeon says, "You got too fat." No clue that he might have botched the surgery. Fracture mends badly, orthopedist says, "You were too active." No hint that the cast was applied incorrectly. Cancer, inoperable, internist tells family, "He should have come to me sooner." No ghost of a suggestion that warning signs may have been missed in the last annual checkup. Cardiac drops dead, cardiologist says, "Well, he never would take care of himself." Never a whisper about the possibility of inadequate medication. Elective surgery, patient dies on table, anesthetist says, "Tch. Difficult case." And who's to know—or who's to tell—that the patient died from too much Pentothal and not enough oxygen?

Well, those were no hypotheses. He'd seen them all happen, and all variations thereof, more often than he cared to remember. And in urology, his own field—oh, the botchings and the lies! Prostatic case. Old man, poor risk, two ways to go: up through the urethra, which is called a transurethral resection, subtle and hard on the doctor, sticking a tube up there and carving out the prostate in a sort of Roto-Rooter way, but easy on the patient, no incision, minimal pain, five days in the hospital and home free; or down through the belly, a suprapubic prostatectomy, easy on the doctor, hard on the patient— big incision through muscle, dig out the prostate, awful pain after, two weeks in hospital, harsh convalescence. And they go that way, with no hint that they do it because the urologist is not skilled enough to go the other way, and patient is deathly ill, maybe dies, and urologist says, "Well, he was an old man. Poor risk." They talked like that.

They? Here was a curious line of thought. Here was the looking glass again. Who were *they?* It was a bad thing to be a patient, it was a nasty revelation, but he had been *they*, he had made his mistakes and made his excuses, and was he now entitled to some larger piety simply because he was looking in from the other side?

He could remember cases . . . one case the year before he'd left practice, and it hurt still to remember, because the patient had been a friend, a lovely old man, and he himself had so wanted for everything to go well. The old man had come to him with a bad infection seated in the prostate. And Hal, hoping to spare him trauma, wanting to get him in and out as quickly as possible, had been hasty. We will treat the infection with pills for a few days, he had said, and then we will do the surgery. But the infection had not been fully cured, and after surgery it had gotten worse—terrible; the patient had been in hospital for three weeks and very nearly died, and had come home like a walking cadaver, thirty pounds lighter than when he'd gone in, and the recovery had taken months.

And what had he told the wife? Oh, yes: "He should have come to me sooner, before the infection got so bad."

And what had the wife said, and her husband too? Why, they had told the world what a prince this was, what a saint, this Dr. Lear, who had snatched his patient from the very claws of death and had been so devoted, so far beyond the contemporary call of duty, as to visit his room every day! twice a day! for all those awful three weeks in hospital, after the nasty infection had gotten so much nastier and given the doctor so much trouble.

Oh, yes. It's Your Fault. And the memory took no sting from hearing Moses, now, saying, "You were trying to do too much," for now he felt not only anger but remorse, either of which was quite enough in itself.

"Did you get a good report card?" I asked.

"Bullshit. I got bullshit. Double-talk." On the bed, shedding the anger in layers, like clothes. "I wouldn't mind if they said, 'I don't know.' But they never say that. In the hospital I would ask, 'Why did I go into failure?' and they would always answer with questions. 'Were you doing anything different from your usual routine? No? Nothing? Are you sure?' Once I told them, 'Well, I did have a Chinese dinner last week.' The residents loved that. They said, 'Aha! A Chinese dinner! That's what did it!' If I told them I tossed salt over my left shoulder, they would say, 'Aha! Salt over your left shoulder! You inhaled some of the salt and it threw you into failure. . . .' Oh, shit. He told me nothing. I had the sense of being rushed. No interest in my mental confusion. No questions about what I've been doing since the hospital. No X-ray. How come? The last X-ray in the hospital showed my heart was enlarged."

"Did he take a cardiogram?"

"Oh, yeah."

"And?"

"Stable. That's what they always say. Stable." His fist began beating the mattress. "Damn it, *who's stable*? Something happened! Is this *stable*? I said to him, 'What happened to me?' And you know what he said?" Beating out the words. "He said, 'You were trying to do too much. I told you not to overdo it.' You remember what they told me?

They told me, 'Go to the gym every day. *Exercise. Exercise.* It's good for your heart.' Well, they were *wrong. Okay.* That's the routine recommendation after cardiac trauma. I can't blame them. But damn it, they shouldn't blame *me.* I said, 'I was walking to the gym all winter, in freezing weather, and doing fine, and suddenly in spring I go into acute failure. *Why?*' And he just shook his head at me and said, 'You need rest. A heart that's been operated on needs time to rest.' What kind of crap is that? I'm a doctor, I know a heart takes three to six months to mend. And here I am, a year and a half post-op, and this thing happens. *Why?* And I say, 'I'm not doing *anything.* I *can't* do anything. I walk two blocks, I'm wiped out, I come home and sleep. Let me tell you what I've been doing. . . .' And he shakes his head. He doesn't have time to listen. He says, 'I know what you've been doing. Too much. You've got to rest.' *Bullshit! I'm not stupid.*" It was a wail of rage. "And then he tells me to come back in two weeks. *To see Peter.*"

Ah. So there had been not only double-talk. The patient had been blamed for his illness, had been handed back his questions, unopened, and had been left feeling rejected, abandoned. Moses, I thought, feeling now a fury of my own, that was a bad thing to do. You do not do such a thing, Moses, to such a patient who comes to you at such a time, humbled by disease. You perhaps have never been deeply and chronically sick; you perhaps do not know from within how sickness humbles—how it clouds and corrodes and befouls the sense of self. I do not know why this should be so, that physical disease plays such cruel vanishing tricks upon the ego, even the sturdiest ego, given time enough. But I have seen it happen here, to this fine strong man, and I have read a bit about such things and I know that this is classic in long chronic disease; this is what the failures of the body do unerringly to the soul. And if I know this much, Moses, surely you know it too. And you are neither an unkind nor an uncaring man. So why do you reject him now, when his ego is so fragile? Could it be that yours is not fragile enough? Too thick a hide, eh? Or that you are angry at this sick patient for remaining so intransigently sick? Or—this being my darkest suspicion—that you can do nothing more for him and so choose, in subliminal ways, to wash your hands? Not that I wish illness upon you, Moses, may you never have illness, but perhaps it would teach doctors something they do not know. Or know only theoretically, which is not enough. Per-

haps there should be a way to induce illness, pseudo illness, something dreadful but safe, with clear parameters, that would last, say,
for a year and wreak all due havoc upon the body and the spirit
before it disappeared. A required course at all medical schools: no
one graduates without two consecutive semesters of chronic, debilitating sickness. What do you think, Moe, old friend, old eminence:
would that make better doctors?

Oh, well.

He took it out on me. How else? Were our situations reversed, I
would have taken it out on him.

Elaborate courtesies: "Of *course*, Martha. Anything you *say*, Martha."

Public put-downs, a thing we had never permitted ourselves: "Why
must you tell that story? I hate gossip." This in the presence of guests,
including members of my women's group. My women's group! What
could be worse? We are known by the contracts we keep. The sociology of the women's group dictates that we will assert the universal-
ity of male chauvinism while implying that our own men are different;
or, at least, redeemable. To be proved wrong *in front of each other*
is monstrous egg on the face.

And after, he says, "You embarrassed me. You drank too much."

Go to hell.

"And you kept interrupting me. You interrupted everyone. You
ruined the evening."

"Go to *hell*."

And I am out the door and down in the elevator and cursing in the
street. Fuck him. What am I knocking myself out for? Caring for him,
fearing for him, and he treats me like this.

But listen: Remember about the displaced rage. Understand about
the displaced rage.

Why should I? I am tired of understanding. Where is it written that
I must be the angel of forbearance?

Come now, angel of forbearance. You are no long-suffering wife.
He is no abuser. This is aberrant. Tell him how you feel. But gently.

Why gently? I am tired of gently, too. But of course, yes, it must be
gently, because of his heart, his sickness entraps me in silence, we
must not aggravate him, must we?, because of his heart, and I am
also bloody damned tired of his heart . . . Stalking the dark streets

with such a ferocity as will surely ward off muggers. And when I come home the kitchen is clean, the lights are out and he is pretending to be asleep, but he is not asleep; he is crying.

Oh, dearest.

And I embrace him and he cries, "You mustn't tell me to go to hell. You mustn't treat me so badly. Not you."

"Oh, dearest. But you treat me badly too."

"How? Tell me." He is truly astonished.

Ah, this and that. "And tonight. Saying I gossiped."

"But that was *true*. You *did* gossip."

"But you needn't have *insulted* me. I would never insult *you* in public."

"Only in *private*. I would never tell *you* to go to hell."

"Your tone of *voice. Patronizing. Denigrating.* I wish you could *hear* your tone of voice."

"That's *exactly* how *you* sound to *me*. I wish you could hear *yours*."

In fact, I do. I hear us both as though on tape. We sound retarded. Soon we will turn cold asses to each other, or get drunk and kiss and make up, and in the morning one will say to the other, "What the hell were we quarreling about?", which is the part I hate most, the What the hell were we quarreling about, the worst mutual insult; if there is going to be quarreling, let it at least be memorable, some style, some logic, not this inane insipid stuff. Effort must be made to salvage us, our dignity, from the What the hell were we quarreling about.

"Listen, Hal, I know you're in a rage . . ."

"We don't need to discuss that," he says.

"Yes, we do. In a rage. In a rage at your doctors and in a rage at your sickness. What surprises me about your rage is that it isn't worse. If I were you, it would be much worse." Check. "But you do not take it out on your doctors. No. You leave them silently and you bring your rage home to me. I do the best I can. What do you think I should do with it?"

He clears his throat. "Okay. I know. My quarrel is not with you. If I haven't made it clear, I think you are splendid. . . ."

"Don't splendid me. Just tell me: what should I do with your rage?"

"And your rage at me for being sick: What do you think *I* should do with it?"

Checkmate. Silence, while we ponder our positions.

"Oh, God," he says finally. "I am sorry. I don't mean to hurt you. I never want to hurt you. I will try very hard not to do it anymore."

"Me too."

"We must be gentle with each other."

"Yes. We must honor each other."

"Yes."

And we kiss. We sleep. But it knits up no ravell'd sleave.

I went with him to the next medical appointment.

After the examination he sat in Mason's office, listless and sullen, frustration upon him like a pox, while Peter spoke soothingly of pills. Silverman entered, bearing his own magnetic field of health and affability.

"Well!" he said. "How's the *shlimazel?*"

It could not have been worse. The word defies translation. Usually it is defined by situation: a *shlemiel* is a fellow who always spills the soup; a *shlimazel* is the one it always gets spilled on. It is a joke of a word, used sometimes wryly and sometimes with contempt and this time with no contempt at all, but it simply could not have been worse.

"I don't know who or how the *shlimazel* is," I said. "As to my husband, his health is none too good."

He apologized instantly. But Hal was beyond placating. He rose, something slaughterous in him.

"Don't you *dare* call me that!" he yelled. "After the last time . . . my coming in here to ask what happened to me . . . That's a legitimate question, damn it! I've never nagged you with nuisance questions, and you giving me that bullshit about exercising too much, you saying such an *asinine thing* . . ."

"I *never*," Moses said, the two of them standing now foot to foot, faces red, arms waving. "I *never* say asinine things."

"*That* is asinine."

"I never—"

"Yes, yes, *asinine things.* Telling me it was *my fault.* What kind of crap—"

Peter intervened. Voices softened. Apologies were exchanged. Talk turned again to pills and other juiceless matters, and we went home with nothing further explained and nothing resolved.

"Switch doctors, then," I said. "Or at least get a consultation. They're not the only game in town."

"Maybe I will," he said.

But the next day Moses called, unbidden, to ask how he was feeling, and his hostility melted in the warmth of that gesture.

"They really care," he said. "I think they fucked up this last time, they missed the boat, but they really do care. They know me. They have an emotional investment in me. It's not all black and white."

And of course there would be this fierce cleaving. It was quite like what happens in analysis, when you have lain on the same couch for too many years, and life seems to be getting no better, and you wonder if it is not time to change couches. Ah, but there is such a history here! Such a habit, this couch molded to every contour of the psyche. Who has the strength to start all over again, to proceed from Square One with a stranger? The very thought is exhausting.

I find myself so much using the word *rage*, again *rage*, always *rage*, to describe what was or how I perceived it to be, plenty in him and not too little in me, impactions and implosions of rage, essence of rage, bottled, sealed, vacuum-packed. The rage was into everything.

We had not tried to make love in a long time, and then one night we did, and quite suddenly he went limp and fell away from me with a groan not of disappointment or anger, nothing so pallid, but of rage; and more, outrage.

I remember trying to comfort him. These things happen, I said. What the hell. We'll rest awhile and start again. And other such irrelevancies.

No. He shook his head No and lay with an arm covering his eyes and a hand covering his heart.

"Can't we talk about it?" I said. Not at all sure that we should. Such a danger. Here, at the very core of it, this banal and painful metaphor for all the kinds of impotence he felt. I put an arm about him, tentatively. "Maybe, if we could talk about it . . ."

He pushed away and sat upright.

"I think you should leave me," he said.

"What are you *talking* about? I don't know what the hell you're *talking* about."

In the soft light from the bathroom I could see him trying, the words trying to get themselves ordered, push themselves past his lips, and the tears, too, falling upon his lips, and finally, with a pain that wrenched my own heart: "I don't know why you should stay with me. I'm a cripple."

"Don't say that. You're *not* a cripple."

"Stop denying." He said it kindly, the rage gone now, a kind of reasoned resignation in its place. "I'm not feeling sorry for myself. It's simply a reality."

But in fact he himself did not accept it as reality. Not in any constant way. When he felt well, or whatever it was that feeling well meant for him, it was as though he had never been down. He kept soaring and crashing and soaring again, no Icarus, and often I thought that such a wildly defiant wingspread could belong only to a colossus or a fool, and he was neither, so I never could figure it at all.

One asks, "How are you?" and the other says, "Well, thanks." *Well* is a neutrality. With him, it was a celebration.

"How do you feel this morning?"

"Well!" Laughing, fist pushing through the air. "*Well*, Mushie! *Completely well!* What are you going to do with a healthy husband?"

Listen, it's *his* body. Maybe he does know. Maybe I should trust.

"A formidable problem. Present it, and I'll think of something."

"Start thinking. I'm going for a walk."

"A walk? It's hot as hell out. Anybody can get tired on a day like this."

"Well, I'll give it a try."

I sit at my typewriter, waiting. Five minutes later the front door opens. I know historically that if he is in animated conversation with the elevator operator, the walk went well. If there is silence, the walk went badly.

And this morning, silence. He goes directly to the bed, lies down, waits till his breathing eases. Then he tells me:

"I walked two blocks. Then I got short of breath. I rested. I had trouble coming back up the hill . . ." Here he smiles weakly. The hill! It is a city block of almost imperceptible elevation. It was level ground until he got sick. ". . . up the hill, and then I rested again, and then I came home."

"Are you still short of breath?"

"No."

"You feel well, then?"

"No." He shrugs. "This is shitty," he says. But still with the smile, which is essentially a kindness to me.

I do not know how to handle the moment. Sometimes, in such

moments, I make jokes. Sometimes he makes jokes. Sometimes it works, sometimes it is awful.

"Now, *look*, Hal, you've got to shape up and stop this business. You promised me you were getting well."

He comes along with me on this foolish little ride. "It just goes to show you," he says. "You can't trust anyone."

He continued up and down like that, and a summer passed again while we spoke of getting, perhaps, to Provincetown next week.

At a dinner party we met a model. Famous, gorgeous, so thin that one might impale oneself upon many of her parts, but with a great sweetness in those bones, something earnest and caring and vaguely, sweetly schizoid. She spoke to Hal of healers and meditators, major and minor gurus. And now, on one terribly hot afternoon, she came, sweatless, to bring him a book by the Maharishi and to speak further of the healing of his heart. Mind–body connections. Slowed pulses. Mystic concentrations. Breathing lessons to reduce the need for oxygen, brain waves to control the heartbeat, peaceful spirits in the blood, *oms* and other secrets. Speaking so sweetly and softly of this doctor she knew whom he, Hal, should see; this doctor who was *very into* meditation; a proper doctor, one understood, an *internist*, who was *very into* the idea of the mind's curative effect upon the heart . . .

And as she spoke on through that hot afternoon, softly and near-hypnotically, I found myself—normally so leery of these healers and meditators, so resistant to anything *weird*—found myself, *om-mmm, om-mmm*, saying, "Yes, I really think you should see this doctor. Yes, let's call him right away."

Yes, let's try. Bring on the meditators, the chanters, the *houngans* and the chickens' blood and all psychics too, magic charms, potions, laying on of hands, drums, signs, tongues; I'll try anything now.

How's the shlimazel? Hell, even a witch doctor has got to do better than that.

That was one fantasy: the mystic one, into which I crept for a harmless hour or two with that sweet, spacey visitor. The other was its opposite number, my own invention, my superrational fantasy, in which I spent a great deal more time: in which that arrangement of plugged and broken parts, arteries, aortas, valves, veins, ventricles, was simply a plumbing system, no more momentous than any other. A naughty toilet, a stubborn kitchen sink. Well, then, fix it. Where's the plumber? Where's the Drano? *Fix it*, you Yellow Page wizards. I'll pay overtime.

I called Mason. "A couple of questions," I said.

"Okay. Shoot."

"He was doing well. Then, suddenly, he was in bad failure. Since the last hospitalization he keeps having his ups and downs, but I think the continuum now is downward. Is that correct?"

"That's a fair statement."

"If you don't know for sure what caused this sudden reversal, I'd like you to take an educated guess."

"Well, I think the pump just isn't pumping as efficiently as it was."

"I know, Peter. But if I could just get a handle on the reason . . ."

"For this sudden decline? What I'm trying to tell you, Martha, is that I don't think it's all that sudden."

"But the fact is, six months ago, in cold weather, he could walk, swim, exercise . . . and suddenly he can't."

"True. But even when he seemed good, he was intermittently in mild failure. We'd increase his diuretics and he'd be better for a time. Then he'd go into failure again."

"But why did he suddenly have this acute episode?"

"I don't know."

Okay. This in no way relieves me. It deepens my dread. But at least it is a fixed point of truth: he doesn't know. I pass to the next question cautiously, hating it:

"Would another angiogram tell you why this happened?"

"It might. And maybe that's something to consider. But I wouldn't want to do it now."

"Why?"

A long pause. He is moving, weighing how far and how fast he can move, toward the edge of it:

"Martha . . . It would probably show us exactly what has happened. And I don't think it would show us anything good. And if we can't offer him anything more surgically, what's the point of putting him through it?"

"What would it show?"

"A deteriorating heart muscle. The surgery helped. It revascularized him to some extent. But you can't revascularize the whole heart. Only part of it. And meanwhile, the vasculatory disease is progressing in him. . . ." He stopped. He sighed. "I'm not giving you good news, Martha," he said. That cost him.

"I know." How cool I am. I am retreating again into that safe reportorial place where I have only a cordial and distant relationship with my husband; and with myself. I may not be able to stay in this place. His doctors have never talked to me so baldly before. But for the moment, we tiptoe politely over this temporary lapse in manners. We talk, with the appropriate detached concern, of juggling the medications again, of the predictable problems: On six diuretic pills a day, the patient is still slightly short of breath. On seven, he is depleted. As a result, he is dispirited. We do not consider it good for him to be dispirited. Perhaps now we will try six, seven, six, seven. Yes, we will try that.

And then I thank him for his efforts, and he thanks me for my interest, and we hang up.

I'm not giving you good news, Martha. This is how they talk, finally, to the relatives of terminal-cancer patients. Terminal bowels, terminal bones. Does he have a terminal heart?

Now it strikes me, for the first time—not as brooding fantasy, not at all on that level, but as inescapable fact—that he is dying. It strikes me that I must write faster or I will not finish in time. And after he is dead, of course, I will not be able to write a word of it. Not a word.

Later, in the middle of the night, I get into bed and edge toward him. He is so still. I put my hand over his heart, fingers spread wide. A shield. Energies flowing out of my will, into my fingertips, deflecting harmful spirits. Get lost, spirits. My love will keep him warm. Harbor of love. No one can hurt him while I'm around. I will kiss it and make it well. I will perform great acts of will. I will *will* him to live.

I near-believed it.

The tendons of my hand began to jump, and I relaxed it into a limp, inefficacious object curved softly around his left nipple, powerless to do anything more than give me the comfort of skin contact.

Chapter 25

"*I* DON'T know how to help him," I said to the psychiatrist Russ. Russ, in a dark blue suit, buttoned vest, starched white shirt, handshake neat, desk top neat, everything neat, cool, a trifle too contained. Russ the passionate table thumper. Where in this neat office were his passions stored?

"I don't know how to help him." Treading carefully, wanting to be absolutely accurate and yet to show my best angle. A shrink, after all; and Hal had talked to him plenty in those months before and after surgery; he probably knew a thing or two about my warts. "I love him so much and it pains me so to see him like this, so angry, so depressed, but I don't know how to help. . . ."

The overly contained Russ suddenly thumped his desk. Behind the silver rims, his eyes flashed. Aha!

"Why *shouldn't* he be depressed? Most people would be much more depressed by now. Mrs. Lear"—shaking a finger at me; I shrank back, not displeased; the psychiatrists I'd known had always been too damned aphysical—"Mrs. Lear, what is striking about your husband is not that he is as depressed as he is but that he is still as *strong* as he is. He is an extraordinary man, Mrs. Lear. I admire him greatly. What he went through in that job, what those bastards did to him . . . With all of the abominable injustices he suffered, and all of the violations later upon his person at the hospital, where he was treated like a slab of meat on a meat rack"—breathing fire now, exhaling smoke—"and with all of the demeaning treatment from certain of his medical doctors, and with the battering he took physically and psychologically . . . how agonized he was by the loss of memory! It was worse than anything that happened to him physically . . . with all of that, he retained his pride and his will, which was an extraordinary and marvelous thing. Now, how can you help him? From what he told me, you do. Your relationship is very strong. He takes great sustenance . . ."

"But now he is so low. He calls himself a cripple. He says I should leave him."

"Do you want to leave him?"

"My God, *no*. Whatever, I value him however, I want him to know . . ."

"Then *tell him*. Make him know that you want him on whatever terms, that you would want him in an iron lung . . ."

But would I, Dr. Russ? In an iron lung? It is very hard to say. A woman I know suggested recently that one good thing about marriage is that you always have a date. And oh, yes, I love him hugely, but if I peer into this darkest part of myself, which I am not about to expose to you, I see this hanky-panky that is composed of need, sheer need, and how much of a date, after all, is a man in an iron lung?

"He's been through so damned much. It's not fair. Is it?"

"It's not."

"Have you had other patients who have been through so much?"

"Very, very rarely."

We sighed and shook hands.

"Please give him my very best wishes," he said. "I think of him often."

An old friend from Connecticut, best man at our wedding, came calling with a book for Hal.

He had had bypass surgery six months earlier. Recovery uneventful. No more angina. And now he works, he walks, he plays, he drives down from Hartford to see some shows on the weekend, he sits in my dining room telling me how, last week, he *jogged*; while my husband lies in the bedroom, asleep, exhausted from a two-block walk this morning.

This is deeply unfair. I love Alex, but it is unfair. I used to resent only strange men walking briskly in the street. Now I feel the old resentment swelling and extending to all healthy men, healthy friends, healthy husbands of friends. I find myself hating muscles, displays of strength. And listening now to Alex, with the scar on his chest (I glimpse the top of it, there, where his shirt is unbuttoned) far fresher and redder than Hal's, speaking of health—of how great he is feeling and how well he is working and how long he jogged last week—I start to cry. Suddenly, bitterly.

This is embarrassing. My tears are drenching the chicken salad. Alex is stunned. What must he do to please me: have a heart attack?

I despise this pettiness in myself. Sometimes I have confessed it, abashedly, to Hal, like a child reporting that she has wet her pants: ". . . and I get this feeling, Why *you*? Why not Alex, or Lewis, or David, or Bob—why *you*?" And he has chastised me: "Oh, come on. That's awful. That's mean-spirited."

Is this genuine? Does no faint vapor of resentment seep out of his own bones?

It has comforted me to learn that my feelings are shared. *Normal*, I am told. *Normal*, they keep assuring me, as though we were engaged in some send-up of self-help therapy: It's okay to feel what you feel because that is what you feel, so it's okay. You're okay, I'm okay. Rhoda told me that when Frankie lay dying of cancer and healthy men came to visit him, the thought would spring at her like a beast, unbidden and unwelcome: Why not *him*? Why *Frankie*? Marilyn told me that when Sidney died, she raged against men who lived. His friends came into her house to mourn, they pressed their wet cheeks against hers, and silently she cursed them for living. Lois told me that when Paul died she strode the streets with her two small children, a transistor radio held to her ear to drown out all sounds of life, and each man who passed was a trespasser, a violator of space, taking up square feet of sidewalk that should have belonged to Paul.

So. Normal.

I have begun to read the obituary pages. Not idly. Avidly. I used to wonder why anyone but the old would read the obits. Now I understand. I keep score. If, on any given morning, I read that a man has died before age 55, it augurs well. It may improve the quality of my day. If several, much the better. The ones who die of external causes, such as plane crashes and murderings, do not count for much. But those who succumb to enemies within—cancers, heart attacks, renal failures, whatever—oh, those score high. They cheer me.

He comes upon me one morning reading the obits. No good news this day.

I say, "There are all these healthy old guys around, and I resent that it didn't happen to them. It happened to you."

"Yes, but a lot of good things happened to me too."

"Name one."

"Ha *ha*," he says, flipping the obit page. "I lived through it."

It was a murderous fall day, in the nineties and airless. Lying outdoors, beneath an awning, he felt faint. His heart felt . . . *funny*. Almost idly, a second-nature reaction, he checked his pulse. It was skipping beats. Normal for 12, or 15, or 26 beats, then a moment's silence: a missed beat. P.V.C.'s, they are called: premature ventricular contractions. He had never felt them before. And the faintness was growing.

He telephoned Mason.

"It's nothing to worry about," Peter said. "When I was training in Houston, we had cardiacs who would go into failure regularly in those heat waves, and develop P.V.C.'s. We'd tell them to get into a cool tub of water, and the pulse would get regular again. Try that. And have Martha buy you some Gatorade."

Gatorade. We'd never heard of it. An over-the-counter item, I supposed. I filled the tub with cool water, saw him out of it and to bed, his pulse still irregular, and rushed off to the drugstore for Gatorade. The pharmacist shrugged. I tried two other drugstores. At the third, a clerk said, "It's a soft drink. You can buy it in a supermarket."

I'd been running around for half an hour; uneasy, now, that Hal, with his quirky pulse—*P.V.C.*, *P.V.C.*, a new rhythm for running, as in *clippity-clop*—was home alone. I cabbed to a supermarket, cabbed home with my emergency supply of Gatorade. He raised an eyebrow at this stuff which looked like cans of Coke, said "*Salut*" and drank one down. Pulse unchanged. Several hours later, in the air-conditioned bedroom, it returned to a regular beat. The next day was cool and he had no P.V.C.'s.

Some days later he asked, Why Gatorade?

Peter reddened and laughed. "I've heard ballplayers use it on hot days. It's supposed to give them more energy in the heat," he said.

I asked my supermarket man.

"Promotion," he said. "What can I tell you? Promotion."

In October he wrote in his journal:

Today, for the first time in almost two years, I feel that this "shattered mind" of mine has mended. Not completely, but significantly. Many scars remain and I know that under some conditions I will regress suddenly and dramatically. But also, I am confident, temporarily.

Today my mind feels clear. I *know* it is Monday, October 18. I *know* we are having dinner with the Ramonds on the 21st. This morning Martha and I walked out of a building and I knew instantly which way was uptown!

I was just out on the terrace. The air is fresh and the light has a prism-like clarity, almost like that glorious October light in Provincetown. With joy—really exultation—I identify with that light. My storms have subsided. My body seems to have reached a homeostatic peace and my mind is returning to me.

Two weeks later he wrote a letter:

Dear David

Thank you for today. Your support has meant so much to me. Yesterday threw me completely. I went into midtown to buy Martha a specific kind of tape recorder she has wanted. The manufacturur had told her it was dincontinued. I called around and found a place that was suppose to have one and went there. They didn't have it and told me to go to another place. I got lost. Because of my own chemistriy and the external stimuli I began "fog out." I hated to leave that district because I knew I could not go back their again so I persisted and became progressive weak, confused, inartirculate and disoriented some stores I visited 2 or 3 times. I tried to cope by writing notes to myself and would reset by sitting on curbstones, leaning against cars etc. I knew I must not get sick again. Finally I got hope by cab but I was more demoralized and emotionay drained than I realized. I usually sleep peacefully. Last nite was a turbulent ocean of nightmares. This morning I sat at my desk trying to deal with paperwork problems which are dificult for me and the problem about the car [This referred to a car repair which the dealer had refused to honor under warranty.] and I found myself sitting here crying. That's when I turned to you for help with the car.

I usually do function adequotely. I have had to accept a lot of reall losss—physical, mental etc. and at times I do grieve for what I have lost. But that loss is real, the grief is transient (moments) and my basic prespective is a very sconscious awareing that I am alive and life is good. But yesterday was just too much for me . . .

He never sent the letter.
Two days later, in a note to himself:

Yesterday was a disaster.
I tried to attend a seminar (2 day) on disorders of consciousness at the hospital. Got to lecture room. Had trouble with course because when a new idea was presented. I would forget the preceding sentence etc. Smae shit as last year.
Then—could not find notes I had taken, and became progressvely incompetent mentally. Had my tape recorder—could not rember how to use it. Misplaced all kinds of things—papers, tapes etc. Retrogressed teribly. Finally—staggered out (could not hold any conversaton during next interminnion. I was very fogey.) Tachycardia. Pulse weak with many PVC's. Went home to bed. Do not do back today.
I am so damn frustrated with these fucking limitation.
Thalked with Jon re movie where a car was scavenged in 60 secs. I am like that. I am there, and then I am not there,
I try not to let Martha see how sad I am. I know it upsets her terribly.
Violent drcam last night. David Norman and I in family environment. I think in the summer cottage. Each on does something "on stage" with skill & applause from the family. I start to sing "Once I built a railroad." Then I stop with explanation that I cant "perform" anymore.
I am ready to cry as I write this . . .

The next day:

Having written last nite—and being extremely depressed, I woke to-day feeling so much better emotionally and intellectually aware of so much that was really bothering me. No cure but it's a beginning.
I have some understanding now of what happened to me since last hospitalization and why I retrogressed.
During convalescence I had made a few assumptions—that I was getting much better. That I was very relaxed. More a type "B" and the old old type "A" competitiveness & value systems were gone. And I was so totally wrong.
All the old journals that piled up while I was recovering during sum-mer—I could not just throw them out. It was important for me to

"keep up" in urology, psychiatry, sexuality, cardiology, general medicine, etc—and for *what what what*??? Day & nite I was reading incesently, tearing and filing. How stupid & unreal! What did I ever remember? I dont know. And what the hell does it matter? I shold not give a dam anymore. I should be out of all that and getting ready for new things.

So what I have learned during the past few days in a way that was very hard are these things:

1. I ain't the relaxed character I thought I was. The body is weak, but I'm still aggressive in the head.

2. If I have these physical & mental limitations almost two years post-op, that's probably how its going to stay. I must *accept* it.

Anyway—I awoke today aware of these realities which I had ignored either through ignorance or denial mechanisms and felt that I'd be ok— accept my limitations, live with them, make a life within them. I will surely have my problems. But I felt that the acceptance was a giant step for me. Now I look forward to seeing where I go from here.

He went downward. In early winter he began to notice, as he had noticed the year before, that he was gaining weight.

As before, he said, "I'm getting fatter. I should diet."

As before, I said, "You're sure it's not fluid retention?"

"Quite sure. I have no symptoms of failure. My chest feels completely dry."

But as the weeks passed I noted the developing signs: the faintly bloated look coming upon him again, the increasingly labored breathing, the growing weariness, all too neatly concatenated. And as before, I began to nag: "Please call the doctor. I think you're going into failure. . . ."

"Oh, God," he said, "why did I have to marry a doctor's wife?"

But he did call Mason and go down for a check. They were always splendid about that, fitting him into jammed schedules on sudden notice.

His heart sounds were stable and his lungs were dry.

There was this odd new symptom, he said: a persistent, highly localized pain on his right side, mid–axillary line. Especially sharp when he inhaled deeply. He was certain it was not cardiac, way out there in the right chest, but what might it be?

Mason consulted with Silverman. Perhaps a minor bronchitis, they thought. Perhaps a touch of pleurisy. Take cough medicine.

He was sure it was neither bronchitis nor pleurisy, but he himself could make no better guess. He did not take cough medicine. "That's a make-work prescription," he said at home. Aspirin helped somewhat.

Lying in bed one afternoon, reading, he found himself suddenly in severe air hunger. The abruptness of it stunned him. Immediately he took an extra Lasix. Then sat up very straight, panting hard, considering causes.

The day before, he had hoisted a case of wine onto a shelf above the kitchen cabinets. (I had been horrified. Ah, my cool-eyed realist, so peaceably resigned to living within his limits. Fucking fool! You could have dropped dead! Okay, okay, I know it was foolish, he had said; don't lecture.)

So he sat now, wondering if the exertion might have caused this dyspnea. Soon the extra diuretic began to work, and his breathing eased.

But the next day it happened again. Worse. He called Mason.

"The extra Lasix helped you yesterday?" Peter asked.

"Yes."

"Good. Continue that, then, and let us have a look at you at the end of the week."

His weight was up now from 155 to 161, and it looked to be all in the face and the belly. His pants were tight. With the extra pill each day, he dropped a couple of pounds and felt better. Mason saw him and found no signs of heart failure.

That didn't seem nearly good enough to me.

"You *know* you're in failure," I said.

He nitpicked: "I know I *was* in failure. Right now I'm not."

"But you go in and out. You're borderline. I don't think enough is being done."

"Enough of *what*?"

"I don't know. I'm not a doctor."

"That's right," he said.

But he put down on paper the doubts he did not express to me:

When I called Pete last Tuesday with dyspnea, shouldn't he have had me come for immediate exam that day?

When I saw him yesterday, shouldn't they have taken a chest X-ray, EKG, blood tests?

Shouldn't I be advised re side effects of diuretics?

I now take seven Lasix daily. No one has ever said anything to me re precautions, side effects, etc.

248

I do not feel well today. Weak, extrelely lethargic.

I feel my pulse. It is very irregular, every fifth or sixth beat missing. It has been irregular on & off for a week. Have not told Martha. Pete said, "It's nothing to worry about."

Also re Peter—he gave me a book called "Risk," about a woman who had heart surgery & he said that I am not *allowed* to read it ! ! ! It was for Martha & I cannot read it because it would be too "disturbing" for me! I laughed & said, "Pete, I've already been there." I know he means well but I guess it is so important for him to maintain a paternal, super-viising & infantalizing role. Just as with the brain damage, which he used to label it psycological—therby of course distancing himself & putting the burden on me. Now I receive trementous reassurance, piternal patts on the back, etc, assurances that I will be "completely normal"— & probably also reassuring himself as well. Moe does this too. Clinicians cannot cope with this sort of thing at all. . . .

Silverman saw him and increased his diuretics again. Still he seemed in a borderline state.

On the second anniversary of his surgery, a few friends came for drinks. He had showered and dressed too quickly and now sat silent in a straight-backed chair, smiling, breathing with difficulty, while the others toasted his health. One had written a poem:

Please don't dance yet on the table—
Not to say that you're not able,
But that Martha might complain
If you kick over the champagne. . . .
So light the candles, bang the drums,
Let the celebration start,
And please accept our Valentine
To your strong but tender heart.

After they left, he cleared up. A tray of dishes undid him, and he lay with his pants unzipped, his midsection bulging with fluid.

I said, "If only you would spend the next few days like an invalid . . ." The word echoed badly. ". . . I mean, really giving yourself a chance to recover, no dish lifting or anything else . . ."

"It's funny," he said. "There was a time when I would have gone into a rage at you for saying such a thing. Now I don't. And I'm so glad. You haven't said anything wrong. We've been through this hell and it's taught us so much about ourselves and each other. We've both kind of grown up in it."

"What a way to grow," I said.

There were many things we could no longer do, none crucial to our well-being, but we did miss them: no theater, no museums, no large parties, no explorations about town; everything planned by the pills, the clock and the availability of emergency help. Now the most modest outings seemed festive.

We liked especially to go to movies on weekday afternoons, when the theaters were near-empty. One day we sat watching a rerun of *Blazing Saddles*, and I was laughing too hard to notice that he had stopped laughing and gone quite rigid. Suddenly he gasped in my ear, "I've got to get out of here right away."

"What is it?"

"My pulse. It's gone crazy. It's up to 144." The average pulse rate is 72. "And my heart is pounding hard."

My own began to pound. The old adrenaline flooded my throat. I helped him out and hailed a cab and sat, close and quiet, while he counted, fingers on the pulse and eyes on the second hand of his watch.

"Something's happening now," he said. "It's slowing down."

"How much?" Visions of its slowing down to a halt.

"A hundred and twenty-four. Weirdest damned thing." He turned and saw what was, I suppose, a look of high tension upon me. He laughed and grabbed my hand. "Take it *easy*, Mushie. I'm going to be okay."

By the time Mason examined him—no more than ten minutes from the onset—his pulse rate was in the nineties.

"One forty-four? It couldn't have been that fast. You're sure you weren't mistaken, Hal?"

"Positive. It was 144."

"What were you doing when it happened?"

"Nothing. We were sitting in a movie theater . . ."

"What movie?"

"*Blazing Saddles*."

"Oh, well, that *explains* it," Peter said. "You were probably laughing too hard."

His pulse did not climb that high again. But often it skipped beats. The pain in his right chest persisted. He had increasing shortness of breath. He felt like hell.

He had a standing medical appointment every two weeks. On a mid-March visit, after the examination, Mason said:

"How do you feel, Hal?"

"Not too well. I've had frequent trouble breathing. I was very dyspneic last night. I thought I had fluid in my lungs."

"There's not much evidence of it now. Your lungs sound dry. Your E.K.G. is stable. Your blood tests are okay. Continue what you're doing and we'll see you in two weeks. But you know you can call us anytime if you think you're in trouble."

I sat listening. *Trouble. Trouble.* Trapped in a semantic blockhouse. We need to put our shoulders to the words and break through. How? We are defeated by the damned circularity of the thing: Listen, Peter, this man is telling you he is in *trouble*, he has *trouble* breathing. But Martha, there is now no evidence of *trouble*, but we want him to call anytime he thinks there is *trouble*. But Peter, remember last spring? You must listen this time. Right now, he thinks there is *trouble*. But right now, Martha, there is no evidence of . . . and so forth.

I stayed silent, which was my mistake.

During the next two weeks he had an irregular pulse for some portion of each day, and we raced frequently down to Mason's office to catch a tracing of it on the electrocardiogram. They caught it a couple of times; more often, not.

Each time, he asked, "What causes it?"

"It's nothing serious. We have patients who have P.V.C.'s all their lives."

"But what causes it?"

"Hal, you know, you do get these cardiac irregularities from time to time."

"Never before last summer."

"Wasn't that during the heat wave? You were probably in a little failure . . ."

"But *what's causing it now?*"

"Well, you know that you have a flabby heart. Don't be afraid to take plenty of potassium, and come see us in two weeks."

Flabby heart. That answer stuck with him. It riled him because it was no answer at all. It was another of those semantic games, a variation on the old It's Your Fault.

"I need a needle and a syringe," he said. "I want to draw a blood sample when I have P.V.C.'s."

"Draw your own blood?"

"Yes. Then you can take it over to the hospital lab and they'll analyze it for me."

"Stick a needle in your own vein? Can you do that?"

"Why not? Junkies do it all the time."

I bought what he needed. His pulsebeat went off that night. He called the hospital at which he had worked and said to the charge nurse in the emergency room, "I'm sending down a blood sample that I want analyzed for potassium, *stat* [immediately]."

He sat down at the dining table. He laid out his materials: the tourniquet, the sterile alcohol sponges, the 10-c.c. syringe with disposable needle, the test tube.

He showed me how to tie the tourniquet around his biceps. He swabbed the crook of his arm with alcohol. He clenched and unclenched his fist several times, until the antecubital vein stood out strong, and then he inserted the needle. I gagged and turned away.

He laughed, although, as he later confessed, he felt queasy. "Not bad for a first try, eh?" he said.

I brought the test tube of blood to the emergency room. Two hours later the report came back: potassium 3.0: slightly below normal, and rather lower than Mason's office had ever recorded.

"How do you account for the difference?" I said.

"You get different readings from different labs. That's common."

"But how do we know which one is right?"

"By *me*. By the way I *feel!*" He was exultant. "That's the answer, kid: a cardiac arrythmia caused by low potassium. That's it! From now on, we're on the way up!"

He called Mason, who was skeptical. "Drawing your own bloods? What do you want to do a thing like that for, Hal? You know every time we've checked, your potassium has been borderline normal, and the lab we use is excellent. And besides, it's only one test, just a little bit low. It doesn't mean anything."

So he did it three times more. Each time, he asked for a copy of the report to be sent to Mason. Soon Peter called him, faintly sheepish but graceful: "Hal, I have four reports. The potassiums are all low."

The difference was not hugely significant, really. It was mostly a victory for the morale: Dr. Lear, Consultant. He increased his potassium intake. It always helped for a time, supplied a sort of instant high; but then the P.V.C.'s would return, and the shortness of breath, and the weakness. Up, down, up, down, the old yo-yo.

A friend, a psychiatrist, was giving a dinner party for Masters and Johnson. Though we never joined such large groups anymore, Hal was fond of the guests of honor, had been graciously entertained by them in St. Louis and wanted very much to go.

He rested for two days. But just hours before party time, his pulse went careening on some unpredictable course and he felt wretched, too weak to take a shower.

"I'll call and explain," I said.

"Not yet. Let's draw a blood."

So he drew it, I tiptoed it down to the hospital lab, we waited, the report came back: potassium below normal; and he took his potassium pill, his fix—quite like Popeye taking spinach, I thought, observing with wonder that patent surge of energy—and we were off to the party.

And he got there looking swell, handsome, and Ginny Johnson hugged him and said, "I thought you were supposed to be *sick*," and people who knew him said to me, "Hey, he looks great!" And strangers asked him, "What do you do?"

What do I do? he thought. I'm trying to stick around. I'm trying to keep my sanity.

He awoke in sudden fear. His heart and his pulse were going mad. Every third beat, every second beat missing: 1, 2, *stop*, 4, *stop*, 6, 7, *stop*, 9, *stop*—like that. It had never been like that before.

Perhaps if he could change the internal pressures . . . He tried changing positions in the bed. It didn't help.

It was 3 A.M. Very quietly—no point waking Martha; what could she do?—he went into the kitchen and dissolved a potassium tablet in orange juice. Then he sat in his study, sipping and waiting, fingers to his demented pulse. Deeply scared.

He called no one. He knew the safest thing would be to go instantly to the hospital, but in this moment he trusted no one but himself. He had the sense that if he sat quietly and kept taking potassium, this awful thing would go away.

... 7, *stop* ... 12, *stop* ... 21, *stop* ... 29, *stop*—much better now.

At 4 A.M. he returned to bed. Immediately his pulse went wild again. Now there were double skipped beats. He went back to the study. He did not dare take another potassium so soon. He sat, sweating.

Suddenly it seemed that his heart stopped. It stopped for so long that he thought it would not start again. He began to cough, frantically, to change the pressures within his chest. Began pounding at his heart with a fist, slamming a fist rhythmically into his chest wall, praying the heartbeat would return before he lost consciousness.

It came back to a more regular beat. He mixed another potassium solution, sipping as he prowled from room to room, trembling. It was 5:30 A.M.

By 6 he had almost a regular sinus rhythm. He sat at his desk, spent, still fearing to go back to bed—what if he never woke up?— but with some instinct that the worst of it was over.

God, that had been frightening. What the hell could have caused it? Daring now to let his concentration slide off his pulse, he leaned back and tried to analyze the thing:

If his heart was stable, as his doctors assured him, perhaps it was the toxic effect of some medication, or interaction of medications.

The heart did return to a regular rhythm when he took potassium. So it must be the potassium deficiency.

Still, his potassium levels had never been critically low. Not low enough to have caused this dreadful episode.

Perhaps, then, it was caused by the diuretics. But no: whatever salts were washed out of him by the diuretics were quickly replaced by the potassium.

There must be a sort of triad. His most important medications: the diuretics, the potassium and the digitalis.

Now: If it wasn't caused by the diuretics, and it wasn't caused by the potassium, might the problem lie in the third corner of this triangle? Some sort of toxic reaction that was produced when the digitalis ...

Digitalis! He realized suddenly that the only one of his drugs which he had taken for granted, with which as a doctor he had felt so

254

familiar that he had never thought to look it up in the *Physician's Desk Reference*, was the digitalis.

He reached for the book. Yes! *Caution: Low potassium levels, in a patient who is taking digitalis, may cause cardiac arrythmias.*

Also: Digitalis toxicity may cause neuralgia.

Of course: the pain in his right chest. The "bronchitis." The "pleurisy."

He called Mason at 8 A.M. Made his report. "I wonder if the digitalis is causing this," he said.

"Well, try skipping the digitalis today, and let's watch it and see what happens," Peter said.

"Okay." That done, he took a Valium and went to sleep.

I woke at 9 and saw him sleeping soundly. Wonderful! I thought. Finally, after all those dyspneas and capricious pulsebeats of the past week, he was getting a good night's sleep.

At noon his pulse woke him again. Not a lunatic pulse, as during those hours which he described to me now, but no sweetheart of a pulse either.

"It's almost a year since you had a consultation," I said. "You remember last spring, how Dr. Corey changed your treatment?"

Paul Corey, a cardiologist whom Hal had known since their training days, had examined him once before and recommended a heavy increase in diuretics; Mason had approved the recommendation, and it had worked dramatically well.

"Yes. I'll go back to Corey. I'm not sure how I'll handle it with Peter and Moe. . . ."

"Make me the heavy," I said.

"No, there's really no problem. I'll say I wanted to get a tracing while I had P.V.C.'s, and Paul's office was so close."

It was in fact two minutes from home, in a hospital building. They had trained together in that building.

Busy place, Corey's office. Waiting room filled, three examining rooms filled, telephones ceaselessly ringing, nurses and secretaries scurrying. I remember it well. I can't help it, I feel the twinge. I remember breezing into Hal's office unannounced, healthy, the patients (the peasants) waiting there, standing room only, the smell of deep worry about kidney stones and bloody pees, the nurse Irene waving me forward, Go right in, he's alone, the sick ones eyeing me, wondering, Who is this woman who is waved inside while we sit on our butts for an hour, some of them recognizing me, smiling with that peculiar respect people have for power once removed—Ah, yes, the doctor's wife—and I go back there and open his door and leap in, Surprise! right into the white-coated lap of power. Hal at his big desk, chair tilted back against the diploma-filled wall: A.M.A.; A.U.A.; A.C.P.S.; Diplomate, American Board of Urology; National Board of Medical Examiners; Resident in Urology, Resident in Pathology, Resident in Medicine and Surgery; St. Louis U.; Alpha Omega Alpha; Yale; With Highest Honors; This is to Certify; For Meritorious Service; In Appreciation of—usually on the phone and always with the cigarette dangling off his lip, giving me the grin and the fast grab, delicious arrogant moments . . . Jesus, how susceptible I was to that particular brand of power. I rubbed up against it and purred. Sexual events, those visits. A wetness in me at the very sight of him there, on his turf, in command and powerful in some ultimate way—because it wasn't legal services he was dispensing, after all; it wasn't soft drinks; it wasn't fur coats or books or stocks and bonds or political patronage; it was life! Health! Surcease from pain! *Help me, Doctor. That* is power. Upon whom are we more dependent? Who else in the world penetrates us literally to the gut, eh? What are politicians beside that! And in his office I would sniff at it, taking it in through my skin. Here, you see how mighty and handsome he is in his white coat? You can talk to him and you can be examined by him and you can be cut open by him and you can admire him and you can desire him but *you can't fuck him.* I can. I can do it anytime I want. Right here, right now if I want, behind this closed door, in this chair, on this desk.

It would have been even more exciting, I suppose, if I had watched him in the operating room, wielding the knife (if I could have borne to look, which I could not). That would have been the ultimate tickle between the legs.

And where did it all go? What a thing, to have stood by and watched him come to every form of impotence. His professional power sucked away first, by both outer and inner spoilers; then his physical power, his sexual power, his mental power, his emotional power, closing steadily down like a lens opening. And is his spirit larger than ever? That would be a fine romance. But no. His spirit, extraordinarily graceful and large for all that he has been through, is nonetheless by necessity smaller, made modest by the diminution of all else.

Oh, Hal. I am not always like this. Ordinarily, with whatever resentments are in me, the bottom line is gratitude. I swear it. Listen, I read the obits every day. The bottom line is gratitude.

On the other hand: At a moment such as this, when all the right strings are plucked and the right buttons pressed, I go crazy. To think of you then, as you were, with your utter confidence and your grace, the patients who waited, Dr. Lear, Dr. Lear, please, I feel worse, I feel better, thank you, bless you . . . And we sit here now, waiting, your hands twisting your brown coat button, the second button down, over the thickest part of your pale scar, buttoning, unbuttoning, buttoning, unbuttoning, unconscious and nervous and weird as Queeg with the steel balls, hands your patients used to call *golden*, sitting here helpless and sick and smelling of worry, and I can't seem to help it. I think of what was and what is and I feel I could cry forever for the loss; I feel this foolish and untenable fury at those who have it still: at the blameless Corey, who strides toward us now in his white coat.

"Hal!" he says, and his face is concerned; his hand dashes out seemingly for a shake but it goes directly to Hal's pulse. "How *are* you?"

"Not too well, Paul," says the pale funny-pulsed invalid to this robust nabob in white. "I've got a very irregular pulse."

"Yes. Gee, Hal. I'd like to see you, but this is a bad day. A crazy day."

"Oh, I know, Paul." Apologetic. "I know how busy you are. I just thought, if we could catch a tracing while my pulse is off . . ."

"*Sure*, Hal. But I won't be able to discuss it with you now. Can you come back later?"

"Anytime, Paul. At your convenience. If we could just get a tracing now . . ."

"*Sure*." Waves to a nurse. "Mary, let's get a tracing on Dr. Lear as soon as a room is free. Can you come back at five, Hal? Then we can talk and I'll examine you."

"Thanks so much, Paul. I'm sorry to barge in on you. I certainly know how busy—"

"Listen, I know *you* understand. A urologist always has to see another prostate. . . ." And smiles, and disappears into his office. I burn. I think it's a needle. See the busy doctor run. Lord, I'm getting paranoid.

Later, after the examination, Corey joined me while Hal was dressing.

"Amazing," he said.

"What's that, Dr. Corey?"

"That body. The guy's got the body of an Adonis, with a heart like that. . . . Amazing." He shook his head.

"About the P.V.C.'s," he told us both. "I'd certainly watch it, but don't worry too much. We can't always tell what causes it. Maybe a change in cardiac reserve, some subtle change in the inner balances . . . these things fluctuate."

A theory, Hal said: Might this be due to the interaction between digitalis and potassium? A digitalis intoxication?

A possibility, Corey said: "Let's see . . . you're taking digoxin once a day and an extra half every other day. Cut it back to just a half every other day. And let me know how you're doing."

It was an immense cutback. At home, Hal said, "I think I'll just try it for a couple of days and see what happens."

"You can't. What good is a consultation if these doctors don't discuss your case together? You *must* tell Peter what Corey recommended."

I was now in the kitchen scrubbing the floor. Therapy.

"What should I tell Peter?" he said.

"Well, tell him that you wanted a cardiogram fast, while you were running P.V.C.'s, and Corey's office was the nearest place. And Corey suggested this cutback and you'd appreciate it if Peter would discuss it with him."

"Okay. That sounds all right."

He goes to the bedroom. I am kneeling on the kitchen floor, Ajaxing away, blessedly absorbed in this mindless task. He comes back:

"Honey, have patience with me."

"Sure." Listen, I don't want to have patience with you. I am tired. Shape up.

"Tell me again: what should I tell Peter?"

"Well, tell him that you wanted a cardiogram fast, while you were . . ."

Tell him whatever. Just don't tell me to have patience. What a bore. I am healthy. I want a healthy husband, skipping around town, hitting the high spots. Leave me alone. Oh, darling, please. Have a regular pulse. I will reward you with my patience and my good temper. When you feel well I am ecstatic, I hug you and kiss you, I *reward* you for health. When you feel sick I am frightened and I

258

retreat. I am getting so damned impatient. Damn it! Can't we ever talk about anything but your goddamn illness? Dearest. Please. Please. Feel well. Otherwise leave me alone to scrub this fucking floor.

"I hate to bother you," he said, "but you'll have to fill out these insurance forms. I just can't do it."

We were living on his disability payments, which were modest, and on whatever I earned as a free lancer. It had never been much. I'd been lazy. I would work only for the top-paying magazines (but for the *Times*; one wrote for the *Times* for prestige) and dawdle for weeks, months over a single assignment, fiddling with adjectives. But now there was a need. Our total savings and holdings would not have carried us a year. No other investments but the real estate: the Provincetown house with a mortgage and the New York apartment with a hefty maintenance. Now I was working as hard and as fast as I could, and perhaps with better results than when I had fiddled. But there were frequent interruptions:

"I hate to bother you, but I'm afraid you'll have to handle the I.R.S. I've tried to get all the papers together, but I get so damned foggy."

We hadn't filed a return in two years. Postponements granted due to organic brain damage, with verifying notes from the doctors. But now our accountant was getting nervous, urging us on. Bills, receipts, diaries, appointment books, bank statements, credit-card statements, business expenses, medical expenses from a two-inch-thick file, interest, depreciations, validations: two years of records to collate.

"I hate to bother you, but can you figure out this bank statement? It's a mess."

"I hate to bother you, but can you call Social Security? I've been going around in circles with them all day. . . . Can you write this letter for me? Three paragraphs, and it's taken me two hours. I *can't* spell. . . . Can you pay these bills? . . . Can you make out these Blue Cross forms? . . . Can you check this with Con Ed? . . . Can you find out about the car insurance? . . . I hate to bother you, but . . ."

Always he had managed the paperwork of our lives, because he did it well, meticulously, and I detested it and botched it. In the healthy days, he would raise periodic objections: "You pile bills on my desk without opening them. You have no concern for our financial obligations. I work hard. I am tired. It is unfair that you leave this whole burden to me." And I, instantly contrite, would say, "You are right. I will manage the checkbook from now on." And of course I would soon muck it up. And he would shake his head over the mess. And I would be appropriately abject: "I *really tried*, but I just . . ." And he would pat my shoulder and say, "Never mind, I'll handle it." A total collusion, as these things always are. A parlor game called Martha Can't Balance the Checkbook.

But now, though he struggled at his desk, he simply could not manage. Papers lost, letters forgotten, calls unreturned, records filed neatly away in places he could not remember. "I hate to bother you, but would you mind . . ."

I minded. I had invested millions in our twopenny game. It drove me crazy to hear the I hate to bother you.

My mother came to visit and we took her one evening to her favorite restaurant, the Madison Avenue Delicatessen.

"Order for me, Mashala," she said.

Why should I seethe? I loved it when my father called me "Mashala." I love it when my husband calls me "Mushie."

"Well, you could have pot roast, or roast chicken . . ."

"No, no, you know what I like. You order it."

Chicken matzoh-ball soup; corned beef sandwich, *very lean*; asserting herself through me to the waiter.

Hal had always tried, with far more compassion than I, to make her feel comfortable, but she was not a comfortable woman. She sat now small and shy and prepared to make gaffes. She spoke tensely of dull things, with the desperation of a woman who knows that she is speaking of dull things, just as I did sometimes; finding myself in her, hating it in us both.

Hal consulted with me: should he have roast beef or scallops? Decided on the scallops. Soon the waiter returned: "Sir, I would advise you to order something else. The scallops are frozen. The sole is very nice. . . ."

"Fine," he said.

I said, "I'm surprised you didn't want the roast beef. We had sole last night."

"You're right," he said. And called back the waiter, and changed it to roast beef. And sat then looking uncomfortable. My mother reached past my face for the salt, saw my annoyance, apologized too profusely. Hal said, "Honey, would you mind awfully if I changed my order again? I think I'm really better off with the sole. . . ."

And I exploded. I hated them both, these two incompetents; I wanted to be anywhere but there, belonging to anyone but them. "I don't give a damn what you order," I snarled. Pounding my lap with my fist. Stop, now; don't make a scene. People at the next table looking at us, sensing trouble, distempers, a woman about to be crazy. What the hell are you looking at? What business is this of yours? Mind your own damned business, eat your drumstick and mind your business. Oh Christ, this rage, I must control it. . . . "Listen, I'm going for a walk," I said. "I'll be back soon," and ran out, others staring and tasting the tastiest appetizer of all, and strode blindly down Madison Avenue, wondering, What the hell will I do? Why must I go back? Why must they be my fate, those two? I want out.

From behind I heard him call, his voice straining: "Martha!"

I turned, terrified now to think what my indulgence was making him pay, and walked back toward him.

"Listen, I understand," he said. "This is part of my problem now. I'm unsure of myself, I can't make decisions. I understand that you get impatient . . ."

"Oh my God," I cried to him. "I have such misery. Such misery. I feel trapped in a triangle of inadequacy—yours, hers, mine. I feel that I am drowning in inadequacy. I can't stand it. . . ."

"Then leave. *Leave*, damn it! How do you think *I* feel?"

How do I think he feels? Oh, charming. It is *his* heart, his battered mind, his fog, his spirit that is being consumed, his pills that poison and keep him alive, his tachycardias and arrythmias and dyspneas and dyslexias, his one-block walks, his days in bed, his skis in cold storage and his bike in chains, his travelogues in the wastebasket, his diplomas in a box in the closet, his work in somebody else's C.V., his past too well remembered and his future closed off, steadily closing in, closing down, and I have taken all this as my own, burdens and fates imposed on me by him, and how do I think he feels?

"I'm so ashamed," I wept. "I love you, I didn't mean it, I couldn't . . ."

"No, wait. You *did* mean it. You always deny these feelings. But they're there, and I understand them. *You* have to understand them. Listen, Martha"—so gentle now—"I know you love me. I also know all your resentments. I cannot escape from my sickness. But you can. Get away from me for a while. Take a vacation away from me."

We embraced and wept, standing there, I for his incomparable dearness. Why doesn't he tell me to fuck off? I must learn to cope with this rage. But that *he* should cope with it so generously: this astounds me.

"*You* ought to leave *me*," I said.

"I would," he said, "but I can't walk."

We went back to the restaurant, where my mother sat silent, scared, like a child who has lost her parents in the crowd. He ate his roast beef dinner and said it was very, very good.

I did go for a long weekend of spring skiing in Vermont. Jon stayed with him, and they enjoyed the three days.

I did not.

That was, he recalled later, the most demoralizing time for him.

The change in medications helped but did not solve his problems, which was a huge disappointment:

"I thought I'd found the magic answer. And I hadn't. I'd feel good, and then suddenly terrible, and I didn't know why. My memory was so wacky that I started a day-by-day diary, to get the patterns of what was happening to me: when my pulse went off, when I felt sick."

(An entry:

4/11. Rx today Lasix IV, digoxin ½, K [potassium] III.

10:00—RSR [regular sinus rhythm], AM medications with breakfast. Feel fine, head clear, etc.

11:30—diuresis began. Slight rregular pulse, 8 stops x minute. Took O.J. & banana & within minutes, RSR and feel great.

12:45—walked two blocks. Dyspneic but no PVC's. On return still slightly winded but not bad, not foggy, *definitely* better than yesterday.

2:00—lunch, RSR, felt fine. Rested two hours.

5:00—walked one block. Very weak, faint, heart pounding & with many PVC's. Difficulty getting home, had to stop twice & then go to bed.

6:15—RSR though still weak.

7:00—Lasix I.

8:00—third K with dinner, then felt *fantastic!!! Totally* well! Head clear as a bell & RSR. Note same pattern as yesterday.

9:30 P.M.—spoke on phone 15 minutes—very dyspneic afterward. Had to rest on bed ½ hour. Feel quite good but note PVC's about 5 x minute . . .)

"I no longer trusted my doctors," he recalled later. "They'd be properly sympathetic and say, 'Come back next week.' That wasn't enough. I was on an emotional roller coaster. When I felt good, I was so hopeful. When bad things happened to me, I was depressed and bewildered.

"It was like the Chinese water torture—drop by drop, just wearing me down. And not understanding *why*—it was so frustrating for me as a doctor not to be able to make a diagnosis.

"Part of me felt I didn't have to be this sick, which made me angry. That was on one level. On another, I had to consider the possibility that this was a progressive deterioration. No matter what my doctors said, I was just going to keep getting worse, and die. And if that was so, I should simply accept it and stop searching for answers in the medications. I mean, I didn't *really* believe that, but I had to consider the possibility."

I was visited by a college chum whom I had not seen in ten years. We exchanged the requisites: "You look exactly the same," she said. "You haven't changed a bit," I said. In fact it was almost true. She had changed startlingly little. This pleased and warmed me. I felt goodwill. I felt safe.

"You remember Hal?" I said; and yes, of course she remembered. I saw her eyes flicker, taking in the change.

She told us what had been happening with her husband. An old war injury had kicked up. He had developed a staph infection in his head, behind his eye, where a steel plate had long ago been inserted. Owing to this infection, his flesh, his very head, had begun to decay from within. His head, she said, had begun coming apart. Last year they had operated and removed all the staph, but they had not attempted reconstructive surgery. Instead, they had made a plastic prosthesis to conceal the decay.

"What kind of prosthesis?" I asked.

"It is a piece of forehead and an eyebrow, and every morning he glues it on before he goes to work. The trouble is that it does not match his own skin color. It is much pastier, the way his skin looked when he left the hospital."

"Why doesn't he have another one made?" Hal said.

"Because he doesn't want to spend the money. He would spend it on anything that he thought was *necessary*, but he thinks this is *cosmetic*. Those things are no good anyway. The edges fray and you have to keep trimming them."

Soon she left, and I thought of this man whose head had decayed and I had in my mind pictures of how this piece of forehead and eyebrow must look, a pasty patch of plastic glued on his brow, trimmed now and again with a cuticle scissors. So he wore his decay on the outside; as though Hal were to wear his heart on his sleeve. Of course, this man was no metaphor for anything. He was beyond metaphor, the thing itself.

I said to Hal, as we lay in bed, "Make a spoon," and he curled himself around me in that way.

"I wish," I said, "that we could build an electrified fence around our lives."

"And we could stay inside it and take care of each other," he said.

Yes. I was pleased and surprised, for usually he would not play such games with me. I pushed it no further. I simply lay there and thought about it, loving it: an electrified fence and we nestled within it, perhaps right here in this bed, in enchanted circles of arms, safe from all intruders, all dangers, various forms of change and decay.

This is a bad nervous time, I wrote. He is in a bad way. Something is happening in him. We don't know what. His P.V.C.'s, everything with its neat cool acronym, persist. In the past week he has been running fevers. Low-grade, but still. I have feverish memories of fevers. Almost a seasonal rhythm: Hal's annual spring fever. To the P.V.C.'s they continue to say, It is not dangerous. To the fevers they say, Take two aspirin and call us tomorrow. I asked Peter if all this could be a recurrence of the postpericardiotomy syndrome, not even remembering when that was. Last spring? The spring before? I said, "Remember when he had those fevers and he said he was dying, you had to do something right away, and you put him on steroids? It was like magic."

But this is different, Peter said. They see the syndrome a few months post-op, but never two and a half years later. Why the fevers? They don't know. Peter says possibly a virus—another of what Hal calls the garbage-pail words. I suspect they are quite convinced that his heart has deteriorated further; and since there is nothing to be done, they don't tell us.

How much does he know? What is in his head? As the patient he may have faith, but what does he believe as the doctor? Or has he now suspended professional judgments?

Yesterday, all day, he felt so fine. Temp normal, pulsebeat normal.

He said, "I feel like I could go out and run. I feel like I'm on the mountaintop. You mustn't let it get you down, Martha. You must remember that I *can* feel like this. Now all we have to figure out is how to keep me from feeling the *other* way." He makes his theories, tests them, changes the timing of pills in relation to meals, breaks up the dosages in different ways—forever struggling to find the chemical key, his own alchemist.

Last night we had series tickets for *The Threepenny Opera* at the Beaumont. I took Ellen. I hadn't been there since a year ago last winter, when we left the theater on a cold snowy night and he turned to me with tears in his eyes and said, "Is my head really getting better?" God, what a long battering he has taken! How does he still, *ever*, keep good spirits?

Afterward Ellen and I went for a drink. She said: "I suppose in a way it is easier to deal with terminal cancer. You know what must come. But with this . . ."

I do not know if this is true, or if it is simply a thing that people say. On the whole it must be easier to hope.

He was waiting up for me: "Did you have a good time? Oh, Mushie dear, I'm *so* glad. I wish you'd go out more."

Always he pushes me to go, to do. I should accept more invitations, he says. I should go to more writers'-group meetings. I should see more of my friends. Why don't I call Abby for lunch? Pushing me toward an alternative life, to get a jump on the eventual void. I suppose if he whined, You leave me alone among my remissions while you go out and have good times, it would not be so hard to bear. But then, that would be another husband.

This morning I looked at him sleeping and thought, Well, I am just so tired. It might not be bad now simply to lie down beside him in our big bed and sleep together, once and for all. I have never had such thoughts before.

He wanted a written copy of his recent history.

"I'm not angry at Moe and Peter," he said angrily. "I know they want to help me. But I also know they can be fallible, and they are busy. I've been too passively accepting the patient's role.

"Last year I said, 'I have severe air hunger.' And they put me on a monitor, instead of getting me out of failure, and three days later I was in the hospital. Now I come in and say, 'I am very short of breath,' and they find no evidence of failure, so they give no credence to *my* description of *my* condition. They are missing the boat again. And I want to have more control at the helm of this boat. I want the history so that if I get another consultant, I can give hard data instead of impressions."

Damn it, he cries. I'm the doctor! I'm the doctor!

He got more than his recent history. He demanded to see the surgeon's operating-room notes. Had it been in my power to keep the notes from him, I do not know, even today, what I would have done. On the one hand, people should not be denied the truth. On the other, why not? I have always had trouble on these levels of ethics.

Anyway, it was not in my power. He read the notes, and that tore it.

"I had another heart attack," he said.

"Does it say that?"

"No. Not in the operative notes. It must have happened immediately afterward. In the recovery room."

"What makes you think so?"

"It fits. According to the notes, it was a totally uneventful operation. I left the O.R. with a normal blood pressure. All my life signs were stable. Everyone who saw the angiogram had assured me I'd have a good result. Bell had said I'd be in the I.C.U. for two days. Instead I was there for nine days, I almost died, I had high fevers and no blood pressure, and I came out with a chunk of my brain dead and so much of my heart gone that I never had a chance of getting well."

I was silent.

"You don't seem surprised," he said. "Did you know?"

"Yes."

"Who told you?"

"Peter."

"When?"

"Last year."

"Why wasn't I told?"

"We thought it best."

"I see." Glacial. "You all put your heads together and decided what was best for me."

"Hal. What possible good could it have done to tell you?"

"What good . . . For God's sake! I've spent all this time thinking . . . I've been living on all the wrong hypotheses. I've presumed all along that when they opened me they found a terrible heart, much worse than they had expected, and they did the best that could be done with this terrible heart, and I was damned lucky to come out alive.

"Now I find I was totally wrong. My heart *wasn't* that terrible. My coronary arteries were shit, but the pump itself wasn't that bad. It was good enough going in so that if I hadn't had that infarct, I could have been fine. Do you understand? This was a patient"—slamming the operative note—"who six months later should have been *fine*. This patient should have been able to swim a mile and jog and work. I was *so close*. I was *there*. It was within my grasp to emerge from this thing *a normal person*. Instead I had another catastrophe from which I'll never recover.

"Moe never told me, 'The surgery went well but this catastrophe happened afterward. I'm so sorry.' He said, 'Well, what can you expect? It was massive surgery.' I don't think there was an invidious cover-up. Moe may not have told me in order to protect me, or himself, and I think that was wrong, but I know he meant well. He didn't understand, though. *None* of you understood: *the truth would have been easier.*"

He rarely mentioned it after that. On occasion, like his fevers, it would erupt. Always he said, "The truth would have been easier." I myself found the truth far harder, and wished that neither of us had ever learned it.

"He's so weak, Peter," I said. *Sotto voce*; Hal resting in the next room. "And he looks very bad."

"I know. And he's confused. He's doing funny things, drawing his own bloods, he's getting depressed with those P.V.C.'s . . ."

Peter, Christ. Who wouldn't get depressed? How would you be after a week in bed with the flu? "Peter, there's nothing funny about drawing his own bloods. He wanted to get samples immediately, while his pulse was wild. That's reasonable. You've assured us that the P.V.C.'s are nothing to worry about. But he looks toxic, he feels toxic, and we don't understand why he has them."

"Well, the worst possibility, of course, is the one we worry about all the time with Hal: further weakening of the heart muscle."

Yes. "How can we determine if that's it?"

"We can't. Not without another angiogram, and I don't recommend that."

"Could something have gone wrong with one of his bypasses?"

"Probably not."

"Could it be due to the medicines? Some toxic reactions?"

"Possibly. We have to experiment with the dosages. We'll change them a little and see how he does over the weekend."

"One last question: Please be straight with me. Do you think it's more likely that he has some toxic reaction, or further weakening of his heart?"

"If we can get him stabilized on the medicines, I think we'll be okay."

"That doesn't answer my question."

"Repeat the question."

"In your opinion, is this more likely a further deterioration of the heart, or a toxic reaction to medicine?"

"Martha, he's always had a weak heart muscle. I think if we can hit on the right formula with the medicines, we can stabilize him."

You've heard me twice. Never mind. Stabilize, labelize, tableize, fableize. So our conversations go.

He was not stabilized. Instead, that Friday, he developed heavy râles, listened to them himself, through his own stethoscope, graced by a yard of extra tubing that he had taped into a Goldbergian device for just such exigencies as these. I held the bell to his back. He said, "Now to the left. Good. Now higher. Good," repeating Good, good, as they always do, though it was not good at all. He went swiftly into acute failure, with desperate pulling for air, and I rushed him down to the doctors.

Nurses took him away. I sat crying in the waiting room. Mason came and put an arm about me and drew me into his office.

"You seem unhappy today," he said.

"I guess. A little."

"Any suggestions about what we should do, Martha?"

I shake my head No, numbly. Yet it seems to me that this is really at the nub of it: they have waited too long, too often, for our suggestions. He and I sit for a moment in silence. Then:

"It's just . . . If he is deteriorating, there is nothing much you can do. I know that. I know that I must handle it better, but it is so hard. He says to me, 'Moe has told me that the disease has not progressed, and I take him at his word. So my problems must have to do with the medications.' A couple of days ago he felt marvelous. He said, 'Look at me, I'm on the mountaintop. Now all we have to do is figure how

268

to keep me from feeling the other way.' And now he makes charts, he takes notes, he goes at it with the doctor's didactic mind, he keeps trying to diagnose it, break it open, find the key. There's something really quite . . . heroic about the way he keeps struggling to beat this thing. . . ."

"That's what we love about him, Martha."

". . . But if it *is* progressive, there is no way he *can* beat it. And if there is this awful gap between the truth and what he thinks is the truth, I can't handle it. I don't know how. And I love him so much, and I am scared of losing him, and it just seems to me . . . I know you and Moe care, I know you are trying your best, but when he comes in here so sick and you examine him and tell him to come back in two weeks, and he leaves here and he can barely walk to the corner . . . that just isn't good enough. There has got to be some better way for you to cope with him and I don't know what it is, but . . ."

"Well, maybe he's right, Martha. Maybe he can be better. In a way I think it's our fault. We didn't treat him vigorously enough when he came in with failure last month."

I tasted bile. "When do you start treating vigorously?"

"We really should pursue a new regimen vigorously now."

"Yes. And I don't even know what that means, but I know that if he can be better, you have got to make a more vigorous effort to keep him better. You and Moe should confer, and there should be some comprehensive scheme for dealing with him, not this hit-or-miss way. And if that means putting him into the hospital and keeping a constant eye on him while you pursue some new regimen, then do it that way. Whatever."

"I think it would be a good idea to hospitalize him. It occurred to me, but I didn't want to depress him. How would he take it?"

"I think he would feel enormously relieved that something was being done. Anything. But just not this 'Let's try thus-and-such, and we'll see you in two weeks,' because I'm telling you, Peter, he's going down the tube again."

Pause. Then he buzzed on the intercom: "Get Dr. Lear on the urgent list for admission."

"Look, don't put him the hospital just to appease me. But if, in your own judgment . . ."

"No, no, I agree. It's fair to give him a good workup. I mean, maybe he's right. You speak of 'going down the tube.' But that means going steadily down, and in fact that's not his picture. He *is* better sometimes."

"But why is he such a yo-yo?"

"Martha, because this is a man with a very borderline cardiac reserve. This is a very bad heart muscle. It's so bad it is barely functioning, and any change—food, heat, fluid, rest, anything—is enough to change its balance. Look: We're not going to keep him around for ten years. You know that. We're not going to keep him around for five years. But maybe we can keep him around for months, or for a year. . . ."

I freeze. For months? For a year? I tune out. I haven't heard him.

"Okay?" He smiles at me warmly. I smile back. "I'll go examine him now. Maybe you'd like just to sit here, have a little rest . . ." And he leaves. I rest. I examine, in depth, a paper clip. I am numb as this paper clip. Numb, deaf, dumb, blind, nothing. I don't know nothing.

And soon he returns with Hal. Hal has had his intravenous shot of diuretics. "I'm *much* better, honey," he says.

Oh, good. For months? For a year?

"We'll try to get you in by Monday," Mason says. "But Hal,"—leans forward, smiling apprehensively—"I want you to try to behave nicely with the house staff. I mean, it will be the usual thing: residents, interns, students, and they'll be popping in and out to take histories and you'll be asked the same questions a hundred times . . ."

Small smirk on my husband's face. "Why are you bringing this up, Pete?"

"Well, you know . . . you've been sort of . . . *irritable* in the past. Just try to remember, they're only doing their jobs. Because the last time, there were some complaints . . ."

Now Hal smiles big. "Sure, Pete," he says. "I'll be nice."

Complained, did they, that my husband was irritable when they took histories? Tch. Let's play Doctor. You lie down. I'll take the history:

Q. *How long have you been sick?*

A. *Two years and ten months.*

Q. *Current status?*

A. *Cardiac cripple.*

Q. *How many hospitalizations?*

A. *Seven.*

Q. *How many heart attacks?*

A. *Three that I know of.*

Q. *What were your symptoms preoperatively?*

A. *Angina.*

Q. *What are your symptoms postoperatively?*

A. *Weakness. Fogginess. Difficulty breathing. Difficulty walking. Difficulty talking. Difficulty reading. Difficulty spelling. Difficulty remembering. Irregular heartbeats. Fevers of Unknown Origin. Heartache.*

Q. *Angina?*

A. *No.*

Q. *Good! To what do you attribute your other symptoms?*

A. *Possible fates. Possible fuck-ups.*

Q. *How long will you live?*

A. *I don't know.*

Q. *How do you feel?*

A. *Sick.*

Q. *When were you well?*

A. *I don't remember.*

Q. *Why are you irritable?*

A. *Who, me?*

I woke several times crying out and each time he reached over to comfort me, asking, "What were you dreaming?"

"I don't know," I said. I felt nauseated, as though poisoned by yesterday. *Months. A year.* How can it be? What was it Hal said recently? "Shape up, Mushie, we've got to shape up for our golden years . . ." Oh, my dearest. There will be no golden years.

At breakfast he confronted me: "Hear me out. I know the night you had. I am worried about the way you handle the strain. I'm no model. But the fact is I could fall apart. It would be so easy. I could just get under the blankets and grieve for myself, and everyone would understand perfectly. Everyone would say, 'Oh, poor bastard, with all he's been through, no wonder he behaves like that.' But what would be the point? What good would it do me?

"So I'm telling you, there's a certain *indulgence* in falling apart, and you shouldn't indulge yourself in that way. You shouldn't be drinking yourself to sleep. You shouldn't be putting the refrigerator into your mouth whenever you get upset. You should say, 'Okay, *we* got stress.

But I'm still *me.'* And don't sit *shiva.* I'm not dead yet. Okay?"

"Okay."

I did just as Hal had done two years earlier. I went doctor-shopping. First to the consultant Corey.

"Tell me," I said.

"Well, so far as surgery goes, you've shot your bolt. That leaves medicines. When you have cardiac function that's this limited, nuances of treatment can make an enormous difference. We have to see if we can give him better function."

"I'm not asking about better function. I'm asking about life."

"I know."

"So?"

"So. You're a bright woman. What can I say? A prognosis of years is . . . unlikely."

"Is what?"

"Unlikely."

I paid a visit to my old analyst William Jody, who had long since become a personal friend. He was in friendship, as he had been years earlier in therapy, a most commonsensical man.

I said, "He is dying."

"Martha, you've always known. Haven't you?"

"Sort of. And yet no. I swear this is true. They had told me in various ways that it was bad. But then you say to yourself, What does bad mean? Bad can mean cancer that takes ten years to kill. And suddenly I'm told a year, or months, and there is no way I can hope for it to be open-ended anymore. The thing has slammed shut. But *he* still manages to hope. He experiments with pills, he talks about consultants, he is beginning again to talk about Provincetown . . ."

"Well, of course," Bill said. "I would want to do the same. Sure, these are denials. But they are also life; they are the business of living."

"What should I do, then? Should I deny with him?"

"I think you have to function on two levels. On one level, you have to be exactly where he is, sharing whatever hopes and illusions he wants to keep. On the other, you have to know within yourself that there are absolutely no illusions."

"Don't say that. God."

"Listen, Martha . . ." He was very gentle. He spoke exactly as Hal would have spoken, had Hal been in that catbird seat. ". . . listen, we

272

could be sitting here next year having this same conversation. But that would be a spit in the eye of fate. What you have to accept is that you could wake up any morning now and find him dead."

"I can't cope with it."

"That's what you said when your father died. You coped."

"This is different. This is my life."

"No, it's not. You'll cope. You've always been much stronger than you gave yourself credit for."

Wrong, Bill.

"I think you're doing very well," he said. "You've been living under great stress for a long time. You haven't run away. You haven't gone into a depression. You haven't suddenly decided that you really don't love your husband anymore and you want a divorce. You haven't started screwing your head off—all things that people have done in such circumstances. You give him love and support . . ."

"Bullshit. He gives *me* support. He tells me, 'You've got to shape up for our golden years.'"

"You give to each other. Look, the two of you are going through an extraordinary experience. It is teaching you . . ."

"A teaching experience?"

"What you're living through now is about the hardest thing in the world: to watch someone you love fading from life, and to be helpless. And when it happens you will have a very, very bad time. But you will come out of it with a great capacity for love, because this experience is teaching you things about love that you might otherwise never have known."

"Bullshit."

"It's true," he said.

That helped. But I was not done with doctor-shopping. I called Mason.

"I'm having a terrible time with what you told me," I said.

"What did I tell you?"

"That we might keep Hal only for months, or maybe a year."

"You misunderstood me. I didn't say that. No one can know that for certain."

Bingo. Just what the doctor ordered.

But finally it was Hal who helped me most.

"You say I shouldn't hoard my fears," I said. "Shall I tell you?"

"Yes. You have no idea how comforting it is that you're willing to discuss this with me."

"I would like to discuss a strategy for survival. If I died, what would you do?"

"If you died," he said, "I would have my time of mourning. That would be an organic process. Slow and very hard. What would help me would be to stay as much as possible involved with people. If I were healthy, to work; and to do things that would keep me active and give me pleasure. Go to the theater. Ski. Make planters for the terrace."

"Then you would stay in this home? I have felt that if you died, I would not be able to stay. I would close the door on it all. You would not?"

"Oh, no. Familiar things would comfort me. The memories of you would be everywhere: there is the picture Martha hung, there is the desk Martha worked at, this is the street we walked down together . . ." We were both crying now. "I would not flee from memories of you," he said. "I would cherish them. But then, there would come a time when I would want more. At some point I would look at myself and say, 'Well, what kind of life do you want now? In what direction will you go?' It would be the death of a part of me. But listen, Martha: there would never be a question of my not surviving. *Never.*"

He was always my own best therapist.

In fact he did not go to the hospital. He improved, for reasons unknown, and the doctors removed his name from the urgent list. The fever disappeared spontaneously. He felt stronger, walked better, checked his pulse each morning and smiled, nodding to its steady beat.

"Oh, God. It's so *good* to feel good," he said. "I'm getting better, kid."

"I know," I said, not understanding how a body could feel good, or even be ambulatory, with a heart that barely functioned and on 280 milligrams of diuretics a day.

As he had done so long ago, he swung half-gallon vodka bottles in the air, manipulating them as weights.

"Oh, my. I haven't seen you do that in a long time."

"I've been doing it every day for a week. After all, I don't want to waste away. Right, Mushie?"

"Right!" I smiled and pressed him close, like a compression dressing.

I saw a faint crack in the face of his front tooth. "Is that new?" I said.

"No, I've had it for a while. But I think I should see the dentist before we leave for the Cape. I should call him and say, 'Listen, you have to fix me up, because I'm scheduled to leave town for an extended period.'"

For an extended period.

We walked. Two blocks, no more, but without symptoms.

We took each other to lunch. *"L'chaim,"* we said over wine. And each evening, at dinner: *"L'chaim."*

On our fifteenth anniversary, in late May, we went to buy him clothes. The first time in two years. A nylon windbreaker—good for the Sunfish, he said; several pairs of jeans; a well-cut blazer, in which he looked supremely healthy and handsome. "Oh, *yes*," I cried, and burst into tears.

The salesman was bewildered. "What's the matter?" he said. "She doesn't like the blazer?"

Hal hugged me. "She likes it," he said.

I asked, "What do you think has happened? How come you are so much better?"

"Don't ask," he said. "Let's just take it."

And we took it, in June, to Provincetown.

Chapter 26

THE dotty old house tilted toward us in greeting. From whatever direction one approached, it tilted in greeting, like an
indiscriminate host. Four stories tall and not a plumb line in it, solid
as ever.

We stood on our bulkhead and looked out at the charmed circle of
our bay. Beyond lay Portugal. The land curved so sharply at this far
tip of Cape Cod, curving back on itself like a snail shell, that one's
sense of direction was tricked. What should have been north was
south. Portugal was out there where Boston should have been, and
Boston stood stubbornly back behind our right shoulders.

Now the great sand flats rippled out to low tide; the toylike
trawlers hugged up against derelict wharves; the tourist schooner
Hindu, out for its sunset ride, was gliding in full sail like a ghost ship
past the lighthouse at Wood Point toward the far cliffs of Truro—
everything etched in a light so flat and cool and pure that I'd always
imagined I could reach out an arm and strike it all down like a stage
set. It was a light artists had worshiped, before fluorescence.

"We made it, kid," Hal said.

I think we were both astonished.

The house, like so much else, was bittersweet. Everywhere I saw his strength: the Sheetrock that he had shoved into walls, the fence posts that he had pounded into the ground, the stairs that he had taken at a run, with hammers and drills and a selection of fifty-cent *How To's* under his arm. The stairs had nagged at me. "Shall we fix up the little room on the first floor for our bedroom?" I had asked before we left New York. "No!" Furious. "Damn it, if I can't make it up to my own bedroom, I don't want to go." He took the stairs slowly, and it was all right.

I had come with other misgivings. The town had a few general practitioners, mostly as old as our house. The nearest hospital was an hour away, in Hyannis. In emergencies one called the Provincetown Rescue Squad, a volunteer crew composed of our electrician, our plumber, our carpenter, our handyman, several firemen. They were well trained and eager, but still.

"No problem," he said. He found a new medical man nearby, a young internist who would administer routine care. He met with the electrician, Ronnie White, and the carpenter, Adam Wolf, and the plumber, Mark Robinson, to plan the management of his case in event of the likelier emergencies: pulmonary edema, ventricular fibrillation, cardiac arrest and such and so. They came on their lunch hour, in their pickup trucks. Proudly they described their new mobile emergency unit, with its radio hookup to Hyannis Hospital, and spoke with assurance of I.V.'s, vasopressor drips, milligrams, defibrillators; they sounded just fine.

Then he relaxed completely. He put on his ancient sawed-off jeans, in which he had tottered through hospital corridors after his first heart attack, and I don't think he ever took them off while the sun shone.

He had arrived looking sick. He tanned quickly, and when he was tan, that face could do no wrong. Our friends marveled at the healing properties of ocean air. And perhaps it was the air, or perhaps some untraceable chemistry between him and this place. Whatever it was, and however weak his body, he simply glowed.

In this place it caused him no distress that he could not work. Among the summer people, nobody worked; at least not too visibly, which would have been bad form in Provincetown. The artists and writers wrestled with their blocks in hidden studios, in the morning hours, and then came out to play. Here he was of the majority, and he sat with the majority on waterfront decks, sipping gin-and-tonics through long afternoons. Sitting with him, I felt part of the normal world. I felt rapture.

He puttered. He waxed and rewaxed the hull of his Sunfish. He had not dreamed that he might ever sail it again, and I thought it a madness to try. We argued:

"I'll go out on a calm day. I'll stay close to shore. I won't heel."

"At least let me go with you."

"I'd like to go alone the first time."

"But you can't swim anymore."

"I'll wear a life jacket. The water's warm."

Neighbors put his boat into the water, and he sailed off. He never knew that they sat on their decks and watched, through binoculars, ready to race out by speedboat if he seemed to be in trouble. I watched too. He looked ecstatic. What the hell, I thought. Maybe months, maybe a year, maybe who knows; better like this than in bed. And managed thereafter to button my lip.

He still could not walk far. But for the first time in years he drove, roaring down the mid-Cape highway at twenty miles an hour in the yellow Jeep, vintage 1956, that I had bought him on our tenth anniversary. He had never dreamed to do that again, either. In the old days we'd had fine adventures in that Jeep, skidding down the high dunes, bumping along on the back beach to picnic in hidden coves. Now the dune rides were gone—he no longer had the stamina for those skids and ruts—but we had lovely drives on the quiet country roads.

I remember particularly a day, a moment, when we were heading out to the Wellfleet lakes—black, still waters surrounded by pines. We were driving down a back road in the old thigh clamp, his hand on my upper leg, mine on his, as we had always driven when we went up to Vermont to ski, or to the Cape for summer vacations. It had been a small ritualized celebration of our mobility: get into the old thigh clamp and go.

The day was so fine that he drove bare-chested. He looked fit, he was wallowing in sun, the hand that gripped my thigh was steady and vital, and if it hadn't been for the scar that ran like a chalk line down the length of his chest, and for the emergency supplies—pills, portable oxygen, vials of fluid, needles, syringe—that lay at my feet, I might have imagined we were as we had always been.

I thought, Awareness of moments is now a substance in the blood, like plasma. This is the happiest moment of my life.

And as I thought this, he threw back his head, and gave a yowl of laughter, and said: "I have never been happier in my life."

Cautiously, we even hit a few of the night spots. It felt like high living to sit in the tackiest bars, listening to the scurviest music, amid hippies who nodded.

There was the White Party, an annual gay gala, held in a venerable joint named The Atlantic House. Gay friends invited us. It would be too mobbed for his comfort, we knew, but he insisted that I go. At 1 A.M. hundreds were pressing through doors and fire exits, seeking frantically to escape from the cool of the street into a small oven where music blasted. They were all in white, white satins and silks, white body paints, white capes and caftans, white sequins, white ostrich plumes, grand plumed fantasies of white, packed rump to rump, sweating hard, shaking and twitching and sniffing and snorting; they held the stuff to my nostrils and spread it on my gums and I flew, shrieked with laughter and shook my stiff rump on that floor like the best of the fag hags and felt graceful as could be, though how I looked was quite another story. At dawn we staggered out. A great white peacock was coming down Commercial Street. He moved slowly, ashimmer with rhinestones, one hand steadying his tall feathered crown, attendants holding the trains and veils that billowed behind him, and as he passed we cried, "Bravo! Bravo!" and clapped our hands, and he gave a small nod of the chin and a tiny tilt of the fingertips, like the Queen Mum in her carriage, and sailed on to the party, and we snorted down to the beach to watch the sun rise. I felt as though there had never been a day's sickness in the family.

Despite his improvement there was not much sex. To be active in sex made him fearfully short of breath, and he refused to be always the passive one.

"Why don't you just lie back and enjoy it?" I said.

"No. It's too damned unilateral. I can't."

"Bloody insulting. I never heard such a thing. If there was one thing they always said about Martha Lucille Weinman, it was that she gave good head. They *all* said that."

He tried to laugh. "They were lying," he said.

So there was not much sex. But there were orgies of tenderness. In the kitchen, preparing meals, we nuzzled each other, making noisy kisses and soft grabs at flesh. We rubbed noses. At dinner we rubbed knees. By the light of fat candles set in red fishnet-covered jars, with the waves slapping against our bulkhead and the buoys clanging mournfully far out in the bay, we devoured mussels and steamers and drank *vinho verde*, a local requisite. *"L'chaim,"* we said. We held hands, fingers twining, stroking, pressing the flesh with reassuring little strokes. I could not leave him alone. How much, I wondered, of my desperation does he sense? May gone, June gone, July half-gone. How many months is "months"?

"We are so lovely with each other, aren't we?" I said. "We are better now than we have ever been, aren't we?"

"Yes."

"Why do you suppose that is? Is it because we live more in the moment?"

"Yes, of course."

"But we talk about the joy we have together. We talk about how nice it is to be together all the time. What if you had simply retired; what if you were home all the time without ever having been sick? Would it be as nice?"

"Retired? I would never have retired. Don't you remember, I used to say that I would retire when I died."

"Oh, yes."

There is no way, I thought, to have the one without the other. To be this happy is definitionally a function of being this scared. Or vice versa.

For Jon and Judy, Provincetown was special too. It no longer drew them as powerfully as it did us, but it had a powerful past. Whatever the disruptions of their childhood, the shredding of a marriage, the departure of a father, the acquisition of a stepmother who acquired them with reluctance, Provincetown had given them summers of stability.

Now they came to visit. Jon came from England, where he was working this year toward his doctorate at Cambridge.

Judy came with her child from Northampton, Mass. He was a sturdy, sunny two-year-old.

"Hello, Grandma," he said.

"Listen, Judy," I said, "straighten this kid out. The name is Martha."

"Sure, Grandma," she said.

They went out one evening, Jon and Judy, and left us to baby-sit. Toward midnight the child woke, scared in a strange dark room, and began to cry. *"Mommy,"* he shrieked. I slipped into his bed and embraced him. He shrieked on.

"Jacob, tomorrow we will make cookies," I said. "What kind of cookies do you like best?"

"I want my mommy!"

"Mommy will be here soon. What kind of cookies should we make? Sugar cookies? Raisin cookies? Oatmeal cookies?"

"Chocolate," he wailed. "And I will eat them all. *Mommy!*"

I'd never had an easy way with children, or wanted children of my own. Now that it was respectable, even environmentally correct, to be childless by choice, I could claim (and often did) that I had simply been ahead of my time.

In the early years of our marriage I had sometimes wavered. What spectacular productions might we bring forth together? Boys to the White House, girls to the sky. Watching a Rinso baby coo on TV, I would go soft. "Let's have a baby," I would say. He left the choice to me. He would have liked to have a family together. If not, no sorrow; he already had one. "Let's do it tonight." "No, not tonight," he would say, having been here before, "but if you still want to next month, we'll do it then." By next month, I never wanted to.

When my father had died, I had longed for a child to name after him. That longing soon had passed. My mother had yearned. "You'll be sorry when it's too late," she had said. "Remember, Mashala. What else is there in life but the children? Daddy always said that." And of course, that was the trouble: I did remember. They had lived for the children, lived through the children, their lives had been footnotes to the children, it was the only model I knew, and I wanted no part of it.

Sometimes I had wondered if I would indeed be sorry when it was, as she said, too late. And here I was in my mid-forties and often I found myself yearning, too late, for a child to name after Hal. A boy child who, had I done this thing when I should have done, would be past his Bar Mitzvah by now, a man, and ready in due time—in months, perhaps; in a year at most—to become a Daddy.

"Mommy," Jacob wailed.

"Sh," I said. "Grandma is here."

In late July Hal slowed down a bit. Took longer siestas, stopped using his boat. He said, "I'm feeling so good, why rock it? Ho ho."

In August the old P.V.C.'s came back. Not badly, but not to be ignored.

He arranged for blood tests in Orleans, a half-hour's drive up the Cape, and left early one morning while I slept.

He was gone two hours. I squirmed. Alone in the car, after all; fasting bloods, no breakfast, no potassium; P.V.C.'s. Finally I called the laboratory. A voice said, "Dr. Lear left an hour ago." "Did he seem all right?" A pause. Then: "Why . . . I think so. He rested; then he seemed better."

An hour later he arrived, looking drained.

"You're all right?" I said.

"Yes."

"Why did you go alone?"

"I didn't want to wake you."

"That's ridiculous. We planned to go together."

"I'm a big boy."

"Terrific. You've been gone three hours. You could have called."

"I suppose I should have. I'm sorry."

"Okay." Mollified. "You seem tired. I think you might feel better if you took a nap. . . ."

"*You* think. *You* think. For Christ's sake, you are not my guardian angel."

Not your guardian angel? Fuck *you*, buddy. *You* try living with someone you love through three years of cardiac crises. *You* walk the tightrope between over- and underprotection, try to keep your balance on that tightrope for three fucking years. Your guardian angel, eh? I resign. Here's the key, here's the house, here's the marriage, goodbye. I'll send you a sympathy card.

"Fuck *you*," I said.

"Don't talk to me like that." He covered his face with his hands.

"Ah, Hal. Darling." Embracing him. Christ, my passions turn on dimes. "It's just that I was so worried."

"I'm sorry. It was terrible not to call you."

"I'm sorry too. For what I said."

"You should be," he said. "That's no way to talk to a *zaydeh*."

Then came a sudden bout of heart failure. He sat upright with pillows behind his head, pale beneath the bronze, pulse rapid, couldn't talk, winking to reassure me and panting, "If I get worse, all you have to do is call the Rescue Squad."

Jesus, not again. I have lost my resiliency, misplaced it somewhere in this golden summer.

When it eased, we called Silverman in New York. Hal always described his own symptoms precisely, rich in detail that might matter, and the doctors who listened were not used to such patients and would begin to tap their feet. Now Silverman broke in abruptly: "Martha, how's your book coming? I wrote fifty pages this weekend. . . ." He had been working on a book, a therapy guide for cardiacs, and loved now to talk writer talk. "Did I tell you I've got a publisher? They're very enthusiastic. They said . . ." And onward, until finally, with Hal breathing heavy on the extension like an obscene caller in the night, I said, "Moe, that's great. I'm so happy for you. But right now I am concerned about what is happening to my husband."

"Oh. Okay. Hal, here's what I want you to do. . . ."

He took extra pills and drained it all out. He rested. He seemed subdued but in good spirits. Despite my own fears, I thought he felt secure.

Then I read his notebook. We'd had an understanding: his notes were sacrosanct, and so were mine. But I opened this notebook by error, a line caught my eye and I read on, transfixed.

Probably I will die rather soon. It is not the prospect of death that is so hard. It is the *process* that is such a bitch. I see a progressive & seemingly inexorable deterioration. Quite insanely I think that I got to survive through Sept because Sept is the nicest month in PTown.

Sense of impending death came with my trip to Orleans. Foolishly I went alone. After 15 miles I felt dizzy and my heart pounding. But I loss too far to drive home again. Stayed in rt-hand lane, untied safety belt to provide maximal abdominal breathing, etc. At lab I collased in a chair, rested, had blood drawn, rested more, ate orange, stagged to car, not sure sure I could make it. Got lost. That's me. Stopped at first diner. Could hardly walk in. Asked waitress to bring O.J. & coffee stat. Resting head on table, hoping I don't faint. Took Lasix, had breakfast, rested & walked very slowly to car. Drove slowly ē maximal slow resperations. Cheked pulse often & prepared to stop at any time. Made PTown. Parked on Bradford & rested a long time before going home ostennsibly relaxed & great. M. started to sob. She had been worried. I had been dumb. I should have awakened her to go with me—or minininally, called her from road to say I was okay. Why didn't I? Testing? Denial?

I am aware of the contrast with last year. My mind is clearer but my heart is much weaker. Last year my daily dose of Lasix was 80 mg. Now it is 280 mg. A rather dramatic increase. Whatever Drs say I know it means a progressive myocardial degeneration. I can only hope rate of dangeration slows down some.

I do not want M. to know my thoughts. I think of our hectic period in NY & how awful she looked then & how lovely she looks now. In NY I would see her face distorted by tension & I would feel like crying because I knew it reflected her terror re me. It hurt so. I am struggling to stay alive, to minimaze my disabilities & concerns to her. And to know that I have failed. In a stupid way I felt guilty. But the worst feeling is one of therrible pain & sorrow that the one I love so much is suffering so much . . .

It went on, but I could bear to read no more. *Probably I will die rather soon . . .* And what could I or should I say now? If I tell him that I have read these notes, his secrets, he will feel doubly burdened. But spirit is so important, the doctors say. If he thinks he will die soon, he will.

I told him. He sank into a chair. "Oh, God, that is terrible. I am so sorry you read that. You had no right."

We talked across chasms. I begged him to talk straight and would not let him talk straight, which was the way I boxed him in all the time. Please share your thoughts with me. And he would open up a bit. And: Oh, I would say, you *must not* think such dreadful thoughts. I can see *clearly* that you are getting better. Locking him in like that, which I did not understand until long after.

And so now he spoke to my needs: "Look, maybe I'm wrong. I'm no cardiologist. Maybe I *am* improving. Maybe I was being over-dramatic when I wrote that. It was a bad day."

"Yes." Soothed.

He assured me repeatedly, since I kept asking, that he was thinking positive thoughts. But often he would sit silent, drawn into himself.

"What are you thinking?"

"Nothing much."

"Please tell me. Don't shut me out."

"Mushie"—proceeding gently—"you've got to let me have some space of my own."

Of course. I cannot demand that he open his mind to me like a ledger. He has a right to privacy in there. And yet it is unbearable that perhaps he is alone with those thoughts again, utterly resigned, unutterably sad, giving himself over to death. I want to comfort him. I want to be comforted. I do not want to be alone with my thoughts.

A friend told me, much later, of a moment that stayed on his mind: He had been sitting with us one evening on our deck. The telephone rang. I jumped up and ran toward it, tripping over a chair, upsetting a lamp, "and suddenly," he said, "you stopped dead. You looked confused. You stared at the ringing telephone, and you stared at Hal, and you said, 'What the hell am I scared of? He's *here*.' I never realized until that moment what you were living with."

Silverman's receptionist sent Hal a note. He read it aloud:

"I'm leaving my job and wanted to say goodbye. I want you to know that I've followed your ups and downs with great concern. After all this time I feel a special way for you. . . . News of your not feeling well has been known to throw all those at the office who care for you into depression. . . . I can't stop caring about the friends I've made among patients, and you rank highest on that list. You are very special. My love to Mrs. Lear, and PLEASE stay well. (Will her book have a happy ending? If it's about you, it better!) . . ."

His voice broke then. "A happy ending. Oh, shit," he said, and started to cry.

Indian Summer is the Cape's royal season. The light transcends even itself. But that year, it turned bleak soon after Labor Day, and remained bleak, and our neighbors boarded up their houses and fled back to Boston and New York. Suddenly it was depressing to be on the water. The white wicker rockers, so right in their season, felt cold and inhospitable. Clothes hung sticky in their closets; the bed sheets were damp.

"Why fight it?" I said. "We can be so comfortable in New York," and we prepared to leave.

In the last days he huddled close to the old Franklin stove, which gave off more charm than heat, rubbing his hands together. The house was just a bit cool, but his hands were always icy.

I wrote:

He is growing weaker before my eyes. A progression measured in every way, his color, his appetite, his posture, his pace, his voice. It pains me so, his voice. In a higher register than it used to be, yet somehow hoarser. Faint, blurred, like a bad connection, a voice running out of timbre, out of time, as though it were transmitting now the sound of the heart itself.

I think in the past two weeks he has been in and out of failure, though he denies it. But I can tell by that cough, from way down deep —a *productive* cough, he once called it. Bad coughs are *productive*, bad lumps are *positive*, good lumps are *negative*; medical language is so perverse. He sleeps propped up high, like last spring (or the spring before? or both?), and after the good months of this summer I feel out of shape for crisis. When things go well for a time you drop guard, you let the belly muscles go soft.

I think of extreme measures. Heart transplants. I think of Peter saying last year what a good candidate Hal would be for a heart transplant, all his other organs good, his other body systems Go, but I know in my own heart that it will not come to that, there is not enough strength left to go through all that.

Mimi W. across the street is dying of lung cancer. She trims her privet with a cigarette stuck always in her mouth. What does it matter now? Each time I see her she seems subtly altered, more yellow and gaunt. I asked Hal, "What causes that?" He said, "Anemia, probably. It's that cachectic look. She won't be here next summer." That cachectic look. Like a phrase out of *Vogue*, meaning some new ethnic fashion, which also won't be here next summer. She knows, everyone knows, they gossip of it (kindly) at Bryant's Market. My dearest will not be here next summer. I know it. Do they gossip of it anywhere? They must.

He hedges his bets. When Rhoda was here over Labor Day, she told me how she and Frankie had talked about everything, open and cool, they had talked of his death and his funeral and what she would do when he was gone. But there was one barrier he would never let down. To the end, when they had both been pushed beyond any reasonable hope, he kept saying to her, "Rhoda, we must check about my disability insurance. It runs out in two years, and then what will we do?"

And now, just today, Hal says to me, "Listen, you really have to hurry and finish the book. We need money. My disability insurance won't go on forever, you know." I said, "When does it stop?" He thought for a moment. "When I'm 62," he said. Then he laughed. It was a laugh to choke on.

Now he makes plans for next summer. He wants to have the house painted. For ten years he has wanted the shingles to weather down to wood (I remember once I said, "That will take twenty years," and he said, "So what's your hurry?") and now he wants it painted. I say, "Let's hold off till spring. We don't have the money now." He says, "We have to make a list for Adam. He should arrange to install a dishwasher. It's been too damn much trouble entertaining this summer." I say, "Good idea." So he will know that though I have vetoed the paint job, it is not because I think he is going to die.

Adam came today and we went over our list, talking and walking from room to room, and afterward Hal was exhausted. He couldn't eat dinner. "Don't look so worried," he said. "Today was a difficult day. Tomorrow will be better." I said, "You yo-yo. What are we going to do about you?" He said, "Well, we did something very good today." "What was that?" "We ordered the dishwasher for next summer."

He flew back to New York. He had no stamina for the six-hour drive. I stayed an extra day to close the house, wallowing in sentiments he would not have tolerated. Each simple act was a last rite: And this is the last time I strip this bed, where for so long the loving was so good. And this is the last time I polish this table, this oak monster at which he sat as a child in Good Eddie's summer cottage, and at which Good Eddie sat as a child in his own father's tailor shop, bolts of tweed spread out for the preppies at Yale, and the father, the grandfather, the preppies long gone, and Hal soon gone, and the table survives; how absurd. And this is the last time I stand on this bulkhead, where for ten years we watched shooting stars. And this is the last time I empty this closet, where we scrawled "*Lear!*" in yellow paint on the floor. Oh, Hal . . .

Oh, shit. Shut up and clean the refrigerator. Take his lead, make investments. Do the laundry. We need clean sheets for next spring.

He called as I was saying a prayerful goodbye to the house.

"I saw Peter," he said.

"What kind of report card did you get?"

"Fair, I guess. He said . . . I don't know. Oh, Mushie. Something about my heart being enlarged . . ." A half-sob.

"I'll start home right away."

"No. *No.* I'm fine now. Please don't rush."

I rushed.

Chapter 27

"*WELCOME* home!" he said.

I shivered. Twenty-four hours apart and I could see him anew. The jut of facial bones, the too-hot glow of the eyes.

"The place looks great," I said.

"Yes. Except the terrace isn't doing too well."

"Oh?" I hadn't wanted to notice. The roses were fungus-ridden. Two Russian olives were sere. Even the live-forever drooped. "Do you suppose they're redeemable?"

"No. The hell with it. Let's throw them out and get some healthy young stock."

At dinner he poured wine and we said the usual "*L'chaim,*" but his eyes did not meet mine.

"What about this enlarged-heart business?" I said.

"It's probably nothing much."

"What does it mean? Does it reflect heart failure?"

"Yes. I guess so."

"What are they doing about it?"

"They've increased my diuretics."

"Is the enlargement reversible?"

"I don't know. Let's talk about nice things. It's our first night home together."

So I talked about invitations that waited and movies we had wanted to see. His eyes stayed unfocused.

"Where are you?" I said.

"I was just wondering how much I'd be able to do. I feel weaker than in Provincetown."

"What did the doctors say to that?"

"They said"—he smiled; still with such a sadness—"they said to take it easy."

Ah. For this they go to medical school. "Could it be because of the increased diuretics?"

"Maybe. But whatever it is, I guess I'll be more limited."

I said, "I'm not trying to jolly you up. But this is important to us: When you could do everything, we did everything and we had a lot of pleasure. Now we have all these limits and it's as though the sensations have been distilled. It's extract of pleasure. There is more pure sensation in walking ten minutes together on a nice day than there ever was in a ski week. You know?"

"Write it down," he said.

"Oh, no. I wish I could say such things in a tough-minded way. It sounds so damned sentimental."

"What's wrong with sentimental? Write it down."

"Then I'll tell you something more. Remember how I used to say that I never knew anything about life until my father died?"

He nodded.

"And then I thought I knew. I was wrong. I know now."

"What do you know?"

"I don't know."

"Write that down too," he said.

We took our little strolls, extracts of pleasure. We would have traded them for lesser joys, the ski weeks; a truth which we spared each other.

I said, "Well, I *do* think you're getting better. Last spring you *never* walked four blocks. What encourages me is, I don't see you going *downward*. You have your crises, but then you get *better* again. Doesn't this encourage you too?"

"Of course," he said. He patted my hand. "Now look," pointing to an ad in the *Times*: "here's a suit I'd like. A gray flannel suit."

"Terrific! Let's go get it."

"Maybe tomorrow," he said kindly.

A bit later I went at it again, as though it were a life raft: "I really *do* think you're better. Don't you?"

"I guess I don't. Not really." I can't play anymore today. I am too tired to keep you afloat.

On the third day home, I called Mason. "Has he deteriorated much?"

"Yes, I think so. His heart is larger than four months ago, and he tells us that he is having trouble. The clinical findings are not good."

"Is there anything to be done?"

"I don't know. We think we should wait a couple of weeks and if there is no improvement, we should consider another catheterization. . . ."

"Catheterization?"

"Angiography."

"Oh." A buzzing in my ears.

"We may have to do it to tell what's going on in there, whether perhaps there is any problem with the surgical corrections that were made, and whether anything more can be done. If there's a chance in a thousand that something can be done, he deserves it."

"Surgically?"

"Maybe. Of course, there are problems that the family would have to consider . . ."

The family. From Peter, old buddy, the language now of economists and coroners. "What problems? The danger of another heart attack?"

"No. There was a risk the other time because it was so soon after an infarct. I wouldn't worry about it now. But I suspect that we'd get a negative finding. Then it's rough. There are two ways he can look at it. He can say, 'Well, that's a relief. I don't have to go through surgery again.' Or he can say, 'This is it. There is nothing more to be done for me.' So it is a very difficult decision, whether to go ahead with a cath. And if we find something that may be correctable surgically, there is the question of whether to take the chance. It's tough, tough, tough."

"Did you discuss it with him?"

"We told him that his heart is enlarged now and that if he doesn't improve on increased medication, we might recommend a cath. The trouble is, Martha . . ."

"Yes?"

"He asked us not to tell you."

What are you thinking? Nothing. What is the matter? Nothing. Are you sad? No; come, let us buy me a gray flannel suit.

"I think I should tell him that I know."

"I do too. Just fix it so he's not too mad at me for telling you."

"He looks so awful. What causes it, this terrible look, like terminal-cancer patients?"

"Cachexia. You mean that wasted look you see on people in concentration camps. . . ."

"Yes, yes." *That cachectic look.* "What causes it?"

"The fatty deposits are disappearing from his face because there is not enough blood supply to support them. So you get these sharp angles, jagged lines, deep hollows . . ."

"Pete. Last spring you said 'months.' September is almost over. How much longer?"

Silence. Then: "He has no heart muscle, Martha."

"His son is due home on vacation next month. He has decisions to make." Jon was finishing at Cambridge. He had the possibility of a fellowship there. He had the possibility of an invitation from Yale. His letters had made clear that if there were no worry about his father, he might prefer to stay in England. "His decisions may depend on what is happening with Hal."

"Send him in to talk to us. We'll give him a clear picture."

"But what if something happens before he gets home? Is it likely?"

"It's not impossible. Hal is worse now."

"Then should I advise him to come home sooner?"

"That might be a good idea. Explain that his father is now a desperately ill man. . . ."

"To come home now, then? It's that urgent?"

"I guess not. Why worry the guy?"

Damn, don't give me options. Give me guidance. "I see. Well, thanks."

"Thanks! For what?"

"For caring and trying."

"We do care, Martha. But we are not doing anything for him. We can't. I'm sorry. What can I tell you?"

Tell me how to make it bearable. "If I could come in and talk to you and Moe for a few minutes . . ."

"Oh, sure, sure. But why don't we wait until our next appointment with Hal? That's in two weeks."

Of course. You cannot tell me how to make it bearable. That is not your specialty. In fact, it is precisely because that is what you cannot do, that being what they never trained you to deal with, that you will now begin to avoid me. Us. Not medically; you would never avoid us medically; but in other, ambiguous ways, none remotely conscious. You will know us rather less well than before. You will call rather less often to ask, "Hal, how're you doing?" and you will sigh when they say, "Mrs. Lear is on the line"; you will not want to speak to Mrs. Lear unless she is a bearer (unlikely) of good or at least neutral tidings. In your place I would do the same. Who wouldn't? (Hal, of course; Hal would be the Compleat Doctor.) Well, you have been plenty caring. I am plenty grateful. And if you now start backing off from this hopeless cause as far as you decently can, I will be, if not *plenty* understanding, at least hip.

He came in from the terrace. "Damn it, it's a gorgeous day. I would so love to go for a walk. I just get wiped out."

Cachectic. More than an hour ago, I swear it.

"Ah, this soup is good." Sitting at the table, beaming. "Just a few sips and I feel better. Maybe I'll rest and we'll walk this afternoon."

"Good idea." Cachectic.

He drinks the soup and I sit scoring debate points:

He has told his doctors to keep certain nasty truths from you. Respect that.

I can't. I love him too much to let him bear these truths alone.

Careful. Remember the last time you invaded his privacy. *"Probably I will die rather soon . . ."* Remember how agonized he was by your invasion. Do not repeat it.

There is a higher priority than privacy. No one should have to endure alone what he is enduring.

He wants to protect you.

I want to help him.

Consider this: Perhaps it makes him feel good to protect you. How many ways does he have left to protect you? Say nothing.

But what of his pain? Pain shared is pain eased.

Say nothing. Say nothing.

I guess you're right.

"Hal. I spoke to Peter today."

"Oh?" Face immediately on the alert. "What did he tell you?"

"Everything. Don't be angry. I made him tell me."

"*Fuck.* You see, this is exactly an example of why I can't tell you things. You go to pieces. Then it's harder for me. . . ."

"No. I go to pieces when I look at you and I know you're troubled and you say you're not. I cannot manage that kind of lie between us."

"Bullshit. You give me double signals. You say, 'Tell me everything, I want to know.' And when I tell you, you start malfunctioning. You don't work, you chain-smoke, you drink too much . . ."

"I will function well. But please, share with me."

"All right. If you'll take it in stride."

And he told me, then:

The trip back to New York had been dreadful. I had suggested, uneasily, that he use wheelchairs in the airline terminals, and he had tossed that one out fast. "A *wheelchair?*" he had said. "Why not a stretcher?" But when he had landed at Logan in Boston and seen where he had to go, he had felt overwhelmed. He had forgotten the length of those concourses.

He had gone slowly, stopping and starting. He carried a briefcase, nothing more in it than his shaving kit and a book, but soon it was a burden. His heart was beginning to pound. No redcaps in sight.

He stopped a passerby: "Pardon me, are you going to Gate 36?" The man rushed on.

He stopped another, who raced away as though from the plague.

He asked a third, and a fourth, and a fifth, until finally in desperation he blocked a couple's path. "I have a heart problem and I can't carry this briefcase. Could you help me?"

The pair looked at him apprehensively.

"What kind of heart problem?" the man said.

"I've had surgery."

"What kind of surgery?"

"A bypass operation."

"How long ago?"

And he thought, if I say two and a half years, the guy will be even more suspicious. So he said, "Four months."

"Got a scar?"

"Yes." And unbuttoned his shirt and showed the scar.

Whereupon the couple had looked at each other, she had flicked her eyelids Okay and the man had taken the briefcase and said, all cordiality now, "You know how it is in airports these days, anyone could be carrying a bomb . . ."

"Of course," he had said.

They had escorted him to his gate, stopping as often as he needed, and delivered him to an attendant.

He had been terribly short of breath. I will not be a fool, he had thought. And asked, loathing to ask it, for a wheelchair to meet him in New York. The pilot had radioed ahead.

In the wheelchair, being rolled past strangers who stared, then looked quickly away, he had hidden his head and wept.

He had taken a cab home. The doorman and the elevator men had all made a grand fuss: "Welcome home, Dr. Lear. Good summer, Dr. Lear?" "Yes, yes," he had said, and gotten upstairs and collapsed upon the bed.

He took extra Lasix. He called Mason. He spent the evening sitting on the floor, upright against the bed, with the telephone beside him and the kit for intravenous injection nearby. The failure peaked and faded.

And then, the old pendulum swing: a long night's rest, breakfast, feeling better, looking good, comes waltzing into the doctors' office and the nurses, sweet familiars, are giving him hugs and kisses, and while one of them takes his chest X-ray she askes if he approves of the treatment she is getting for her cystitis, and while another takes his cardiogram, she asks something about her father's prostate, and so he has given a couple of urological consultations before he sees a doctor, and that makes him feel pretty nice.

Mason examines him. Then he dresses and goes into Mason's office and the X-ray is sitting up there on the viewing box, beside his previous X-ray, and Peter says: "How are you doing?"

"I've been pretty weak, Pete. Yesterday I had trouble getting home."

"What do you think is going on?"

He glances up at the X-ray. Fluid in the right costophrenic sinus, there in the lung cavity. As to the heart, he can't much read it. He doesn't have to.

"I think my condition is deteriorating," he says.

"I think you're right," Peter says. He picks up the intercom. "Ask Dr. Silverman if he's free now."

Moses has just come back from taping a TV show and now he is off to talk to his publishers about his book. But no, it surely isn't these distractions which keep Moses from meeting his eye; it is something rather less . . . efficacious.

"Now, here's the X-ray we just took," Peter murmurs to Moe, "and here's the one from five months ago. And you see how this has enlarged? It's much bigger. . . ."

"Yup. And this," Moe murmurs back, "there's a change here too. . . ."

Turning from the picture to each other, morosely shaking their heads.

As though he, Lear, were not in the room at all. As though he did not exist, except up there on the viewing box.

"Look here, you see this? Maybe one of the bypasses is closed off. Or there could even be another aneurysm," says Moe.

"Let's see, now, how did Dr. Bell close that other aneurysm? With a purse-string suture, wasn't it?" says Pete.

"Yes."

"I think we have to investigate this."

"I agree."

"Well, then, maybe we should arrange for a cath and see what's going on."

"Um."

"We may find out there's just nothing more to be done surgically. But at least we'll know."

"Okay," says Moe. "But before we schedule angiography, let's get an echo cardiogram. Let's start with a noninvasive procedure, and see where we go from there."

"Okay," says Pete.

The senior man nods and walks out, and the associate turns to Lear, who is suddenly again alive and present.

"Let's see," he says conversationally, "you are now taking four Lasix in the morning and three in the afternoon. Right?"

Lear nods numbly. *Maybe one of the bypasses is closed off. . . .*

"I want you to increase the Lasix to five and four. All other medications the same. Have one of the girls make an appointment with the lab for an echo cardiogram next week. See you in two weeks. So long." Walks him to the door, slaps his shoulder, sees him out. Lear stands motionless in the waiting room, trying to get his bearings, like a blind man. . . . *Or there could even be another aneurysm. . . .*

"So *you're* Dr. Lear!" It is the new receptionist. "I never would have guessed it. You don't look sick at *all!*"

He smiles and says thank you and goes home.

"So that's what happened. I walked out of there thinking, What if I had pulled that on one of them? 'Well, Peter, you have a little blood in your urine. You'll need some tests to see whether it's cancer. If it is, maybe we'll take out your kidney. Or we may find out there's just nothing more to be done. Have the secretary make an appointment for those tests. So long, Pete. See you in two weeks.' . . ."

"How should they have handled it?" I said.

"As though I were human. As though I had ears. Doctors have to have these discussions, and I'm glad they talked straight in front of me. I've always wanted the truth. But they should have talked *to* me. Given me explanations. I mean, what's the good news? If the tests show that I need surgery, is that good or bad? And what if I'm inoperable—what does that mean? *Tell* me."

He shook his head and sat numbly for a moment. Then: "So yesterday I took the extra diuretics and I went out for a two-block walk and I had to take a cab home. *A cab home*, Martha!" He pounded the table twice, once for each miserable block. "I'm so weak. I don't know what to do."

Taking the longest possible route between two points, lessons learned from Mother, I edged toward what had been for months on my mind.

"Wouldn't it be nice," I said, casual as a crutch, "if there were some kind of machine they could hook up to a person in left heart failure that would do the work of the left ventricle, the way a dialysis machine does for people in kidney failure."

"Very nice."

"Are they working on anything like that?"

"No. Nothing external. The kidney machine is a much simpler thing. It's just a filtering system, that's all."

"What about heart transplants? They've made great progress, haven't they?"

"Not great. The mortality rates are still awful. But I'm following something else," he said. "I happened to read in one of my journals" —voice low and cool, cordial as my own—"about a left-ventricular bypass. They've got this device that is inserted and takes over for the ventricle. Very simple insertion."

"Really! How interesting. Shouldn't we look into that?"

"Well, there's just one problem with it."

"Yes?" Politely.

"It's still in the experimental stage. They only use it on calves." Big grin. "I hope they hurry up."

Two nights later, there sat Moses, his smart mournful rumpled face peering out at us from a television talk show. And with him sat an eminent cardiovascular surgeon, and they were talking about hearts. Talking about this new device, this left ventricle made of plastic, which is being implanted now in calves. The surgeon has a sample with him. The camera dollies in on it—neat little thing, smooth, curvaceous, cuddled there in his palm. It is not ready for humans, he says; the operations go well, but the calves all die within ten days.

They turn to talk of heart transplants. What's happened? the host asks. Heart transplants were such a hot item just a few years ago.

It is very quiet in our bedroom as we listen. Well, the surgeon says, he himself no longer does them. The problems of money and donors and rejection phenomena . . . It's just too tough. As a matter of fact, practically the only man in the country who is still doing transplants is Shumway, up there in Stanford. He's done some nine hundred by now. About a third survive the first year.

Only a third survive? the host says.

Moses shrugs: Well, that's not too bad, thirty percent.

Oh, my friends. Cardiovascular technicians, *Americans.* The limits of your know-how are obscenely low. A heart: what is it, after all? A piece of plumbing, an electrical circuit, a muscle, a pound of flesh; one rotten pound of flesh in the body of an Adonis, as the man said; one small malfunctioning part in an otherwise splendid machine, pish-pash compared with the malfunctions of a rocket; and what can you do about it, eh? To the moon and back, triumphantly, and on to Mars, and Jupiter I suppose waiting in the wings. And what do I care for moon rocks? What do I care for dead planets, or even live planets, universes, galaxies in space? What comfort can they be in bed? I curse those galactic adventures, for in the way of my primitive logic, it is very clear that if they had not gone out there, with their billions and their brains, they would long since have come in here and learned how to make it all right. In these small inner spaces. In Hal's heart.

I ask you: Where would we be now if the Russians had created the first viable heart transplant, instead of Sputnik? Don't tell me. I can't bear to hear it.

I said, "This period between now and the echo cardiogram—I feel we're living in limbo."

"We are," he said. "It's interesting what happens psychologically: I get the feeling that my doctors are trying to distance themselves."

"Why do you think that is?"

"Because I'm an unpleasant problem for them. So they would rather avoid me. I'm sure it's unconscious. I used to do this with certain patients, fail them in this way."

"You did?"

"Sure. There was a particular group. I can't quite define what they had in common. . . ." His voice trailed off.

"They were patients whom you didn't know how to help?"

"Whom I *knew* I could help no more. For whom I *knew* there was no more hope. That's what we're talking about, of course." We stared at each other. He did not blink, and I do not believe that I did either.

"But even among those terminal patients," he said, going slowly now, trying to understand it, "there were some I failed and some I didn't, and I'm not sure I can explain the difference. I remember many of them who looked to me to make it more bearable, and I gave them more of myself, or tried to, than I ever gave other patients. I remember one who was in kidney failure. This was before we had the dialysis machines. There was no way he could live more than another day or two, and he knew it. He always demanded the truth. He was so brave. And I stayed with him all night in his hospital room, and I remember that the medical man on the case was astonished that I should do that. But it was simply that I could do nothing else, nothing else, and I wanted to be there if I could comfort him in any way.

"So it wasn't that I failed the hopeless ones. No. The ones I failed were . . . I guess they were the ones who wanted me to lie. They would say, 'How am I doing? Tell me the truth.' But you got to know who meant it and who didn't; you knew which ones were really saying, 'Tell me I am doing well. Tell me I am going to live.' And I couldn't do it. I couldn't keep going into their rooms day after day and giving them hope when I knew there was no hope. So I stopped going. I would say to the medical man, 'Tell Mr. So-and-So that I got tied up in the operating room, but I was asking for him and I hope he's feeling better today.' I failed those people. I am very ashamed of that now."

We sat quietly. He made one of those large rabbinical shrugs. Suddenly we began to laugh. I cannot say why. One moment we were sitting in despair and the next moment he shrugged, and then, quite suddenly, we were howling.

"Mushie, isn't this *preposterous?*" he said. "For us to have come to this. Can you believe it?"

"Not really. Can you?"

"I think I'm beginning to," he said.

His need for sleep grew. Ten, twelve hours a night, and two or three more in the afternoon, and he would wake from these siestas saying, "That was a marvelous rest. I feel great now." Quite as though it were all benign, a sound body in a sound snooze, quite as though he were not a doctor and did not understand what the weariness really meant. Once he even said, "Who knows? I might fool you and *shlep* along like this for the next twenty years."

Instant replays. This is the way it used to be, in those pale gray days after the surgery, when I would tiptoe in while he slept to hold mirrors beneath his nose.

But my God, he never slept like this! It is afternoon; we went to sleep shortly after midnight: he has slept around the clock and more. I have been racing back and forth like a terrier, doing my best not to bark, racing at first every fifteen minutes and then every ten and now every five and he is breathing, yes, the sheet goes up and down, but it is 1:15 and he is still asleep, and what's more, so deeply asleep that when I finally could keep hands off no longer and bent down and caressed his shoulder and made little kisses up and down his arm (Are you crazy? why in heaven's name are you doing this? The man is sick, he needs his sleep), he didn't even stir. What kind of a sleep is this? What kind of a breathing is this? How marginal?

Hello, Moses, listen, it's 1:15 and he is still sleeping, what should I do? Echoes of the Quinlan case, poor lump . . . Could it happen here? Could this be how a heart fades away, fading into long limp sleep, coma, going out like a light on one of those dimmer gadgets? Moe! What should I do?

The buzzer sounds from the lobby to announce that mail is coming up. A bloody loud buzzer. Will not even this wake him? And I go yet again, frantic this time, stomping loud and heavy down the corridor to the bedroom. He has turned in the bed. His back is to me. He is motionless. As I watch, one hand comes around his shoulder and waves an animated hello. Saved by the bell. *"Hel-lo!"* I shriek, and bound onto the bed, as children do in the morning.

My own sleep was bad. I dreamed of high cold winds blowing over our bed, auguring a great hurricane, and I reached out in sleep to protect him from these winds, cried out to warn him, and woke realizing instantly that the cold I felt was the feel of his feet against mine.

Soon after, I dreamed that someone was opening the door to our apartment. I heard the lock click. I screamed, and awoke on my own high note. Already Hal was bending over me: "Martha. Martha, what were you dreaming?"

"No dream," I whispered harshly. "Someone is opening the door."

"Sh. You were dreaming."

"No dream. *Someone is there.* Where's your gun?"

"Martha, for heaven's sake . . ."

"Let me go." I picked up a scissors that lay glinting on my bureau and padded out to the foyer, fully expecting to face the intruder there. Nobody. Moonlight. Door lock undisturbed.

Trembling, I went back to bed and crept into the thin circle of his arms and laid my head upon his frail chest and slept amid memories of brawn.

So managing not terrifically, certainly not as well as I had promised, I sought help. Went back to the psychiatrist Russ.

"He says, 'I might *shlep* along for the next twenty years.' What is in his head? As a doctor he must know the truth. As a patient he manages to deny, but on some level he damned well knows. And this drives me crazy, to think that he struggles with it alone. If we could face it together . . ."

"No! That's for *your* sake. That would comfort *you.*" A point, Doctor. "This whole trend toward being so open about death and dying— 'Put your head on my bosom and tell me all your fears; I do not want you to suffer them alone'—what crap! Sure, on some level he knows he is dying. But if it is important for him to feel that he can handle this alone, with dignity and self-respect, without confiding—you must allow him that. He is a very proud man. The best thing you can do for him is to let him keep that pride.

"Another thing: He must make his own decisions about what will be done to him medically. No winking between you and his doctors. I hope he will decide not to have an angiogram. But it must be *his* decision. Agreed?"

"Agreed."

I think everyone hoped he would decide against an angiogram. Instead, he pushed for it ferociously. He said, "Listen, I know it's a million-to-one shot that anything more can be done for me surgically. But if it could, wouldn't that be wonderful?"

"You'd be willing, then, to take the risk?"

"Willing? Are you kidding? In a minute!"

"But the risk . . ." Hands off, Martha.

"In a *minute*."

His old swimming buddy Chelsea called. "He said all the boys at the Y ask for me all the time. I asked how he was and he said, '*Physically*, I'm great. *Physically*, I'm walking four miles a day. *Physically*, my muscles are better than ever. *Physically* . . .' So I said, 'How are you doing emotionally, Chelsea?' and he said, 'Well, I guess I'm sort of depressed. . . .'

"And I thought, Jesus! I would trade with him so happily for either one: the four miles a day or his clear mind. And he's depressed. What a joke! I don't begrudge him. I'm *happy* for him. But why this double whammy on *me*? Anyway . . ." He sighed. "I'm sorry, kid. This is feeling-sorry-for-myself night. On the other hand: Frankie isn't feeling sorry for himself. Frankie's widow isn't worrying about—"

"No! I don't want to be a widow!"

"Then *take vitamins*, damn it."

I stared at him. He grinned. We rolled on the bed in laughter. Take vitamins!

The echo cardiogram, a benign procedure, told them nothing. For information, they would need to do angiography. But it kept getting delayed, and he kept getting worse. He could never anymore negotiate two blocks. "Maybe I should just walk the first block," he said. "I do a terrific first block."

Heart failure woke him at night. His doctors were out of town. We called the consultant Corey, who suggested self-administering Lasix intramuscularly.

"Not intravenously?" Hal said.

"No, that gets a little hairy. Intramuscular will be good enough."

So he did it a couple of times, but it was clear we could not go on like this. And then came a very bad night in late November, and he was admitted to the hospital, not for angiography but in the routine way: emergency admission, acute congestive heart failure. Even then he would not go by ambulance.

"I'm feeling much better now," he said in the cab. That too was routine.

"You're certainly in better shape than the last time we went to the hospital. That's progress."

"Yes," he said, "I think I'm in the best shape I've been for any of my admissions. Wish me a *mazeltov*."

But in the hospital, as the elevator doors opened on the sixteenth floor and his wheelchair rolled down the long corridor, he hunched into his sheepskin. "Oh, it is all so fucking familiar," he cried softly. "Oh, I can't bear to be here again."

An orderly said, "You're back? It's nice to see you. I mean, I'm so sorry."

In his room, a nurse said, "This is the best of all our views."

"I know," he said.

"How do you know?"

"I've seen them all."

Almost immediately they scheduled angiography. Jon and Judy came home.

He said the night before the test, "Hope what I hope."

"Which is what?"

"That I need surgery. That they find something they can correct surgically."

He telephoned us soon after the test. He sounded alert. "It went very well," he said. "It was really fascinating to watch this time, not at all frightening. Come on down and I'll tell you all about it. Oh"— smoothly—"and I definitely don't need surgery. So we don't have to worry about *that*."

I called various people who waited for the news.

"How's that for graceful?" I asked his cousin Norman.

"That's graceful," he said.

They warned us at the nurses' station: "He's okay, but he's pretty angry. The nurse wouldn't tell him what his blood pressure was, and he raised hell."

Good. He's feeling good.

"What's this about your getting the nurses all upset?" I said to him.

"Oh, you heard. Well, why the hell shouldn't she tell me what my pressure is? She said it's against hospital policy. That's bullshit. When she came back to take my pressure again, I said, 'Are you sure it's against hospital policy?' and she said, 'It's against *my* policy.' And she started to put the cuff around my arm, and I said, 'Listen, if it's against *your* policy to tell patients their blood pressure, you're not taking mine, because it's against *my* policy to let my pressure be taken by anyone who won't tell me what it is.' So she left in a huff. Fuck her."

Feisty. Marvelous.

Mason came into the room. He was meeting no one's eyes. "Well," he said, "there's absolutely nothing we would recommend to be done surgically. There is no aneurysm. The bypass is working beautifully. The heart function is not as bad as we would have anticipated. The bottom of the heart is flaccid, which I think is an appropriate word to use when speaking to a sex therapist . . ."

"Then pronounce it right: *flaksid*," Hal said. Oh, feisty.

". . . but the sides contract fairly well. And one interesting thing we found was that when they gave you nitroglycerin, the sides worked better. So hopefully, nitro will help you. Now, you certainly have plenty of disease in there. I'm not saying you don't. But what I *am* saying is that we have seen worse. I feel we have something we can work with, and frankly, that's better than I'd hoped. I don't think you've been doing as well as you can, and I don't think we've been doing as well as we can. We have to review it all and regulate you. You've been walking half a block. I think we can do better. I think we can get it up to one, two, maybe three blocks. . . ."

"What about the other bypass?" Hal said.

"What?"

"You said the *bypass* is working beautifully. I had two bypasses. What about the other one?"

"Oh. Well. The other one couldn't be visualized."

He left soon after. I said to Hal, "What does that mean, 'couldn't be visualized'?"

"That means closed," he said. "That's what happened. The second bypass closed."

Later I called Mason. "Is there space between what you told him and what is?"

"Yes. The heart functioned very poorly. Just barely. The bottom just lay there. I'll tell you, it was god-awful. But I was telling him the truth when I said contraction of the sides improved with nitro. That was encouraging. So maybe we can do something with the nitro. Get him walking better."

"For how long?"

"I don't know. But look, he's had three years."

It was the first time I'd heard the tenses switched. "No more prognoses?" I said. "You must have had other patients in his condition."

"No."

"No?"

"No. We've had patients in worse condition and they go downhill fast and die. But we've had no one who has stayed alive as long as he has with such severe disease."

I told Judy and Jon. She wept.

Jon said, "I'm very encouraged by how he came through this test. I think he can have time ahead yet and we can all have good times together."

"How much time?" she said.

"I don't know," his son said, "but I just feel pretty good about it."

He looked and sounded remarkably well. But even with daily shots into the vein they were not able to rid him of the râles, those watery crackles in his chest.

A Dr. Benton, an elderly internist whom we knew slightly through friends, stopped me one day in the corridor. He said, "It seems to me that you ought to investigate the possibility of heart transplantation."

I was rattled. "Transplantation? But I understand the mortality rates are dreadful. Only Shumway is still doing it."

"No, there's a new team at the University of Virginia," he said, "and the statistics are much better now."

"What are they?"

"I don't know. But you could find out easily."

"How?"

"Through Doctors Silverman and Mason. I would even suggest, confidentially"—drawing closer to me—"that if they are reluctant, you should pursue the matter yourself. Certainly inquiries should be made."

"You think so?"

"Oh, I do. With that angiogram"—he shrugged—"what have you got to lose? That's what I told your husband."

"You *what?*"

He drew back. He blinked. "Why . . . yes. I went in for a little chat with him this morning, and I suggested this. . . ."

"What did he say?"

"He thanked me. He said he would consider it. I hope you don't mind. I hope you don't think I was interfering. I felt, in the circumstances . . ."

He was making soft little clucks of contrition. I do not know if he realized then, or ever, what a cardinal dumbness he had committed.

Hal never spoke of it. Not a word. In his notebook, he wrote:

Yesterday Dr. Benton dropped in to say hello. I thought that was very nice of him. . . . I was astounded when he proceded to talk about me medically & that I should look into heart transplants. This was so grossly improper & unethical I thought he must be crazy or perhaps a little senile.

If I saw a pt. in consultation & thought his kidney should be removed, I would never tell it to the pt. I would tell the primary physician. If we disagried & I felt strongly, I might say that I have been called in consultation & in all conscience I must give the pt. my opinion. But *only* after talking ē his doctor. And in this case Benton had not been invited by anyone to render an opinion.

Moe & Peter has assured me that the angiogram was encouraging. And then Dr. Benton tells me, "You have nothing to lose by looking into transplantation." The gross stupidity was compounded by the fact that he didn't even know the statistics. I know since I have kept up ē the literature and I know why my drs. do not discuss transplant ē me. It is because 1, the mortality rates, 2, I am probly no longer a good candidate. I was a year ago but now general condition have deteriorated, no longer have resiliency etc. 3, I might not be accepted as a candidate anyway because of age. So why discuss it? Instead they emphisize the positive (good response to nitroglycerin etc.) They don't lie exactly but emphisize the positive. I have done the same thing a thousand times. So I deduce from this that the finding were quite discouraging & that there is nothing to be done. . . .

Silverman called me. Hard work, that call:

"Well, I can't say he's got a great heart. I mean, the outlook to perform any useful, uh, I mean, any *measurable* activity is, uh, guarded. Now, as Peter told you, one bypass is, uh, closed. Not that we worry about it, because there is no function anyway in that part of the heart . . ." Well, of course not. Do you think I am some sort of dummy? If the bypass closed, how could that part of the heart have stayed alive? Stop giving it to me backward. ". . . and the other bypass, to that area that is still functioning, is, uh, good. Some parts of the heart do not contract. Others do, with the nitroglycerin. So it is not a problem of flow. There is enough contraction so that he can lead a, uh, comfortable but limited activity. Thank God for his good bypass. It's certainly good that we have that. Now, I've been saying all along that he needs rest. I know he says he's been getting plenty of rest, but I mean really *loads* of rest. A guy at Tulane has done some very interesting new research that shows that rest may improve the contractility . . ."

"Moe, you speak of rest. Peter spoke of—"

"I know what Peter spoke of."

"Wait, Moe. It's important for you to know what Peter told Hal. . . ."

"I know what Peter told Hal."

"*Moe.*" My voice bulled through his, taking us both aback. "Peter told Hal he could do better and might be able to walk a block or two or three. . . ."

He exploded now: "I don't care what Peter told him! I don't care about the fucking block! I care about keeping him out of this paroxysmal dyspnea!"

Good. If he explodes I can stay cool.

"And what *I* care about, Moe, is that he get consistent instructions at a time when contradictory instructions would be very confusing and demoralizing."

"Don't worry." Controlled now. "He'll get consistent instructions. I'm not talking about, uh, indefinite confinement. But at least let him rest a month before he starts walking. . . ." An Rx: Reassure. Which won't. It gives him so damned much space between the lines; space enough to fall into, chasms.

"But you're sending him home on exactly the same diuretics he was taking before this admission: ten pills a day. If it wasn't enough to keep him out of failure before, what will keep him out of failure now?"

"Well, more rest. More discreet diet."

"He has been doing nothing *but* resting. And we have been exquisitely discreet with his diet."

"You have been, eh?"

"Yes. And so how will things be different now without more diuretics?"

"Martha. We can't give him any more diuretics." Finally. We had shot the bolt not only surgically but medically. "You get up to those dosages . . . We're afraid it would damage his kidneys."

"Then what is to be done?"

"Well, as I said: more rest, more discreet diet . . ."

So I quit that. I said, "Dr. Benton saw Hal yesterday."

"Benton? Who sent him?"

"Nobody. A social visit. But listen, Moe: he talked to Hal about heart transplants."

"What? That stupid . . . God damn it, how stupid!"

"It's done. Now my question: Should we be talking about heart transplants?"

"No. It's premature. Let's wait until we can no longer maintain him on medications."

We had a belated Thanksgiving dinner. While Jon and I brought him home from the hospital, Judy set it out: turkey, brisket, potato pancakes, pumpkin pie. Discreetly saltless.

"How nice," he said at the table. Smiling, eating slowly, knife and fork trembling in hands that had held deadlier knives without a tremor. "How lovely this is, the four of us together. What a wonderful Thanksgiving!" And, raising the wineglass, *"L'chaim!"*

Now a great green oxygen tank stood like a sentinel in our bedroom. Such things had to be anthropomorphized, not for his sake but for mine. He dubbed it Big George.

He rested the requisite month, taking oxygen after meals to ease the strain on his heart during digestion, and then he wanted to walk.

We went out on a mild December day. He was wobbly and held my arm for support. People rushed by, coatless, carrying parcels wrapped for Christmas. He shivered in his ski parka.

Suddenly, as a man came toward us, Hal threw off my arm. He averted his face and began striding unsteadily ahead, fast, fast, like a running drunk. I thought he would fall.

"Hal, what the *hell*—"

"I don't want to see him, the bastard, the bastard," and kept striding, and collapsed in a chair in our lobby.

It cost him a day in bed.

"Who was that man?" I said.

"Buschel. The bastard who told me I'd be in trouble."

"In trouble? What do you mean?" Knowing instantly.

"Koerner's hatchet man. The one who told me . . . You don't remember? Let me give it to you chronologically: Koerner promised me funding for five years. A year later that bastard came to me and said, 'You'll have to earn your own salary, or you're in serious trouble.' Then, when my program got to be so successful, I heard Psychiatry was trying to take it away from me. I went to Koerner, and he said, 'No one is going to take your program away' "—and told again the whole stinking story, wounds frozen so deep that in the retelling he used precisely the same phrases he had used two, three years earlier —"and then we had that meeting when Gross said, 'Dr. Peron is going to be head of the program.' And I said, 'You can't *do* that. It's *my program.*' And Gross said, 'Sorry, Hal,' and Koerner just sat there. . . . That was the worst thing they could do to me. That hurt so much. . . ."

Oh, those spoilers. What did I wish them? Curses; shames; chronic and debilitating diseases of the soul.

Did it hurt so much still? I asked him.

Nah, he said. A momentary thing, just seeing that bastard in the street. I hardly ever think of it anymore.

Then it got very cold and he seldom left the house.

We did go, insanely, to a New Year's Eve party. His cousins Norman and Frances came to town. We four were to spend the evening at home; but we had all been invited to the same party, a limousine waited downstairs and I thought Hal really wanted to go, and he thought they really wanted to go, and really no one wanted to go, so we went. Went off shortly before midnight into a bitter cold; dismissed the driver at the wrong address, a mere half-block short of our destination, but there was no way he could navigate that distance in those winds. He huddled miserably in a doorway while Frances and Norman raced about in the street, screaming for cabs through the first ten minutes of the New Year, I trying to shield him from the wind, thinking, He may just end it here, like the winos who freeze to death in doorways, and he shook and whispered, "I'm so cold," and finally a cab came and drove us twenty yards to the proper door. But it was a brownstone, stairs up to the living rooms. Men wanted to make a seat of their hands and carry him up, but he would have none of that; he rested, took the stairs and then sat amid the partygoers dazed, staring wordlessly, as though this were a psychiatric ward, at these creatures in dinner jackets and gold caftans who chattered and drank champagne.

He changed in the New Year. Grew sharper around the edges of his character. He became both more and less tolerant—sympathetic as ever to the troubles of others, but suffering no phonies or whiners. "I have no patience with the old farts' grumbling," he said once. "They don't know. They just don't know." He refused to spend time with gossips, bad-mouthers, professional bearers of chicken soup—all those in whom he had always urged me to seek the saving graces. "I have no time to waste," he said.

But he loved to see the people he liked. He entertained them often in our bedroom, lying back among the pillows, nitroglycerine under his tongue, swigging oxygen through the nasal prongs that pressed down to give vaguely the look of a harelip; swigging vodka in the usual way.

More than pleasant, these visits were crucial. They bridged his growing isolation. He felt a sensory deprivation, he often said. He felt like a housewife left behind. The movers and doers would come to call, and he did not have much to talk about—or felt that he did not; it was the same thing—except himself, and he did not want to talk about himself.

He still could not read in any sustained way. He began to watch the television newscasts with a notebook before him, as though Cronkite and Brinkley were lecturers. He would make notes about the top stories and study these notes, hard, so that he might discuss with his guests what was happening in Lebanon and Congress. "It's good exercise for me," he said.

One morning he came bare-assed and agitated into my study. "I had a bad dream. I feel like a child, waking from a bad dream."

He had dreamed that he was at a party. Interesting people were scattered through many rooms. He wandered among them, trying to participate in conversations, and could not. "I couldn't remember how to talk. I began feeling more and more like a vegetable among these vital, vivacious people. I became progressively confused and decided to go back to my room. But it was in a sort of hotel, and I couldn't remember my room number. I couldn't find my room. I was totally lost. . . ." He began to cry.

"I think you are incredible," I said to him. "I think you have made the most incredible adjustment. But it is so much to manage alone. Do you think it might help in this period to be seeing Dr. Russ?"

"Ah, no!" he says, grinning fiercely now, eyes flashing that wild cachectic blaze. "I'm not in any bad depression. And with just a little help from my friends, I have lots of fun!"

Each day, he said, "Should I try walking today?"
"What do you think?"
"I think maybe not. I feel so good when I do nothing. If I don't try to do too much, I can do a lot. Right?"
"Right." Silverman's words echoing from long ago: "And then he'll get to a point where he's grateful just to be alive. . . ."
"I just hope . . . If I could just get better enough for sex . . ." How much had earlier been physiological and how much psychological, the weight of anxieties that might crush the libido, hardly mattered anymore. It was gone. He felt not only loss but guilt: "My sickness has deprived you of so much. And for you to be deprived of sex too— that makes me feel terribly sad. I would feel better if you went out and got laid."
"Indeed. You are a saint."
"Oh, fuck off. Just don't tell me about it," he said.

For me it was no longer a sadness. It was irrelevant. My libido was gone too, lost, frightened away by near-crises in and out of bed. I didn't yearn, I didn't care. Pleasure was to kiss his face. Often he walked about the house naked, his ravaged body lovely still, and I would look at his penis and want to reach for it, cuddle it like a face, nuzzle it, stroke it, press my eyes against it, take it into my mouth not to coax it to life, for these impulses were not in the least genital, but simply to speak in loving ways, the mother tongue. But of course, such things could not be done. They would seem to demand performance.

Now his doctors sometimes called unbidden. Just checking in, they would say. We were both grateful. Moses told me once, "We must reassure him that he isn't just a cardiac cripple going inexorably downhill. It is very important in these cases not to let them lose hope," and as he said this, there was a soft click on the line. Hal had heard.

"I am not losing hope," he said later. "I know I'm not going to get any better. That's hard to take. What always helped me in the past was thinking, Later I'll be better. I don't think that anymore"— wiping his eyes—"but I'm not giving up. I'm simply accepting my realities. I may challenge them sporadically, but my denial is much less now. The closer people can be to their realities, the better off they are.

"The paradox is that in many ways I'm happier now than I've ever been. I never thought about how I might cope with sickness. I was *the doctor*. Now I look back at all these things that happened to me, emerging from these experiences with holes in my head, and I wonder how I was able to cope. What was there in me that allowed me to survive as well as I did emotionally? Why aren't I in a deep depression? I don't know. I guess it's still my father. 'You've got to make the best of it.' That's what he always told me. And I try to, and I'll *never give up*."

He decided to buy a good camera. He knew a bit about photography. He would learn more. It would be a fine hobby, he said, for a man who could not walk much. "I'll specialize in faces. I'll be your resident portraitist."

A month later I received a check for reprint fees. It was March, shortly before his fifty-sixth birthday; eleven months since Mason had given me that message from the depths, *Maybe months, maybe a year*.

"What would you like for your birthday?" I said. "This will buy a pretty good camera."

"A camera? *Hell*, no. What about my uh . . . my, uh . . ." And he makes steering motions with his hands.

Oh, yes. He wants a Moped for next summer.

Chapter *28*

---

*S*O there was his fifty-sixth birthday, a gift. A spit in the eye of fate, Bill Jody had called it, at a time when neither of us had thought that it would come to be.

My work was not going well. For more than two years I had been interviewing Hal. There were dozens of notebooks, scores of hours on tape. From time to time I would read him pages, he would clarify or expand and I would revise. But now I was coming to material that I had not, in this past year, dreamed he would live to read: Mason's dire prognosis, my own counting of the months. "What are you writing?" he would say. "You haven't read to me for a while," and I fudged and began to lock up notes, dreading what he might discover at my desk. It was no way to work. It froze me.

Quite suddenly, there came an opportunity to go to the MacDowell Colony, the artists' and writers' retreat in New Hampshire. I longed yet feared to go.

He argued, pushing me as he always did, with that gritty generosity, into a future of my own: "I don't need you to hand me my pills. I need to see you functioning well in your own life. *Please* go. It would be good for you."

One had to apply, usually, months in advance. But there had been a cancellation, a studio was available, Jon would be home for a two-week spring vacation and would be happy to spend it with his father. The MacDowell people kindly cut through many red tapes, and in two days the matter was settled: I went.

It was a revelation. I had never before been to such a place, never imagined such a place, where all else existed so that one might work. And this being the case, I worked. Nine hours each day in my little studio in the woods, lunch left on the doorstep by gnomes, no sound outside but the drift of snow and, inside, the wood crackling in my fireplace, the typewriter clacking away loose and easy, I was lost in it, couldn't get enough of it, clinging there each day until the supper hour; I, who always detested to write and did it pathetically slow and hard, like a constipated ancient.

It happens to everyone, the veterans said. It is what happens when all the energies are freed for work. And this was surely true, but I thought it had more to do with commitment. It was why I needed a program to stop smoking. It was why I needed a contract to make a marriage. The formalization of commitments. Philosophically I disapproved, but these were characterological things. Some people need the formalization of commitments; without it, we are slobs.

I called Hal every night. I crooned tenderness on the telephone: Oh, Hersh, dearest Hersh, I miss you so. And of course this was true and not true at all; I was ecstatic to be alone for these two weeks, free, absorbed in my work, relieved of his constant sickness. He felt great, he said. Jon was taking splendid care of him, cooking lovely salt-free meals. And he was walking *very* well. There had been, yes, just a touch of failure. He had gone to Mason and gotten his dry-out shot two days early, and also Mason had started him on a new medication called hydralazine, a revolutionary new treatment which everyone had been talking about at the last cardiologists' convention in Las Vegas. And he was completely dry now, and I was not to worry.

I left MacDowell on a high, fifty new pages in my pocket. I picked up Judy on the way home. It was Friday, April 1. Hal was radiant. His wife had returned, his son was still there, his daughter was visiting: a family weekend. And he looked marvelous, for him, the deadly gauntness gone from his face. "You're so *handsome*," I said. "I *know*," he said, and we laughed and slapped palms, as the football players did after a touchdown, and grabbed at each other.

April Fool. By night he had an irregular pulse and a low-grade fever.

Saturday, he felt awful. I called Mason. It sounds like a virus, he said. Garbage-pail words again. Unidentified flying fevers. Take aspirin, he said. Hal, lying there with the old pallor, as though yesterday's look of health had been a dream, a figment of my own fevered imagination, said, "Ask him if we shouldn't stop the new medication. We should get rid of the variables." Quite so, Mason said; stop the hydralazine.

Saturday night his fever was higher.

Jon left for London Sunday morning. Judy left for Massachusetts. Goodbye, darlings, Hal said, smiling, too weak to lift his head much off the pillow but eager to make good last impressions.

Mason appeared late Sunday. He'd been playing squash in the neighborhood, he said. A house call? How quaint, how lovely of him! Hal huddled beneath blankets. Yes, probably a virus, Mason said, concern clear upon his kind, plump face. Push the aspirin. Come in tomorrow for blood tests.

Another bad night. Chills, fever to 103. He dozed intermittently, his breathing labored. Finally I slept, and dreamed:

"How long do I have?" Hal asks Mason. "Maybe months, maybe a year." "Two years, maybe?" "No, I think two years is too optimistic," Peter says. I stand crying. Hal smiles at me with a sad transcendent sweetness. "Never mind, Mushie," he says. "What do they know? They're only doctors."

Monday we went to Mason's office. Hal had tremors. Peter was angry with me. "*Why* aren't you keeping the fever down? I told you to keep pushing aspirin, two every four hours. . . ."

"Peter, I was pushing even harder. Two every three hours. We still couldn't control the temperature. Would he be safer in the hospital?"

"They couldn't do much more than you're doing at home. There's not much to be done for a virus."

"But can't these high temperatures affect his heart? Weaken his heart?" The two of us discussing Hal as though in his absence. He sat quietly, staring at the floor.

"High temperatures weaken all parts of the body. In everyone. But then they recover."

"I mean *irreversible* weakening. Can the fever do any irreversible damage?" Like a heart attack?

"No. Fevers generally don't work that way. Keep after it vigorously with the aspirin and let's observe. . . ."

Observe. A nurse's voice came up on the intercom: "Mr. Schneider wants to know, about that sebaceous cyst, should he come in to have it drained?" Mason said, "Tell him if it's full and ready to be lanced, to come in and—" And suddenly, from no conscious impulse, I snarled, "Tell him to take his sebaceous cyst and shove it up his ass."

Mason was shocked. Hal, who had been sitting like a bundle of rags, gave me the fierce blue glare. That was where he stored all the starch he had left: in his eyes. "That's *terrible*," he said. "Other people's problems are serious to them. You should be ashamed."

Of course. "I'm sorry," I told them. And do take your sebaceous cyst, Mr. Schneider, and shove it up your ass.

So we observed. It deteriorated quickly into the same terrible old syndrome, the April madness, the raging fevers, the uncontrollable shakes, the layers of blankets, the drenchings, the clutchings, the blue lips, the rasping breath, the dazedness, the whole damned old thing. It was as if someone had pulled a switch and set it in motion; and then it speeded up and kept going for two hideous weeks. He was in crisis and I was feeding him aspirin, holding the water glass to his clattering teeth, and every night I lay down beside his racked body wondering, What the hell kind of virus is this? wondering if he would be dead in the morning, and wishing I were back at MacDowell.

Shit! I wrote in that first week. I came home from MacDowell five days ago. Eons ago. I cannot even remember what it was like, except that I felt so fine and strong, and now back here five days and I have not written a line, mired again in the shit. Thanks so much for taking such good care of me, darling, the father says, and the son says, It was my pleasure, Dad, and waves goodbye. Thanks so much for coming to see me this weekend, darling, the father says, and the daughter says, Please feel better, Daddy, and waves goodbye. And I am here, I see, I say Listen, I think you should be in the hospital, and to me he says, Don't play doctor. I remember that play, *The Shadow Box*: male lovers, one is dying of cancer and the other tends his death, and there aren't many laughs. Then someone comes to visit, she brings fun like baggage brought in from the outside world of health, she makes the doomed man laugh and his lover is bitter. He tells her, "You come waltzing in and out of here like a fucking Christmas tree, but some of us are here for the duration." I choked on that line, I cried and wrote it down in the dark of the theater, because that was how I felt about the nearest and dearest who can make him smile because they are never around long enough to go sour—Judy, Jon, Norman, David, all those beloveds who never anger him because they do not tell him, Please don't do this, please let me do that, let's check your temp, remember your pills . . . Not being around for the duration, they need never nag, simply come and go and lighten his load with their twinkles, and I am the heavy and it hurts. To me he says, eternally to me, Let's not tell Judy this, let's not tell Jonny that, no need to worry them with all this shit; the children, save the children, he is only twenty-seven, after all, she is only twenty-five, why worry and soil the children?

David called yesterday. "And how about *you*," he says, with Hal on the extension. "How's your work going?" An awkward silence while I muster my rages. "Not too well," I say. "Life keeps interfering with nonfiction." Rotten thing to say. How hurtful to Hal.

"She's had to baby-sit with me . . ." he says finally.

"Don't say that," I snap. "I hate it when you say that."

He feels so guilty about being a burden, which in fact he strains not to be. I think of other men and how they would be in his life. They would want the grapes peeled for them and whine if the toast was too dark. He with his guilt, and I with my rage, each the obverse of the other. We are both in such a bind.

Perhaps because he feels so little control over his own life, he has become overcontrolling with me. He tells me what I must say on the telephone and what I must write in the letter. It infuriates me.

His memory is worse now. He says, "What day is today?" "Tuesday." Ten minutes later: "What day is today?" "Tuesday." Soon again: "What day did you say this is?" *"Tuesday."* "Don't yell at me," he says.

He is lonely. Whenever I come into the bedroom he says, "Where have you been?" "In my study." "What are you doing?" Damn it, I am not *doing*, I am *being*, in privacy for a time, away from you and your sickness. Oh, God.

Last night, in his sleep, he had diarrhea. Shit! Palpable. It was the first gastric symptom of virus, which relieved me, because I had been wondering whether possibly it was all cardiac. Perhaps now he will begin to get better. But he is too weak to put on his bathrobe alone. My life here, now, is nursemaid to a man gone strangely old from sickness and garrulous from loneliness, clutching at sleeves, wanting to talk to confirm that he still exists, and I ache for him but I resent him as well, this sick, sunken man who is my beautiful Hal whom I adore. The intensity of the anger that hovers here, beneath what I take to be love, is frightening. I understand the wretched banality of such an anger as this, I do not have to be a professor of whatever to understand the how and the why of such an anger, yet it shames and appalls me. And of course, he knows.

Of course he knew, for I wore my anger like warts.

These angry feelings were normal and logical, he thought. Not for everyone, by no means for everyone, but for many people; certainly for someone like Martha, who had low tolerance when life did not go as she thought it should. And look how her life had gone. It was no prize. I love you I love you I love you, she said all the time. And he would wonder, What is this love she feels? In part it is love. In part it is guilt. In part it is fear. For many months she had been loving him too lavishly, with too much display of affection, and always he felt an air of desperation about it, he felt like saying: "I'm still alive. Let me alone."

So the I love you was not simple. When was it? The truth of it was, she was entrapped, and on some level hostility was a natural response. He understood it. He even sympathized with it. He simply did not want to be the butt of it. It was a terrible thing to be so dependent upon someone who in many ways resented him, although of course she loved him. When she cut him short, or answered him in hostile ways, or listened to him with ostentatious impatience—at such times he fiercely resented her; although, of course, he loved her.

In a barely decipherable hand he wrote in his notebook, filled now with recent chartings of fever and other clinical notes: "I find this progressive dependency demoralize & intolerable. I am very tempted to just flee. Live in a warm climate alone & last as long as I am destined to. . . ."

But of course there was no place to go and he was in no shape to get there. He could not get to the bathroom alone. In any event these were not constant thoughts at all. They surged and subsided, like my hostilities.

It was terrible. It was two hideous weeks in that house with those fires that consumed him, turned him red and blue. That first week I watched the mercury descend much too slowly, from 103.6 to 102.8 to

102.1. When I called Mason he spoke of watching, waiting, observing. "The fever is going down," he said. But fast enough? Surely this was not fast enough for such a tenuous heart. Mightn't such a heart collapse under such a stress, simply stop beating?

Observing. He lay spent on sweat-soaked sheets, too weak to move. "Let me help you to a chair; I'll change the sheets." "No. Just shove a towel under me." The diarrhea was severe. One night he tried to make it on his own to the bathroom and fell heavily to the floor. I shrieked, certain that he had dropped dead. "Something is happening to me," he mumbled dazedly, and I wondered if something had not already happened, whether the fevers had not taken some further part of his heart with them, or whether his good bypass, the one vessel that remained to keep him alive, was perhaps not so good anymore. I gave him more aspirin. I saw that he was bloated and got him onto a scale, held him there as he swayed, and found that his weight was up five pounds. Body fluid, it had to be. He had eaten practically nothing for eight days.

We went for another office visit. Other patients stared, trying not to. His eyes were almost closed, his head lolled.

Peter beckoned me into his office. "He's getting dressed. He was a little moist. I gave him the Lasix, and now we'll see. . . ."

"I keep wondering about the strain on his heart. I wonder if he wouldn't be better off in the hospital. . . ."

From the examining room we heard him call, "Help." We dashed in. He slumped in a chair, trousers halfway on, a sock in one hand, head dangling down near his knees.

"Please," he said, "help me get dressed."

I saw Peter's eyes flicker in alarm. I helped my husband into his clothes and led him into the office, and Peter said:

"Hal, Martha seems to think you'd be better off in the hospital. What do you think?"

"Not unless you feel there's a medical reason."

"Well, I don't know what more it could do for you. You need rest, which you can get at home. But Martha seems anxious, and certainly, if you're anxious too . . ."

"No. Then I don't want to go."

Still at home, then, we moved into the second dreadful week. The fevers subsided, but now he began the familiar descent into acute heart failure.

"You're coughing a lot. Do you think it's failure?"

"No. The cough is superficial, in my throat."

"Are you sure? Is it possible you're in failure and don't know it?"

"Martha." Reddening. "I know when I'm in failure. I've *been* there, remember?"

Oh, yes. And so have I, and I know when you are denying. That sound is coming from fluid-filled lungs.

On Wednesday, twelve days after the siege had begun, I called Mason again: "He is coughing heavily. He is panting. He is beginning to wheeze."

"Okay. He's due in the office Friday. Let's watch him and keep him on aspirin, and if he is still coughing then, we'll reevaluate it."

If he is still *coughing*? Fools, both of you! If he is still *breathing*. Why does no one listen to me? Why is no one trusting my observation? If not the patient, whose medical judgment can no longer be trusted because he is committed now to denial, why at least not the doctor?

Thursday the wheeze came louder from those saturated lungs, and I said to him, "I tell you that you are in failure. Please listen. You should be in the hospital."

"I have had plenty of hospitals. If my doctor sees no diagnostic or therapeutic reason for me to be there, I don't want to be there. I don't want to be admitted as therapy for you."

At dawn Friday he woke me. Gently, so as not to frighten me. He was sitting upright, in the familiar angle-iron way. Big George bubbled. Beneath the old adrenal rush I felt something slow and tired.

"I think we better get to the hospital," he said.

I thought, I would like that very much. I could work. I could read. I could sleep and not have to worry about whether he is fevered or chilled or drenched or dead. I could be alone.

Wait. You will be alone plenty. You will lie alone in this bed unable to comprehend that he no longer exists, and shudder with pain, and remember that you wanted to be alone.

He said, "I can feel the fluid in my lungs. The cough is different now. Listen." I listened. It was the same cough I had been hearing for days.

"You'd better arrange for Peter to admit me," he said.

"Should I leave word for Moses too?"

"What for?" he wheezed. "I've been underwhelmed by communications from Moses. Maybe I should buy a yacht."

❖ ❖ ❖

Within an hour we were in a hospital room.

The telephone rang as a nurse was settling him in the bed. It was Mason.

"Well," he said, "I'm sure it's reassuring for both of you to have him in the hospital. Probably we should have pushed him in earlier. But I guess he just didn't want to go, eh?"

Three days running they pumped him full of diuretics, and still they could not get him out of failure.

"Is this reversible?" I asked the intern. Lover, I called him—handsome, pouty, forever posing for the nurses, forever shaking his head and rolling his eyes to show how hard he worked; too self-involved, I thought, to be much involved with medicine.

"Reversible?" he said. "Why, uh, I would think so. Of course, with these cases we never know."

On Sunday he was still in failure, but better enough to start giving them hell. If he could not piss it out in one way, he would in another. And he knew what to give hell about. He knew every botch and blunder.

"You're damn right I was angry!" he growled when I came in. "First of all, his technique was obscene! I said, 'Is that the needle you're going to use to inject me?' He says, 'Yeah.' I say, 'Well, for Christ's sake! That's a bare needle lying on my bedspread! Do you know you've contaminated it?' He nods at me. *Duh. Duh.* I say, 'Get a clean needle.' So he goes off mumbling, and then he comes back and injects me. Unbelievable. I say, '*Wait* a minute. You haven't taken off the goddamned tourniquet!' And I rip it off my arm. He says, 'Gee. I'm sorry. I forgot.' Then *I* felt bad. I told him, 'Look, I may have been a little harsh, but these veins are getting stuck every day. It's important for me to preserve them as well as I can.' He says, 'I understand.' *Duh.* I asked him, 'Who ordered this injection?' He said, 'The resident said I should give you the Lasix if I heard râles.' So then I wondered: If this *shmucky* intern contaminates a needle and forgets to remove the tourniquet when he injects me, does he know how a râle sounds? So when the covering doctor came by, I said, 'Hey, listen to my chest, will you? Do I have râles?' He said, 'You sure do.' So then, of course, I felt *much* better."

"Of course," I said.

A nurse brought pills. "What's the blue one?" I asked.

"Ah, the blue one," says my husband, who lies at that moment with the oxygen in his nose and the E.K.G. discs on his chest and the thermometer in his anus and an I.V. in his arm. "That's my aphrodisiac."

Monday morning I telephoned Mason. "I gather they just can't get him out of failure. Is it because of the fevers he had?"

"We don't know," he said.

"*Was* it a virus? Do you still think that?"

"We don't know."

"Is it reversible?"

"We just don't know. There's no question he's much worse. He's been in the hospital seventy-two hours and he hasn't responded. He's a very sick man now. That fever, which might not affect another person so much, made his heart beat faster, and his heart doesn't want to beat faster. It can't take it." Echoes of another talk with Peter, two weeks ago to the day . . . Can these fevers do any permanent damage? No, fevers generally don't work that way. . . .

"We want to try these new medications, these vasodilators," he said now. "We're going to put him back on the hydralazine today. Let's see what that will do."

"I must ask this," I said, knowing all the while that I must not. "He seemed to be doing well until two weeks ago. And then this siege began, and it tipped him into this awful failure, and what I don't understand is why someone with such low cardiac reserve wasn't hospitalized earlier, so the strain on his heart could be relieved faster. . . ."

"Martha, I don't understand this whole conversation! He didn't *want* to go to the hospital. I certainly would have had no objection to admitting him. . . ."

"But it seems to me I was telling you clearly. . . ." Keep quiet, idiot. Back off. Why have you not learned, why do you never learn, that you only impale yourself upon confrontations? ". . . I told you we couldn't control the fever, I asked if he shouldn't be hospitalized, I told you I could see him going into deeper failure. . . ."

"Come on, Martha!" Furiously defensive now. "We would have been happy to hospitalize him. I asked him, and he said he didn't want to go."

"If you had said, 'I think you should be in the hospital,' he would have gone willingly."

"Well, then, you were giving us mixed signals. How are we supposed to understand those mixed signals?"

Signals! Why are you talking about *signals*? Where was your *medi-*

cal judgment? I mean to say, I aim to say, I am bursting to say . . .
No. Stop. Stop. These words are knives that will cut off my nose.

We hung up with ice between us.

That afternoon they put him back on hydralazine. At 9 P.M. his
temperature spiked suddenly to 105, and the nightmare began.

How odd, that through all of his hospitalizations, through all the
crises of his illness, I have never once spent a night in his room. Never
even a night in the visitors' lounge. I have been a good guest, a
meticulous observer of visiting hours. Out when the bell rings, or
shortly thereafter. I put this to you, all you nurses who race like mice
from one nocturnal crisis to another, and you doctors who lumber like
sleepy bears, to indicate that I am not your standard hospital hysteric,
a repeat offender, chewing handkerchiefs through the night in the
lounge down the hall, pleading for a cot to be placed in his room,
wringing of hands and clutching at the sleeves of white coats—that
has not been my style at all. I have never even requested—this too
surprises me now—a private nurse. When authority has said, "Go
home and relax. Everything that can be done is being done," I have
gone home and, if not relaxed, at least believed.

But when I called him at 9 to say good night and he whispered,
his voice trembling and receding as on a bad overseas connection,
"You wouldn't believe it. The same thing, all over again. I'm so sick,"
some sure sense warned me, propelled me here, toward a crunch that
I already knew was coming.

First I called his doctors. The service answered. Mason was un-
available; Silverman was in a restaurant. I said, "Get him. Tell him to
call me instantly." He did, instantly. We hadn't spoken in months. I
said, "What's happening? Hal is running 105, he sounds horrible . . ."

"Relax," Moses said. "Apparently he's been having these febrile
episodes at home. . . ."

"*Apparently?* Do you know what's been going *on?*"

"I'm sorry. I mean, he *has* been having these episodes. Now, we
thought this new medication would help him. He was doing well, and
then these episodes began. . . ."

"Then you think the medication caused it?"

"We don't know. Apparently at first there was some question that it
might be a virus . . ."

"Do you have any idea how sick he's been? Were you informed?"

"Martha, I know you think that I've sort of . . . sloughed Hal off.

But that is absolutely untrue. I want you to know that. I am always very concerned about him, I care deeply about him, I have said repeatedly that I want to be consulted about him, to see him when he comes into the office. But sometimes I don't even know he's coming in."

"Why wasn't he hospitalized earlier?"

"Well . . ." Guarded now. "If I had known . . . I mean, if I had known *in detail* the course of his illness, I might have admitted him earlier. The younger men are reluctant to hospitalize a patient because of a virus. The house staff doesn't like to be bothered with it. I must admit, with a patient like Hal, I would have treated it more aggressively. But that's past. The important thing—"

"What's being done right now? A fever of 105 . . ."

"Take it easy. It's being taken care of. The important thing now is to make him better and decide upon the best course of long-range therapy. . . ."

I chased down there, arrived in his room at 10:00 P.M. His fever now was 104. His eyes were glazed. When he saw me coming he tried to sit, but couldn't, and instead opened his arms wide toward me and croaked out a fanfare: "Welcome, Mushie! *Ta-dah!*"

This room was so tiny that although my chair was wedged deeply into a corner, I was no more than three feet from his bed. The space was lit by a dim, nasty overhead—when they are this bad, a nurse confided, we like to keep the light on—and the icy blue of the television screen, and it was all small enough so that I could see and hear with no trouble the water bubbling away in the oxygen wall unit, I could hear his shallow, hard, rapid intakes of oxygen through the nasal prongs and I wondered about this—if his lungs are filled with fluid, why are they giving him oxygen? where can the oxygen go?— and I could reach out a hand and feel that the sheets were drenched again, as at home, and that he was wet and tremorous, as at home.

I sat in that corner and spent the night watching him go down. The most hideous night of mistakes, bad judgments, oversights, fatigue, neglect, institutional paralysis, the very worst of institutional medicine turned its face to me that night, as I sat there watching him go down.

11:00 P.M. Lover came to listen to his lungs.

"Breathe deep," he says, scowling to show me how hard he is listening. He leaves the room and soon returns with a resident.

"We'd like to listen to your lungs again. Breathe, please. Good.

323

Again, please. Good," and the resident and Lover look at each other, and I know that it is not good at all. "Well, I guess we'd better give you some more Lasix. . . ."

"Oh, no," Hal says. "I didn't sleep at all last night."

Lover says, "He had a toxic reaction to the Lasix that kept him up all night. Dr. Mason says that whenever he hears râles in this patient, that means he's in failure, and he plies him with Lasix. But I wouldn't be too crazy about giving him more diuretics tonight. I'd be more concerned about what happens to the fever."

"Okay," says the resident. "We'll wait till morning." And out they go, perhaps having committed—I could not know it then—the first abominable error of the night.

I follow them to the nurses' station.

"His râles are worse now than when this episode began?" I ask Lover.

"Oh, yes. The sudden fever has put him into worse heart failure."

"Can he get a heart attack from this?"

"That's not the problem. The problem is he has such low cardiac reserve that his heart can't meet the demand this fever puts on it."

I go back to his room. "Where were you?" he says.

"In the lounge. I had a cigarette."

"Oh, Mushie, I worry about you," he says. "I wish you would stop smoking."

Midnight. A little nurse, a ninety-pounder, comes scurrying in. The way she moves reminds me of the terns that scurry along the back shore in Provincetown. But she is not a tern, she is a Lark. This Lark is a darling, achingly eager to heal, the dedication shines on her like dew, but it is one of the bleak failures of institutional medicine that she is on this case, for she is a novice, fresh out of nursing school, and he is a supine crisis, requiring veterans.

"How're you *doing*, Dr. Lear?" she chirps. "How's the *breathing*? Are you having more trouble *breathing*?"

He nods, and she does something with the dial on the oxygen supply unit. I can see the water suddenly bubbling faster.

His fever is 103.6. She takes his blood pressure, wrapping the cuff lovingly about his arm.

"What is it?" he says.

"Ninety over 56."

"Very good."

He lies propped high on pillows to ease the breathing. He keeps fiddling with the cannula, adjusting its prongs this way and that in his nostrils. "I'm so tired," he says.

"Why don't we turn off the TV and see if you can sleep?"

"I'd like Basil Rathbone chasing Moriarty," he says. "If that's not on, the hell with it."

So I switch it off and settle back in my chair, watching him. Suddenly he begins to sneeze, repeatedly, violently, and each time he has to remove the nasal prongs. "My God, my nose hurts. My nose is burning. I can't breathe. I can't use this thing. Tell them," he says, and I go out to the nurses' station, where a clerk sits reading a newspaper, and I say, "My husband is having trouble breathing. Can we get a nurse?" She says, sullen, "They're busy now. Can't you see no one's here?" and I say, "But if you could get someone. We're having trouble. . . ." And she says, "When they're free, they will come. *There are other sick people here too, you know.*" Giving me that stare, that hauteur of headwaiters.

When I get back to the room he is in a paroxysm of sneezing, he can't stop; each sneeze jerks his head forward, and then it falls back, limp, against the pillows. He looks dazed. "Got to stop it," he pants. "Got to stop. I can't breathe." And I go out again, not knowing what to do. A strange nurse walks by. "Please!" I say, and she races into the room with me and sees him there, sneezing and struggling to breathe, and she grabs the cannula and holds it to her face, and then turns toward the oxygen unit.

"What the *hell* . . ." she says. "Who the *hell* turned this up?"

It is set at 10: ten liters of oxygen per minute, twice as high as it should be, and it has burned the mucous membranes of his nose. He is in agony. They bring unguents, gently they daub the burnt membranes, and soon he is sneezing only occasionally, but he cannot wear the nasal prongs at all now, and he cannot breathe. They bring an oxygen mask. They fit it over his face. "Got to sleep," he mutters. "I'm so tired."

1:15 A.M. Lark comes to check his signs again.

"Well?" he says.

"Your fever's about the same."

"Blood pressure?"

"A little lower. Eighty-six over 56."

From across the hall a voice shrieks, "Help! Help! Help!" Lark goes running. In a moment she is back, clutching her heart. "Whew, did I get scared! But it's just Mrs. Healy. She's pretty whacked-out."

I have seen Mrs. Healy. Yesterday she appeared in the doorway and began throwing cellophane-wrapped candies at Hal. "What's the matter with her?" I ask.

"She had cardiac surgery a few weeks ago, and she's been pretty crazy ever since. You know, sometimes cardiac surgery does funny things to people."

"I know," he says.

He dozes, but only two or three minutes at a time, and then he pulls the mask off his face and begins to gasp. He says, "I can't breathe. It's like breathing in a paper bag."

I adjust the mask. Sweat pouring down his face. "Try to relax." Wasn't that what Moses had told me? Relax. And he dozes again for a moment or two and then his head begins to toss from left to right, fighting the mask, and again in his sleep he pulls it off and wakes gasping.

"What's the matter, Hal?"

"I can't . . . Feel this. You feel anything?"

I hold the mask over my face. Nothing. Again out to the nurses' station. The sullen aide, still reading, but now Lark is there too, and she comes rushing back to the room with me.

"Can't breathe," he rasps. His hand is clutching air.

She puts the mask over her face, as I did.

"Listen," I say. "I hear a hissing sound."

Lark turns toward the wall unit. *"Oh, my God, my God, my God,"* she says. *"How did this happen?"*

The tube is disconnected. It lies on the floor. Oxygen hisses freely into the room.

2:00 A.M. I sit here close beside him. In sleep he wipes a finger across the bridge of his nose, where the cold sweat is dripping under his mask. I sop up the sweat with a Kleenex. Every few minutes he wakes to his own pantings.

"So tired," he groans. "Ask them for more Valium. I need sleep." And I go back to the desk and ask Lover, who sits writing notes and yawning deeply, and Lover asks a nurse, "When is Dr. Lear due for Valium?" "Not for another two hours," she says. "But he's desperate for sleep," I say. "Who isn't?" Lover says. "Okay, give him the Valium. Give him any damned thing he wants."

And still he sleeps so fitfully.

His splendid profile is all bones, pure. He looks younger than he has looked in years. No more fatty deposits anywhere. The bags beneath his eyes are gone. His skin is tight, taut. A young, taut, beautiful face; a death mask.

2:30 A.M. Lark comes back for the blood pressure.

"What is it?" he asks.

"A *little* lower now. Eighty-two over 56." His temperature is 102.6. She checks the oxygen supply unit. It is working.

An aide comes to give him an alcohol rub. "Oh, that feels so good," he groans. "Turn on your side," she says. He cannot do it. She calls an orderly to help turn him. She finishes and starts to leave.

"Wait," he says.

She pays no attention.

"Wait. I feel faint. What should my wife do if I faint?"

She continues out.

"No, *wait*. I've got to go to the bathroom. Please help me get up."

"I'll be back in a minute," she says.

"No. No time. I'll soil myself. *Please* . . ." But she is gone.

"Hal, wait for a nurse."

"*Now*—I've got to go *now*, oh, God, help me. . . ."

He is rearing out of the bed. I grab him as he is about to fall. "Hurry, hurry," he says, and already he has soiled himself, it is the most violent diarrhea, and I half-drag him to the bathroom and loosen his pajama pants and ease him down upon the toilet seat.

"Go out. Close the door," he tells me. In all those years of marriage we have never used the toilet in each other's presence—an eccentricity, a mutual aesthetic preference—and he is not about to start now.

I call through the door, "Let me know when I can help you," and he takes so long that I keep calling: "Hal. Hal. Can I help you out now?"

"No. Not yet." And finally, in a voice worn down to its nub: "I need help now."

He sits boneless on the toilet, too weak to move, the soiled trousers crumpled about his ankles. This fastidious man. The stench makes me gag. There are fresh pajamas on the shelf. Somehow I get them on him, and he puts his arm about my shoulders and I drag him back to the bed. "I'm so weak. God, I'm so weak," he says.

3:30 A.M. "Please put a cold compress on my head," he says. "Oh, that feels better. I'm getting weaker. I don't know what to do. I must sleep. I need sleep. Please get more Valium."

Lark is at the desk. "He isn't due another Valium until 6," she says.

"Ask the intern."

"He's gone to sleep. Mrs. Lear"—she looks at me anxiously—"I hope you'll understand. I can't wake the intern for a Valium. Not if I want to keep my job."

"But I think my husband's sleep at this point is more crucial than the intern's sleep."

"I'm sorry," she says.

4:00 A M. His breathing is much worse. What shall I say? To whom? I watch him failing steadily, visibly, and the nurses keep coming in and out, checking his vital signs, checking the numbers, but nobody is *doing* anything. I feel that we are alone in this place. He is sliding downhill, down, down, and the brakes are here, somewhere, the medicines are here, the emergency measures are here, the doctors are here, and in this vast place, in this one small, dim room of this great medical center, we are utterly alone.

He keeps slipping down in the bed. Every few minutes he says, "Please lift me higher. I can't breathe," and I put a hand under his shoulders and he braces his feet and we say, "One, two, three, *go*," and he pushes and I pull and we manage to get him inches higher in the bed. But soon he is too weak to brace his feet, and I have to go find someone to help lift him. And minutes later he has slid down again and I go again for help, but no one is there. Not even the bitch clerk.

He says, "I don't know what to do."

"About what, darling?"

"Me."

5:00 A.M. Here's Lark. "How're you *doing*, Dr. Lear?"

"I'm getting worse," he says. "Please tell the doctor."

"Okay." She comes back. "He says there is nothing more to do right now. He'll be in to see you soon."

Alone. Alone.

"Oh, God. Oh, God," he says. Suddenly he smiles at me, a smile of such sweet irony as I have never seen. "This is a *Mona Lisa* smile," he says.

"What does it mean?"

"Only I know."

I go running out. "Lark, I'm scared. *Do* something."

She does the only thing she can think to do: comes back to take another blood pressure.

"What is it now?" he says. His head rolls freely. His speech is slurred. His eyes are blind.

"About the same," she says. But there is an urgency in the way she scurries out of the room, some fearful bit of body language, and I follow her out and ask, "Is his pressure really the same?" and she says, "No. It's in the low 70's." She shakes a little fist in the air. "I don't like the way this is going," she mutters. "I'm going to wake the doctor. If he hasn't had much sleep—well, neither has anyone else."

5:30. Hal is saying repeatedly now, "Help me. Lift me higher. I can't breathe." Rolling his head in desperation. "Tell them I need help."

"Yes, darling. The doctor is coming."

5:45. Hal clammy-cold now, shocky. Lover finally appears. He is indolent-faced. "I understand you're not feeling too well," he says.

Hal points thumbs down.

"Let's listen to your back. Would you lean forward?"

"I can't. Help me."

The sleepy eyes widen in sudden alarm. He helps Hal forward, listens, says, "I'll be right back."

Hal's head turns frantically on the pillows. "They have to do something fast," he says.

"Yes, darling. They will." I squeeze his hand, but he cannot squeeze back.

The intern returns. "I've called Dr. Mason. We have agreed to stop all your medications and do nothing more until the doctors see you on rounds at 8 o'clock. Meanwhile, I'm going to start an I.V. on you."

I understand this. They are establishing a line. If they need suddenly to pour some lifesaving potion into his veins, the needle will be in place.

He jabs, and perforates the vein. "Press here," he directs me. I press down hard on a gauze pad over the vein. He sticks the other arm and gets the needle in properly.

"Okay, that's set. We'll see you at about 8," he says. And goes. He is *gone*. Can this be? Should I call Peter? But the intern has just called Peter. They agreed to do nothing until rounds. Two hours from now. We seem not to have two hours to spare. "They must hurry," Hal is saying. "I am getting very bad." Should I simply run into the corridor and begin to scream, and never stop until help comes? But then they would kick me out into the dawn. We cannot have you screaming in the corridors. We have sick people here. They would kick me out, and he would be alone, at the mercy of, unprotected from, the medical establishment. I know for sure that if he had been alone through this night, lying alone amid their botches, he would already be dead. Absolutely I know that. And listen, this is a *good* hospital; can you imagine how many patients, in how many good hospitals, not to contemplate the bad, have died this night due to the ministerings of the medical establishment? Propped up here, struggling to breathe, with the useless oxygen mask flung to the floor, with no breath to call for help, no strength to stagger out for help, no wife or other overnight guest to protect him from his hosts, he would have gasped his last, and what would they have told me? Of course, it had to be expected, they would have said; he had such a bad heart, it was a miracle he lasted as long as he did; and so forth. Imagine how many families will hear such and-so-forths this morning.

Now I understand what it was that so agonized him, and about which he would not speak, when his mother died. We had been married a year. She died back there in Hartford, in the hospital where he was president of the medical staff. The charge nurse called him in the middle of the night and said, "Dr. Lear, I am calling to tell you that your mother has just expired." The cause of death was heart failure; and when they told him that, the agony came over his face, and he said, "I wonder . . . Oh, God, I can't help wondering . . ." "What?" I asked. "No, nothing." "Tell me." "No. I don't want to talk about it. What's done is done. It can't be changed." And I never knew what he meant, and now, suddenly, I know. He wondered if his mother had died for lack of supervision. People do not die suddenly of pulmonary edema. That death is slow. He wondered how long his mother had lain there, unsupervised, gasping, drowning, conscious, before she died. For that is the horror of dying of pulmonary edema, as he is dying now. The victims are fully conscious, as he is now. It is not like renal failure, wherein they simply drift off and away, or even like the final hours of cancer, wherein, usually—the conscious horrors having come earlier—they are in coma; no, when the lungs are filling with water they know it, they are experiencing it fully, struggling and thrashing in panic, like a drowning in mid-ocean but slowly, slowly, a drowning that may take hours, and conscious to the end.

At 6 A.M., in the grayest light of dawn, Lark came back to take a blood pressure. She could not hear it.

"What does that mean?" I whispered to her.

He answered loudly: "It means that I am dying."

And then he did something quite remarkable. Somehow he managed to rouse himself out of incipient shock, managed to cut through the terror of his own drowning and become again the doctor, a more observant doctor than any of them had been all night, and to give her a totally lucid medical assessment.

"Listen to me," he told her. "I am very dehydrated. I can barely feel my pulse. I have put out no urine since my fever spiked last night. My kidneys have stopped functioning. Tell them they must hurry or I will die."

She looked terrified. "Yes, Dr. Lear. They will be here soon. Don't you worry. Hang on."

And from 6 to 8 we hung on. Thinking back on it later, I could not fathom how I allowed such an interlude to be. What was I doing, what the hell did I think I was doing, sitting there? I simply submitted, entered upon their institutional madness, sat and waited while life flowed down the drain, assuming, because it is a symptom of mass madness to make such assumptions, that there was a guiding intelligence, accepting that help would come when it was scheduled to come, and that I could make it come no sooner, and that this was a rational course of events, moving deeper and deeper into his catastrophe with no clear understanding of how or why it was happening, as though it were a war.

I clutched him. At 6:15 he asked, "What time is it?" "Almost 7," I said. And at 6:20, "What time is it?" "Almost 7:30," and he kept pulling off the mask and sneezing, and soon he was saying over and over and over again, "I need help. I can't breathe. They must hurry," and I was saying, "Soon. Soon. Hang on, darling," hanging on to him tight, his face soaked with cold sweat, his eyes empty, gasping, thrashing, pleading, "Help me. Help me. Help me," and nurses glided in and out and I asked again and again, "Can't we get the doctors now?" "Soon," they said. And then he began to mutter, "I don't know what to do. I don't know what to do," and I knew what he meant; he meant that he was dying and he knew what had to be done, but he did not know how to make anyone do anything, and so he simply continued to pant, "Help me. Hurry. I can't hang on," and I sat gripping him hard and watching him go and knowing that nothing more would be done until 8, because 8 is when doctors make rounds.

*　*　*

They came early, actually. At ten minutes before the hour. A clutch of them, the chief resident and his satellites, and they clustered around the bed, smiling cordially, and the chief resident said loudly, as though the patient were deaf, "Good morning, sir. How're you doing?"

He gestured thumbs down, as he had hours earlier.

"Would you wait outside, ma'am?"

I waited. Soon they came out to the corridor and stood in a circle, whispering, and I went back into the room.

"Move my head. Move me up. I can't breathe," he said, tossing his head wildly about on the pillows, and I tried to pull him upright but he was a dead weight. I ran out to that tight little circle. I said, "Can someone help me sit him up? He can't breathe." And the chief resident said, "Would you wait, please. We are having a conference here. Someone will be with you in a minute," as though I had asked for a salesclerk, and I nodded, as though this too were rational.

A strange doctor came. The head of the coronary-care unit, I learned later. He took one look and shook his head and spoke sharply to the resident. Nurses went rushing for drip bottles. Peter arrived. Then Moses. Hal's head bobbed from side to side, and he kept gasping, "I don't know what to do. I don't know what to do." Peter said, "Hal, *we* know what to do. We are taking you to the C.C.U., where they can dry you out. We'll be taking you soon," and "I can't wait," Hal rasped, his head thrashing now like a fish on deck; "Martha, *tell* them. I am dying. *Hurry. Help me.* I don't know what to do."

Suddenly they exploded into action. They pushed his bed out of the room and went racing with it down the hall, Moses and Peter pulling the headboard and two other doctors pushing the footboard, and nurses running alongside carrying the drip bottles, pushing the E.K.G. machine, the bed careening wildly down the hall, bumping into walls and supply carts, Peter so nervous, I remember, that he laughed giddily as the bed hit walls and yelled, "Hey, *watch* it there!" and I running behind this maniacal procession, facing Hal, who was racing away from me backward, a nurse holding him propped up. They came to a halt at the elevator bank and now, with this desperate urgency upon them, moved into purest farce, for they could not fit the bed into the elevator, not with all the people and all the equipment that had to accompany this bed, and they tried first this way and then that, shouting to one another, "Push it out again and angle it in foot first" and "Come on, *come on,* you can squeeze into this corner," several of them laughing hysterically by now, like children past all control, and finally they got everyone and everything wedged in, all but me, and I stood out there in the hall as the doors began to close on the face of my husband, who stared at me unseeingly and sighed, "Hurry. Hurry. Hurry."

"What floor?" I yelled to Moses.

"Four! Four!" he yelled back.

I took the stairs and caught up with them and ran with them to the coronary-care unit, where an orderly blocked my way—"Stay!" he said—and they rushed him through the swinging doors and a team converged upon him to perform what are called heroic measures.

I stood there. A cart rolled by with Hal's clothes. His robe, his shoes, his shirt, stuffed into paper bags. It seemed to me that these clothes in paper bags were all that was left of him now. I grabbed his shirt and began to sob into it. Even as I did this, I felt powerfully as though it were someone else's gesture. It was in a tradition that distressed me, the tearing of clothes and the beating of breasts, that damp tropical theater of grief in which my mother had mourned when her husband had died, and her mother too, every sound and gesture being large, significant, therapeutic; the larger the gesture, the greater the grief. I wanted desperately to be contained and Americanized, as Hal would have been, as Hal would have liked, yet I did as the mothers had done and cried big to show big grief.

A nurse took the shirt from me, gently.

"Don't do that," she said. "Isn't there anyone you would like to call?"

Yes. David. He was having breakfast. He would leave immediately.

"What should I do now?" I said to the nurse.

"Wait until they come for you."

"Where?"

"Here. In the waiting room."

Another woman waited in the waiting room. Mrs. Bailey, from Boston. We smiled at each other.

"My husband is dying," I said.

"Oh, don't lose hope yet," she said. "My husband dropped at Kennedy. He was waiting for a plane to Brazil, and he dropped. It's a good thing he wasn't on the plane. That would have been the end. They took him to ———— Hospital. Have you ever been there?"

"No."

"Oh, that's a terrible hospital." Mrs. Bailey seemed in her mid-50's; a large, muscular woman with leathery skin and a husky voice. A country-club golfer and drinker, I thought. "Perfectly terrible hospital. But I must say they were very nice to him. They transferred him here this morning. Now, in this place, who can you believe? One doctor says he's in danger, one doctor says he'll be all right. It's crazy, isn't it?"

"Yes."

Moses and Peter came into the waiting room. They looked at their shoes, like mourners.

"It's over?" I said.

"Almost," Moses said.

They took seats opposite me. Mrs. Bailey moved several seats away. They talked—mostly Moe talking, mostly Peter nodding. They said that it had been predictable, since his heart was so bad, and that he had lasted, really, longer than they had hoped. And so forth.

I asked why he had gone into failure.

Moe explained that something had happened. I could not understand what it was. The words were too technical.

I said, "What is happening now?"

Moe said, "They're still working on him, but it looks pretty hopeless."

"Is he conscious?"

"Completely. That's the trouble. I wish he was less conscious. He keeps asking questions: 'What's this you're doing? What's that?' He's got to know everything. He's so adorable."

"I want to see him before he dies."

Peter said, "Okay. Let me go back there and see if they're ready for you. They're getting him cleaned up."

"What do you mean, cleaned up?"

"When they have to make cutdowns to get the lines in fast, it gets pretty messy."

"I see." I didn't. It didn't matter. "What about his children? Should they come now?"

"Wait. No point calling now. In the next hour either he'll die or he won't. If he dies, they can't get here in time anyway."

"Will you tell me when to call them?"

"We'll tell you," Peter said.

Moe said, "I want you to know they've tried everything. They have made a truly heroic effort."

They both left. Mrs. Bailey rejoined me.

"He is dying now," I said.

"Don't lose hope yet," she said.

Now a doctor came for her, and I moved off, but in that small space it was impossible not to hear.

"He must be operated on," the doctor said. "His aorta is ripped open. Without surgery, he has no chance."

"And with surgery?" asked Mrs. Bailey.

"A fifty-percent chance. But I must warn you, he may go sour on the table. It is a very long operation. Four to five hours."

"When are you doing it?" she asked.

"Immediately."

He left, she sat down again, I moved back toward her, in that minuet of the waiting room that we had both learned with such speed. Again we smiled at each other.

"He may go sour on the table," she said.

"Don't lose hope yet," I said.

David arrived. It was 9:25.

"This is Mrs. Bailey," I said. "Her husband has a ripped aorta. They are going to operate."

"How do you do?" David said. "I just saw Moe in the hall. He told me it is very bad."

"Yes. They said I can see him before he dies. Do you want to see him too?"

"Yes. Funny, he must have had a premonition. We were talking Sunday. He said, 'It's just a matter of time. I'm a doctor. I know. But I put the best face on for Martha, and Silverman and Mason put the best face on for me.'"

Peter came in. He bent his best face down toward me—it was woebegone and very, very red; poor, dear Peter—and in a voice that quivered to hold its nonchalance, he said this: "They're ready. Why don't you go in now and say hello?"

I began to laugh. "Hello!" I said. "Hello, hello, goodbye, hello!"

David said, "Come on. You can't go in looking like this. Go wash your face."

"Yes." I went and washed my face. I combed my hair and put on blusher.

"That's much better," Peter said. "About the children—you'd better get them here."

We went down the long hall and through the swinging doors. The area seemed to be brilliantly lit, as though for a film. My husband was propped high on a bed. He was surrounded by machines. He was naked, covered from the groin down by a sheet. There were many lines. There was blood. His eyes were closed. His face was yellow. He was panting, but he looked dead.

"Here," somebody whispered. "Stand here." Many people seemed to be waiting there, silent, watching, as though I were standing now at the open coffin. What should I do? What should I say? How do I bid him goodbye?

I bent and brought my lips to his ear, inhaling the smell of him. I kissed his earlobe. He did not stir. I whispered urgently, "Hello, darling. It's me. You've got to hang on. *Hang on. Hang on. Hang on.*"

His eyelids fluttered. Softly he sighed, "How do I do that?"

"*Just hang on,*" I hissed, and kissed his cheek, murmuring in silence Goodbye, and turned and walked away.

A woman embraced me. She was plump and warm. She led me back toward the waiting room, hand holding mine, and talked steadily and soothingly. Her name was Bonnie, she said. She was the head nurse. It was not yet hopeless. Quite true, it was very bad, but it was not yet hopeless. They had done this and that, and such and so had happened, he had not responded, but they were going to continue trying, and I was to wait in the waiting room, and not lose hope, not lose hope, and she would come back and tell me, she said, whatever more there was to tell, as soon as there was anything more to tell. And in this way she sat me down, and petted me, and plumped herself about me, as though she were a comforter. I wanted to sink into her and sleep.

So we waited, David and I. Mrs. Bailey was gone now. We sat alone, composing an obituary.

"I want it to be in the *Times*," I said. "You will call the *Times*?"

"Yes. Is it still Whitman? Does he still edit the obituary page?"

"No. He's retired. I don't know the editor. But I think they'll run Hal's obit. Wouldn't you think so? After all, I worked there."

Silently we pondered the weight of this clout. Would it reserve courtesy space on the *Times* obituary page? And if so, how many inches? A photo, possibly? Of course, much would depend upon who else died this day. The chances of making the obit page were always better on a slow day.

"And if it isn't enough that I worked there, tell them about his program. That was important, you know. Those bastards took it away from him, but he created it. 'Dr. Harold A. Lear, the founder and first director of the Medical Center Sexuality Program, one of the country's first . . .'"

"Hold it." David was taking notes on the back of an envelope. "The medical what?"

"Medical Center Sexuality Program. Got that?"

"Yes. Go on."

"'. . . died today after a long cardiac illness. He was fifty-six . . .'" Et cetera.

I smiled at him, savoring efficiency. This was much better. This was as American as I could wish. "Now, about funeral arrangements," I said. "If I could just tell you . . ."

"Of course."

"He wanted to be cremated."

"Okay."

"He always said, No fuss. Short and simple."

"Okay."

"But I would like it if you would give a eulogy. Will you do that?"

"Of course. I'll be honored."

"And Norman too."

"I'll tell him. We've already contacted him."

"And two other friends. Here, I'll give you their names."

He pocketed the information.

"Where do you want the service held?" he said.

"I don't know. We don't belong to a congregation. Any suggestions?"

"How about Campbell's? That's nice. Dignified."

"Who would conduct the service? I'd hate to have a stranger conducting the service." Should a rabbi preside? We knew no rabbis in New York. Hal had not been to a religious service in years, and I not since childhood. There was a rabbi in Hartford, an old friend, but perhaps there were questions of courtesy privileges, as in hospitals: could a Connecticut rabbi conduct a service in a nonsectarian funeral parlor in New York? How good it would be to have rules. My father had been buried by rules that seemed to have been passed down like genetic traits; and he had been mourned by the rules, in a *shul* where he had sat all the high holy days of his adult life, in a certain seat, among people who knew all the rules, led by a rabbi who had known the deceased for years and could bear witness to his probity and sweetness of character. What comfort that had been. In what rules would our comfort lie? "Can a nonsectarian person conduct a funeral service?" I asked.

"I just don't know. I'll find out," David said.

It was 10:50. Mrs. Bailey stood in the doorway. She said, "I came back to find out how your husband is doing."

"Why, Mrs. Bailey, how thoughtful. He's still dying. We're going over the funeral arrangements."

"I'm so sorry," she said.

"And your husband, Mrs. Bailey?"

"They're operating now. They seem pretty hopeful."

"I'm so glad."

Now Moses appeared. His head shook slowly from side to side. "Gone?"

"No. He's not gone. He's better."

We stared at him. "*Better?*"

"*Better.* He's being a pain in the ass. He wants to know every detail of treatment. He's driving them all crazy in there. It's unbelievable. It's something spiritual, that fight, that fight that keeps him alive."

"*Better?*"

Moe shrugged. He was still shaking his head, as from palsy or shell shock. "Unbelievable," he said.

Bonnie, the head nurse, beckoned me.

I tiptoed back with her into that white cave, and past the flashing objects that kept us from him, as the television cameras on their dollies keep the studio audience from the star, and she guided me beneath the cameras, as it were, and past the cables, to where he lay still panting, his eyes closed, his face remote behind the mask, and I wondered, *Better?* But surely they are wrong. How can anyone who looks like this be *better?* And I bent down again, Bonnie smiling sweet encouragement and beckoning me toward him, and whispered, "Darling. You're *much better.* You've got to *fight.* You're going to *make* it. You're going to *make* it. You're going to *make* it."

And with one sudden swift move he ripped the mask off his face and turned to confront me directly. His eyes consumed me. *"I've already made it,"* he said.

"At 8:25 A.M.," the intern in the coronary-care unit recalled later, "we got a guy with an infiltrated intravenous. So he wasn't getting dopamine, the drug to maintain blood pressure. He had no palpable blood pressure and yet he was able to talk to us. This in itself was unusual. We had to feel the blood pressure by hand. We thought we were getting around 70. He was in cardiac shock: blood pressure too low to maintain life; no urine; decreased mentation; clammy extremities. I would have thought that his chances of coming through were very, very small. We got to work on him instantly."

"Who were 'we'?" I asked, for this was a proper interview, notebook in my lap.

"Doctors Silverman and Mason; our Attending in Cardiology; two residents; the intern—myself; medical students and nurses. We all descended on different parts of him: making cutdowns, putting in lines. Do you understand this? In such a situation it is crucial to get lines instantly into arteries and veins to deliver medications, to measure different things. There is no time for niceties. We simply cut. When we can, we put a superficial anesthetic on the skin. Then we make the cutdown.

"A cutdown was made on the right side to insert the dopamine line.

"A cutdown was made on the left side to insert an arterial line. That is to measure the systemic blood pressure. We couldn't get it in. Then we tried the femoral artery. It wasn't easy. It wasn't a nice, juicy artery pumping with blood.

"A cutdown was made and a Swann-Ganz catheter inserted into the arm and threaded through the vein into the right side of the heart. That is to measure pressures in the heart.

"A Foley catheter was inserted to measure the urine.

"Throughout the entire period he was fully conscious. He was asking questions and I was telling him everything we were doing.

"While we were putting the lines in, he became extremely short of breath and started frothing at the mouth. That is 'bubbling.' In such a case, we may use any of the modalities whose first letters spell MAD DOG: morphine, aminophylline, diuretics, digitalis, oxygen and general procedures. 'General procedures' means sitting him up, reassuring him and putting on tourniquets to keep fluid in the arms and legs from coming to the heart.

"We gave him diuretics—five hundred milligrams Lasix intravenously.

"We followed general procedures.

"We also removed a pint of blood to lessen body fluid. That is called a phlebotomy. We do it in the most acute cases.

"At that point we were giving up hope. He had life-threatening high potassium. Everything was going in the wrong direction. Systems were breaking down. It is a cycle: the breakdown of one system triggers the breakdown of another. You've got to break into that cycle at some point and reverse it; otherwise there is no chance. With the patient in shock, pulmonary edema, potassium and lactic acidosis, no urine, and seeing the numbers from the laboratory, which were crazy, we felt there was no hope. We felt, Well, we will keep trying, but it is not going to work. I remember—do you want the asides?"

"Yes. Please."

"I remember a couple of doctors came in and saw what was going on, and one of them said, 'You're all crazy. Why don't you quit? There's no chance.'

"Within half an hour he was better. Things started turning around. Easing of the pulmonary edema led to decreased demand on the heart, which decreased the size of the left ventricle, which increased the blood pressure, which increased the profusion to his kidneys, which reversed acidosis and peripheral tissue destruction—and all systems started feeding into each other. From then on, it was pretty much a matter of watching. The cycle was reversed. Of course, it could switch again at any moment. But it had been reversed.

"I would have to say that I was amazed. In all my time in the C.C.U., I had only seen one other instance of a patient being brought back from that degree of extremis.

"I would also have to say that the crisis is indicative that the same thing could easily happen again. But of course, you probably know that."

"Soon?"

"I would have to say, probably yes."

Despite the reversal of that deadly cycle, they did not really expect to keep him alive. We sat through the day in the waiting room, friends and relatives, waiting for some final notice. People kissed me and murmured to me and chattered to each other of ordinary things, which I resented. Chatterers, I thought. His daughter did not chat. She and I sat silent, huddled close, pressing flesh and damp Kleenex. This was a comfort. This was, in some way, a rule.

Mrs. Bailey visited several times. We held hands, like intimates. Her husband was still in surgery. "Boy, it's really something, isn't it?" she said. "It sure is," I said.

The nurse Bonnie came and went. Big Mama, so exquisitely attuned to countless women like me, whom she had consoled in this waiting room, that she seemed to be inside my head, to know exactly what images were trapped in there and how best to pet and soothe. Draping herself now about Judy and me, whispering news bulletins and cautionary notes: ". . . still holding his own . . . we just don't know . . . moment to moment . . ." I felt that I needed no cautions. It never occurred to me that we might beat this rap.

In midafternoon she came to us and said, "We think he may have had another infarct."

"Infarct?" Judy said.

"Heart attack," I said.

My God, another infarct. Of course. Hadn't I dreaded precisely this, dipping my toe into this dread whenever I'd asked of Mason, "Can these fevers damage his heart?" At what point in the long night had it happened? When he had moaned, "Oh, God, help me" and slumped down, that proud and beautiful man, upon a toilet seat, soiled as a baby, too weak to move? Or later, toward dawn, when he began to drown, pleading, "Hurry, hurry, hurry," with that thing in his eyes, that which has always been least bearable for me, a full consciousness in a terrible terminal moment—had it been then? Or earlier, perhaps even at home, at some fatal moment during those two preposterous weeks at home, when he was being treated with aspirin while his fevers spiked and smoldered? "God, another infarct. When? Why?" And Bonnie said, "The shock . . . such low blood pressure over a period of time—that certainly could have done it. He was very shocky. At least, now he is no longer in pulmonary edema. The ones we have a bad problem with are those who stay in pulmonary edema for two hours. That's a real problem. He came in with edema and we got him out of it and three hours later he was in edema again and we got him out of it again. That's more encouraging. We got him"— whispering liltingly, as though this were a song title—"just in time."

"But shouldn't he have been in here last night? With that fever and that heart, and the terrible weakness and struggling to breathe and saying, 'I'm getting weaker, help me' . . . oh, Bonnie, how it hurt to hear him begging for help . . ."

"I know, I know."

". . . shouldn't he have been in here then?"

"I can't say. I don't know what his situation was."

"It was bad. You should read the charts."

"Yes, that would be interesting. Certainly we would have preferred to have him in here last night. But nobody consulted us. We didn't hear about him until this morning."

Didn't hear. Nobody had heard. How strange, that we should scream all night and nobody had heard. My God, my God, another infarct.

He was the only optimist in that crowd.

"Hello, Daddy," Judy whispered—both of us whispering in his presence, as though timbre might kill him—and his eyes opened. "How are you, Daddy?"

He grinned. "*Much* better, darling. I thought I was going to die this morning, but I'm much better now."

It was a large room with two beds, the other bed now empty, and dominated by all the machinery of heroic measures. Nurses and doctors stood about. He could not move his arms. They were taped to splintlike boards, elbow to wrist, to hold the lines secure. He gestured me close with his chin, pulled me down with his eyes. "These people worked their asses off for me," he whispered. "Some change from last night, eh, Mushie?"

Oh, some change. Those others . . . sweet neophytes or seasoned bunglers, in the end it's all the same, isn't it? As incompetent as those others had been, that was how splendid these people were. Bonnie, introducing me to various staff members: "And this is Lois, who will be with him till 11 tonight. And Ginny will be watching him too. He is in good hands"—Lois smiling at me with something I might have sworn was love, Ginny squeezing my arm, both of them children, yet I swayed toward them as though they were books of knowledge; ". . . and have you met Dr. Corona, our chief resident?" —another child, pudgy, unprepossessing, the one who had ordered them to rush Hal to this place, blushing now as I fell upon him: "Ah, Dr. Corona, how can I ever thank you, thank you, thank you, thank you, thank you . . ." "No, please," he said. "We don't know . . . we hope . . . we'll try . . . we don't know . . ." And Bonnie whispering to me, "You should go home, get something to eat, get some sleep, it's late, there's nothing you can do here, you can call us anytime . . ." And Lois, pressing a telephone number into my hand: "Yes, here, a direct number, *anytime*, middle of the night, any questions . . ."

So we left at 10. Went out to dinner, a small knot of family—the daughter, the wife, a few relatives. I got drunk fast and wept wildly. There were a couple of cousins who had never gotten on too well. Now I wept to them of reconciliation. "For his sake," I wept. "He would not want bad feeling between you; I know this hurt him always; he always wanted the family to be close, to be together"—"My God, another Eddie," one of the cousins said—"to be close and stay close and stay together," I wept, and the truth was, Hal had never given a damn about that. It had nothing to do with Hal. It was for me: Abide, damn it, abide with me.

That was a Tuesday, April 19.

And on Wednesday, I was not a widow. Mrs. Bailey from Boston was a widow. Her husband, to whom they had given a 50-percent chance, had gone sour on the table.

I never saw her again. I had felt so close to her. I wrote her a note, which she did not answer, and very soon I forgot what she looked like. It was like that in the waiting room.

My husband, to whom they had given zip, was somewhat better, they said. They seemed astonished. When they brought me to him, he held his splinted arms straight out like a sleepwalker, which was as close as he could come to the fighter's victory sign, and said, "We *beat* them! Right, Mushie?"

He is some fighter, they said. But they were not betting on him. Nothing to bet on. The chief resident, Corona, told me, "This is a man who, despite his young age, has what we call an end-stage heart. It is barely functioning. He has severe damage in almost all parts of a myocardium that is highly diseased to begin with."

End-stage heart. What a phrase. What precision. It resonated even as he spoke, and I thought it would echo always in my head, like *may go sour on the table.*

Thursday.

Of all the rooms in which I have waited through all of the crises, this is the worst. Its banality is uncivil. Small, beige, with brown carpeting; blue-and-beige-striped draperies; eight chairs, four blue, four beige. And on the wall, a colorful diagram: YOUR HEART AND HOW IT WORKS. They come into this room in an endless procession, women mostly, incipient widows mostly; they move through a sort of revolving door into the terror of one another's lives, stay a brief time, make intimacies, intense and rootless, and then they part and move on to celebrate or to mourn; mostly to mourn. I do not think there are pen pals. Beyond this room, we will not exist for one another.

Tuesday there was Mrs. Bailey from Boston, that doughty lady, who kept telling me not to lose hope. And now her husband has gone to that great sour in the sky.

Yesterday there were a dowager, elegant in gray silks, and her two elegant sons, vested suits, good Italian shoes. All morning they sat murmuring together in a corner. At one point a nurse came and asked, "The doctors want to know, how old is your husband?" "Eighty," the woman said. That would be okay, I thought, to be sitting here worrying over losing Hal, age eighty. Then I felt ashamed. You really must learn, I said to myself, that your own grief does not diminish anyone else's. Perhaps in fact her grief would be harder to bear. She had been married—what? Forty, fifty, sixty years? A far older habit than mine, harder to break.

When they came to tell her that her husband had died, she said nothing. She simply shrank. The sons brought her gently to her feet and bore her away.

Today there is a lovely young woman. Rather like the actress Marlo Thomas, with the long dark hair sweetly clumped upon each breast. Her name is Susan. She was sitting here crying when I arrived.

"My husband is here," she said, as though this explained all the secrets of life.

Her husband! I would have supposed she was crying for her father.

"He is thirty-four. And this is his second attack. And I just can't help feeling . . . I mean, *no* time is a good time, but it doesn't seem fair. He's so young. Isn't he?"

I nodded.

"Is your husband here too?"

"Yes."

"How old is he?"

"He is fifty-six," I said; and saw clearly in her face that she was contemplating fifty-six as I had contemplated eighty.

This afternoon she got word that her husband was better, and left. "I hope you have good news. I'll see you tomorrow," she said.

Then there were two elderly women. They held hands and spoke in Yiddish. One said, "Why did it have to happen to him?" and the other one said, "God knows."

Is this room ever empty?

I marvel at the staff. These are extraordinary people. Never through any of his hospitalizations have I seen such people as these. I expect competence, but not caring. It is easy to find caring on obstetric floors. Obstetrics is happy medicine. But here, in this wretched place, where people cry their hearts out every day, how does the staff manage to remain so emotionally available? How is it that they have not grown indifferent, or sealed themselves off? I told Bonnie, "I don't know how you all bear it." She said, "It's hard. Many times we go home at night and cry."

He is weaker today. He had an "incident." During the night his blood pressure dropped steeply, spontaneously, and they had to increase the dopamine. These vasopressors are powerful stuff. They force the blood pressure higher, but they also make the heart work harder. Not the drugs of choice for end-stage hearts, if one had a choice, which they don't.

Hal has two basic problems, Dr. Corona says: his blood pressure and his heart failure. The old Sex and My Mother. Without the vasopressors, his pressure drops to nothing. Without the diuretics, huge amounts of diuretics, he would start drowning again. And the situation has an agonizing circularity, because not only do the vasopressors put extra strain on his heart, but the diuretics tend to lower his blood pressure even more. Corona said, "All we can do is keep working on both problems. It's a delicate balance."

I met one of the day nurses from the third floor. She said, "I knew something terrible must have happened, because just after I came on duty Tuesday morning, someone came running down to the nurses' lounge yelling that we had to get a dopamine drip started on Dr. Lear. It's very rare to use dopamine on the floor. By the time they're that bad, they're usually in the C.C.U. And then I heard that Lark had a terrible night. What happened?"

I told her a bit. I told her about the sleepy Lover.

"Oh, *him*," she said. "No wonder." And then: "I'll tell you something else, but don't quote me: I heard that when Dr. Mason came in and saw how bad things were, he was furious that they hadn't called him earlier. He raised hell."

Vasopressors. After Hal's surgery, he had been on vasopressors. It was like this after the surgery: a heart attack, high fevers, low blood pressure. That was the heart attack they never mentioned until a year later, and then only to me. And not a word about this most recent attack from Moe or Peter. I haven't seen or spoken to either of them since Tuesday morning, when Peter told me it was time to go say hello to my husband.

"Lobster claws" he calls his splinted arms, moving them in a faint swimming motion in the air. He cannot touch his face. Today he asked Judy to blow his nose. He said, "You blow Jacob's nose, you're probably pretty good at it. It's my right nostril that's congested, so press the left and let me blow. . . . Ah. Fine. You *are* good at it." I know he does this to comfort us. He assigns us tasks: he asks Judy to blow his nose and Jon to wash his face and Martha to peel his orange.

Judy, feeling so torn, left today. Jacob was crying for her. Jon came home yesterday, exhausted by the flight and the fear. Astonished, I think, to find that he still had a father.

They grew tremulous, greeting each other, but managed to keep it cool. We are all recognizing the necessity for cool.

Yesterday Bonnie said, "If we can get him through tonight we'll breathe easier. But you must be prepared—tomorrow he'll be can-tankerous, irritated, depressed . . ."

Instead he makes jokes. Mostly orange-juice jokes, for he is parched from the diuretics and they dole out the fluids drop by drop and he is obsessed by thoughts of orange juice.

"Would you prefer a half-cup of tea or a quarter-cup of orange juice?" the dietitian asks him.

"Are you kidding?" he says. "Three hundred and seventy-five dol-lars a day and you're offering me *a quarter-cup of orange juice?*"

The nurse Lois asks him to take some pills.

"Bring in a quart of orange juice and we'll negotiate it," he says.

Lois tells him, "But I don't like orange juice."

"Bring vodka too. You'll like it."

And later: "Listen, Lois, let's make a deal. I'll trade you three of my Lapsang Souchong tea bags for one orange."

They have asked us to hold our visits to a minute or two. But he won't let go.

346

"Wait, wait," he says to me. "I have something important to tell you."

"What is it, darling? The nurses want us to leave."

"But this is *important*. I want you and Jon to go to Shun Lee Palace tonight. The Lake Tung shrimp is delicious. I recommend it highly. The hot-and-sour soup—"

"Hal, the nurses are giving us the high sign."

"Fuck them. Wait, *wait* . . ."

He reminds me of a child stalling at bedtime. But this is the ultimate bedtime and he refuses to say good night. He knows everything. The end-stage heart, everything. I am sure of this. It all goes on at once: The patient denies, the doctor knows. He flashes the grin at us, and makes his jokes, but I see how his head swivels and his eyes dart, in that desperate way, to note how the troops are dispersed. He must make sure that help will be there when he needs it. Because Monday night, it was not.

Friday.

I woke in the night and called the C.C.U. The nurses are lovely about my nocturnal calls. We whisper like roommates, sighing together over sorrows that they seem to share. Through Hal's various crises I have come to see how many doctors and nurses, especially doctors, have the psychological astuteness of a toad. But these people —what a breed! This one, Maureen, tells me:

"I'm letting him run the show. I didn't want to let him sit because I was afraid of disturbing his arterial line. Then he told the doctor, 'I can't sit up, I can't wipe my nose, I can't do anything for myself.' We hadn't realized how angry he was about feeling helpless. Then we knew we had to lower the limits and let him feel more control.

"He is in constant communication with that body of his that's letting him down. He is fighting," Maureen says as I listen in gratitude and awe, "to hang on to his own idea of immortality. Heart disease like his . . . these people . . . my heart goes out to them, these people who struggle and struggle and won't give up. You see different types. Some of them, they come in here and they deny and they just sleep from one end of the day to the other. Others never stop struggling. He's a struggler."

"Is he . . . Oh, well. I can't think of any more questions to ask."

"You don't need questions. If you just want to talk, we're here. Call anytime," Maureen says.

347

At 8 A.M. I call again.

Another nurse says, "You should be prepared: he may look more tired than yesterday."

"Why is that?"

"Well, he's exhausted. We removed the left armboard and he was able to feed himself, and we helped him wash, but he was worn out after that. It doesn't take much, I'm afraid. And also, it's not easy to sleep in that bed, with all those attachments and having his vital signs checked all the time."

In three minutes she calls me back: "Mrs. Lear: He says to bring oranges."

I start to laugh. They have their vital signs, I have mine. And though I do not for a moment believe he is going to leave the hospital alive, I love this vital sign.

He was feeding himself when we came in. His hand was having difficulty finding his mouth. Finally the spoon full of lima beans arrived at his lips, several having dropped en route.

"A bagful of gold," I said, displaying the oranges.

"Good. Let's hide them," he said.

"Where?"

"Wait a minute. Katherine"—calling a nurse. "I have something here of great value about which I will take you into my confidence. . . ."

"What is it?"

"Five oranges. I want you to hide them where nobody can steal them."

As she goes off, he winks at Jon and me and shows us an orange that he has palmed from the bag. Now he puts it under the bed sheet. "Sh!" he says.

He's had a busy morning. They had to replace the Swann-Ganz line, which was not in the right spot in his heart. "And they couldn't do it through my arm, so they did it through the femoral artery. It was like Old Home Week, the same angiography team. Except they didn't have to use dye, so that helped." Suddenly he winces. "Yah! The damn Foley catheter is giving me such spasms. For twenty years I did this to people. This is retribution." Now he hands Jon a small ginger ale bottle. "Hide it," he says.

"Why?" Jon and I look at each other. Is he confused?

348

"To confuse the enemy," he says. "It's like World War Two, when they used to throw tinfoil out the airplane windows."

"Why did they do that?" I ask.

Jon, laughing now, explains: "To mess up the radar readings."

There is a newcomer in the waiting room. She sits alone in a corner and curses. The young woman Susan, whose 34-year-old husband has suffered his second heart attack, asked her some time ago if she might like to talk, and was told to piss off. There are many therapeutic modalities in the waiting room.

Susan reads *Cosmopolitan*. Often she thrusts it aside and files her nails, which are long and pale and frosted. She speaks, in part to her nails, in part to her mother, who sits beside her, and to me.

"Now I know what hell is," she says. "Hell is this waiting room. I'm so glad I'm working now. It's really keeping me sane. Last year, when he had his attack, I fell completely apart. I kept a big bottle of pills by my bed and they were my crutch. I thought, Well, if things get bad enough, I'll just swallow them all and go to sleep and never wake up. I don't mean to say that I love my husband more than anyone else loves theirs. But I am so *dependent* on him. He's much older than I am. He just cares for me so completely. I just went," Susan says, while her mother nods thoughtfully, "from very protective parents to a very protective husband. I don't do anything. I don't pay the bills— nothing. I don't know how to do any of that. And it's no good. I know that now. It's just no good at all to let others do everything for you. But I'm not like that anymore. I hope I'm not. I think I've grown since last year."

I listen to her, stunned. Almost it could be my voice. I am close to twice her age, I have worked for more years than she has lived, I am self-supporting, I am experienced, I am in various senses worldly, I am ferocious in my parlor feminism, and here we are, twins of de- pendency. The two of us, this raw girl and I, clutching at Oedipal straws.

Bonnie says, "He is quite apprehensive."

"How does he show it?" I ask.

"He says, 'Are you sure all my lines are in right? Because I go into shock if my lines aren't in.' And he's getting demanding. He says, 'My blanket is crooked. The light is in my eyes.' These are all ways of testing us, to make sure we're there when he needs us. . . ." Damn right. "They are ways of expressing his fear. But we'd much rather he express it than hold it in."

"What's his status today?"

"Well, we still can't get him off the dopamine. That's the big problem."

"He complains about the aspirin. Is that what gives him drenching sweats at night?"

"Yes. But we have to keep giving it to him because of the cardiac rub. Aspirin is anti-inflammatory."

"The cardiac rub. What is that?"

"When there has been death of tissue, there is the reaction of fluid rubbing against the lining of the heart."

"Death of tissue. You mean the heart attack?"

She nods.

"And what could have caused the heart attack? Could it have been the strain put on his heart by those fever spikes?"

She shrugs guardedly. Bonnie has been more candid than most. But she belongs, after all, to the institution. "Who knows?" she says. "With a heart like his, anything can cause it."

"Like prolonged fever and congestive heart failure?"

"Well, possibly. That could cause a weakening of tissue, or an infarct, which is lack of oxygenation, which results in death of tissue. But we've been over and over the charts of last Monday night, and during the night the signs just weren't that bad. In the morning, there was a sudden acute episode. . . ."

"That's not true! I was there all night, Bonnie. I took constant notes."

"But the charts show—"

"My notes show a steady deterioration. The nurse noted labored breathing at 2 A.M. She noted a low blood pressure at 2:30 A.M. She noted the blood pressure dropping over a three-hour period. She woke the intern at 5:30 A.M. because the pressure was so low. The pressure was in the seventies, and the intern did nothing but start an I.V. My husband himself noted that his kidneys were failing. He told them that at 6 A.M. All this is in my notes. And nothing was done until rounds at 8 A.M."

Bonnie regards me sadly. She says, "Mrs. Lear. I wish I could say such things never happen in medicine. But they do."

Now I am satisfied. Blood from stones, blood from hearts. What does it matter? We stare at each other silently. There is here a deep mutual defeat.

Damn it, it matters! This is how they neutralize their own mistakes: they say, You cannot dwell, you cannot relive, you cannot redo, let us now look to the future. And they expect the likes of me to go with them into this future, and if I will not go, if I keep dragging my feet and looking back, poking here, prodding there, why, then, I am a *pest*, am I not? A past-obsessed pest. And finally they will neutralize me as well, by reducing me to a chronic irritation.

"Is it still considered a possibility that hydralazine precipitated these crises?"

"Yes. It is a possibility. All we can find that seems to correlate exactly to his episodes is the hydralazine. We've called the manufacturer. Dr. Mason has been calling all over the country. We've read all the literature. Our lab people are working on it, trying to determine whether this drug could have such effects . . . but we still don't know. You may get a bad batch. Sometimes you never know. And of course the drug companies will protect themselves. They want you to use their products."

We had dinner, Jon and I, at David's house. Each time the telephone rang we all stiffened, and we talked of how that ring, coming at odd hours, makes us crazy. It is like the old show-business joke, David said: When you are hired for a part, the management has ten days to drop you. Notice may come by wire or registered letter. There is an actor who is always hired and always fired within the allotted ten days: a desperate fellow. Now he gets a part. He goes home and locks his door and stuffs rags into the crack beneath the door, so that no one can slip in a letter; and lets his telephone ring, so that no one can call in a wire; and he never pokes his face beyond that door. And at 11:59 P.M., on the last day of the crucial ten, there comes a knock. A voice says, "Western Union." He does not answer. The voice says, "Come on, come on, I know you're in there. The landlord told me." Cursing, he opens the door, takes the wire, reads it and cries out, "Thank God! *My mother died.*"

Just so, David said, when his telephone rang at 7 this morning, and it was a friend with an agonizing backache, who wanted the name of David's orthopedist, he said to himself, Thank God! My friend has an agonizing backache.

Moses has been calling David regularly with medical reports.

I said, "He has not called me once since the night Hal went bad. Isn't it strange that he calls you and not me?"

"Well, he's afraid of you."

"Afraid? Why?"

"He knows you're angry, you feel Hal should have been hospitalized earlier. So I guess he finds it easier to avoid you. Martha"—he is coming on to me now, as Bonnie came on to me in the hospital—"you can't let that bitterness get to you. It will just make you sadder. It will make it all the more painful."

"But can you imagine if it had been Joyce? And they had let her go through that night in that way?"

"I would not let myself be bitter," he said. "What good does it do?"

But I think he would be bitter. He would make great waves.

Don't be bitter.

Why not? Where is it written that this is a playing field upon which we must all be good sports?

I feel a fierce need to point the finger. But at whom? It is not a simple thing. There is no way to say, cleanly and with authority, that the butler did it.

There perhaps had been other times, he thought—wrongly—when he had come closer to death. As in that week after surgery, fighting pain; but he had not been alert and aware, as he was now; as he had been since this episode began.

That terrible night, when Martha had sat with him, gripping him, his mind had been absolutely clear. He had known that his lungs were filling with water and that he was dying. He had known the precise look of his lungs. Often enough he had seen such lungs. When he had been a resident in Pathology, doing autopsies, he would cut sections of lung, like wedges of cheese, out of each lobe, and examine them for fluid. There were three degrees of diagnostic precision. The first was gross observation, a crude measure: he would hold this bit of lung, squeeze it between his fingers, note how squishy it felt. For greater precision, he might drop a wedge of lung into water. The lung in many ways was like sponge: a dry piece would float; a fluid-filled piece would sink. Most precise was the microscopic examination of tissue. If he took one of those wedges that sank in water and put it beneath the microscope, he would see that the alveoli, the holes in this human sponge, were waterlogged.

Often, doing the water test, he would find that those sections he had snipped from low in the lungs would sink and the upper sections would float; and then he would know that the deceased had had moderate pulmonary edema, confined to the base of the lungs. It would be as it was now, with him, when doctors listened to his chest and said that he was wet in the base of each lung. But if the top sections of lung sank too, he would know that the deceased had been in total pulmonary edema; brim-full; overflowing; and it was damned close to this, he knew, that his lungs had been on that night. The image had come to him then, it had come out of well-remembered autopsy rooms to flood his mind as fluid flooded his lungs, and he had been able to see those lungs, except that they were his now, filled with water all the way up to the apices, with just a tiny bit of space, way up there near the top, that could still take oxygen. He'd kept begging Martha to sit him up higher, higher, so that air could get into that crawl space. And he had known that help had to come fast, those sponges had to be squeezed dry fast, or soon in some autopsy room in the bowels of this building a pink-faced resident would be snipping out wedges of his, Lear's, lungs, and dropping them into water, and watching them sink.

In his medical opinion, the pulmonary edema could have been prevented. He felt that some part of him had died on that night, and it was the part that had always looked on the sunny sides, sipped from the cups half-full, crooned the On the Other Hands. After that, no more. If he survived this one, he would no longer trust. I've been someplace, he thought, and I can never be the same.

Lying there in the C.C.U., not yet at all sure that he was going to live, though he played the optimist for Martha and Jon—and not yet suspecting, for he simply could not allow himself to suspect it, that he had had another heart attack—he wondered why this thing, which in his opinion had not had to happen, had happened.

It seemed to him that there had been a chain of failures. He himself had failed at the beginning to confront his symptoms. Peter had failed to act fast and aggressively, although he had acted with kindness. A resident and an intern, on the night he went bad, had heard the wheezings in his chest, yet had failed to treat him with diuretics: a critical error that had set off the deadly downward spiral. A nurse had failed to see, until he himself had warned her, that he was possibly in kidney failure, a dire sign of the breakdown of body systems. The nurse had failed in almost everything except compassion. But really, her failure was not that she did not know; an inexperienced nurse should not have been assigned this case. Her failure was that she did not, soon enough or urgently enough, call those who *would* know. That was her training: it was that whole harsh hierarchical system in which a young nurse might be so intimidated that she would be afraid to awaken an intern to come to the aid of a patient. She was a defect of the system. Then there had been the failure of the intern: either a poorly trained or a stupid intern, who did not appreciate the significance of what he saw; or a lazy intern, who cared most about his sleep; or an intimidated intern, quite like the nurse herself, so intimidated that he had hesitated to call the patient's doctor, at home, in the middle of the night. That too was the system: You handle it yourself. You do not wake up the doctor. And when finally he had called, he may have failed to give an accurate report; yes, the intern figured large in this chain of failure.

They almost killed me, he thought; and felt his heart pound with dangerous rage.

But there was no *J'accuse*. At some point, it seemed to him, human failure melded into and became inseparable from institutional failure, the two together forging such a formidable instrument for failure as to dictate more horror stories than the public ever dreamed of.

Saturday.

"I'm terrific! It's the first good night's sleep I've had. I'm running my own show now, Mushie. Last night they brought aspirin. I said, 'What is the indication for aspirin?' They said, 'So you won't get a temperature tonight.' I said, 'I'll tell you the indication *against* aspirin. So I won't get a drench and I'll be able to sleep. I refuse to take the aspirin.' So I didn't, and I had a wonderful night's sleep!"

His failure is under control, they say. This seems to mean not that he is dry, but less wet than he was. They were able to lower the dopamine two drops, to 25. They taper it a drop an hour. If his blood pressure goes below 85, they push up the dopamine again. But this time, when they tapered it, his pressure held at 90. The most encouraging sign we've had.

In a script that is still a scrawl, but beginning now to be legible, he has prepared a list of questions for the doctors:

1. How will we calibrate my potassium & my heart pressure when I get home?

2. How come I am getting no potassium supplement?

3. What is my X-ray report of yesterday?
4. What happened to me? (*no bullshit!!!*)
5. When will I be able to go to Provincetown?

Sunday.

Dopamine down to eight drops an hour, and blood pressure holding steady. From eight drops, Bonnie says, they sometimes bring it down to zero. They will try that later today. "But we do have a problem. We got a couple of P.V.C. doubles before."

"Doubles?"

"Two P.V.C.'s at once. That can be very dangerous. But his pulse reverts to normal when we give him more potassium. It correlates exactly, which is lucky. With some patients, those doubles persist no matter what we do."

After lunch, the crucial test: they take him off the dopamine. His blood pressure drops to 88, and holds there. A triumphant moment. Seven days he has been on the stuff.

"Goodbye to my old friend dopamine," he says. "I hope we've parted permanently. I hope it's not just off duty for the weekend."

Later I take one of the residents aside. "I suppose"—pushing myself yet again, like a madwoman or a fool, precisely where I do not want to go—"I suppose that even if he pulls out of this acute episode, you cannot prognosticate more than—what? Months?"

She nods sadly. Opens her mouth to reply. *No, don't! That was a trick question!* "I'm afraid so," she says. "Sometimes surprising things happen. But with as little heart as he has left, that is usually the best you can hope for: months."

Fool. To assume, simply because I ask for the truth, that the truth is what I want—what kind of idiot assumption is that? But too late now. We must follow this through. "I was told more than a year ago that he might have months. How about that?"

"You were lucky," she says.

"I was with him that night. I saw it. It was horrible."

"Yes. It is always horrible," she says, "to see someone in that distress. Pulmonary edema is about the worst way there is to go out."

"And of course, he knows all this. Everything we are saying to each other."

"Yes. I think that makes it much harder."

"If you had gotten him earlier, that night, would it have made any significant difference?"

She sighs. "Not really. It might have been somewhat easier on him. He wouldn't have been so exhausted, so desperate for breath. But we would have had to do the same things to him. That's what we hate, when they are in such pain and we have to cause them more pain, cutting down for the lines and so forth. We hate when one goes sour while we're cutting down. We would prefer to let them go out more pleasantly."

"And it is likely to happen again?" How many sources must I check? Is this my reportorial instinct, my masochistic instinct, my catharsis, what?

"Yes. Next time we would have to get him earlier."

Aha! Then why did you say it would have made no difference if you had gotten him earlier?

"If there were little hope, might they—"

"Treat him less aggressively?"

"Yes."

"It would depend on the doctors involved. Probably they would work on him very aggressively and if he didn't improve fast, they would draw back a little."

Draw back a little. I see them, drawing back, slowly shaking their heads. "Is that how he is most likely to die?"

"Well, there are three possibilities. The first is that his heart simply gives out. You wake up some morning and find him dead—in which case there is no more to do than pull the sheet over his head. The second is a recurrence of pulmonary edema. The third is that he might throw an embolus. He can't afford that."

"Then the first is to be hoped for?"

"Devoutly," she says.

We stand on either side of his bed, Jon and I. Hal is doing his oxygen-mask number. "This is my magic mask," he says. "When they start bugging me, I simply put it on and disappear. They think I am here, but I am not."

"Where are you?" Jon says.

"Why the fuck should I tell you?" He laughs, and begins to cough.

"Should I hit your back?" I say.

Suddenly he is apathetic: "It makes no difference."

"You don't like being hit, eh?" Jon says.

"I'd rather hit, to tell you the truth. What's that column in *Newsweek*?—'My Turn'? Yes. My turn."

On either side of the bed, our fingers secretly touching his shoulders, his arms, his cheeks.

At dinner—which I think might be Hal's fondest vision going out: his wife and his children sitting in some perfect harmony, warmer than blood, over the hot-and-sour soup—Jon and I spoke of heart transplants.

We are down now to this bottom line. It is the only hope, if it is a hope at all.

I know Moses does not think it is a hope. I remember how enraged Moses was, last fall, when Hal had angiography and the uninvited Dr. Benton came into his room and spoke of heart transplants. "God, how stupid!" Moses said, and would not talk of transplants.

So it's up to us, isn't it? The family. Three times, now, I have felt that I should act aggressively when the doctors did not. And I did not. And shall I now compound those errors? Shouldn't we push and punch our way to Shumway the transplant man? What is there to lose?

I asked Jon these questions as we clicked our chopsticks.

"We certainly should ask the doctors to explore it," he said.

We decided that Jon would broach the subject to Mason. "I don't want to do nothing and just let him go," Jon said. "On the other hand"—echoing his father, though Jon is less the optimist; Jon weighs pros and cons and shrugs his shoulders at the sum and says, That's life—"on the other hand, I don't have any desperate feeling that I must hang on at any price. The past three years have included a lot of hell, but they have also included some of the loveliest times we have all had together. I feel he and I have both grown and come to a truly incredible understanding. He has lived a good life, he has helped people, he has used his mind and been greatly loved, and I feel peaceful about it."

This both comforts and unnerves me. It is a fine thing to say: loving, civilized. But oh, Jon, I have a less civilized sense of the matter. I do feel, since this is my life, that I must hang on at any price.

Monday.

A large bloodstain on the sheet, by his groin. "Why is there blood?" I asked.

"Ah, we had a problem. They took out my arterial line. I kept applying pressure, but I felt the wetness. I knew it needed a compression dressing. The artery might thrombose and then, when they have to get a line in there again, they will have more trouble." He does not say *if*. He says *when*. "So I knew I needed help, but there was nobody in the room. I reached for the emergency bell and it wasn't there. I wondered, How the hell do I get their attention? Then I thought, Ha! I pulled out this thing that attaches to my electrocardiograph"— pointing to a four-pronged plug by his thigh—" and man oh man, did they come running!" Triumphantly he grins at us.

He is chatty today. "There's this little rabbi wandering around. Every day he comes in here and says, 'How are you doing, my friend?' He makes me very nervous. I asked the nurse, 'Who the hell is that little rabbi and what does he want from me?' She says he's from the Greek Orthodox Church, but I think he's really a rabbi. This morning he came in when I was washing my face. He said, 'Cleanliness is next to godliness.' I told him, 'I've been a little too close to godliness lately. Let's keep me a little dirty.' Right?" Grinning again.

"Right!" we say.

It is a week today since his crisis began. Dr. Corona says he has improved enough that they will let him dangle his legs tomorrow.

"We're very happy with his progress," Corona says.

"I guess it's been quite a surprise for you."

"Oh, yes! In all the time I've been on this service, I've only had two such surprises. One was your husband and the other was a woman whose heart kept stopping, and we thought for sure she was a goner. She made it. We love surprises like these. We don't get them often. Usually, the ones you expect to die—they die."

Young Susan's husband is much better and has been sent to a private floor. Before she left the waiting room, we embraced and wished each other well. We agreed that we must get together sometime. We won't.

Jon has told Mason that we would like him aggressively to pursue all the latest information on heart transplantation. Peter agreed. He will contact Stanford. I wonder if this is the best way. What if the Shumway people immediately foreclose on Hal because of his age; mightn't it be wiser to approach them through someone with clout, perhaps someone who knows Shumway directly? If a routine request falls into a routine hopper, we've had it.

It is extraordinary that neither Peter nor Moses has called me once since this crisis began. Hal told me today, "They have both mentioned to me that they thought you were angry. I told them, 'Why shouldn't she have been? I was dying and the hospital was doing nothing!' But you should try to be very nice to them. They have been working so hard for me."

So I will have to mend fences. I see David too turning away from my anger. I myself wish that I could turn away from it, and yet it would seem somehow obscene not to feel anger. I think of that woman who lost her son to friendly fire in Vietnam and kept sifting through the ashes and asking Why? until all the world turned from her, even the journalist who was writing her story, much to his own dismay.

Tuesday.

I am sleeping impossibly long hours. I hide in bed and count months like sheep. Why burden people with the truth? Classes in bereavement; the art of constructive mourning. This will change, of course. This fad will play out, as all sociomedical fads do; new research will show that an abundance of truth does not make incipient mourners free; truth enslaves us to truth, deadens our spirits, vitiates our energies, gives us headaches, blurred vision, constipation, bad dreams, causes us to lie through the night counting months. Truth may be, *may* be, good and well for those who are leaving and want, as we say, to put their affairs in order, but for those of us who must stick around, truth is a crock. The new research will show this and the medical sages will come full circle, back to the comforting lie. "Who knows?" they will say, shrugging and smiling in a most encouraging way. "There are miracles every day of the week." And so forth. And in fact, who *does* know? Already Hal has beaten them out by a month. Their truths are only guesses. Why bother with such truths?

For the past two days, the waiting room has been filled with Indians. The wife: she weeps constantly, making no sound. Other women, all in saris, bend and sway about her. They jockey for closeness. They hold damp towels to her swollen eyes and plead with her to eat something, to come take a little walk, to go home and sleep, none of which she will do. She simply weeps. There are many men, small and moustached, who stand shaking their heads gravely. They seem all to be related—brothers, cousins, aunts, in-laws—and I am filled with envy of this extended family, massed here like a mountain. We are not massed. We are tucked away, all the well-heeled natives, tucked away in our tight little nests, you and me and baby makes three, and I always knew this was dangerous. I always knew there was safety in such numbers as these, this mass of vital nutrients, soothing sounds, mountains of flesh to press, networks, lifelines, bloodlines, systems; continuities. I have the sense that she will never be lonely. But of course, this is illusory.

Today, when we came in, Hal was dangling his legs over the side of the bed. It seemed almost unnatural to see him sitting without support.

"Well, " we said, "look at that!" Look at that, indeed: wasted.

He smiled proudly. "Now that I can dangle, I'll start using a commode. There's a triumph!"

His lunch had been sitting for several hours, but he was too weak to eat it. In the morning they had removed a line and he had hemorrhaged. Now he was anemic. They were going to give him blood.

He said, "I was so hoping that I'd be able to get all cleaned up and get my hair combed today, and then I'd dazzle you. Maybe tomorrow. Just wait till I get my transfusion. *Then* . . ." And he held up both arms like an iron pumper, flashing biceps that were no longer there.

"Incredible," Jon muttered.

Yesterday Hal had a roommate, briefly. Jon and I had been there when they wheeled her in. Most of the ones who come to this place are too sick for words, but this woman had been loud and abusive.

"Do you mind if we examine you?" a doctor had asked, and we had heard her yell from her curtained bed, "Yes! Nobody in this place is going to examine me, you sons of bitches! Get away from me! It's your fault this happened! No I don't *want* that medicine, damn you!"

An intern and I had raised eyebrows at each other. "Is it fear?" I had asked.

"No, I think it's personality," he had said.

Today she was gone. Cardiac arrest in the night.

"She cursed for hours," Hal said. "Then suddenly there was silence.

They rolled in the defibrillation cart, and I knew she had arrested, and then they started screaming commands at each other, and I knew they had gotten her heart started up, and then it all turned very quiet again. . . ."

"And she went out with a curse?"

"No. She just went out." He reflected on this. "So I think I should get the hell out of here myself. Get out one way before I go out another."

It had not been personality, I learned later. It had been sound fury. She had come into the hospital for a valve replacement. She had been scheduled for surgery today. Yesterday they did a routine coronary catheterization and in the midst of it she had a heart attack, and *knew* it, poor wretch, and cursed them for it.

"It can happen during a cath," a nurse said. "We always explain that to the patients beforehand and get their permission in writing."

Bonnie said they will move him tomorrow, out of this room which is reserved for the worst of the worst. "We'll take him to one of those cubicles down the hall. It's time for a change of scene. He's isolated here, he keeps hearing awful things happening in the other bed, he's beginning to get a little confused about night and day. . . . He's getting a bad case of C.C.U.-itis."

Wednesday.

"I've got some story for you. Listen to this. Have you got your pencil, Martha?

"There's a new nurse here. This morning I asked for an orange and she gave it to me. Then I realized they hadn't checked my potassium level. I said to her, 'They haven't taken my fasting bloods yet, have they?' She said, 'No.' I said, 'Then I shouldn't have the orange, should I?' And you know what she said? She said, 'Oh, *don't be such a hypochondriac.'*"

"What did you say?"

"I said, 'Come here.'" And as he girded himself for the telling, his eyes flashed, he pulled off the oxygen mask, color came into his face and his voice took on timbre. "'Come here. *Who the hell are you to call me a hypochondriac?* How *dare* you"—all the frustration spilling out of him now—"*dare* you call me a hypochondriac? And even if I *were* a hypochondriac, that would reflect my illness. Your job is to *help* the patient, not to express your hostility to the patient. And if you can't do that, you have *no damned business being a nurse.*'"

"Good for you!"

"Damn right. Cheers," he said, and took a slug of potassium. "They say I'm better. Ah, here's Dr. Corona. Dr. Corona! If I stay this well, can I use the commode tomorrow?"

"Sure."

"Did you all hear that? Let it be broadcast loud and clear. Blow the bugles, bury the bedpan. I have permission to use the commode."

The Indians are here in droves. They come, they go, a changing cast. Now there are nine. Earlier they overflowed from the waiting room and clogged the hall.

The women sweep by, weeping, with the soft rustle of saris. They cluster about her. She is fat, and her face, full anyway, is swollen now by her agony. She has sat here for three days and nights. The women whisper to her in some Indian dialect, sad, rapid birdlike sounds. The moustached men stand silent, smoking. New faces constantly, dozens, scores of them, and again I feel a sharp thrust of yearning for a huge family of my own, for dozens of warming, caring, blood-related bodies.

I had thought the husband was a heart-attack victim. But no, it is worse. It is absurd: Two of their children had chicken pox. He caught it. The infection infiltrated his lungs, and he was rushed here with a fever of 106 and with an almost nonexistent blood pressure, so that there was no oxygen, no profusion to the brain, vast brain damage; now he lies there, a vegetable, and they are waiting only to pull the plug.

Now the relatives are all begging to visit this vegetable, and each one who enters his room must wear a surgical gown, and a mask and gloves, and wash hands upon leaving.

A nurse says to me, "We try to keep them out. We tell them, 'Why go in there? You can't do him any good.' We are afraid they will all go home and pass the chicken pox on to their children. But they insist. There is nothing we can do."

Chicken pox. "How can such a thing happen?" I ask.

"We see it very rarely. And almost always it is a foreigner. Almost always from those parts of the world . . ." She waves a hand vaguely toward a window. "They have never developed an immunity to it."

The wife is persuaded, finally, to go home. The children need her.

Flanked by a dozen relatives, weeping silently, she is led to the elevator and away.

Chicken pox.

When we got home, Jon went immediately to his room. Suddenly he came storming out. He paced. "Are you all right?" I said. "I am terrible," he said, "but I don't want to talk about it," and strode back into his room. There was for the moment nothing more to be said or done. How painful it must be, I thought, to be the son and watch, to the very last drop, the slow seepage of paternal omnipotence. He has been here almost two weeks. His father, who is in the short range better and in the long range worse, lingers. How long should he linger while his father lingers? People must go back into their own lives. I wish I had such a distance to go, but I am already there.

Friday.

They played it cool, saying goodbye. They talked of summer and Provincetown, all of us together again in that safe harbor.

"It won't be long!" Hal said, smiling and shrunken-faced within the oxygen mask. He held Jon's arm with his own black-and-blue hand and said, "Now I'll tell you where I've been going when I put on my magic mask. I've been millions of light-years away, in Tralfamadore."

"Tralfamadore?"

"Don't you remember? Where Billy Pilgrim used to go in that Vonnegut book. But now I've decided that I don't have to go where Billy Pilgrim went. Why the hell should I be limited by Vonnegut's imagination? I can go anywhere I want to go."

"Where do you want to go?" Jon said.

"Provincetown."

They kissed goodbye. Jon cried on the way to the airport. A nurse told me after that Hal had cried too.

I asked Dr. Corona, "Do you think he can get to Provincetown this summer?"

He looked at me as though I were insane.

"Well, then. Do you think he can live through the summer?"

"I just don't know," he said.

The chicken pox man died last night. I asked Bonnie, "Naturally, or with a pull of the plug?" She hesitated a beat. "Naturally," she said. What the hell. Why should she tell me?

So today the Indians were gone. It was as though they had never been. I sat alone in the waiting room with a woman whose husband has been here several days. A doctor came and told her, "He is doing well. We are going to move him soon." She asked, "How will I know when?" The doctor said, "If you come here and he is not here, it means he is somewhere else." "Of course. Forgive me. Thank you, Doctor," she said.

Saturday.

Hal seemed stronger today, but still has great gastric distress. Anything taken by mouth doubles him over. It is quite possible, one of the nurses told me, that he has developed an ulcer; not uncommon for people who have been on heavy doses of potassium for long periods of time.

They are moving him back to a private room tomorrow. To a room on the third floor, where he spent that long night's dying; where Lover still slumbers, I suppose, and Lark still chirps. I asked, "Why *that* floor? Why not any other?" But space is tight, Dr. Corona says, and also Dr. Mason feels that it will be an advantage to have him there, since the third-floor people know his recent history. *Know* it? For Christ's sake, they *made* it. I would like to make complaints, insist upon another floor, but I feel powerless. Dr. Mason has communicated nothing of this advantage to me. Dr. Mason has not given me the sound of his voice since that morning almost two weeks ago when he told me to go bid my husband hello and goodbye. Dr. Silverman, the same: zip.

Nobody is behaving in a remotely congratulatory way about this move. Nobody is saying, Whew: we made it. They seem rather to be shoring Hal up and battening him down, like flood fighters, against further storms that must come. Friends say, "Well?" and I tell them he is better, and they say, "Wonderful!" and I cannot explain how it is both wonderful and not. I cannot explain that he is recovering in order to die.

These C.C.U. people have been our lifeline. I am so frightened to leave them. I feel that to be put back into a regular room, at the mercy of regular house staff, is to be cast out into the world. I am terribly apprehensive about this move. I know he is, too.

Chapter 29

ON moving day I dampened their white shoulders with my thanks.

The charge nurse, Bonnie, gathered me in and whispered, "Don't lose hope." The resident, Corona, said, "Let's hope for the best. He sure has the spirit." As I followed Hal's stretcher down the hall, a nurse came running. "We all love him. Tell him," she said. The receptionist signaled to me to wait. "Frank, we've got one here for the morgue," she said into the telephone; then hung up and clasped my hands and wished us luck. Moving past that waiting room for the last time, I saw two strange women, one dazed, one convulsed. They had nothing to do with me. I moved on.

The intern Lover buried his face in a chart when he saw me. I knocked on the chart as though it were a door. "Don't you remember me, Doctor?" He reddened. "Yes, of course," he mumbled, and buried his face again. Those were the only words we exchanged, though Hal stayed on that floor for a month.

Mason and Silverman came to see him each day, devoutly attentive, as they had been since the morning of his crisis. But neither called me.

The little nurse Lark still scurried. "I'm *so* glad to see you," she told Hal. "That was *such* an awful night." Once I took her for coffee. I said that I wanted to reconstruct the events of that night, but I handled it badly, reportorially, came on too hard with my questions, and she scratched her face nervously, and said, "Mrs. Lear, I'm just a nurse. I can't question the intern's judgment. I know how I *felt*, but I can't . . . please don't ask me . . . my job . . ." And I thanked her and let her be. What did I need of her, anyway? I'd been there.

It was rotten from the very first hour, when a doctor accidentally tipped a urinal, its contents drenching the bed sheets. "I'll send a nurse's aide," he said. Two hours later Hal was still lying on wet sheets, his bedsores marinating in the uric acid; and no one had come to help him dangle, a critical recuperative measure; and no one had come to relieve the gastric pain of which he'd been complaining for hours. I marched to the nurses' station. An aide said, "The nurses are in conference now. Someone will come when they're free." I said, "And what am I supposed to do meanwhile about this patient who is in acute gastric distress and cannot move out of a wet bed?" She gave a Tch of disgust. She knocked at the conference-room door: "Mrs. Lear says her husband has gastric pain. I told her you were in confer-ence, but she insists he needs a nurse now." I heard one of them say, "Oh, damn." I marveled, as I had before: He is a doctor; he is white and middle-class; he has a wife who can make demands in his name; he is a private-room patient in a great medical institution; he is gravely sick; what the bloody hell goes on in the wards?

For two weeks he needed private-duty nurses around the clock. The first one said, "Oh, I see you did your pee-pee," and I thought he might explode. He told me, "Cancel her. I won't have her in my room again."

So she was cancelled, and from then on we were lucky. We drew privates who were wonderfully competent and kind. They saved him from the house staff.

He interviewed each as though for an office job:

"Do you know my blood pressure?"

"Yes. It's stable around 80 over 60."

"Do you know my pulse irregularities?"

"Yes. You have frequent P.V.C.'s. In the C.C.U. you had some doubles."

"Do you know if I am allergic to any medications?"

"I know you have a possible allergy to hydralazine."

"Do you know my occupation?"

"I know you are a doctor. You are a urologist. You switched to doing some kind of therapy."

"Okay. I mention this because it's important for you to understand that I know more about my body than any of these doctors, these kids. I know my own body very well. And that's a mixed blessing for you, because it means I can help you take care of me. But it also means I can be stubborn. I can be a pain in the ass. I know that."

She nods.

"Do you know my recent history? Have you read the charts?"

"Yes."

"Then you know that one of the sequelae of my illness is a memory problem. Not for past memory, but immediate memory. I may meet you and talk to you for ten minutes, and two minutes later I cannot remember your name or anything we've said. So I must depend on you to be my memory."

"Very well. Anything else?"

"Yes. I expect to be treated like a person. I am not a disease. I am a person with feelings and intelligence. When I ask what my blood pressure is, I expect to be told. Is that clear?"

"It is." Confronting him eye to eye. She would do. "Anything else?"

"Not right now." He fell back panting and closed his eyes, exhausted.

He could assert himself in this way. But his memory had retrogressed—"We have to treat the head by treating the heart," Moses had said long ago—and physically he was helpless. The first week, he simply lay back, often allowing himself to be fed; made ecstatic, when it was absent, by the absence of gastric pain. His arms lay limp, the black threads hanging from his cutdowns, at the elbows, at the wrists, like hairs from a witch's wart.

His day nurse was in an advanced pregnancy, her first, and her care was lavished upon him now as though in rehearsal for the real thing. Gently she helped him shift to his side in the bed so that she could treat his buttocks: shrunken, flame-red with bedsores.

"Oh, it's much better now," he says, "since they put the sheepskin under me. Before that, it hurt so much. Who brought me the sheepskin, Gladys? You?"

"No, Miss Dickens brought it," she says.

"When? This morning?"

"No. Miss Dickens is your evening nurse. She brought it two evenings ago."

"Oh. Is it evening now?"

"It's afternoon now. It's one o'clock."

"One o'clock. Did I have my lunch yet?"

"Yes. That nice piece of broiled fish—do you remember? And the yogurt . . ."

"Oh, yes, the yogurt. That was ambrosia. That made the pain go away."

"I know," she says, smiling, stroking his spine, as though he were indeed her newborn and worthy of the most tender respect.

With soap and warm water she began to wash his poor macerated ass, massaging gently.

"Oh, that feels so good," he groans.

I say, "Perhaps I should watch, so I'll know how to do it when you come home."

"That's a good idea," she says. "You see, you massage in circles, like this, to help bring back the circulation. And then you rinse it and dry it, like this. And then baby powder . . ." as she sprinkles on the Johnson's. "But you probably won't need this at home. As soon as you're getting out of bed, Dr. Lear, this will get better."

"Of course," I say, relief flooding my throat. The preposterousness of this, my Hal, lying here moaning as a nurse sprinkles baby powder upon an ass that had risen and descended through hundreds of nights, humping me powerfully, as I lay moaning; and how long would it be before I would come to some crisis of bitterness, washing his ass, powdering his ass, playing nurse to this poor ravaged body? Oh, I want him home. I want it. I dread it. I no longer have any notion what I want.

She finishes the job and says, "Now we are going to sit you up and get you in a chair while I straighten the bed. Move slowly"—she and I supporting him on either side. "Now you can tilt a little. . . ."

"Where am I going, Gladys?"

"To this chair. Right here." She drapes a thermal blanket across the chair, hanging on to him with one hand. "Now if you'll stand slowly . . ."

"Which way should I face, Gladys?"

"This way. Turn slowly. . . . Yes. Good. Now you're right in front of the chair. You can let yourself down."

And finally he is seated, his gown twisted up around bony thighs—

my God, the thigh muscles he once had! like rocks—and she drapes the blanket about his neck and shoulders and his legs, and adjusts the oxygen mask on his face.

I look at him, this faint apparition in white. "Well, well," I say heartily. "You look like a pasha in a Turkish bath."

He looks like death. It is strange that we find this look acceptable, predictable, for cancer, but not for heart disease. This must have to do with metaphors, which Sontag has discussed at eloquent length. But end-stage bowel, end-stage heart, what the hell is the difference? Dying slow is dying slow. Except, of course, for the crucial difference that there is no morphine here, nor will be. A blessing to be counted.

But there were curses too. His mind. Hal's *particular* curse, the psychiatrist Russ had once told me: to be fully aware of what was happening to his mind. Not like senile people, who are blessed by their own forgetfulness; but aware, analytical, introspective, watching his own fine mind go down the drain.

"Did you have any visitors today?"

His brow furrows. He thinks a long time. "Yes. But I can't remember his name. Isn't that funny?"

"Who? A doctor?"

"I think so."

"Michael?"

"No. Please help me. The senior man—what's his name?"

"Moses?"

"Yes. Thank you. I'll be *damned*. I couldn't remember his name."

"What did he have to say?"

"He said I'm doing very well. My lungs are clear. My pulse is slow. My heart sounds are wonderful."

Wonderful. "That's marvelous. And did he have any jokes for you today?"

"No. The joke was that I couldn't remember his name. Moe would die."

In his absence, plumbing repairs were being made in our home; and crumbling walls, the stuff of my dreams, were being replastered in fact. He asked, "Have they fixed that thing in the living room?"

"What thing?"

"You know. Where you turn on those"—making faucet-turning motions in the air—"those *things*."

"What things, Hal? Where in the living room? Can you tell me?"

"When you are standing in the middle of the living room, facing"—grimacing; struggling with directions—"facing . . . *west*. Okay?"

"Okay."

"What is that thing you face, when you face west?"

"The fireplace?"

"Yes. I think so. And what do you call that thing above the fireplace?"

"The mantel?"

"Is that it?" Dubiously. "What's the thing you draw to keep out the . . . to keep out the . . . *you* know."

"The screen? To keep out the sparks?"

"No!" Shakes his head furiously. His struggle is deepening. My dread too. "What do you do in that thing?"

"Light a fire?"

"No! No! Oh, I'd better give up. I can't seem to . . ." He clenches his fists, starts again: "What is that plastic thing that hangs from the mantel? The thing you draw to keep out the . . . the . . ."

Now I am listening on two levels. I am scared, chilled. I am also fascinated, a clinical observer, no relation whatever. "Hal," gently, "are you confusing the living room with the bathroom? There is no plastic hanging from the mantel."

"There isn't?" He stares at me in astonishment. "Of course there is! You draw it to keep out the . . . the . . . I mean, the plastic thing hangs there, and you turn on those *things*"—making faucet-turning gestures again—"that start the . . . the . . . Help me. Jesus. I can't do it."

"The faucets? To start the water? To start the shower?"

"Is that it? I don't know."

"But that's in the bathroom, Hal."

"No, damn it. In the *living room*. The plastic thing hangs down, and you turn on those things, and then you draw the plastic thing to keep out the . . . Oh, my God." He is exhausted. "What is the thing I tell you to do sometimes, when you feel tired and you have to keep working? What do I suggest that you do so you'll feel refreshed?"

"Take a shower?"

"Maybe. Where do you do that?"

"In the bathroom. I draw the plastic curtain, and then I turn on the faucets and take a shower. Is that what you mean?"

"Yes. I guess so. And that's not in the living room?"

"No, darling. That's in the bathroom."

"What's in the living room?"

"The fireplace. Where we make fires." We are both trembling. "In the bathroom there is the tub, where we take showers. . . ."

"Yes! *Tub!* Jesus, isn't that crazy? I confused the fireplace with the *tub!*" Momentarily he is triumphant. Then his face crumples, a map of inner agonies. "Oh, God. I couldn't say 'bathtub.' Wasn't that weird?"

"It *was* weird, darling." I must not pretend nothing much has happened. I must validate. But I must also reassure. I must find precisely the right tone. I don't know how. "Yes, it was damned weird. As though the wires crossed for a moment. But I'm sure it was just a transitory thing. . . ."

"Oh, yes. I'm not worried about it. Really I'm not." He is sweating. I sit with him longer, holding hands, hating to leave him like this, but already I have kept Judith waiting a half-hour on a street corner. Finally I kiss him good night. I say, "Get a good night's sleep and call me when you wake up."

"I will. And Martha . . ."

"Yes?"

"Have a wonderful time. I'm fine now, really. Don't be worried. Have a *wonderful* time."

At dinner I try to describe it to Judith. But the surreal sound and the texture of it are difficult to convey. And his agony is impossible to convey, and I don't know the half of it anyway. Only he knows.

I had been with him for just minutes. He was merry. He had been wakened from a sound sleep so that medical students could listen to his heart—collecting heart sounds, he said, as though they were bird sounds—and he had told them off. "I'm not just an interesting heart sound," he had told them. "I'm a tired *person*." Now he used a urinal, held it up. "That's for *my* team," he said.

I saw the nurse eyeing his monitor. She seemed skittish. She left the room, and I followed, heard her telling an intern that Dr. Lear was having coupled P.V.C.'s. Then she took me aside. "When he sees you," she said, stroking my arm so as to assuage, "he gets happy and excited and his heart works harder. He should rest now."

That tenuous, then.

It was 8 P.M. I felt an urgent need to buy a dress. Where might one buy a dress at this hour? Of course: I got the car out onto the highway and sped up toward Loehmann's, bargain capital of the Bronx—in whatever state of distress, the bargain mentality would not desert me—to buy a dress, assuring myself of the soundness of this expedition. What did I own, after all? Pants. A few evening skirts. I had not worn a dress in years. What would I wear to the funeral if suddenly he died? I needed a dress—not *necessarily* a funeral dress, but an all-purpose dress, subdued, suitable for various small subdued occasions; every wardrobe should have such a dress at the ready; speeding northward toward the Bronx, weaving in and out through fast heavy traffic, horns cursing me all the way, I arrived there a half-hour before closing time, ripped through the racks, filled my arms with masses of navys, browns, grays, no blacks, dashed into a fitting room and tossed them on and off, grimly, amid idle murmurs of women. . . .

"Janet, it looks lousy on you. Is it okay to say that? Are we still friends?"

"Of course, Muriel. I didn't bring you here to lie to me. But why does it look so lousy?"

And left the place empty-handed and drove home slowly, now hugging the right lane, the lane of caution and despondency, and so to bed.

I telephoned Mason. We had not spoken in almost three weeks. Had he made inquiry yet about heart transplantation? Not yet, he said. He had reason to believe that the Shumway people were adamant on their cutoff point—they would operate on no one over age 50—but he would pursue the matter and get back to me.

Hal had felt perky in the morning, Gladys told me. But then medical students had come to take a history and stayed for more than an hour. "So he's a little tired now," she said, tenderly rubbing his neck. Clearly she disapproved of these history-takings, but could say nothing. It was not her place.

Now a doctor with five students in tow entered the room.

"Dr. Lear, I'm Dr. Fell. These are the students who examined you this morning. Would you mind if we examined you a bit more now?"

I touched Hal's elbow. "Hal, are you strong enough for this?"

"I'm strong enough to say what I want to say." Then to Fell, his voice coming slow and faint from behind the mask, "Doctor, as you may know, I am very tenuous. On several occasions, house staff who know nothing of my condition have come in here to examine me without telling me why, without asking if I felt up to it. Those are bad medical manners. That is bad medical practice."

"Well, Dr. Lear, those things are certainly wrong, and I apologize."

"Please don't misunderstand. I know these young people need the experience. I want to cooperate fully whenever I can. Perhaps later today . . ."

I took my chance. "I'd like to interject something," I said, and felt Hal stiffen. "Doctor, you understand that my husband, being a doctor himself, feels a particular obligation to help medical students."

"Oh, he shouldn't."

"That's not the point. He *feels* it. He hesitated to refuse them this morning, and his nurse told me that he was much weaker after they left than before they arrived. That distresses me."

"I don't blame you. From now on, we'll make sure that no students examine your husband without his consent."

"I'm trying to explain why he may give his consent even when he feels too weak. I would be reassured to know that no students will ask to examine him until he is significantly stronger."

"Very well, Mrs. Lear. We'll arrange that."

To the students, who stood looking sober and vaguely frightened, as though by a parental quarrel, I said, "No offense."

"Oh, no. Of course," they murmured, filing out, and one of them said, "If it was my dad in that bed, I guess I'd feel the same way."

I waited for his wrath. It never descended.

"Fine," he said. "You said exactly the right thing."

He squeezed my hand, and I wondered at the surge of comfort, almost pleasure, that I felt. Then I understood: I had played a role; perhaps been of help; release of trapped energies; deployment of the adrenal troops.

Ah, no mystery. Bricks fall on me like rare insights.

I have such an envy of couples. Women who say, "I'm meeting Sidney at the office and we're going down to the Village for dinner." Hal. Imagine the miracle of such normalities, if we could meet at the office and go down to the Village for dinner.

Couples who get on nicely together I envy in benign ways. I wish them well. Couples who treat each other badly make me turn vicious within.

"Sweetie," he says, "you always buy the lousiest wines." "Sweetie," she says, "come off it. You don't know a thing about wines."

And I, sitting at their table, turned instantly vicious. She would be no more than inconvenienced if he dropped dead right now. He, the same. Why us? Why Hal? What is needed is a modified form of triage: those who love each other will get top priority; those who hate each other will be left on the field; the rest will be treated when the medics have time.

I left them to each other at 10 and returned to the hospital. "I have to meet Dr. Lear upstairs," I told a guard, and was let by.

His night nurse sat outside his door. He would never let nurses sit through the nights in his room; he wanted his privacy, he said. And now she told me:

"I can understand that. Going into the hospital . . . it's like losing your identity, in a way. He keeps fighting for his identity. He wanted water tonight. He's still on restricted fluids and I wouldn't give him more, and he blew up. He said, 'Oh, damn it, what's another fifteen c.c.'s going to do?' But you take a guy like that, and just a little bit too much can do it. Usually, when they're that sick, they're depressed. He's not depressed. He's aggressive. He keeps asking, 'What's my blood pressure? Is my pulse regular?' Of course, being a doctor, he'd be more inquisitive. He talks a lot about how much better he's getting. That's often a sign of anxiety."

I peeked in. Hal lay in a fetal ball, facing me. He stirred, opened his eyes, and in the dim light from the corridor he saw me and said, "What are you doing here?"

The coupled P.V.C.'s. His heart will work harder. He must rest. "Sh. I'm just leaving. Go to sleep."

"No, wait. Mushie, darling, I'm *so* glad you're here. I'm *so* much better. Come give me a kiss, but don't wake me up."

The oxygen mask was removed for the kiss, then readjusted. "Now *sleep*," I said, thrusting my fingers forward as in a hypnotist's command, and in our old game his head instantly rolled to one side, his eyes closed, and he slept again. I tiptoed out.

"Quite the lovebirds, aren't you?" the nurse said.

"It's not that. It's just . . . I like to see him. He's such a lovely man, and I know I'm not going to have him much longer."

374

"Uh-huh." A straight, friendly look. No *Don't give up hope.* Just "Uh-huh." So again I had asked and wished I hadn't.

"Where is my help button?" he says. "Where is my urinal? Where are my eyeglasses? Where are my pens and my notebook? Where is my antacid? Where is my cracked ice?" His imperatives. He smiles and puts his arms about the hospital-bed table that holds most of these imperatives, as though he would embrace it, and says, "It's like the James Ardrey territorial imperative. This is my territory. Anyone who comes near this, I'll cut their fucking fingers off." And a moment later: "Yes, that's how it feels. Just like the Gene Autry territorial imperative."

"You're really going to trust me to shave you today?" I ask.

"I'll give you a trial."

"When will you do it?" asks the nurse.

"Now, or when you come back from lunch," I tell her. "Whenever you decide."

"Whenever *I* decide," he says, eyes blazing.

"A bit irritable today, isn't he?" she murmurs to me.

"He's entitled." Don't tell me about his irritability. That's for *me* to say, not you. Bitch.

"What's happening at home?" he said.

Plaster dust all over. Bad canvas on the bedroom walls; the painter says it would be easier to leave the country than strip the stuff off.

"Then we'll leave!" says my husband, clutching with those large, splay-fingered, tenacious hands at a future no one else believes he will have. "Why bother with the apartment? After all, we'll be spending our summers in Provincetown, and you'll finish the book and be a superstar, and we'll spend our winters in warm climates . . ."

"Right, darling! Right!"

It is hardest for me when he soars like this; it is in these moments that the prospect of losing him becomes most insupportable. It is when pain and anxiety turn him rude, querulous, demanding—"Don't interrupt me." "*Water.* I need it near me." "Where is my box of Kleenex? *Not* that one. The one I wrote something on. Where *is* it?"—that it is easiest to accept what I must. I think, Very well. If you are going to die, die. I am as ready as I will ever be. Get on with it, then, and for Christ's sake let me get on with remaking my life.

"And I don't tell these thoughts to anyone," I said to his cousin Frankie's widow. "I am ashamed."

"Then I will tell you what I never told anyone," she said. "In the last nine months of Frankie's life, there were times when I said aloud in the shower—because I couldn't say it anywhere else, or to anyone else—'What are we waiting for? If it's got to happen, let it happen now.' Those are totally normal feelings."

"Rhoda, don't give me pap. I know they're normal feelings. I'm just trying to find a way to live with them. One question."

"Okay."

"If someone you love drops dead suddenly, it's an unspeakable trauma. If it happens slowly, and you know it must happen, does that make it any easier in the end?"

A long pause. Then: "No. As a matter of fact—possibly I shouldn't tell you this, but I will—after he is gone, there will be times when you will look back to when he was the way you are so afraid he is going to be, bedridden, with you as the nurse, and you will think that you would give anything to have him back on those terms."

The next day, Mother's Day, flowers came. He had sent them every year, in a salute to the stepmother. And now a ravishing bouquet, with a card: "To my Mushie. To the next fifteen years."

He was euphoric. He was laughing. What he felt was the absence of pain, which made him feel much stronger than he was.

"You can't imagine how much better I'm getting, how fast," he said. "I feel *wonderful*."

"I think *you're* wonderful. I think you're an incredible man."

"Why?" Genuinely puzzled. "I'm lucky! I'm healing! My body is healing!"

It did seem so. Two weeks out of the C.C.U. now, and still not walking. But his pulse was more regular. His color was improved. He moved more easily in the bed. He sat up, erect and alert, for his dinner.

I said, "You look lovely."

"I try to keep up appearances," he said, adjusting the safety pin on his pajama bottoms.

"Hal"—venturing into Elysian fields where we had not played for months—"I would like to make a toast: *L'chaim*."

"Damn *right*," he said, and we clicked teacups.

He gazed at me hard, gauging something. "My God, you look *so much better*," he said. "I've been very worried about you."

Still no word from Mason. I called Silverman. We had not spoken in five weeks, since the first morning in that wretched waiting room. Now such silences. The ears could melt from such silences.

I said, "Since you're most concerned now with the state of his heart . . ."

"Yes. Precarious."

"I don't suppose his gastric distress is a high priority. But do you think he has an ulcer?"

"It's hard to know. He could have a stress ulcer from everything he's been through. Or maybe one of the medicines burned his esophagus. But we can't subject him to a barium enema with this fragile state he is in now. I do think he may have had another heart attack. . . ."

Finally.

"When, would you think? Before he was hospitalized?"

"I can't be sure. I would think . . . yes, maybe before he was hospitalized. I haven't told him."

"Of course not. Now, Jon and I have asked about a transplant. It seems that Hal—at best—may come home and be virtually bedridden for a few months, and then die." He said nothing. "So I don't see that we have anything to lose."

"Except the massive suffering it may put him through." Guilt, with a trowel.

"We don't want him to suffer. But if he's a good candidate, and if they would take him, and if it's his only chance, he deserves to be presented with the option and to make his own decision. That's why at least we want the information, we want the current statistics, we want his case presented."

"Okay. We'll follow up."

"One more question. I know how preposterous it is, but he's talking about Provincetown. . . ."

"Oh, *no*."

"Yes. And he's going to ask you whether there is any possibility . . ."

"No. No. We'll tell him we want him to stick around this summer."

And I told Hal, "I've been thinking . . . it's so pretty out on the terrace now. They're putting up the awning next week. You could have a nice slow convalescence right here in New York."

"You mean, not go to Provincetown?" Wary voice.

"Well, just not *hurry* to get there. We can be very comfortable here."

"Of course not hurry. But certainly by July."

Sweet dreamer. Dream one for me.

When the stitches were removed from his cutdowns, one wound, in the crook of his arm, continued to fester. Stitches must still be in there, he said. Certainly not, the floor doctors said. He persisted. They ignored. Finally one resident took time to probe the oozing wound. "I'll be damned," he said poking with his forceps at a stitch that was looped completely around the vein. "And here's another! And another!"

Above his bent head, Hal winked at me.

The cutdown healed clean.

"Your hematocrit is a little low," a doctor told him. Hematocrit: the ratio of red blood cells to whole blood volume. "It's 29."

Hal whistled. "That's *damned* low. But of course, I had that phlebotomy."

"Yes, but we would have expected it to regenerate by now. We may give you some packed cells."

Hal told me after, "That's a serious problem potentially, and they never even mentioned it before. It's amazing, the things they don't tell you. You find out by accident. Yesterday a nurse said, 'I see your B.U.N. has come down nicely, from 80 to 45.' B.U.N. is a measure of kidney function. Eighty! That means *terrible* kidney function. Dangerous, possibly even fatal! And nobody told me."

"Isn't it a matter of judgment? Expecially since you're a doctor and would understand the danger. When you were practicing urology, you didn't always tell a patient—"

"You're right. It is a matter of judgment. They may have felt, Why worry him? We'll watch it and and worry for him. I can understand that. It's legitimate. But this blood situation is different. A red-cell count of 29 means that I have only three-quarters of my normal blood cells. The red cells carry oxygen. With such a low count, I'm getting greatly reduced oxygen when I need it most. But it's easily treatable. Why didn't they tell me? Why haven't I been given packed cells yet?"

"Maybe they just found out."

378

"That's unlikely. But I'll check. I don't trust anyone anymore."

"Why not?"

"Oh, Martha," he said, "you know why not."

"Shall I tell you how I think I am going crazy?" he said, sipping his antacid slowly. "No, not crazy. Paranoid. I think I may have become a little paranoid. I've been wondering if I should see a shrink."

"Why?"

"I'm not sure. You know me: I always want to do it myself. But now something in my head says, 'You really want to see a shrink.' I've tried to think why. There is nothing here that frightens me. I don't think I'm depressed. Physically I'm getting better. By the way—did I tell you?—I've decided that my heartburn is psychogenic. Not altogether, but there is a strong psychogenic element."

"How do you know?"

"I'll give you two examples. When Dr. Chin probed my wound and I saw that it was finally clean, and when he assured me that they would be watching over my hematocrit, a funny thing happened: I suddenly knew—I *knew*—that I would go to sleep and not wake up with gastric pain. And last night, for the first time since I've been in this room, I had an uninterrupted sleep.

"Another example: The other day you and I quarreled about something. I don't remember what. Do you remember?"

"Yes." Wobbling from his bed to the bathroom, a distance he had just begun to navigate on his own, he had picked up a wastebasket. I had said, reflexively, "Don't," and he had turned wrathful. "Why *don't?*" he had said. "Have you asked my doctors if I am forbidden to pick up a wastebasket with three Kleenex in it? Do you know if I am allowed to move a chair, like this?" Shoving it hard. "Do you know if I am allowed to roll a hospital table, like this?" Slamming it against a wall. "Who are you to set my limits? If you are going to keep saying *don't* and creating tension, maybe I shouldn't come home. . . ." And so forth. "Yes. We quarreled about the wastebasket."

"That's right. The wastebasket. I got angry, and I was rude to you. I feel terrible when I'm rude to you. I kept thinking about it when you left, feeling very upset about it, and that night I had severe pain. I was up for hours, sipping this shit, trying to coat my stomach mucosa with three inches of grease. That was when I realized that there had to be correlations between this pain and my state of mind.

"Now, about the psychiatrist: I thought, the only reason I would want to see a psychiatrist would be fear that I couldn't cope with something. What do I think I can't cope with? What's frightening me? Why should I suddenly think that I may be paranoid? Someone said to me, 'You're in good hands now. You can trust your doctors.' My answer was 'I can't trust anyone.' And then I knew: I was frightened of my rage. I had the most terrible rage that I was not ready to confront. I kept acting like Scarlett—I'll think about it tomorrow— and then I couldn't hide from it anymore. This is a terrible thing that has happened, I've got to work this out, I am filled with rage, the most consuming rage, Martha, because I believe that if I had been hospitalized immediately, none of this"—extending his cut-down arms toward me—"would have been necessary, and if they had given me one goddamn shot of Lasix my lungs wouldn't have filled with fluid that night, I wouldn't have spent that night dying, I wouldn't have died, none of it had to happen, none of it, and not just this, everything, everything that's happened to me in these three fucking years, I can't be Pollyanna about it forever, I can't go on forever saying On the other hand, other guys have died in these three years and I'm still here, other guys haven't died, they've had bypasses and aneurectomies and they're out on the tennis courts, they don't have holes in their heads, they're not in chronic failure, nobody else in their fucking practice is on as much Lasix as I am—did you know that? I asked one of their nurses, Does anyone else take this much? and she said, No, only you, and I think of how much has changed, how broken I have been, I have become, I have been made, and sometimes I have to ask, Why me? Why me? Okay, I've got a fucked-up heart, I can manage that, I know the incidence of infarcts during surgery, the percentages were there and I was on the bad side of the percentages, maybe with somebody else I would have been on the right side, I don't know, the surgeon did his best, I can't blame him, but my *brain*, why my *brain*?, who else do you know this has happened to?, no one, no one, and all the shit since, and now these fucking cutdowns, my almost dying, the whole fucking thing, I've been mismanaged and I am filled with such fucking rage I don't know what to do with it, it's always the patient's fault, they told me, 'Well, you had a bad heart going into surgery,' but I *didn't*, my *vessels* were bad but not my *heart*, the operative note said nothing about a bad heart, it would have said on the operative note—"

"Hal. Hal." Yes, this rage might consume him. "The entire anterior wall of your heart was destroyed in your first attack." It was true. But it was also true that his heart function before surgery had been "pretty good." Mason had told me that. No one had told Hal. "The entire anterior wall, Hal."

"How do you know?"

"The first angiography report. Peter read it to me."

"Really? Well, that's good news. That makes me feel better." A smile. Then, suddenly: "My memory is getting much worse. I know that I ask you the same question four times. I try to hang on to the answer, but I can't. And sometimes you get a little impatient with me. I understand that. If someone asked me the same question four fucking times I might get a little impatient too, and that's why I try t-t-to do things, to arrest the process, I try to write letters, but I can't spell, I mix things up, I leave out words and parts of words, I can't talk on the phone, I am lonely, and reading, I try, I read Doris Lessing, but she's not talking to me, or a piece by Gary Wills, a marvelous piece, but I can't say, 'But Gary . . .'

"Bastards. Oh, bastards. I've accepted so much of the crap—'You had a bad heart, you had a virus, get Gatorade'—*crap*. But I don't accept the brain damage. I don't. I don't accept it as being an immutable sequela of my disease. I'm convinced somebody fucked up in that operating room . . . Who? The anesthesiologist? The surgeon? I don't know . . . but *somebody* fucked up, and they left me a s-s-semivegetable."

I gasped sharply, and he said, "Yes! There! There's where I feel lonely! Because my head is *different* from other people's. When my head isn't functioning right, I'm alone, utterly. No one can be with me there.

"Something happened to me that night. Something significant. I can't verbalize it well. Part of it was my awareness: I was dying and I knew I was dying. I was aware of the fuck-ups. Now I think I see . . . I think of doctors as wearing transparent facades. And this is strange for me, because I am a doctor. The white coat and mask of 'the doctor' are transparent to me now. I see my doctors as pretty much what they are. In many ways they have been darlings. I am aware of their strengths and their devotion. But I am also aware of their weaknesses, their mistakes, their professional affectations. . . . I am aware of their guilts."

"You think they feel guilts?"

"Oh, yeah. Don't you? It's a fucked-up case, Martha! And I'm still alive, and I keep coming back to haunt them. They can't wash their hands of me—yet. I'll tell you something"—leaning conspiratorially close, but hell, no, not paranoid; he knew precisely whereof he spoke—"when the bag of tricks is empty, when nothing more can be done, do you know what doctors wish? They wish that the patient would die. Not consciously, of course, but that is what they wish. Because as long as that patient lives, he is a reproach. He is a constant reminder of what doctors do not want to face."

He telephoned me at home that night. "I don't want you to worry," he said. "Talking about it was a great relief. I'm fine now."

Mason reported that the limits appeared firm: Shumway's heart-transplant team did not want candidates over age 50. I could see, it was plain enough, why this would be so. Candidates over 50 would yield higher mortality rates. They would make bad statistics. Bad statistics would not attract grant money. In this game of hearts, my husband was not a 56-year-old individual who might, or might not, be a good bet for survival; he was a statistical probability.

Could Hal, age aside, still be considered a good candidate? Yes, Mason said. Various body systems had deteriorated in the critical period but had since recovered. He had told this to his Stanford contacts. He had said that the candidate, but for his heart, had the body of a much younger man. That had cut no ice. But if we wished to present the case, they would consider our application. A committee would decide.

I said, "Maybe we can push through the age barrier. Let's apply fast, since the prognosis is so bad anyway."

"Okay. I'll discuss it with Moe, and then we three will meet. I must tell you that I would put the prognosis now at four to eight months. A few weeks ago, I wouldn't even have given him that."

"I see." What did I see? I looked in the mirror. Schizoid, I thought. I can see something schizoid growing in my face. There are two distinct I's. One takes a pill and too much booze and goes to bed well buzzed, and often wakes screaming; the other listens, with a fine dispassion, and makes notes for a book.

And I went to sleep, and reared up from some instantly forgotten nightmare, screaming, "*No!*"

So we met, we three. I sat in their waiting room while a detail man fidgeted opposite me. Always I had felt so sorry for detail men. I remembered them fidgeting in Hal's waiting room, men waiting long hours in summer in polyester suits, ball-point pens in their shirt pockets, vinyl attaché cases filled with pharmaceutical hopes, nervous when the nurses finally beckoned them into those inner sanctums, girding themselves for presentations in court. . . . I sat opposite this fidgeter and studied my notes, my little dispassionate presentation, scrawled that morning in some heated resolve to stay cool, nonaccusing, nonthreatening; and then I blew it.

I start far too strong by saying that I feel Moses must intervene at the top: directly to Shumway.

Mason interrupts: "I've already written to my contact on Shumway's team, outlining Hal's case. There is no point twisting Shumway's arm—"

Silverman interrupts: "Listen, I don't mind twisting his arm. The hell with that. I have already told David"—Ah, David, eh? He has told David—"that I would be prepared to go out there *personally* to talk with Shumway. But this surgery. This is not a decision that you or Harold's children can make. The mortality rates are dreadful. . . ."

I: "What are they?"

Silverman: "I don't have them at my fingertips, but they're dreadful. And it's such a horrible thing. If he's accepted—*if* he's accepted— then you have to move out there, uproot him. And *if* he survives, then there is the pain; there are months of living in a sterile atmosphere; no privacy—it's like living in a goldfish bowl. It's a horrible thing."

I: "Please. Let me say what I have to say, and then I would appreciate hearing what you have to say. First, of course, neither Jon nor Judy nor I nor anyone else can make this decision for Hal. It is his. But it would be too cruel to broach the subject to him unless we knew that Shumway would take his case. All we are asking you to do is this: if age is the only deterrent, pursue it with Shumway directly; and as aggressively as possible. *If* age is the only deterrent—which, I understand from Peter, is the case."

Silverman: "Well, no. There's another. This operation is so psychologically traumatic that they will consider only patients with absolute mental integrity. Hal doesn't have that. Since his surgery, he has had . . . uh . . . a deficiency." So. This is the first time that either of them has acknowledged the brain damage. "So he wouldn't qualify on that ground either. And there is something else we must consider: His general physical state is precarious. How much further tissue damage

383

has there been? We don't know. After all, we have to consider what caused this whole episode. . . ."

I: "Oh, please, no. I don't want to get into that."

Silverman: "What do you mean, you don't want to get into that? Listen, Martha, we can't just talk about what *you* want to talk about. We believe now that this whole episode may have happened because Hal had another infarct."

My lips burn. I am about to blow it, but I cannot let this pass. "He had another infarct because his heart could not stand the stress of two weeks of spiking fevers. . . ."

"Oh, no. Heart attacks don't happen like that. Look, Martha, you are grasping at straws. I don't blame you. But a transplant is not a viable alternative. It is tantamount to a death sentence. It's not therapy they're doing out there, it is experimental work. Someone has to keep experimenting, so they're doing it. Maybe in another five years they will have solved the problem of rejection. But right now, it is not viable. I could not recommend it for anyone."

"Not for your wife?" Oh, Martha, such a dumbness. Take it back.

"Not if it were my *wife*, not if it were my *children*"—he is taut with anger now—"not if it were *anyone I care about*. Why should I differentiate with Hal? I would not subject *anyone* to this procedure, in *any* circumstance. We're not simply concerned with the *length* of his life, after all, but the *quality* of his life. And I understand how you feel, but I think maybe you're just considering it because of the emotional strain you're under, from all the shock you've been through"
—Yes. A slight madness. Hysterical wife. I have no mental integrity either. Oh, they're pulling out all the stops. Guilt. Guilt—"and furthermore, nobody can say for sure how long Hal will live. He's fooled us before. He has amazing will. . . ."

"Peter has already told me, and I appreciated his forthrightness, that he considers the prognosis now to be four to eight months."

Mason reddens. Silverman purples.

"How could you *say* such a thing to her? How do you *know*, Peter? How many cases just like this have you *seen*?"

Peter, dear Peter, who cares deeply for Hal, squirms a bit like the detail man, a diffident smile on his face, and says, "I think in all honesty I would still have to hold to that prognosis, Moe."

"You shouldn't have told her that, Peter! That's what this whole damn thing is about! She hears 'months,' so she's grasping at straws. I tell you, *nobody knows*. Three weeks ago I wouldn't have given Hal two days. And *look* at him now: he's beginning to walk, he's in good spirits. I don't know how long he may last, but I'll tell you this: I think his chances for survival are a hell of a lot better without transplant than with it."

I say, "I only want information. I am only asking you to present the case without bias."

"You are asking me to argue aggressively and vigorously for a procedure I cannot recommend. If you insist, I'll talk to Shumway. I'll present the facts and tell him that the family is very eager. But I don't believe Hal should have this procedure, and I have to let Shumway know that."

He stands up. The interview is over.

"One other thing," I say at the door. "He talks constantly of getting to Provincetown. It's his Eretz Yisrael, in a way. If this transplant business comes to nothing, don't you suppose we may as well go? And let whatever happens happen."

"Why not?" Peter says. "He always feels good there. . . ."

"I would be adamantly opposed," Moses says, glaring at his associate.

Blown. There are assigned roles in the doctor's office. They hold the power. I am supposed to be the docile wife, bowing respectfully to power, leaning on recommendations as though they were crutches. I should have been conciliatory, but I have never had a gift for conciliation. When I think I am *right*, I must confront head on, I never did learn that one does not win by being so goddamn *right*, one does it by wooing, weaning, praising, seducing. Powerful men do this to each other all the time; why does it have such a bad name when women do it to men? It is not merely sexual politics in a doctor's office, after all; everyone comes helpless into a doctor's office; it is power politics, and the stakes were very high, and I had played it all wrong.

Silverman delivered the information: Ten to 15 percent of transplant patients died on the operating table. The first-year mortality rate was 75 percent. The two-year rate, 40 percent. A "handful," as unspecified as a handful of all-purpose flour, had survived beyond five years. None beyond seven years. All chosen candidates had to move to Stanford for six months to a year; preferably, for life. Some hundred were accepted each year. They went out there and waited for donor hearts—ah, such a waiting game. Of these hundred, twenty-four received transplants. Of the ones who were not operated on, all—*all*—died within a year.

Silverman said, "I am told there is no way they will take Hal, because of the age cutoff. I can try to push. I repeat, I would not recommend it. But if you want me to pursue it, I will do everything in my power to get them to consider Hal's case."

Ambivalence ate at my vital organs. I called the psychiatrist Russ. I said, "I am in deep trouble. Can I see you tomorrow?"

And I told him the whole story, from that beginning six weeks earlier, with the scathing fevers that had started at home, and the failure, the emergency admission, that long night's drowning, *Help me, I'm dying, I don't know what to do* . . .

Weeping copiously now. Russ handed me a Kleenex. "Oh, my," he said. "Oh, my. I have never heard such a terrible story."

"So the only hope we have left is the transplant. It is eating me up. I don't know what to do. On the one hand, this terrible long shot. On the other, four to eight months."

"What do you want?" Russ said.

"I don't know. They're against it—they will push if I want, but they're against it—and I just don't know."

"You want someone to help you decide?"

"Yes!"

"Well, then," he said, and reached behind him to a stack of periodicals.

"Look here. I just happen to have this recent report from the last journal of the A.P.A."—waving it at me: "The Role of Denial in Prolonging Life in Terminal Patients." "Denial can work wonders. Not passive denial, but a fighting denial like your husband's. We are learning remarkable things about it.

"Your husband has the most amazing will," he said. "Those transplant statistics . . . you call those a good bet? I would bet on his will *any* day. It has performed *miracles*. Would you take it from him, face him with this prognosis, uproot him from his home, his friends, everything he values, to sit in a bed in California waiting and waiting for a heart that he may never get? And for what odds?"

And suddenly it was resolved. Of course: If Hal could perform such acts of will, if he could say to me each day, "Oh, I am *so much better*," if he had managed to create this fierce protective balance for himself, would I dare tip it? Oh, no. I would put my money on Hal's will. Deny with him, damn right, I can deny with him; be a rock for him; fill whatever time we have left with as much joy as we and the fates can provide; let that time be choice; and then, when I must, let him go. Let go.

And I left there feeling, finally, at peace.

Now I know that there was a failure of will. Not his. Ours. Mine. We closed that book because it was too hard to read. It was too overwhelming a scenario of logistics and stress and uncertainty. It was easier on the nerves to take the prognosis gracefully and then, in time, make a graceful funeral.

Had we given him options, I know what Hal would have chosen. Had we said, "These are the numbers, and your chance is a thousand to one," he would have taken it. He would have grabbed it.

Not that we had options to give. In no circumstance would the transplant team have taken him. I learned that later. So it is a moot point. The moot points are always the ones that congeal in the brain, as impotent rage congeals in the gut, having no place else to go. But as a moral issue, it is not moot. I know what I know.

He kept telling us how much better he was getting, and we all smiled and looked away, pained by his faith, and then he started, in fact, getting much better. Where the resiliency came from, no one knew. In the third week he began to walk in the hallways, leaning heavily on his private nurse, and then he discharged his nurses and walked on his own, and then came an afternoon when he was waiting for me, robed and combed and shaven, and offered me the crook of his arm.

"We're going for a stroll?" I said.

"Stroll! Are you kidding? I'm a *hiker!* Tell me," he said, as he had said every time, at some point in the upswing of every crisis, "what are you going to do with a healthy husband?"

I thought, with gratitude, his rage saves him from depression and his optimism saves him from rage. It is built in. He is too long fixed in the habit of optimism to change in any permanent way.

So we walked, and all along the way there was a cheering section. An orderly said, "Looking *good*, Dr. Lear." Another called softly, "Go! Go! Go!" and gave him the raised-fist salute, which Hal returned, and instantly I heard echoes of a hundred Mexican doctors, a hundred years ago, shouting, *"To-re-ro! To-re-ro! To-re-ro!"* when my

Tequila-pissed husband jumped into the ring to fight the bull. It stretched behind and ahead of me, straight and plain as the length of this hospital corridor: where we had come from, what we had come to, where we had yet to go.

"Come on," he said, for I had stopped walking. "We've got to go on."

"How far?"

"As far as we can," he said.

Back in his room, he motioned me to the bed. I lay down beside him and he put his arms around me and I buried my face in his neck in the old way. I felt transported. I wanted more acutely then, I think, than at any other moment to fall into a final sleep beside him.

He said, "Pretty soon, kid."

"Pretty soon," I said.

In the sixth week, on our fifteenth wedding anniversary, Hal came home in triumph.

It was short-lived. Very soon he was running fevers again, and Silverman, chancing nothing this time, put him back into the hospital immediately. That almost, but not quite, broke his spirit.

These fevers were not high. He felt stronger. His mind was clear. Now he struggled to play a role in his own care, to be acknowledged as a doctor who knew a thing or two about this case, and repeatedly he was denied. The weight of the institution was crushing.

The professors descended upon him now with their tests, as they had on previous febrile occasions. They moved in the magnetic fields of their own expertise—the blood experts, the endocrine experts, the tropical-disease experts; they ordered the tests and rarely gave him the courtesy of personal reports, and he festered. He asked them, and I asked too, when I could find them, whether this might be some sort of autoimmune reaction. We clung to this, he and I, remembering how the fevers had first appeared just months after his surgery, how he had staggered steadily downhill, staggering finally into Mason's office to say, "You can no longer simply observe me, or you will simply observe me die"; and how Mason had taken a shot in the dark of this disorder, put him on steriods for the treatment of an autoimmune disease called postpericardiotomy syndrome, and immediately he had started to improve and within months was walking, by God, to the gym.

But now the professors said simply, No. Autoimmune reactions occurred months after surgery; this was well documented in the literature. But years after surgery? No; that was unheard of in the literature. If it did not appear in The Literature, it did not exist.

An infectious-diseases specialist came, did a cursory examination and left before Hal could ask all his questions. He called the man's office. The doctor said, "I don't have time to talk to you now," and hung up.

Hal stared at the telephone, gone dead in his hand. He called again. "That was unforgivable," he said. "I never hung up on a patient in my *life*. I never *heard* of such a thing. How *could* you . . ."

"I told you. I don't have time for you now," the man said, and hung up again.

Hal seethed. He told me, "I want to get the hell out of here. I won't take that shit from people anymore. My mental difficulty is bad enough. It's devastating to my self-esteem. On top of that, to take this shit from doctors—I won't have it. I *won't*."

And then, while he lay hot with fever and temper, a nurse's aide hung up on him. She said, "When I have time" when he buzzed the intercom to ask for oxygen; and after an hour had passed and neither she nor the oxygen had appeared, he buzzed again, and she clicked him off. Simply, wordlessly, clicked him off. And he buzzed a third time, and she did the same, and a fourth, and she did the same, and now all of his rage, all of his fear and his futility were focused on this, to be clicked off, turned off, by a nurse's aide, to be powerless, mute, nonexistent. He marched into the hall and stopped nurses in their tracks to tell them about it; he told the orderlies, he told the intern, he told the resident, and when Mason came on rounds told him too, and kept repeating to me in a fury that was on the edge of a howl, "She clicked me off!" He couldn't let go of it. It was the ultimate insult. The ultimate loss: clicked off, cancelled, out.

He scrawled this in his notebook: *I am not a dog in a kennel.*

The brushfire raged on.
He called me one morning, his voice shaking with wrath.
"Come take me home."
"What's happened?"

"I don't know. Fuck it. I don't give a damn anymore. The chief dental surgeon saw me. He said I have two infected teeth."

"So?"

"So now they're telling me that that may be the cause of the fever. My teeth. It's preposterous. It's obscene."

"I know. But they're groping around. . . ."

"Yeah. And now they can all stop groping and land on my teeth, and it gets them off the hook. It's bullshit. *Bullshit. Bullshit.* And I . . . Oh, Mushie"—abruptly his voice switched into a faint, agonized croak—"I've had it. I'm too tired."

I told Silverman, "Moe, for God's sake, it's not his teeth. You know that."

"Yes. But we're testing everything. Whenever there's an F.U.O., it's standard procedure to test the teeth. He does have a bad abscess. And in a situation like this, I'm committed to following up on *any* lead."

"Of course. But he's beside himself. He is dying and he knows it and they're talking dentistry."

"Yes. I know."

We all knew. Kicking and flailing about like a drowning man, which was precisely what he was, while they spoke to him of teeth.

"And beyond this, what more can be done?" I asked Silverman.

"Nothing."

So. An extraction and a root-canal.

"Well," I told him, "you and I know that it's not the root, ho ho, of the problem, but you may as well get it taken care of."

"Oh, sure. I'll have it done before I get out of here. No point leaving with an abscess that may flare up when we get to Provincetown."

To Provincetown.

"And Martha, I want it done right away. Then *out.*"

"Moe may want you to hang around for a couple of weeks, just to make sure you're stabilized."

"I don't want to hang around for a couple of weeks."

"You misunderstand, Hal. I don't mean in the hospital. I mean here at home, in New York."

"*You* misunderstand, Martha. I mean I don't want to hang around New York for a couple of weeks. I want to get to Provincetown *fast.*"

He submitted graciously to the dental surgeon. "As long as your hands are in my mouth," he said, "my mouth is in your hands."

The work was done. Hours later he lay curled on his left side, hipbone near sharp enough to pierce the flesh, temperature 101, with violent shakes, skin of his arms turned to goosebumps, right side of his face grotesquely swollen, lips tugging to the left in a Novocain-frozen smile.

"I'm glad that's d-done," he said. "I don't think the P-Province-town Rescue Squad does d-d-dental work."

The fevers continued.

Silverman talked straight: "Martha, I'm stumped. We're all stumped. We've done every test in the world. At first we were getting all negative findings. In the last few days we've gotten some positives. These signs often point to S.B.E., even though you can't find it in the blood cultures." S.B.E.: subacute bacterial endocarditis—inflammation of the heart lining. Treatment, six weeks of intravenous penicillin. It was the treatment Hal had refused, for lack of proof that he had S.B.E., when he had first developed fevers three years earlier. That was when Mason had started him on steroids. "We are left with two alternatives. One is nihilistic and the other is therapeutic. And I can't in any good conscience pursue the first. We've got to do *something*. Now, I cannot commit this guy to six weeks in the hospital with I.V. penicillin. It would devastate him psychologically. He'd go out the window. But maybe we can work out a compromise: send him home, and have him come into the office each week for a million units of penicillin intramuscularly. We might get results. Cases of S.B.E. with negative cultures are rare. We would be treating it blindly and hoping that we make a hit. But if the fevers don't subside, I think that is the route we will have to go, because it is the last and only thing we can think to do. Ah"—he sighed, sad and exhausted—"it's so hard for me to go into that room every day. It's such a strain. Poor guy. Today he says to me, 'I feel so good! Is it possible the fever broke through some infection and I'm getting better now?' He's fighting so hard. It hurts. It's not like that for the other doctors. They feel sorry for him, but they go from Room 353 to 354 to 355. . . . But for Peter and me— he's part of our medical family by now. We love the guy. It hurts."

The fevers subsided spontaneously. They sent him home in mid-July, holding the penicillin in abeyance.

Outside, the mercury rose into the upper 90s. In our air-conditioned apartment we waited, tiptoeing around each other's anxieties, for the mercury to rise again.

"I've had no fever for two days," he said, "so I figure we can be in Provincetown by next week."

Hal. You have had another heart attack. You have an end-stage heart, Hal. A terminal heart and an interminable will. Do you know that you will die soon? On what level do you know it? Do you know that I know it? Do you want to speak of it? What are you thinking at this moment? You believe, really, then, that you will make it to Provincetown, with all of its resonances? "He is a doctor. He knows," the consultant Paul Corey told me once. I said, "But he is also a patient. The doctor knows. The patient denies." Which are you more of now, Hal? A smile into my eyes, and then you are light-years away, within yourself. Contemplating hopes or inevitabilities? I do not know. My God, the aloneness within our intimacy! As for myself, there is only this: I do not want to let you go. I refuse. I reject. I will not have it. At night I wake moaning, Hal, Hal, I do not want to let you go, and sometimes you wake and you turn, even now in your excruciating weakness, and kiss and comfort me. You do not hear the words, my unconscious spares us both that; only the moans. But of course, you know the words. You know the melody, which has been whistling through this house like the wind, shaking walls, for such a bloody long time. What an awesome silence there will be when you are gone. As after every holocaust. How can six million strangers, Hal, mean as much to me as you?

"So what do you think? If my temp stays normal, can you be ready to leave in a week?"

"Sure." How do I support and stall? I have been told to support and stall. "But if you do get a bit of fever and they want to treat you for S.B.E., we can still get to Provincetown by Labor Day."

"What do you mean, Labor Day? I can have the treatment there."

"How? With an I.V.?"

"Sure!"

"Don't you have to lie in bed all during the treatment?"

"Of course not. You can move around."

"How do you move around with a needle in you?"

"The same way you do it in the hospital: we just wind the tubing around and secure it, and I take my little drip bottle of penicillin and I go. I could even go to the *movies*, for Christ's sake."

I stared at him, dumbfounded.

"I mean, I may need a bottle-bearer," he said. "Are you available?"

And on August 1 we packed our summer duds in luggage, and I packed the prognosis in my pocket, and we ordered the wheelchair and flew up to Provincetown and broke open the wine and made the usual toast.

Afterword

*H*AL died on September 13, 1978: two years after the worst of
prognoses and six months after the best.

Not knowing how long he might live, I had decided months earlier
to make a cutoff point for this book. That point would be in August of
1977, when we flew to Provincetown against the prevailing winds. My
editor had said, "If he dies before the book is done, you will have to
write an epilogue." "Of course," I had said, and had promptly told a
friend, "My editor says that if Hal dies before my work is done, I will
have to write an epitaph."

That August in Provincetown was both sun and shadow. He lay on
our deck and watched neighbors sailing his boat. Toward month's
end he began to speak of how he had always loved autumn in New
York, how fine it would be to start going again to restaurants and
films. In New York he had no tolerance for cold, and it was clear that
a housebound winter would devastate his morale. We went, by intri-
cate logistics, to Florida. Through January and February he lay on a
little terrace, failing steadily, speaking of the healing properties of
sun. In March he began to talk of how he had always loved spring-
time in New York. Always he was preparing to feel stronger someplace else. He never did.

In Florida, counting months, I raised again the question of heart transplantation. I spoke with his uncle, the cardiologist Victor Kay, who cared for him through that winter. Victor sent Hal's records to Stanford. The answer came back unequivocal: No; not simply because of age, but because his general condition was now too tenuous.

In the last months, back in New York, I was astonished by the will that he imposed upon his limitations. His routines hardened. Every day that he was not in hospital, including days when he was so weak that he staggered, he worked hours at his desk, imposing order. I do not know if he understood that it was metaphor.

He paid bills. He wrote letters. He kept a dictionary at hand to check monosyllabic words. In one fully characteristic moment, he grinned and said, "You know, it's really exciting to learn to spell again. I'm getting much better at it."

He clipped from the medical journals. He could not read much, but my God, how he could clip. Most of the articles were about heart disease. He made notes in the margins and piled the stuff neatly, to be read later, when his mind improved. In one pile was an article titled "Hypokalemia May Trigger Ventricular Fibrillation." He wrote on it, *Discuss with Moe and Pete.* Heading another pile was a journal with the cover line PSYCHOSOMATIC LINKS IN CARDIOVASCULAR DISORDERS, and here he had written, *Very good! Save. Read.* There was a mound of miscellany labeled *Martha—F.Y.I.* It contained an article titled "Hopelessness Following Illness in Middle Age," subtitled "The Middle-Aged Man Who Gives Up the Ghost," and it was for me to read in order that I might understand that this was precisely what he would never do. Also in that pile was a letter from a sports club, advertising ski trips. On the envelope he had scrawled: "M—*please* go! We can resolve any possibel assosiated problems." It was postmarked six days before his death.

He was stern about my working every day. "Hurry up and finish the damned thing," he would say. "We need the money." But of course, it was not the money. It was control. The process of dying could be controlled only by the normal process of living.

He wrote this passage, which I did not discover until after his death:

Thought go rushing through my mind like the torrential rapids of a stream rushing down a mountain a storm & covering & uncovering protruding rocky boulders. But my mind goes in many directions con-

395

currently & sometimes simultaniously & sometime concurrently. Often I feel like am jolting down a wild unknown stream in a rubber raft & not sure what thoughts or feelings will be the next turn.

"My father died at 57. I am now 57. Will I live longer. I do not belabor this, but it must be there, persistent, sublimminally. Of course I have had the advantage of modern medical therapy including surgery. I wonder how much they have really helped me. What if I had just taken nitroglteran for for angina PRN. My ventrical has deterorated, my bypass has block & 1 struggle constantly to cope with the brain damage which occured during the surgery.

I did not mean to dwell on this either, but I guess it too is in there subliminally. I know that I have almost no cardiac reserve & that I am dying. What I do not know is the rate of progress of the cardiac deteiroation. However I no one can tell me & I have realized that I may very well be the best judge.

I am not repressing. I know whats happening to me & what will. But I dont want to be externaly a sickie. I dont want to enjoy poor health. Im determined to keep my emotions under control. I want to take pride in myself & to be groomed & well-dressed & in minimazing my illness to the outside world & not to dwell on them externally. It becomes almost a senile things—how much did you urinate & did you have a bowel movement today. That is how senile become when their world narrows. I dont want to be like that. I dont want to tunnel myself. In wahtever time I have left I want to grow larger.

What are the things which actively & consciously bother me? I gues that #1 would be my continous struggle to cope with my brain damage & 2 my dependency upon other people for almost everything. I think it is is impossible to change a type "A" personality. But I have been very lucky that I could channel the intensely success oriented personality to the goal of copeing with adversities. I am so fortunate that I did not just go plunk into deep depression. But I had been carefully tuaght as a child to succed & I have manage & I have managed to evoke that core within me & direct it toward the goal of surrmounting the physical, psychological & enotional adversities with which I am enveloped. . . .

He reordered his personal stationery—a thousand sheets. *Yes, damn it, he would live a thousand days to write a thousand letters.* The paths his anger found!: enraged Letters to the Editor and other parties, Con Ed for demanding a payment long since made, Shell Oil for billing him a thirteen-cent carrying charge. And when I raised an eyebrow at that, he laughed and said, "Well, I've got to keep my mind exercised."

He slept all day, huddled in his robe, and when he woke he would say, "That was a good nap. I feel great now," and one evening removed the robe, shaved—he could no longer bathe without help—and combed his hair carefully and came to the dinner table looking like parchment, in jeans and a red sweater.

I said, "Dressing for dinner, eh?"

"Damn right," he said. "Why should you have to look at sickness all the time? I wanted you to look at a *healthy*." And unbuttoned the sweater coyly, as in a striptease, to show me that underneath he was wearing his favorite Provincetown shirt, patchwork denim, and in this gesture there was everything.

He said, "I don't look too bad, do I?"

I grabbed him. "You look *fabulous*," I said, nuzzling, nibbling, French-kissing the flesh of his cheek. "*You, fabulous*."

"Enough of this lovemaking," he said. "I want food. I want"—thumping the table, half-grinning, as though about to make a good joke; and then it broke: "*I want a new ventricle*."

Sudden stillness in the room. I sat and buried my face in his crotch and he stroked my hair and we cried. He recovered first. "Isn't this *ridiculous*, Mushie?" he said, as he had said a hundred times before. "For us, to have come to this."

Oh, it is, I thought. I cannot make peace with it. I believed I could, but I cannot. Simply to stand by and let his heart, this part that should be a replaceable part, keep slowing down, fizzling out ("*Fizzling?*" he had said a few days earlier, when he had demanded that we discuss my fears. "Oh, Mushie dear, don't worry about that. You know I don't fizzle. I snap, crackle and pop"); and then he is gone.

"Imagine," I wrote that night, "wandering through these rooms calling Hal, Hal, and he nowhere, not to exist, a nothingness. How can that be? I suppose because he is a doctor, death is natural to him. A natural enemy. To me it is irrational, an obscene perversion of natural order. So often I have found comfort in the thought that when this perversion takes him it can take me too. I know which of his pills would do the job. But I know too that I have never meant it. That is the option for depressives. I am not a depressive. I am a hysteric, and for hysterics life is precious. There is always something else to be hysterical about."

On June 19 he was hit, as suddenly as though by a car, by the same old crisis of fevers and failure. He had long since put me on notice that if—which always meant when—it happened again, he would not return to that hospital to which he had been admitted eight times, and in which he had come so close to death the year before. "Why should I go back there?" he had said. "They almost killed me in that place." He knew this was irrational. There were bunglers everywhere. But he had a fix, and when the time came his fix held, and we returned to that hospital to which he had traveled by wheelchair, caroming crazily down a city street and feeling his own pulse fade, on the occasion of his first heart attack.

Silverman and Mason had no staff privileges in that place. The doctor of his choice was away. The covering doctor was an Andrew Fried, very young, very intense. When we came in, Hal's temperature was close to 105 and he had the severe shaking chills called rigors. Fried gave him a 40-percent chance.

I told him briefly of that long night's drowning the year before. I told him of the doctor who had said that the next time it happened, as it was bound to happen, they might draw back sooner, to spare him. I said, "If it comes to that, what will you do?"

Fried said, "I have known your husband just ten minutes. But it is already clear to me that this is a guy with incredible will. We get people in here who tell us, 'I'm tired. Just let me go.' But this guy isn't telling us that. He wants ferociously to live. I must tell you that I would feel a responsibility to him to subject him to any discomfort, even torture if necessary, to give him every possible chance."

Ten minutes, I thought, and he sees my husband clear. My terrors have made me blind.

It did not come to such choices. Hal beat the odds. By midnight he was sitting up in bed, in the C.C.U., bitching because he could get nothing to eat.

Jon came home from England. He was home permanently now. In the fall he would take up a teaching post at Yale, a move dictated in no small part, after countless flights home in moments of crisis, by the desire to be closer to his father. Judy arrived from Massachusetts with Jacob. The child could not be brought into the hospital. She positioned him beside a hot-dog vendor's umbrella in the street, and Hal stood with Jon at his hospital-room window and waved to the grandchild whom, as it developed, he would never see again.

He stayed in the hospital for six weeks. His fevers persisted. His recent memory was shot. They tested the hell out of him, arriving at no answers.

I began to ask again about autoimmune reactions. I was not exploring in a vacuum. My own internist, to whom I had given the briefest description of Hal's symptoms, had said, "Sounds to me as though it might be an autoimmune problem." Hal's uncle Victor had called me from Florida and said, "I don't know why they aren't trying steroids." I had said, "They tell me they have never seen an autoimmune reaction so long after surgery. What does that mean?" Victor had said, "It means that they have never seen it. I have."

So I persisted, and in the fifth week they put him on steroids. But it was a Mickey Mouse dose, simply to placate me. It helped him only slightly.

I said, "I know you don't believe this is an autoimmune problem. But even if steroids are not the answer, they do suppress fevers, don't they?"

True, they said.

"Then why not increase the dosage, simply to make him more comfortable?"

Very well, they said, and tripled the dosage. Within twenty-four hours the fevers and shakes were gone, and within the week Hal was home, played out but euphoric.

Now he took as his primary physician young Dr. Fried, who had tended him that first night in the emergency room and had often visited him thereafter. He said, "The guy doesn't have much clinical experience, but he's bright and he listens. I like him."

So Andy Fried became Hal's doctor for the last six weeks of his life, and he paid attention and respect, which at that point seemed more important to me than lifetimes of clinical experience.

When the end finally came, it happened like this:

On September 12 Hal slept very late. At 1 P.M., I went into the bedroom and found him lying quietly, eyes open.

"Why did you wake me?" he said.

Clearly I hadn't wakened him. I said, "It's afternoon. You haven't had any medicine yet."

"Sleep is more important than medicine. My body needs sleep. You shouldn't wake me."

"I'm sorry." I brought him the pills. "Perhaps you'll be able to sleep some more now."

"I doubt it. I'll try."

At 1:30 he padded into the kitchen, looking cross. He sipped orange juice. He said, "I was lying there trying to think what could possibly rationalize waking me when I am sick and need sleep. And I had a completely irrational thought. I thought, The only possible justification for waking me would be if my mother was calling."

We stared at each other. His mother had been dead for fifteen years. I put my arms about him, and we both wept.

At 2:15 he began to shake violently. "Here we go," he said.

The thermometer registered 102.

I said, "I'm going to call Andy now."

"Not yet. I want to watch the fever. My notebook."

I brought him the notebook, but his hand could not control the pen. He dictated to me the clinical note: "2:15. Severe rigors. Temp 102."

Five minutes later it was 103, and I listened to him no more. I called for an ambulance.

At 2:30 two police officers were at our door. Hal's shakes had subsided slightly. He rose from the bed and began stumbling about, collecting things. "I'll need socks. My feet are cold," he said, and rummaged in a drawer.

I said, "Hal, come on. They're here."

"They can wait. I need my electric razor." And he continued to stumble about, clearly trying to impose order, to pack in a reasonable way for a reasonable trip; but he was dazed, he was picking up objects and looking at them blankly, putting them down. He shoved a toothbrush into the right pocket of his robe and a pen into the left. "My notebook. My eyeglasses," he said.

"I have them. Please, Hal, let's go."

"Don't rush me. My pants."

"You don't need pants. You have a robe on. We're going right to the hospital."

He glared at me. "*I want to wear pants*. My lightweight jeans."

I sat him down and somehow got the jeans on him, pulled them up under his robe.

"My shoes."

"Never mind your shoes. Come on."

Finally he submitted. We shuffled out to the foyer.

"You want a stretcher, sir?" a cop asked.

"No."

They took him, one at each elbow, and supported him into the elevator and through the lobby. Outside were an ambulance and a patrol car.

"You want to go by ambulance, sir?"

"No."

They settled him into the back seat of the car, and I got in beside him. He felt his pulse.

"What time is it?" he said.

"Two thirty-five."

"Please write: 2:35. Shaking chills subsided. Weakness. Irregular pulse."

A wheelchair took him through the emergency room into a cubicle. They put him on a stretcher and got an E.K.G. started, and an intravenous. His fever was 105. Yet he seemed to me somewhat better now. We chatted; I don't remember about what. I do recall that he said, several times, "Take it easy, Mushie."

A doctor asked him, "Dr. Lear, how old are you?"

"Fifty-seven."

She turned from her notes to look at him, and he grinned and said, "But I've been *sick*," and winked at me.

She listened to his chest. "Have you ever had atrial fibrillations before?" she asked.

"No."

She moved off to a corner. I approached her and whispered, "Is that what he's having now?"

"Yes. But they're not too fast."

Some minutes later Fried appeared, examined Hal, then took me aside. "He says he's feeling better now. He is not in bad failure. I don't know what the hell is going on. They'll keep him down here overnight, watch him closely. If his fever comes down and he feels better in the morning, I think we should send him home. With his prognosis, there's no point holding him in the hospital and starting tests again. Okay?"

I nodded.

"And I'll come back in an hour to see how he's doing."

He left. A resident said, "We're sending you for chest X-rays now, Dr. Lear."

"Can my wife come?"

"Sure."

I walked alongside as an orderly rolled his stretcher down the hall and parked it by the X-ray room. Now we were alone.

Hal said, "I'm cold." They had pulled back his robe to take the E.K.G. His chest was bare. "Can you wrap this thing?"

I did so.

He said, "My notebook . . ."

He reached into his left pocket and pulled out his pen. He looked at it as though he could not fathom what it was. Then he fell back, his eyelids fluttered shut, his face began to twitch, his mouth, his nose, his eyes, all twitching in odd, rapid, unsynchronized ways, like the features of a severe spastic, and this twitching lasted for an eternity, perhaps twenty seconds or more, and then he slumped and was still.

I screamed. People stared. I screamed, "Get a doctor. *Do* something." A man said, "I'm a doctor," but he did nothing, just stood there staring. I was shoved aside, and soon there were many people around his body. I couldn't see clearly, but I could make out that someone was pushing rhythmically on his chest, and someone else seemed to be breathing into his mouth, and of course the image that came was of Hal pounding on my father's chest and breathing into my father's mouth, while I watched, and here now Hal, while I watched, and I began to shout. A guard told me later that I kept shouting, "Fuck! I *knew* this would happen. Fuck! I *knew* this would happen," and then someone pushed me through swinging doors and guards stood on the other side of the doors and would not let me through, but the upper halves of those doors were glass and I kept looking, though now all I could see was a mass of bodies around a stretcher, I could not see my husband at all, and then I heard a rattling, something being rushed toward the stretcher, and even before I saw the damned thing I knew what it was; it was the defibrillation cart; it was the cart Hal had bought back there in Hartford, when he had been president of the medical staff and rammed a four-bed coronary-care unit down the throats of a budget-minded board of directors; it was the cart he had described so often, knowing its sounds, describing precisely its sounds, hearing it come in the midst of so many nights, in so many coronary-care units, for so many people who had gone into cardiac arrest while he himself had lain nearby; and now the cart was coming for him.

And when I saw that, I walked away from the doors and sat down.

I began to write in Hal's notebook, describing these events, and I felt quite calm.

Vaguely I heard people. Someone said, "I think it's her husband." Someone else said, "Is he dead?" A nurse knelt beside me and asked, "Can I get anything for you?" and I said, "Yes, please, a cigarette," and a man who sat nearby, twitching not at all as Hal had twitched but simply like a crazy person, shouted, "Yeah, sure! Smoke! Smoke! You'll get a heart attack!" and someone yelled to him, "Shut up!" and he moved away.

Once I walked back to the doors. White coats were like walls around the stretcher. I saw a great deal of blood on the floor. I remember feeling both agitated and detached, and thinking, Oh; they have cut open his chest and are massaging his heart.

Then I sat down again. A social worker came. "Do you want to wait in my office?" she asked. I said No. "Can we get you anything? Water? Coffee?" I said No. "I must say that you seem very calm," she said. I believe that I said, "I am," and this unnerved her. She said, "Can we call anyone? Friends? Relatives?"

His cousins Norman and Frances had been planning to have drinks with us. I asked her to call their hotel.

Soon Fried came through the swinging doors. He said, "It's amazing. They've shocked him out of arrest."

"Is he conscious?"

"No. By the time I got there they had already moved more aggressively than I might have wanted them to. There's a pacemaker in him now."

I felt a sudden nausea, taking this to mean that they had indeed cut Hal open and attached a pacemaker to his heart, but Fried explained that No, this was an external attachment; a wire hooked up to a pacemaker box had been threaded through a vein in Hal's neck into his heart.

I said, "What made the blood?"

"When they put in the wire. It's a small insertion, but he's been on such heavy anticoagulants that he's bleeding a lot."

"What do you think?" I said.

"I don't know. It's pretty dismal. But who knows? The guy has amazed us before. They'll be taking him up to the C.C.U. soon."

I sat a time longer. It was 5 o'clock. They had been working on him in that corridor for an hour and a half. Soon I saw them rushing the stretcher away, escorted by the paraphernalia that had escorted him the year before: the drip bottles on poles, the portable E.K.G. monitor, all that. Frances and Norman came, and we went up to the C.C.U.

There are in every large hospital signs leading the way to one pavillion and another, and often there are tape or paint markers on the floors—Follow the blue stripe to get to Maternity, Follow the yellow stripe to get to the West Wing, and so forth—but this time there was no need for directions. We simply followed the path of Hal's blood. Wet dollops of Hal's blood on the floor led us along corridors and around corners and through wings and up an elevator and down a hall, and Hal's blood delivered us directly to the door of the C.C.U.

We were shown to a waiting room. Vaguely I remembered this waiting room. I had sat here when Hal had suffered his first heart attack.

We called Jon, who would take a train from New Haven. We called Judy, who would fly in from Massachusetts. David came. We sat. All I could think of was the twitching. I kept pushing it away and it kept coming back, that dear face contorted by the twitching, and I thought, Oh, God, if only I hadn't been watching in those seconds, if only I had escaped them, getting a drink of water, talking to a nurse, asking someone for the time of day, anything, anywhere, but only not to have been watching in those seconds, watching the twitching, the twitching, and now surely it would convulse my nights and my waking hours too, it would keep sneaking back into my gallery of images, where Hal was still being raced down a corridor the year before, propped high in a bed that careened off walls, pleading, "Hurry. Hurry. Hurry," and now the goddamn twitching too, and I thought, There is simply no more room in this gallery, the place is overcrowded, the basement is full, the gallery is jammed, it may take years before the exhibition is changed, and what ever will I do about the twitching? Weeks later, when I was still obsessed with it, someone said, "But of course, Martha, that was not *Hal*. That was simply electrical circuits going crazy. It is as though you have a friend who is an epileptic, and suddenly he is lying on the floor, twitching and frothing, but that is not your *friend*. And then he recovers and says Hello, and it is your friend again." Which helped. Although Hal never recovered to say Hello.

After a long while a doctor came. Chief Resident in the C.C.U., a young man looking bone-worn, with a yarmulke perched atop a great head of bushy hair. Dr. Alvin Goldin.

He said, "We don't really know anything yet. His blood pressure is being maintained on its own, without vasopressors, if you know what those are"—Oh, yes. Oh, yes—"and that is a good sign. The pacemaker is working. He is beginning to try to breathe on his own, fighting the intubator"—the device stuck through his mouth down deep into him, pumping oxygen into him.

"Does it hurt, the intubator?"

"No. But it is uncomfortable and frightening. We keep telling him to relax and let us breathe for him, but he is showing some agitation."

"He is conscious, then?"

"We don't know. Probably not. But it is very difficult in these cases to know what degree of consciousness there is."

"Then how is he showing agitation?"

"He is moving his extremities a bit. He is withdrawing appropriately from pain. When we stick him with a pin, he withdraws. But he is not responding to verbal commands. You must be prepared. If he survives, there is no way to know what degree of mentation he will have."

I had known this from the first moment of the twitching. I had been waiting to be told this. Cardiac arrest; no flow of oxygen to the brain: within four minutes, I recalled this detail from some reading way back, within four minutes there is irreversible brain damage. And how long had it been before they had shocked his heart back into some semblance of a beat? I had no idea. No sense of time. But for sure far longer than four minutes.

"What would be your guess?" I said.

"I can't guess. As to his life, there is a guarded optimism. But you must understand that it is *very* guarded. As to his brain, in these cases of cardiac arrest it takes from twelve to forty-eight hours to determine how much cerebral function may be recovered."

We all stared at the floor, as though it held secrets. Hal's mind. His agony at the first, his agony at the last, that was the secret he had borne alone, and I prayed now that he was beyond it.

"Do you want to see him?" Goldin said.

"Would he know me?"

"No."

"Then I don't want to see him."

He nodded, his little black yarmulke nodding sadly on that great bush of hair, and walked back toward the C.C.U.

Norman and David went with him. Frances and I sat alone. She sat with me and I sat with the twitchings. It was 7 o'clock now, darkening outside. Heavy rain. In the waiting room adjacent to ours, a television set was blaring. I remembered wondering, when I had sat here after his first heart attack, why there should be two waiting rooms, adjacent, only one with a television set, and now I understood that one was for boredom and one was for despair: an arrangement dictated, no doubt, by grant proposals and studies-in-depth. "What do you *mean*, you don't want to study venereal disease in Harlem?" the cruel fools had asked him years earlier. *"They're willing to fund it."*

The men were gone a very long time, perhaps an hour. "What are they *doing* down there?" Frances said, and I said, "Damn, why is it that when there is crisis, the men take over?" And we marched, driven in this moment by some displacement of feminist fury, down the hall to join them, just outside the C.C.U. door.

This door too was glass-plated. "Where is he?" I said.

"There." Norman pointed to a cubicle where many white coats surrounded a bed, and I saw instantly that it was adjacent to the cubicle in which he had lain more than four years earlier, when I had come home from France and knelt by his bed, crying, and he had whispered to me, "Don't worry. Everything will be the same as it was," and I turned my back to the door. But soon it opened. Supplies were being wheeled through. Clearly I heard a voice saying, "Dr. Lear, can you hear me? If you hear me, please squeeze my hand. Thank you, sir," so gently and respectfully, in the way that all the white coats should have addressed him down through the years, and again: "Dr. Lear, can you hear me? If you hear me, please squeeze my hand. Thank you, sir," and I covered my ears, and then the door swung shut.

Soon Goldin came out. "Things look a bit better," he said.

I gaped at him. *Gone?* In that other waiting room, the year before. *No, he's not gone. He's better.*

And now Goldin: "We think we're getting more response. A couple of times, when we asked him to squeeze, we think he squeezed back. But other times he didn't. We're not sure whether he understands, or whether he is simply withdrawing from all stimuli. But it may be a true response."

I said, "Would he know me now?"

"I very much doubt it."

I pondered this doubt. How reliable was it? If there was any chance that he might know me, I could perhaps help him impose another act of will upon his body. I could grab his hand and say, "Hal, it's me. It's not them, it's *me. Martha. Jon. Judy.* We have to get to *Provincetown.* We have to get to our *golden years.* Remember *L'chaim. Squeeze my hand. Squeeze my hand. You're going to make it,*" give him all the buzz words, in some way cut through the electrical jumble and reach him in that spiritual space we had shared, and of course he could not speak with that thing in his throat, but perhaps he would squeeze back and his eyes would say, as his voice had said the year before, *"I've already made it,"* and it would be all right. But if I went in and said these things to a body, a twitching vacancy, I would not be able to bear it, it would in some sense kill me, and so I had a failure of nerve; I simply was not brave enough to take the chance, and I did not go in.

Afterward, of course, I was obsessed by questions of whether it might have made a difference, and they all assured me that it would have made no difference whatever, and I wanted to be kind to myself and believe them. But I could not. It tormented me to wonder whether he was conscious in those hours that he lingered, what terrors might have been in his head, whether he might have known me and been comforted by my presence. It torments me still; as, on occasion, do the twitchings.

We returned to the waiting room. People began to say, as people do in such circumstances, "Go home. You can do nothing here. We'll call if there is any change," and I resisted for a time, but an hour later there was still no change and I understood that it was stupid to sit in this place staring away from one another when we could be home, slugging down drinks.

Jon soon arrived at the house, looking grim. "Is he dead?" he said. No, I told him, not dead, but like this and like that, and soon after the same story to Judy, and then we all sat around eating and drinking and it got mighty jolly—jokes, family anecdotes, fond memories: a prewake.

At midnight I called Goldin. He said, "He is still not responsive to verbal command. A neurologist has seen him. We can't know how far he will come back neurologically. He is moving his extremities more. I can tell you on the basis of studies—but you *must* understand"—being so gentle and careful—"that statistics mean very little in such cases; each case is highly individual, and you must not rely on this—that when they have this much function of the extremities so soon after an arrest, it's generally a good sign."

I made this report to the group. Norman said, before leaving, "Who knows, Martha?" and I said, "I know," and I did.

I shared with Judy the fine big bed I knew I would never again share with Hal, woke several times and telephoned Goldin, who told me, "No change." At 8 A.M. he called us and said, "His blood pressure is dropping. You'd better get here fast," and we got there fast, and Goldin said, "If you want to see him, come now." I asked, "Would he know me?" and Goldin said, emphatically, "No," so I declined, having already bidden him goodbye. But Jon and Judy went to make their own goodbyes; they went in there just for moments and when they came out they would not speak of it at all, nor did I want to hear, except that Judy, weeping, said, "It wasn't Daddy." And at 9:30 Wednesday morning, September 13, 1978, eighteen hours after an arrest which a heart such as his had no business surmounting for moments, Hal finally died; not for the first time, but for the last.

"I will never give up," he had said long ago. And the sweet son-of-a-bitch never did.

We settled on Friday the fifteenth at Campbell's Funeral Chapel.

Two hours after Hal's death, I went there with Norman to make arrangements. We were shown the main chapel, which I had last visited when a friend had thrown herself out a window the year before, thereby dying, as the *Times* always reported in such cases, after a long illness at home. It was a large, formal, pew-filled space, imposing by its very formality certain imperatives that I hated, and that Hal had hated, such as white lilies, organ music, the original funereal silence. I asked "What else have you got?" and was told that there was another *facility* upstairs, though a corpse awaiting a funeral was in it at the moment. I said that this would be quite all right with me, so long as the casket was—as of course it was, was it not?—closed. It happened in fact to be open. We asked if the lid could be lowered while we checked out this facility, but it seemed no simple matter; there were certain protocols involved, and several staff members held a whispered conference before it was decided that, yes, they might close the damned thing for a moment. So we went upstairs, I dreading already to find a smaller, shabbier version of the main chapel, and found instead a large sunny room furnished quite like the lobby of an intimate European hotel, where organ music would have resonated badly and one might hear, instead, clusters of friends talking sunnily of what a swell guy he had been, and I said, Sold.

I was presented options as to the ashes. If I wanted them, there was a selection of urns. I most devoutly did not want the ashes. Well, then, the man said, two alternatives remained: either the ashes could be scattered on a common ground of ash, somewhere in New Jersey, I believe; or, for an extra $50 charge, they might be scattered over water. Over water, I said. He then asked the requisite biographical questions and showed me the dotted lines upon which to sign, and he went about this so cordially, comfortably, that I was moved to ask how long he had been in this line of work. Twenty years, he said. Did he own a piece of the action? No, he regretted, none. And did he like his job? Why, yes, he said, in fact he did; except, of course, when the deceased were children—one never got hardened to that; but apart from that, it was a good enough job. And I quite liked him for this forthcomingness, not the least unctuous, no embalmed smile, no polite wringing of hands. I thanked him for his services and we left.

And in the car home, it suddenly hit me. "*Scattered over water*," I said. "That could mean a toilet bowl, for God's sake."

So that detail was changed, and in time I received a letter certifying that the cremains of Dr. Harold Lear had been interred in the waters of Provincetown, Mass., by a licensed agent of the R.L.W. Flying Service, and a bill for an extra $350. A bargain, all options considered.

I wanted to look splendid for Hal's funeral. Lacking that competence, I wanted to look as well as I possibly could. I wanted also to see every guest and hear every word that was spoken. These were urgencies that astonished me, tipped me off that I would have surprises, for when my father had died I had looked like hell and must suppose that I had wanted to look like hell, in order that everyone should see the proportions of my grief, and I had been numb to every nuance of the occasion.

On the afternoon of Hal's death I went with Frances, who sustained me that day, as she would in the days to come, with her thin, elegant arms that were like life belts, to buy what I referred to, several times, as my wedding dress.

On the next afternoon, I had my hair set. I went to a salon I had not visited in a decade, to the hairdresser who had arranged my wedding coiffure. I told him my situation. He pointed to a woman who was having a manicure. "She has been widowed too," he said. I asked for an introduction.

"When did your husband die?" I asked her.

"Four years ago."

"My husband died yesterday."

The poor woman flinched and drew back. It was a ghastly line to impose on a stranger, but I was yielding to every impulse.

I asked, "How long did it take you to get over the worst of it?"

She said, "I'm still getting over it," and now I drew back, as though she were contagious, and mumbled Good luck, and fled.

I dreamed that night that Hal lay with his eyes closed and the intubator in his mouth. It looked not like an intubator but like a length of white cord, roughly twice the thickness of telephone cord, and his hand was reaching up to smoke it. I woke smiling. Toward morning I dreamed again, I could not remember what, but awoke screaming, and Judy hushed and mothered me.

I dressed with care for the service, fussed with the eyeliner and the mascara, wore sunglasses to hide swollen lids, measured myself in the mirror, smiled at Hal's picture; and he, holding a champagne glass toward the camera in a photograph taken the previous New Year's Eve, when impending death had been clear upon his face, smiled brilliantly back.

"You have grown more than you know," he had said to me then. "You are stronger than you think. You will cope." And I said now, aloud, to his picture, "I'll be damned, Hal. I think you were right."

It was a sunny memorial service. Young Dr. Fried spoke first. He had telephoned me the night before, and said lovely things about Hal, and I had invited him on impulse to give a eulogy. Now, in that unformidably hushed room, I saw Moses Silverman and Peter Mason and I felt a dreadful qualm, wondering what sort of ingrate they might take me to be, for they had given my husband four years, and this eulogist had given him six weeks, and I thought, Well, I will expla ι to them later about the telephone call and the impulse.

But Fried made it all right. He said, "Since the way a man dies, just as the way he lives, is often a solid measure of his spirit, it is appropriate that we share perceptions of his very last days. . . . Consider this," he said. "Harold Lear was a physician who understood every detail of his pathology and prognosis. He knew exactly the conditions of battle, he was not awed, and he fought like hell. . . ."

David spoke; Norman spoke; a psalm from Corinthians; memories of a shared childhood; tributes to the grown man, the doctor, the cousin, to the gallantry with which he endured what he had to endure, to the spirit of his final hours: ". . . and through the door I kept hearing the doctors say, 'Dr. Lear, put your hand down. It's all right. We're taking care of you. *Put your hand down*, Dr. Lear. . . .' and I had the feeling that that was Hal, whether he was conscious or not, trying to get in on it, trying to let them know what they ought to be doing. . . ."

And I sat thinking, This is all very well, but when will they speak of *us*? I want that. I want it on the record.

Jon spoke last. He began, "In my life I have known many people who have loved mankind very much, and had difficulty getting along with individuals. My father did have a passing interest in mankind— but, God, how he loved individuals! It was reflected in the way he cared for his patients"—recalling how, when he and Judy were small, their father would take them on hospital rounds; recalling the gentleness with which he touched his patients—"As a child, I always thought that happiness was having your pulse taken by my father"; recalling the way he talked and listened to his patients, "for he had an ability," Jon said, "to talk and be talked to that outstripped anything I've come in contact with in my life. Judy and I could say anything to him. . . ." And I thought, What about *us*, Jonny? What about the things he and I could say to each other, and did? Please, Jonny.

And Jon said then, "My father was passionately in love. It was a very romantic marriage. And for me and for Judy, that was a wonderful thing. Just to see the two of them, fooling around and nuzzling each other, calling each other Mushie and Hershie, and laughing and loving each other, made an enormous impact on us. My father was a very special, very remarkable, very happy person, but he didn't come in on a clamshell. He very much *became* the person he ended up being, and a lot of that growth was because of the love they shared. . . ."

I relaxed. I wept. It was true, damn it, and I wanted it on the record.

Three days later came the autopsy report. I had ordered this autopsy. Hal had to his last conscious moment been a doctor; his last conscious act had been to reach for a pen with which to make a clinical note; he had burned to the end with scalding questions about his surgery and his brain damage and his F.U.O.'s, and I had wanted answers on his behalf. It had seemed a legacy.

And there were no answers. No clear causes. No explanations for the brain damage, no endocarditis, no proof of autoimmune reactions. The Fevers of Unknown Origin remained just so: unknown. Hal's mysteries had been interred with his ashes in the waters of Provincetown Harbor.

At first it drove me crazy. Fried told me, "Medical students ask us questions, and we cannot answer them. If a patient has cancer in different organs, but enough is left of these organs to sustain life, yet the patient dwindles and on a given day stops living—why? The students ask us this, and we simply don't know. That's a common instance. Hal's was rare. There could have been some sort of autoimmune process: the body becomes allergic to itself, or to its own tissues that have been altered in some way, perhaps during surgery. There could have been a malfunction in the brain: the thermostat going crazy and causing those fevers. We can't know." And then, gently: "When are you going to let go of it?"

Now he is four months dead, and I am beginning to let go. The finality of it still eludes me. Judy says, "I keep thinking, Okay, Daddy, it's been long enough. The joke's over. Come on back now." It is like that for me too, and will remain so for a time, I suppose.

But in other ways there has been a decent accommodation to realities. I have spent much of these months trying to come to terms with bitter feelings. They are corrosive. I want to be rid of them.

His surgery: Hal's life after his surgery was unalterably changed for the worse, and I must wonder, as he wondered and wrote, whether perhaps he would not have been better off saying No, thanks, to the surgery, and taking his nitroglycerin and his chances. But I am convinced that competent people made the best decisions they could make at the time. There is no bitterness on that score.

His doctors: I do believe, as he did, that mistakes were made. I believe that doctors most grievously failed him as to the agony of his brain damage. I believe that doctors sloughed him off who would be horrified to think that they sloughed him off; and this was one of the things that turned his perceptions and his guts inside out, bewildered him as a patient and pained him as a doctor.

But I also have come to believe that the doctor does not exist who could treat such a gravely ill patient for such a long time without making mistakes; and that given their mortal limitations, they were more than good; and that much of the anger I felt was simply, primitively, because they could not do the impossible: they could not make him well.

It must be that grief is more bearable in the absence of guilt. And I, who was always addicted to guilt, feel comfortingly little of it now that he is gone. There is nothing that was not said between us. There are no If onlys. There are few regrets. We knew and said that we gave each other joy, he knew that he was profoundly loved and respected by his wife and his children, he knew that his life had counted, that he had grown and never stopped growing, and that is perhaps more than most of us know before we die; and though he said Bullshit whenever I told him that I admired him more than anyone else I had ever met, I think he knew that this was true too.

And I feel, finally, blessed by that passionate affection we shared, and by the generosity with which he helped me prepare for the loss of it. This was his final gift. I had no way to know its immensity until he was gone.

"If I died, what would you do?" I asked him long ago.

And he told me, "I would have my time of mourning. That would be slow and very hard. But there would come a time when I would look at myself and say, 'Well, what kind of life do you want now? In what direction will you go?' It would be the death of a part of me. But listen, Martha: There would never be a question of my not surviving. *Never*."

Hal. *L'chaim*.

January, 1979